The High Times READER

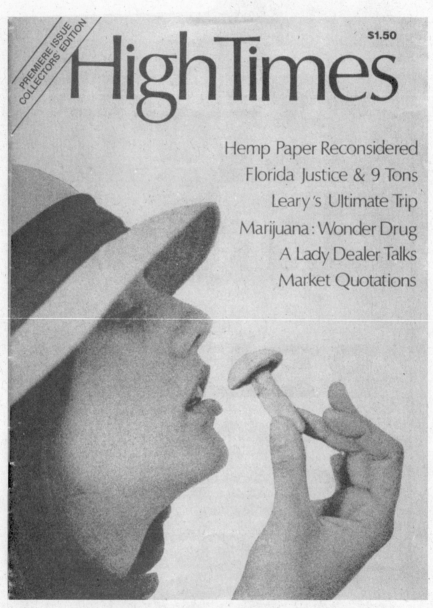

$1.50

PREMIERE ISSUE
COLLECTORS EDITION

High Times

Hemp Paper Reconsidered
Florida Justice & 9 Tons
Leary's Ultimate Trip
Marijuana: Wonder Drug
A Lady Dealer Talks
Market Quotations

High Times #1, 1974

The High Times

READER

Edited by Annie Nocenti & Ruth Baldwin
Introduction by Paul Krassner

NATION BOOKS
NEW YORK

THE HIGH TIMES READER

Copyright © 2004 by High Times
Introduction copyright © 2004 by Paul Krassner

Published by
Nation Books
An Imprint of Avalon Publishing Group
245 West 17th St., 11th Floor
New York, NY 10011

AVALON
publishing group incorporated

Nation Books is a co-publishing venture of the Nation Institute
and Avalon Publishing Group Incorporated.

Library of Congress Cataloging-in-Publication Data is available.

ISBN 1-56025-624-9

9 8 7 6 5 4 3 2 1

Book Design by Maria E. Torres

Printed in Canada on recycled paper
Distributed by Publishers Group West

Thomas King Forçade
(1945–1978)

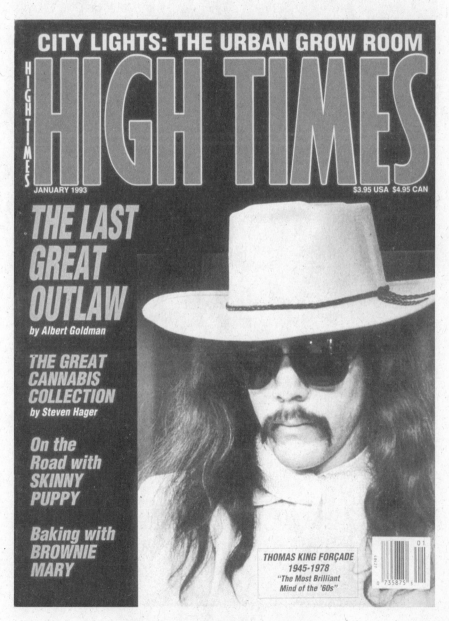

High Times #209, January 1993

DOES GRASS REALLY MAKE YOUR BREASTS GROW?

High Times

Oct/Nov

$1.50

Aldous Huxley on Moksha
Yagé: Amazon Wonder Vine
World Harvest Report
Dope Behind Bars

Pictorials:
The Fields of Mexico
American Beauty
Fashions & Comix

Exclusive
Interview:
The Dalai Lama
on Sex,
Drugs
and
Violence

DEEP DARK SECRETS OF
CHOCOLATE

High Times #6, October 1975

CONTENTS

INTRODUCTION

Paul Krassner

In college, Tom Forçade majored in business administration and minored in hot-rodding. He would eventually morph himself into a mysterious character who wore all-black clothes and drove a black Cadillac with a Plexiglass bubble-top. It was at the Revolutionary Media Conference, held in Ann Arbor, Michigan in 1969, that Forçade became director of the Underground Press Syndicate (UPS).

At UPS he issued "repression reports," one claiming that the percentage of underground press staffers involved in drug arrests was one hundred times that of the general population. By 1969, UPS reported that sixty percent of the papers loosely grouped as "underground" were experiencing major repression, and many failed to survive.

In the summer of 1971, Forçade had this warning for a gathering of underground-press editors in Oyster River, Colorado:

> The UPS papers, as advance scouts for journalism in America and the world, often find themselves in conflict with the last vestiges of honky mentality, uptight Smokey-the-Bears of the totalitarian forest rushing around with para-legal shovels and axe-wielding blue meanie henchmen, stomping out the fires of a people who have found their voice and are using it. You're going to have to identify some sort of base that the straight press can't co-opt. Either sex, drugs or politics.

Three years later, following his own advice, Forçade launched *High Times* out of the UPS office. It was supposed to be a joke—a one-shot lampoon of *Playboy,* substituting dope for sex—but it turned out to be a unique magazine that has lasted thirty years. *High Times* is about much more than getting stoned, though. Marijuana is a metaphor for civil liberties. Smoking a joint serves as a gateway to outlaw consciousness.

As long as any government can arbitrarily decide which drugs are legal and which drugs are illegal, then all those who serve time behind bars for illegal drugs are actually political prisoners. In 2004, the White House anti-drug campaign spent $170 million on insidious propaganda, working closely with the Partnership for a Drug-Free America, which was founded and funded by tobacco, alcohol, and pharmaceutical companies. The war on drugs is really a war on some people who use some drugs.

The priorities are insane. Cigarettes cause 1200 deaths every day in America alone—not to mention 2.41 million deaths annually in the developing countries—but the worst that can happen with marijuana is maybe you'll get the munchies and raid the refrigerator. As for alcohol, each year 16,000 Americans are killed in alcohol-related crashes; alcohol is directly linked to about one-quarter of suicides, almost half of all violent crimes, and two-thirds of domestic abuse. Then there's prescription drugs, a $100 billion industry that annually takes 100,000 lives across the nation.

Every year, the United States government spends more than $33 billion prosecuting the drug war, and makes 1.5 million arrests. Of those, over 1.2 million are for simple possession. Just as we now consider barbaric the tradition of human sacrifice by priests at the ancient Inca temples who cut the hearts out of their own innocent worshippers, anthropologists of the future will surely declare that we ourselves have been living through a barbaric era.

Meanwhile, you hold in your hands *The High Times Reader,* featuring articles and interviews that span three decades, with material ranging from the irreverent to the spiritual, from the hysterical to the historical, from "My Scrotum Flew Tourist" to "Why the Miss America Pageant Should Be Banned," from "The Secret Life of Walt Disney" to "The Strange Story of Lyndon LaRouche: Sinister Mastermind of the National Anti-Drug Coalition," from "I was JFK's Dealer" to "Fear and Loathing in Baghdad." Within these pages, you'll find the print version of a countercultural theme park.

One thing you won't find in this book, however, is a reader survey that *High Times* published, including this question: "Is it possible to smoke too much pot?"

To which a reader responded: "I don't understand the question."

PUBLISHING STATEMENT

On the Principles Behind Publishing High Times

THOMAS KING FORÇADE

NOVEMBER 1976

DOPE PANIC

A TERRIFYING SHORTAGE OF marijuana has been gradually spreading across the land, the droughts between dope shipments have been lengthening, and fear is in the air. We have previously explained in this space the reasons for the dope shortage: 1) steeply rising demand yet the same acreage planted to marijuana; 2) DEA efforts to defoliate or burn the marijuana fields (à la Vietnam); 3) a DEA–Coast Guard blockade in the Caribbean and a DEA–border Patrol electronic battlefield along the Mexican border; 4) the devaluation of the dollar has meant mucho marijuana and particularly hashish has been diverted to more profitable markets than the U.S.A.

Now, the dope shortage has reached crisis proportions, with no end in sight. Repeat: no end in sight. Although there is always a drought in the summer, this time the drought will *not* end. The old scene is *over*, baby. The reason is that the government is currently applying massive antidope programs to Colombia and Mexico. These programs were developed in Jamaica, which was used as an island test lab for DEA techniques. The test study involved a blockade by the Jamaican Coast Guard, intensive surveillance by the Jamaican intelligence community, defoliation and burning of fields, and gigantic sums of U.S. tax money to buy the cooperation of everyone in sight. Orchestrating the whole show were the CIA planners currently assigned to and running the DEA. So much money was poured into Jamaica that it became more profitable to deal information than ganja, and thus the Jamaican connection was wiped out three years ago.

Last year, these same methods were applied to Colombia and Mexico, except this time *hundreds of millions* of U.S. tax dollars were used. The program did not interdict the flow of dope (just as the bombing of the Ho

Chi Minh Trail never stopped the supply of armaments to the Viet Cong), but it has certainly reduced the flow. This does not stop marijuana use, just raises the price. So what's the point? Isn't the cost of living high enough already without wasting tax dollars on driving the cost up further?

ODBC (the Organization of Dope Exporting Countries) is being effectively "established," just as the CIA and ITT destabilized Chile. The smart money is going out of the import game and into domestic cultivation. America is the greatest agricultural producer the world has ever known, and there is no reason this agriculture cannot include that nearly unkillable weed called marijuana. Meanwhile, smart consumers are saving their seeds and growing their own. One good seed grown to maturity equals one full pound of good marijuana. Can you really afford to throw them away? The luxury of imported dope is nearly over for most people, and that's a plain fact. Imported dope is becoming as much a luxury as French wine. If people in America want to get high, they're going to have to grow their own. As those who have gotten into high horticulture know, *the best dope in the world is grown in windowboxes and closets.* After all, you can give your few plants far more attention than a farmer can give thousands of plants, right? The techniques of growing good pot are readily learned—books on the subject abound. And excellent weed can be grown *anywhere* in the United States.

The only hope for a high America is a return to the Victory Gardens that helped win World War II. Operation Intercept in 1970 (generaled by G. Gordon Liddy) was Dope War I. Now we are faced with Dope War II. Final victory must be achieved. Marijuana ecology demands that seeds be saved and planted.

WHEN FREEDOM IS OUTLAWED, ONLY OUTLAWS WILL BE FREE

The general public (us) has no idea who really owns, controls, and manages *Time* magazine, the *Washington Post*, the *New York Times*, the three monopolistic TV networks, Random House, Simon & Schuster and so on. Nor do we have any idea what their goals are. And the public will never learn from the aforementioned sources, either. Many fine people work for the straight media, but as A. J. Liebling said, freedom of the press belongs to those who own one. We own one, and this is an important point. After all, it was the media that made marijuana illegal! Their pot scare campaigns created the temporary popular support that made it politically expedient to outlaw marijuana. The media (except for the underground press) fully cooperated in getting us in and keeping us in the Vietnam War and, after ten years of mass demonstrations, the media finally helped get us out. The media put Nixon in (over ninety percent of the daily newspapers endorsed his candidacy in 1972, Watergate notwithstanding), and the media finally got rid of Nixon just a year later by publishing the truth. So you have a right to know.

Trans-High Corporation (THC—the parent company of *High Times*) was started to bring new consciousness projects into reality, particularly projects within the media. As we stated some time ago, we have no particular interest in manufacturing rolling papers or hash pipes, or starting *High Times* key clubs. We are mainly interested in opening up communication, providing access to information. One of the first THC projects was *High Times* magazine. It was a coldly conceived concept, there was nothing accidental about it, and we definitely expected it to succeed, eventually. Instead, it took off like a rocket, right from the beginning, and our main problem has been holding on. Holding on—to our personal identities, to our editorial independence, to our corporate independence, to reality, to our rapport and unique communication with our readers, to our sanity. Coping with the staggering business-financial-organizational problems caused by our rapid growth. Finding honest, competent, creative people to be the staff. And retaining our perspective amidst a barrage of publicity— all of it strangely favorable.

To outsiders, the *High Times* "success story" appears to be a typical capitalist trip, with one or more individuals on top raking in tons of money to be used for buying Lamborghini sports cars, MacIntosh stereos, penthouses, Peruvian flake, and sexual companionship that resembles the people in the cigarette ads as closely as possible. While we assure you that we at *High Times* fully appreciate the value of hedonism (learned in part from that pioneering personal researcher in the field, Hugh M. Hefner), the fact is that *THC is owned by a non-profit trust fund* and the staff makes very modest salaries indeed. Should we make any excess profits, they will be given to organizations concerned with social, cultural, political, and economic change. We'd like to own Macintosh stereos, but other things are more important to us. Like putting out the best magazine imaginable. A magazine that has always been far more than a "dope" magazine. Lately, as you have seen, we have been broadening our editorial scope even more. It is obvious that our readers want to hear about a broad range of contemporary and historical subjects. We have no desire to be limited to being the magazine of substances that people put in their mouths. In this issue, you will notice more general news, more diverse features, much more music coverage, and more cultural and political coverage than ever before. We have added the National Weed section, continued and expanded our policy of using name authors and experts from every field, including top-notch investigative reporters, fiction writers, new journalists, old journalists, better editing, and hard-core dopers who know what they're talking about (we've been there, too, folks). Meanwhile, we will continue to have the best, the most accurate, the most interesting and entertaining, the most wideranging, creative, wildest, courageous coverage of dope anywhere. If you see any serious competition, let us know.

When *High Times* began, many people thought it was so slick and professional that it was surely a Madison Avenue production designed to "rip off" the dope culture. The reality is that the people who put out *High Times* were (and the hard core still are) admitted children of the sixties—veterans of the civil rights movement, the underground press, SDS, White Panthers, Y.I.P., the preunderground Weathermen, Amorphia (an early legalize-pot organization) and all the rest. Since then we have added a sprinkling of straight professionals, particularly in the business area, to keep the economic wheels turning and the records straight. We hope those who deal with us have noticed a vast improvement. We have also added a sprinkling of magazine professionals from such places as *Penthouse, Playboy, Oui, Good Housekeeping,* Harcourt Brace, and so on. Most of these people were actively supporting what this magazine stands for long before coming here. Our average age is about twenty-four.

Outsiders must also wonder: just how massive are the profits from such an obviously successful magazine as *High Times*? In the last six month accounting period, THC lost $33,000. During the same period, we gave

$25,000 to NORML and lesser amounts to various other projects. Why are we losing money and why are we giving money away as well?

First of all, *High Times* is extremely expensive to put out. We spend a lot of money on research, top-level writers, extensive editing, expensive high-quality art work, four-color printing, sophisticated independent marketing, top quality organization. We give money to NORML and other organizations because we know that they are barely surviving, that they work very hard, and it is not fair for us to have money when they need money—as long as we don't undermine our survival. We don't think we are undermining our survival; we think we are insuring it by supporting organizations for change including NORML.

We are also losing money because although the circulation of High Times is currently around 420,000, it is extremely expensive to have to service that size circulation without a national distributor. The Big Five national distribution monopoly has boycotted *High Times* because of THC's radical structure. Obviously, any magazine that can sell 420,000 without a national distributor represents a serious threat to the hegemonic monopolistic control of the Big Five over what the public will be allowed to read. The Big Five are now financing a brace of "dope" magazines (*High Times* is *not* a dope magazine) intended to break the back of THC. But we have bad news for the Big Five and the establishment that controls them—there is room for plenty of counterculture magazines. But such a magazine must have a contemporary corporate structure or it is just another money-making media scheme available for purchase by the highest bidder. Remember Deep Throat's admonishment to Woodstein—follow the money!

Making money is not enough for us. Money and political "power" (often a goal in publishing) strike us as irrelevant. We are faced with a future that needs help. We know that as far as the future is concerned, we are playing for keeps. Our goal is to go all the way, whatever that may bring.

"I WAS JFK'S DEALER"

Ed Dwyer

Fall 1974

THE MAN WHO CLAIMED to know the Kennedys leaned over his *pâté* and confided to me.

"Before I contacted you, I investigated a bit to see if *High Times* was legitimate."

Across his suite, he assayed the departing waitress from room service.

"Yes, we had you checked out, too," I said. I told him how I'd been making discreet inquiries for a week to determine if he did indeed move in the Kennedy circles and had only then confirmed the interview. We agreed to meet at his suite at the Sherry-Netherland Hotel. I was met by a dapper, politely tanned man in his mid-forties. He greeted me unhurriedly and began what was a fluent, one-sided conversation.

"You see, I feel that what I know about Jack, Bobby, and Ted is in no way harmful to their reputations. In fact, I'm willing to wager that, had Jack lived into a second term or Bobby been elected president, the marijuana laws would have been stricken."

He paused, reached inside his corduroy sport jacket, produced a tortoise shell cigarette case and flipped it open.

"Like to turn on?" he asked, smiling.

"Sure," I said.

I asked him to give me some background: how he had come into the Kennedy circle and how he related to their lifestyle. He stared down at his cuff and then looked up.

"Well, I can't really be considered part of the inner circle. You know about people like Kenny O'Donnell, Paul Fay, Dave Powers, Joey Gargan and the rest who were always by the Kennedys. That's not my people. My background is like a lot of those fellows, but it's taken me a long way from the power plays and inner workings of the family. I graduated from Harvard in 1954."

"Did you turn on at Harvard?"

"No, not at Harvard. Somewhere along the line I decided that I wanted to be a writer, and after graduation I took a job with a major news magazine. By 1957, I had gotten myself assigned to Havana. That's where I first turned on. Batista's regime was at its rottenest, but the place was rife with dope, gambling, and colorful characters. In fact, it was going to Cuba that brought me into contact with the Kennedys again."

"What was Cuba like in those days?"

"If you remember, the late 50's saw Fidel Castro's star rise. We all felt sympathetic toward Castro—it was the romantic thing to feel in those days—but we never dreamed he'd get in. As it happened, I was among the first to be booted out.

"But I had made the right contacts in Cuba, especially in the black market and government—there was little difference—so when I returned to the States, I was considered something of an authority on Caribbean affairs. At this time I was thirty years old, smoking a lot of excellent grass, dealing a little to my less well-connected friends, and becoming a surprising success. And I made sure to maintain all my contacts, too."

"But how does this bring you to the Kennedys?"

"At Harvard I knew Ted Kennedy; we ran in the same circles, were both rather jockish as undergraduates and our fraternities mingled at parties and things. I remember I supported Jack's candidacy for the Senate in 1952 and worked the campus trying to drum up votes." He laughed ruefully. "I would run into Ted around the commons doing the same thing. Hell, I even remember the flap when Ted was caught cheating in a Spanish final.

"So I wasn't really surprised when, several months after I returned from Cuba and Jack was president, I was contacted by a friend of Ted's at the White House and asked to submit a report on my work down there and any recommendations I had. I knew the President had a love for fine Cuban cigars, so I took down a beautiful handmade humidor full of a custom blend of Cuban tobacco, hand-rolled in Jamaica. It turned out the meeting wasn't private but a debriefing of four journalists who had covered the Cuban revolution. After the meeting, I handed him the cigars and he thanked me. Then he took a good look at the cigars and when he did, he invited me to stay and smoke one with him."

He sucked on his Scotch and leaned back.

"You know, Jack's back was always giving him trouble. He had been seeing a doctor who was later written up in *New York* magazine as "Dr. Feelgood," getting shots that were a combination of speed, vitamins, cocaine, and cortisone. His back was bothering him the day we met and I suggested he try something to ease his pain that wouldn't dull or agitate him like the drugs he was taking. I gave him a quick rundown on marijuana: its effects, its history, my experiences with it and the archaic laws surrounding its use. He was genuinely curious. It was something to which he had never given much thought, even during his investigative days in the Senate."

"Do you mean that he was completely ignorant about pot?"

"Oh, of course not. You couldn't possibly party with the show business types and international celebrities that the Kennedys favored and not know something about grass. And, of course, he was always sharp as hell and wasn't easily buffaloed by anti-pot propaganda. The late fifties saw a lot of drastic changes in lifestyles . . . beatniks, avant-guardists, abstractionists, and movie stars like Brando and Dean who cashed in on rebellion. Jack was a consummate politician; he was aware of all these changes in taste. He'd just never tried pot until I turned him on. At least as far as I know."

I had visions of handsome John Kennedy toking away behind his captain's desk, easing his backpain, while a dour Lyndon Johnson is kept cooling his heels with Mrs. Lincoln in the antechamber.

"Of course, I didn't turn on with him. I just arranged to have the weed delivered to him," he added.

"How much did you give him?"

"At the time I had old friends from my Caribbean days sending me a few pounds a week. In fact, they still do! I'd joined the International bureau of a large weekly news magazine and in those days a package from Mexico City or Bogata wasn't cause for undue suspicion. . . .

"Early one evening I received a phone call at my apartment in Georgetown. It was one of Jack's most trusted press liaisons, who informed me the President was planning a short vacation. He was taking his boat out with family and friends, and I was asked if I could provide him with the memos I had drawn up in accordance with our conversation two weeks earlier. Could I have everything ready by ten o'clock that night? I knew exactly what was meant by the call, because the President hadn't asked me to draw up any memos. By ten I had prepared a manila folder full of blank paper. Inside was an ounce of fresh Panamanian from a shipment I'd received the day before. At ten on the dot I answered the door to find a familiar press officer who took my 'notes'. You know, Red Fay wrote about Jack's habit of taking late night rides through Washington. I think he overlooked one very important ride, because I swear Jack was inside the black limousine parked at my curb."

"Did the President ever contact you again?"

The gentleman's face sagged slightly.

"No, not exactly. I received a letter shortly after that night, thanking me for my cooperation and expressing hope that we might meet again for an informal chat. The limousine came several more times, but I'm not really sure who was getting the stuff. His stay was so short you know, one thousand days they say, that many of us caught only the quickest glimpse of the real John Kennedy . . . the Kennedy who was so open to life that he was willing to expose himself to a virtual stranger and try something he knew the public might find horrifying."

"Would you know if Jackie turns on?"

"I can't really say for sure that Jack smoked the dope, though I assume he did, considering my later contacts with Bob and Ted. I've never met Jackie, but you know I've heard talk that Onassis made some of his fortune smuggling cocaine and heroin after the war." A *pâté* finished, he was now drawing heavily on his second Scotch. "Of course, you can hear anything down in the islands."

"You just mentioned your later contacts with Bobby and Ted. Could you tell us about them?"

"Do you remember Allen Ginsberg's account of his talk with Bobby in 1968, where he asks Bobby if he had ever smoked pot and Bobby refuses to answer him directly, but keeps evading the question?" he asked.

"The interview when Ginsberg chanted the Hare Krishna chant in Bobby's office?"

"Correct. Well, Allen thought Bobby was being insensitive by not giving a direct answer. He didn't understand Bobby's style, the intensity at which Bobby worked. By 1968, I think Bobby had decided the pot laws should be changed, but he wanted to approach the issue when it could be won and he was storing up all the impact of his decision for the right moment.

"I first met Bobby in Los Angeles at the 1964 Democratic Convention. Earlier in the year I had lost my job—drinking—and I had driven down to the Convention, knowing I could get freelance assignments. Like many others, I expected Bobby to be chosen as Vice-Presidential candidate. And I was absolutely awestruck by his reaction to the crowd. Understand, the public impression of Bobby had always been one of ruthlessness—the little fellow who tore after the Teamsters, miffed Lyndon Johnson, and shoved civil rights down the racist throats of America. But there he was, absolutely vulnerable and in tears at the accolade.

"Later, at a cocktail reception, I spoke with him for about two minutes. I told him if I could be any help in the future, to let me know. What was unnerving was his spontaneous recognition of me. When I approached him, I expected that Kennedy coolness, especially to someone on the fringes. I didn't cruise the same circles as, say, Arthur Schlesinger, Joseph Kraft, Murray Kempton, or the others who were coming on board for his New York Senate campaign. We were introduced, I think by Pete Edelman, and I'll be damned if he didn't know who I was. He said he'd be glad to have my help."

"Did you speak about grass?"

"No, but I suspect part of his interest in me was a result of my contact with his brother. He seemed overeager to meet me, if you know what I mean. It wasn't until 1966, when I moved to New York that I saw him again. That was at another party; all the society mavens were there: Truman Capote, George Plimpton, Pete Hammil, that type, and I didn't get to speak to him. However, Ted was there and we had a dandy conversation about the days at Harvard. Around that time Ted had just returned from a trip to Vietnam and we talked about that a bit and made some conversation about his bad back and his marriage, which always seemed a bit haunted. He invited me up to Squaw Island for a few days and I told him I'd try to make it some time. He promised we'd go sailing; I remembered

Jack's vacation 'sailing' trip, but all I did was joke that I hoped his sailing was better than his flying."

He continued. "Also at the party were Steve Smith and Peter Lawford, who were both married to Kennedy women. Now I'd met Lawford at parties before and he really believes in high living. Steven Smith, on the other hand, is a real tight ass, Mr. Park Avenue Associates. I noticed them looking very friendly, very stoned in fact, and I excused myself from Ted, who was wandering in the direction of Joan. I wanted to talk to Peter and Steve. I was surprised to find them talking about dope and both seemed to agree that Bob should make a motion to decriminalize marijuana. I was especially shocked at Steve, who was touted as the no-nonsense moneyman of the Kennedy clan. Then I realized that first impressions do count. They were both, ah, stoned. I felt surrounded by history's hidden heads; Ted and his sailing trip, Peter and Steve with their talk of decriminalization. All this at a party for Bobby, the Senator from New York."

We both paused to take quick bites at the last of our hors-d'oeuvres.

"I met that crowd several times after that night and got high with them, so I wasn't surprised when they wondered aloud if I was able to obtain some good weed. I still had my connections in South America, and I was dealing a little of my best to friends. Soon after that I began receiving calls from people I knew were close to Bob and Ted asking if I could perform small favors. This was about the time Bob was being challenged by Eugene McCarthy for the right to topple LBJ in 1968. McCarthy's appeal was to the leftish upper-middle class, mobile American student pothead. Bob probably felt the need to commit himself to try what his brother had tried. To Bobby, you had to feel deeply toward a topic to support it. When he decided to soften on marijuana, as everyone in the press was aware, it wasn't an intellectual exercise like Jack tried. I think it was because he had tried it and liked it, and believed it was not harmful." Sitting back in his chair, he sipped the last of his Scotch. We poured another round and I sensed that time was getting short. He had glanced at his watch several times.

"And you think it was grass that began the changes in Bobby Kennedy?"

"Could be. I find it more than a coincidence that shortly after I sold some exceptional grass to Bobby's acquaintances, Arthur Schlesinger was pushed into the pool at Hickory Hill (the Kennedy home in Virginia), that

Bobby decided to enter the primaries, and that later, he decided to hire prankster Dick Tuck as an aide."

"Did many of the people around Bobby get high?"

"Ask Frank Mankewiecz, Jimmy Breslin, or Andy Williamson on that question. They would be better able to answer it than me."

"But you're certain that Bobby turned on?"

"Definitely. It's just that with so many kids of his own he wasn't going to force the legalization issue and exhaust it before he became President. It is ironic that he was killed by a Palestinian."

"Did any of your friends deal with the Kennedys?"

"Well, most of us who worked the South American or Middle Eastern regions for the government or press in the early '60s were continually turned onto excellent grass and hash. Some of us have made some profit from our experience. I know many of these people were in a position to deal with Kennedy people."

"Have you ever dealt to Ted Kennedy?"

"Funny enough, not as closely as one would assume from our early acquaintance. I've followed his rise, though. He's quite a go-getter—loves to party—and generally I admire his politics, but we've never gotten together and been high. However, I did hear an interesting story from a reliable dealer friend of mine who works at the Agriculture Department." He cleared his throat.

"Ted has always been pretty free with his good times. His best ability has always been to pull together when he had let go too much. But I suppose the Chappaquidick incident at the Dike Bridge was the first time his ability, and his integrity, were ever really tested.

"From what I was told, and despite what Paul Markham and Joey Gargan say, Ted was thoroughly wasted on something the night of the incident. It was a bad habit he'd had since Bob's assassination, when his back began hurting him and the pressure of being the last male Kennedy became too heavy to handle. This friend of mine swears Ted was dosed with some of his sunshine in Edgartown before the party at Lawrence Cabin. It was his first trip, and they figured the cabin was the best place for it.

"The party was perfectly innocent, just old friends getting high and trying to loosen up after a hard year. But Mary Jo got unhinged and Ted offered her a ride back to town with him; he, too, was several sheets to the wind and was getting claustrophobia. After the accident, Ted tried repeatedly to save the girl, but there was no way. The reason he didn't go straight to the authorities was because it took several hours for him to come down."

My host suddenly stood up, and I asked one more question.

"As far as heads go, some of the Kennedy children seem the genuine article. What do you think?"

"All I can tell you is that they are beautiful, independent children who love to get high in as many ways as there are kids. But keep an eye on John Jr; with his taste for rock, I wouldn't be surprised if he turns out to be a bigger head than Bobby's two eldest sons. I just hope that all of the kids live to fulfill the potential of their fathers, who were great heads in more ways than one."

It was obvious that our chat was at an end. We shook hands and I thanked him for the story—which amounted to a beguiling explanation of over a decade of American history. If true.

"Listen," I said, "you've given me a great story, if it checks out. Maybe we could get together some time again, and talk things over, in general, you know." He smiled.

Well, I'll say one thing for him. His dope was indeed Commander-in-Chief in quality.

THIS MAN IS SEEING GOD

and God Says He Smokes Only the Best.
This Man is Bob Marley and He Smokes with God.

ED DWYER

SEPTEMBER 1976

BOB MARLEY IS THE fastest-rising, highest-flying star in music today. Like most members of Jamaica's Rastafarian religion, Bob smokes about a pound of marijuana, or "herb," a week. *High Times* visited with Bob on his most recent American tour, and we found a lot of things to talk about.

High Times: Have you seen *High Times* magazine?

Marley: Hard times? Ooo-eee! Ooo-eee! *High Times!* Dis supposed to 'ave de bes' high in de worl'. *High Times,* only de bes'.

High Times: Some Thai weed?

[*Pause*]

High Times: Do you think herb will be legalized?

Marley: I don' know if dis government will, but I know Christ's government will.

High Times: What about the Jamaican government? Mr. Manley, the Prime Minister?

Marley: Him? Legalize herb? Boy, I jus' don' know. It's kinda legalized already. Me don't t'ink is really him, y'know. The realization of de truth. I don't know if Michael Manley will be de one, or who, but y'know, every-t'ing will reveal right out to de flat truth.

High Times: Now when you go back to Jamaica as a big star, are you able to talk to different people and get some things done that you'd like to happen?

Marley: Down dere? See, Jamaica jus' run outa politics today . . . ya can't have anything happening. But ya have people who will do t'ings for ya, like ya brethren, y'know. But when ya talk about de people in power, ya haffa be a politics-man. Me don't deal wit' no politics—me deal wit' de truth.

High Times: Your audience here is mostly white. What do you think about that?

Marley: Well, I hear dat we not gettin' through to black people. Well, me tell de R & B guy now, he must play dis record because I wan' get to de people. We're not talkin' about no make me no superstar. Don' ever make me no star. Me no wan' be no star. But in de meantime, every knee shall bow and every tongue confess. Dat mean, de guy dat make de record, play for de people. Don' put me in no bracket, y'know what I mean? So dat is wit' de D.J. Him mus' realized dis is reggae music. I mean, it's music.

High Times: Do you consider yourself an outlaw?

Marley: Outlaw? No, no outlaw. Right in time.

High Times: You talk about dancing a lot in your songs. Do you see dancing as a form of communion with Jah?

Marley: When ya dance, ya just are Jah. Ya mus' dance.

High Times: When was the first time you got high on herb?

Marley: As a yout'. Was in de Sixties.

High Times: What was the best weed you ever smoked?

Marley: One time I was in Jamaica, was doin' a show, an' a man come up to me, and he gave me a spliff. Now, das de bes' herb I ever smoke. Yeah, man! Neva get an extra herb like dat again! No, no, no. Just like one tree in de earth, y'know?

High Times: Just one tree?

Marley: Jus' one tree. Sometimes ya just find a tree. It lamb's bread.

High Times: What's lamb's bread?

Marley: De ability what de herb 'ave ya call lamb's bread. Some a dem ya call Bethlehem's bread. Dat is when ya really get good herb, y'know what I mean?

High Times: Well, the Jamaican that's coming into the States now is not as good as it was.

Marley: Ya don' get no good herb because too much sell in Jamaica. And ya find alla people who plant herb fertilize it, so nobody really take care of de herb like first time. Ya use fertilizer, it come quick. Dem fertilize it an' cut it before time.

High Times: Do you guys find it hard to get good herb?

Marley: Me fin' it hard to get in England.

High Times: In England they always mix it with tobacco. It's really foul.

Marley: Yeah, man. It's time to let de people get good herbs an' smoke. Government's a joke. All dey wan' is ya smoke cigarettes and cigar. Some cigar wickeder den herb. Yeah, man, ya can't smoke cigar. Smoke herb.

Some big cigar me see man wit', God bless! Me tell him must smoke herb. Ya see, de people come together because is not de buildin', is not de buildin' me wanna see, me wanna see a nice level piece of green grass. Don' wanna haffa go in no elevator, gwan upstairs, and talk wit' some people in a square place. Me wanna go out in a earth, man. Righteousness cover de earth like water cover de sea. Where I gwan is, me don' have time to be in building all de while, when de miracles happening all de while outside. For some time miracles happen outta de sky. Is good for ya to see it, y'know. Among some green trees, yes man? I mean, ya 'ave green trees in America.

High Times: Have you ever tried acid?

Marley: Me hear 'bout people who do it. No, me meet people who do it, an' dem tell me. And when dem tell me, I travel to de same place. I mean, when a guy explain it an' ya listen, ya can go all de way up to de same place as him.

High Times: Who told you about it?

Marley: Well, one mustn't call people names, y'know. What keepeth its mouth, keepeth its life.

High Times: Do you think herb takes you to the same place?

Marley: I feel like ya 'ave thousands of different types of herb. If when ya plant it, if ya meditation not high, it don't come like de right type of herb.

High Times: It's very hard to find the right type of herb.

Marley: Yeah, man.

High Times: One of the reasons we're into this is to try to find it.

Marley: Well, ya see, dat herb, ya can't find dat herb.

High Times: Where is it?

Marley: Y'know what happen to dat herb? I tell ya where dat herb go now. Just like ya 'ave some apple trees, an' dis year something happen to dat apple tree dere, an' dis year dat tree taste better den dat tree. Ya find dat a seed planted de right day, de right minute, den dere's tree, ya find it, nobody plant it. A seed show, an' it grow, an' ya start nurse it, an' it become the best tree. Well, ya can get plenty a dat—de best herb dere. Jus' one tree, sometime a guy have. Ya might pass bye an' get a spliff. Ya say, "Where ya get dis?" Him say, "Dis come from St. Ann." So ya go down to St. Ann's an' ya don't find it again.

High Times: Your new album cover and the promotional sacks are burlap. Why?

Marley: We call dis a crocus bag. It has roots material, sackcloth. Ya associate wit' de poor man. If ya see a man walkin' down de street wit' dis, y'know 'es really poor, 'es a sufferer.

High Times: Like sackcloth and ashes?

Marley: Yeah, but ya see, de t'ing is, de first shall be de las' and de las' first. Is jus' like de Rastaman. Like Christ. Why did de whole worl' crucify? Him find, say in dis time de Rastaman is de only truth. So even de crocus bag stand out!

High Times: So this is how you educate Americans?

Marley: Yeah, man!

High Times: Who in Jamaica wants the American DEA down there?

Marley: What is DEA?

High Times: The Drug Enforcement Administration, the top narcs in the U.S. They're the ones that donate the helicopters and defoliants and things to countries like Jamaica. They try to squash the grass-smuggling trade. They send field agents to Mexico, Colombia, and Jamaica. We've been told that there are quite a few agents down there going around with the Jamaican police. Do you have any opinion as to why they're doing it, or who in Jamaica wants them down there?

Marley: Jamaica and America 'ave a deal. Ya mean, why would Jamaica invite a t'ing like dat? I tell ya, man, is in Jamaica interest. Same system, same people who control America. I don' know if is President Ford or whoever de president is. But what I know—de same force what control de system look de same in my eye. I t'ink de same force control Jamaica dat control all dem type a t'ings, y'know. I t'ink dem devil. For de devil 'ave a fight against de rights, y'know.

High Times: Manley is a socialist. Isn't he changing things?

Marley: Manley supposed to be a socialist. See, I don't have nuttin' ta say 'bout Manley, Manley personal self, man to man. But me no unnerstan', me no educated to know about big words like democratic socialism. Do it, let me see it, don't tell me 'bout it. Live de life.

High Times: What about Seaga, the capitalist who's running against Manley?

Marley: Ya 'ave two powers in Jamaica. One name Labor Party, an' one named PNP [People's National Party, Manley's ruling party]. An' every year now dis one [the PNP] win. Well now, I like to give de guy a chance, de one who win. I find it look like before him can get papers together, is votin' time again! So somebody set de trap fa dem, for before him can really check out Jamaica, an' find out how much Jamaica owe America or Jamaica owe Canada. I mean, what is de backside doin'?

High Times: Didn't Manley use a reggae song for his campaign?

Marley: Yeah, "Better Must Come." One t'ing is, ya can't blame Michael Manley, ya can't blame dem guys. Da t'ing is, de system set dat dey maintain de power.

High Times: Who sets the system?

Marley: De system been set! Manley come, comes ta someone. Dat someone, dere was someone before dat, someone comin' from where it was comin' from in England. It comin' down from England now. I don't know how financial dem set up, how much money Jamaica borrow from England, or what kinda plan Jamaica an' England 'ave, but I know Jamaica owe money to certain people. And if de politician run for politics an jus' wanna run for politics and don't unnerstand de runnings a all de t'ings a' gonna face him, den he gonna run away from de system, an' if ya run from de system, de people kill you! Y'unnerstan'?

Dat is when ya dare to go up 'gainst God, fight 'gainst God. If ya come to do somet'ing, ya do it. But if ya come to do something an' ya don't do it, ya fighting 'gainst God. An' all de people ya trick all de while. So where's de system settin' from? I don' know de business deal dem have, but dey can't just look upon Jamaica an' say, "All right Jamaica, we give ya some a dis an' some a dat. All right Jamaica, we're withdrawin' from ya," or whatever. Because either you swing wit' capitalism, or ya go wit de other "ism"—socialism. Tell 'em 'bout some more "isms." See, ya govern by dis "ism" or dat "ism." We gotta trim it in right dere; no middle way. Even if ya go upon dis "ism," him don' wanna lose friendship wit' America. Let me tell ya something—de same situation dat put de people in gonna catch 'em. Devil trick devil. I find now people want Africa. But if America help Africa, I don' even want dat neither. But what de people want is Africa.

High Times: They want to go back?

Marley: Forward. Yeah, man. I mean, we love Jamaica, an' we love de earth. But dere's a part a de eart' where it need plenty help—Africa.

High Times: Would you be willing to get a big boat and take people back and forth?

Marley: No, dat is not de t'ing. Dat is not de t'ing. Y'see, when Marcus Garvey come, he have de *Blackstar Liner*. Dat is not de problem. De problem is, ya gotta get de people's heads togetha. Why ya go to Africa? No sinner shall enter dere. Dat's why Africa become a place dat ya don' want to be like 'ere. Me don' wanna talk 'bout Africa too much, but I love to talk 'bout Africa. Yeah, because Africa is my land. Just like de Englishmen 'ave England an' de Indians 'ave India. Africa! *[Bob points to himself]*. It should be a t'ing where everybody help me go home, because dem supposed to be my brother. "But until dat day when de African continent will know peace . . ." I don' unnerstan' why when people talk about Africa dey wanna push Africa to one side. Now we know dat as de children of God, not as de children of America or as de children of Jamaica, but as de children of God, we know dat Africa need help. Poverty, y'know, it's not dat. De type a help Africa need is unity. Any time ya say Africa, is unity. If ya can't cite Africa, ya still in Babylon. Don' care who—anytime ya cite Africa, ya in unity. Until dat day, no have no peace Rasta! Yeah. But y'know when people talk 'bout Africa, dey talk like ya can't go dere, is a jungle, y'know what I mean? Yeah.

High Times: Have you been to Africa?

Marley: I'm going dere, yeah.

High Times: Soon?

Marley: Yeah, man. Africa teach all over de earth. Civilization, everywhere, every corner of de earth is African civilization. Now, a man hafta know himself. Ya can't tell me he's American or he's Jamaican or wherever he is. We know Noah had three sons. De las' destruction t'ing, three son him have: Ham, Shem, and Japhet. De three brothers, three colors. Dat mean, I don't know if I can tell a white man him come, say, live in Africa. My duty is to talk to de people who want to hear, who listen. If dey ask me a question, dey want to learn an' I 'ave somet'ing I can tell, den Jah will give me de inspiration to answer it. De whole earth start in Africa, de whole creation. But yet de people today come say, "Boy, de people dem starve in Africa." Money control whole lotta t'ings. But y'know, dem t'ings jus' reveal demselves out to de youth. Because if I don' unnerstand, my son will because de truth is always dere. Den ya realize dere's somet'ing going on about de place. Go up in a White House, go check it out an' find out de president don' even know. Go check it again. Maybe it end up inna other room. Maybe some big Catholic guy control. Ya don' know where it end up, y'know.

High Times: Huh?

Marley: Ya don't know. *[He laughs.]* It might end up here, y'unnerstan? Yeah? So, ya have to be careful—de whole t'ing is truth.

High Times: What was that?

Marley: Be careful, y'know?

High Times: Be careful? Yeah.

Marley: Whole t'ing is truth.

High Times: Amen.

PETER TOSH ON HERB

MARK JACOBSON

SEPTEMBER 1976

ASK A DREADLOCK JAMAICAN about the Wailers, and he'll tell you about Peter Tosh, Bunny Livingstone, the Barrett brothers, and Bob Marley. That's because Marley emerged as the leader of the top Rasta band only after the departure of Livingstone and Tosh. Bunny is now recording a solo album for Island Records. And Peter Tosh will be making a lot of noise in America from now on.

Peter's song, "Legalize It," is a Rasta anthem that hit number one in Jamaica a few days after Prime Minister Michael Manley overturned the ban on its airplay. Can it happen here? With Columbia Records releasing the album *Legalize It* we haven't ruled out that possibility. And if "Legalize It" hits number one, can the real thing be far off? We asked Peter what he thinks a record can do.

Man of all description, man and men of all different category, you know? Just go in a studio, an' sit down, turn on a mike an' say I am a lawyer an' I smoke herb, or anything you wanna call it—marijuana, or pot, or anyt'ing, every man would be wit herb irrespective of how big him t'ink him in society.

A man is not too big in society if herb is degradation of society, because accordin' to de law of herb, only de small man get deprive, or go to prison, or bein' brutalize by police for herb. Only de small man.

Me come to de conclusion that de whole earth—well let's say 99 percent of de earth—have some form affiliation wit' de herb, because dem call it ganja, an don't know ganja is a t'ing dat grow. Ganga is a bird in Australia, or ganja is a place in Russia, an' ganja is whole lotta different t'ing, but nothin' pertainin' to what him callin' it, legal t'ing. And the poor man who don' know him constitutional right, just get fucked.

Well, we like herb for free man. Because it is fuckin' up de whole earth, an' is not fuckin' up de whole earth. *Is* fuckin' up de small man, cause only de small man at all time go to blood-clot jeal for herb, an' de beeg man just pass in him limousine. An' if he can have on him certain identification that society see man, o-so-well-it's-mister-Brown don'-touch-it/blood-clot-let-him-go-on. An' oh, *Yes man!* Just right! *Me smoke herb!* Me smoke herb, me pass my herb, me goin' free. You bigger, you smoke herb an' you pass it, an' you goin' free. But because you bigger an' you drive a bigger can dan me, an' you live up a Beverly Hill an' dem bum-clot, then you mus' come, you dominate de whole earth. An now dem jine dat rahs-clot Christopher Columbus, rahs-clot, Pirate Morgan, Francis Drake. All dem same, dem fuckers. Dem kinda work used to work, man, legal laws, dem sit around an' drink dem blood-clot whiskey and say, "Haw, haw, haw, *Let us make a law*" callin em fucker an' t'ing, *yess mon!* Ya man, an' is just de small man *feel it at all times*. An de small man, is not only domination of herb him feel . . . *incrimination* of herb; evryt'ing, every illegal law is put up to fight against the small man. An' is de small man who is buildin' up the resource of the earth.

Yess mon! Slavery abolish! Dat was from about eighteenth or so sixteenth *blood-clot* century ago, dem say slavery abolish! Do right an' let every man be satisfied. Earth resource must be distribute right. Herb was made for the use of man, an' not for de use of some blood-clot drunkard. Herb was made for de use of man, an' not *men* in dem likkle blood-clot *chamber!* An' man must get herb cause man keep de earth runnin' till today. Not *men* in him likkle limousine, dem likkle blood-clot luxurious fucker. An dem make de law. Rahs-clot! Dem t'ing get me mad. Yeah, man. It's not me alone dat get mad. It's in some kinda madhouse de rahs-clot where some stay consciously mad and have to just *abide* wit' de situation, until de situation changes, y'know? But man, bum-clot, come to dat now, man.

Economical pressure, dem raise up everyting an' herb will keep you from t'inkin' about what's going on now. Dem wanna come *dominate*. Dem put out, dem wanna bring out dem drugs. Come spring it up on us, fucker! Dem trip, dem fuck up your head. Wise man use herb. We can do dat. *We have to get out of hell man,* whadayamean, *or let hell get out of us.* What you t'ink man? Too heavy for dem? Well, I *know* it is right.

Dem say dat herb is a dangerous drug, and pie-zen an' every day I pie-zen myself an' nevah die. So why? Fight against I? Pure Babylon. Fertilizer come from oil. An' rubbish. Oil an' herb don't mix. Yes, man: Herb must as plant a come by nature. Jus' grow, an' it *don't care* how it come. If it knot, or if it spread out. It nice same way. But as soon ya fertilize it, man, it pure fucker. Your belly hurt. Ah, ya feel bad like ya wanna vomit, man. Yes, man. But if you smoke some nice herb an' put your mind somewhere where inspiration flows, herb so nice.

MICHAEL KENNEDY

An Interview

RON ROSENBAUM

JANUARY 1977

MICHAEL KENNEDY IS A radical dope lawyer whose clients have included Dr. Timothy Leary and Nick Sand, a chemist indicted by the U.S. government for allegedly manufacturing enough LSD to turn on the entire world indefinitely. Mr. Kennedy is also one of the top political lawyers in America and had among his clients members of the Weather Underground, the United Farm Workers, GI-coffeehouse organizers, Los Siete de la Raza, Wounded Knee, Jack and Micki Scott, who harbored Patty Hearst, and lately the Puerto Rican Socialist Party.

Kennedy was born in Spokane, Washington. When he was ten he moved to California's San Joaquin Valley. He graduated from the University of California at Berkeley and took his law degree at Hastings College of Law in San Francisco. In 1963 he was admitted to the bar and joined Hoberg, Finger, Brown and Abramson, the best trial firm in California, whose specialty was personal injury claims against insurance companies. But before Kennedy tried many cases, he was hauled into the Army, where he graduated 154th in a class of 155 at Fort Benning's basic training.

It was military service that radicalized Kennedy. He was already unpopular with the Army for participating in radical activities while in law school. In the Army he learned about our secretly escalating involvement in Vietnam and made a number of antiwar speeches while in uniform. This did nothing to lessen his harassment by Army Intelligence, and by the time he returned to civilian life he was radicalized. The war was escalating, and insurance trials had begun to bore him, so in 1967 he took up an offer to be staff counsel for the National Emergency Civil Liberties Committee (an offshoot of the ACLU, formed when the ACLU introduced an anticommunist pledge and loyalty oath during the McCarthy era). It didn't take Kennedy long to learn the ropes of political trial work, and he got into dope work because dope and politics seemed to overlap naturally.

Kennedy has just recently moved to New York from San Francisco because he feels there is more political work in New York now, and he is involved in counseling the Puerto Rican independence movement in New York. By a happy coincidence, New York has the worst drug laws in the nation, and Mr. Kennedy should be able to make a decent living springing dopers in fun city.

High Times: What were those first dope cases like?

Kennedy: Marijuana charges. The first dope case that I took was a kid named Gypsy Peterson, who was the organizer of a GI coffeehouse at Fort Hood, Texas. He had been found with eight seeds in the lining of his pocket and was given eight years—a year a seed—by a Texas court. I took over his appeal, and we ultimately got the conviction set aside. That was the first time I got into detailed study of the dope laws and the search and seizure rules, particularly the Fourth Amendment defenses.

High Times: Did you get him off on a Fourth?

Kennedy: Yes, based upon an illegal search. The primary thing was that they violated his civil rights. Also, I think I was able to demonstrate that they wanted Gypsy for political reasons and would have done anything to get him, including possibly planting eight seeds.

I knew Gypsy as a result of having handled the Fort Hood 43 case, the 43 black GI's who refused to go to Chicago for antiriot duty in '68.

High Times: Is that the reason many radical lawyers also became dope lawyers: the political prosecution of their clients on dope charges?

Kennedy: I don't think so. I don't know if my experience is unique. Most radical lawyers ended up in dope law primarily because it was the only source of money in their practice. There are some dope clients who can pay, and there are some who cannot. There are some who are political, and there are some who are not. The vast majority of dopers, in my view, aren't political. No, I think most radical lawyers do dope work for money, in order to have enough income to be able to do the political cases. Because I have never made a dime on a political case.

High Times: You just said that most people who smoke dope are not political.

Kennedy: I really meant dealers. I didn't mean that the people who smoke dope are not political, because I don't think that that is accurate. But I don't think most dope dealers are.

High Times: Do you feel that dope has helped radicalize people politically?

Kennedy: Definitely. Dope obviously gives you a different perception of the society you live in and causes you to question some of the things that may have been traditionally unquestioned values.

The other thing is getting busted—that can radicalize you in a big hurry. When you see the heavy-handed way in which narcs, who are the primary fascist force in this country, treat people for offenses that are no greater than smoking flowers or expanding their consciousness, you've got to know that there is some other motivation going. And that that other motivation from the narc standpoint is political.

High Times: Why do you say that the narcs are the primary fascist force?

Kennedy: Well, I don't think it is a happenstance that Liddy and a lot of the most influential cop advisors in the Nixon administration and in a number of administrations before Nixon had had a heavy antidope background or dope prosecutorial background. The DEA, the Drug Enforcement Administration, and the state narcotics enforcement bureau, especially in states like California and New York, are probably the largest single-minded police force in the country. More money is being spent now on narcotics prosecutions and narcotics law enforcement than any other aspect of law. And there is more money to be made in the field of narcotics law enforcement than any other field of law enforcement. So it has all of the ingredients that would cause a very evil-minded person to want to get into it.

It also has the guise of law and order on its side. The laws are ill-advised for the most part, stupid and unenforceable and unintelligent. But police can, under the guise of law, break into people's homes and search them and violate their rights in a whole variety of ways. And they can do this with impunity.

High Times: Do you believe in the abolition of all penalties for use of drugs from heroin on down?

Kennedy: I think one area where we might maintain a narcotics law is where a cop is found stealing smack from the public coffers and dealing it. I think that is a criminal offense that ought to stay on the books permanently.

But aside from that, I don't think there is a dope law in this country that makes any sense at all. And I don't know if there can be any sensible dope laws in this country that can accomplish a prohuman purpose. The theoretical prohuman purpose of dope laws is to protect ourselves from our own ignorance. That assumes we are stupid. I don't think that is a very prohuman premise. We ought to be allowed to do anything we want to our own bodies.

If, as a result of ingesting something we then involve ourselves in collateral criminal activity, if they can prove that the substance ingested caused the criminal activity—which they will probably never be able to do—then maybe they should say that there is a cause and effect. But they shouldn't assume that dope is the problem, because dope itself is not the problem.

High Times: What is your feeling about the marijuana high itself? You say unrealistic laws against it radicalize people. Do you have a feeling that the high itself is a positive thing?

Kennedy: Yes, I haven't seen anything to indicate that there are any harmful side effects whatsoever from smoking marijuana. I think a great number of people get tremendous enjoyment out of it. It is clearly less harmful than tobacco. It is less harmful than alcohol and the things that our parents and earlier generations used. Alcohol was their marijuana, and despite the evidence that this was extremely harmful to them, they continued to imbibe. Yet despite the fact that the evidence is overwhelming and almost completely un-contradicted that marijuana is not harmful at all, and does in fact have some not only psychological but medical advantages to it, they still keep the laws on the books.

High Times: Tell us about the legal situation in California now. Do people smoke in public?

Kennedy: Oh, yes. People have been smoking in California for a number of years. I think I handled the last single-joint case in San Francisco. That was about three years ago.

A cop busted a kid near the City Lights Bookstore for smoking what a cop with a keen sense of smell suspected to be marijuana. He grabbed the cigarette from the kid and busted him. It was, in fact, a marijuana cigarette. And I argued to the judge that it was nonsense. I didn't make it a legal argument. I said, "This is totally ridiculous. Are you going to try and pop everybody who smokes a joint?" The judge threw the case out.

Then the DA quietly said to the police, we don't want you busting anyone for smoking. We have real crime in the streets. Next to Miami, San Francisco has the largest ripoff crime rate in the country. They haven't solved a burglary in San Francisco in many years. Stop the harassment of people who smoke.

High Times: What precautions would you say people have to take these days? Can they smoke on the street in California? Can they carry an ounce of dope around?

Kennedy: California is not really a monolithic entity. Because, for example, when the marijuana laws were decriminialized in California, the first thing that Ed Davis—who is the chief of police in Los Angeles and who has to be one of the craziest bastards in the world, in addition to being just stoned mean—issued an ounce scale to every cop. So that they could make the distinction right on the street between writing you a citation like a traffic ticket if you have an ounce of grass, or a felony rap.

So L.A. is a little weird. If you want to do anything enjoyable, do it in someplace other than L.A. In northern California there have been no significant problems with people smoking dope in public for years now.

High Times: Have narcs harassed you because of your success in getting people off legally?

Kennedy: I couldn't win a popularity contest with the narcs, that is a fact. They have harassed us.

High Times: What sorts of things?

Kennedy: When we were handling the Brotherhood cases down in Orange County, I was representing Michael Randall. And Michael had been out on bail and we had been going through 54 suppression motions. We were living down there, doing nothing but that case. We had a little beach house in Laguna Beach.

The narcs got a passport complaint out of the District Court in Los Angeles against Randall. They held it for about a week and waited to serve it until Friday night at eight o'clock at my house, where Randall was with his wife, cooking Mexican food for us. The narcs came, about ten of them, to serve this warrant when they could have served it that very day in court. And the narcs were the same narcs that we had on the stand every day for the past six or eight weeks, and we had really kicked some ass with them.

The doorbell rang, I looked out the window and I recognized two of the narcs. I turned around and said to everybody, "Cool it, it's the narcs." They kicked the door in, and Don Strange, who is the head of the Southern California Task Force of the Drug Enforcement Administration, stuck a gun that looked like a cannon right in my nose, and his eyes were big and his hand was shaking. I thought he was going to blow us away, because he was really scared.

They thereafter charged me with six misdemeanors in California and brought me to trial. We ultimately beat the charges because I wasn't guilty. They charged me with using obscenity in the presence of women and children. The only women there were Mrs. Kennedy and Mrs. Randall, and the only children I could perceive were the narcs themselves. The charges were all thrown out. But that is an example.

Many narcs have said to me, "We will get you one of these days." They don't like it when they go to a great deal of trouble—usually illegal trouble—to make a case, and you are able to persuade a judge and jury of the illegalities inherent in the case, and the client gets off. And the narcs are also convinced that some of the dope lawyers in the country must be involved in the trafficking of drugs. Although this has not happened to me, a number of lawyers have been set up by narcs.

High Times: What are some of the strategies that you favor in dope cases? There are obviously the search and seizure illegalities, but have you come up with any other particular things that have outsmarted the narcs?

Kennedy: I think the primary success has been due to some imaginative work in the Fourth Amendment area, the search and seizure area. Other than that, we have used the cannabis defense. And as you know, that has been chopped out of the law.

High Times: That there are alternate forms of the plant?

Kennedy: Right, they can't prove that it is *Cannabis sativa,* for example. It could be *Cannabis indica.* Also, we have convinced juries that even though the client may have in fact been in possession of contraband—marijuana, LSD—that in fact there were so many outrageous things done by the narcs that they are inherently not believable.

Most narcotics officers cannot help but gild the lily in their case, even if they made what would constitute a straight, legal bust. They always have to embellish it in some fashion in order to make themselves look better. I think they are probably insecure. So when you get their reports or their prior statements and you compare them to other clear facts and you find some variance, then the juries begin to worry about who is telling the truth.

And jurors are not so surprised that a defendant may come up with some strange defenses that may or may not bear some resemblance to the truth. But when a cop does that, his duty is to tell the truth and to uphold the law, not to get a conviction. The jurors tend to be very hard on the cops.

High Times: How bad is search and seizure case law now?

Kennedy: Well, the United States Supreme Court has been systematically whittling away at the Fourth Amendment. The Supreme Court under Warren, and for some years after, made it very clear that illegally obtained evidence would have to be suppressed, could not be used for any purpose whatsoever. That is not to protect a guilty person or a person who is in possession of contraband or an illegal substance, but because they understood that it is far more outrageous and far more dangerous to allow state officers or federal officers to go unpunished when they violate the rights of the citizenry. Their responsibility is to protect the citizenry, not to violate them. That is theoretically the difference between the democratic government and the totalitarian government, although that difference is becoming less clear as things develop in this country.

Now the Supreme Court says that illegally obtained evidence, no matter how illegally obtained, can be used in a grand jury, for example, to obtain an indictment. There are indications that illegally obtained evidence can now be used for impeachment purposes. There are a variety of other ways in which the Supreme Court has taken apart the Fourth Amendment.

This is not true for states such as California, however, which still give very strong Fourth-Amendment rights in the search and seizure area. In California they have to demonstrate very strong probable cause in order to substantiate a bust. The classic cases were the automobile cases where a person with a beard and long hair was going through a small town in northern California or someplace and a cop would pull him over allegedly because his tail light was faulty or his license plate was hanging off. And the cop would invariably say, "Well, just as I started to pull the person over. I put my light and my siren on and I saw him make some type of furtive movement." He was putting his hand down his crotch, or bending down over here or something like that.

The Supreme Court of California pointed out those activities are as consistent with innocence as they are with guilt, and you have to assume that the person is innocent. And that does not give you probable cause to then ransack and roust that person. But under federal law they could probably get away with it.

High Times: What about that classic automobile case in other states?

Kennedy: In most other states the rule would be the same as in California. In most other states you would have to demonstrate strong probable cause. It is the federal busts that are the more complicated. And because in so many states the rules with reference to the Fourth Amendment are much better for the defendant than for the narcs, a lot of times state officers make a bust that they know they can't win under their state rules, they'll turn it over to the feds and try to bring a federal case against the individual to get around the more lenient and protective laws. However, in New York, federal busts are frequently turned over to the state for prosecution in order to take advantage of New York's oppressive dope laws.

High Times: They can do that?

Kennedy: It is illegal for them to do it, but they do it.

High Times: What is the "In Plain View Doctrine" regarding your own premises?

Kennedy: The Plain View Doctrine is that if something is in plain view, then finding it does not constitute a search and is not an invasion of your rights against an unreasonable search and seizure.

Well, the cops in their typically ambitious style extended that and began crawling up fire escapes, peering in windows and hanging out in toilets. It got so outrageous that finally the courts began cutting back and they said, "All right, plain view is not a search—when you are in a place that you have a right to be. But when you are in a place where you don't have a right to be, where an individual has a reasonable expectation of privacy, you are in fact searching with your eyes." So now when the cops are hanging out in the toilets, trying to watch people, or if they had to climb up a tree to look in your window to catch you rolling a joint, that would be illegal, and you can win your case then.

The area around which the court has cut back most significantly is in the entrapment area. Entrapment is critical in dope law. I have had many cases where the defendant could not possibly have gotten involved in a criminal activity without the provocation of the cops.

And the classic case was a case up in Seattle that the Supreme Court decided a year ago. This guy wanted to make amphetamine, and he didn't have a critical ingredient. There was no way that he could get this ingredient. He talked to a guy who he heard through the grapevine had the ingredient that he needed. The guy was a narcotics officer. So the officer provided the critical ingredient without which the speed could not have been made, without which the crime could not have been committed. If that is not a case of entrapment, one couldn't exist.

The Supreme Court says it doesn't matter that the cop did that. If the defendant has any criminal propensity himself at all, any criminal attitude in his mind, that is enough. And the entrapment goes out the window. But fortunately, it is not the law in California. It is not the law in most states. But it is the law in federal cases.

There is basically no entrapment defense in federal cases anymore. And that is what makes them very difficult to defend, because the police entrap a great deal. I mean, the traditional political bust for black political people has been to plant a bag of heroin on them.

High Times: What about the area of smell these days? If they can smell the smoke can they make a search?

Kennedy: There is a doctrine called the "Plain Smell Doctrine." A rather remarkable thing happened. Suddenly every cop in the country developed an extraordinary sense of smell. "I smelled marijuana on him." And it got to the point where that became such a subjective and such a ludicrous test that the court started throwing it out.

Smell by itself is not enough. They've got to have something else. Because you can take a narcotics officer's nose and the dogs' noses and run tests with them that they can't possibly pass. Most of them can't distinguish burning oregano from burning marijuana or burning pepper weed. So smell is not the significant factor.

High Times: Well, what was your association with Leary, and when did that begin?

Kennedy: I was hired by Timothy Leary to handle his California appeal, just after his California conviction in March of 1970. The first time I met him was in Orange County jail just after his sentencing. I agreed to take the appeal. I undertook it and wrote what I consider to be an extraordinary brief. And we took the brief down to him on a day in early September. I remember it had to be filed like on a Tuesday. We took it down to him on Saturday. He read it and made a lot of corrections. He was always very actively involved in the legal process. A very bright guy. And then on the next Sunday he went over the wall.

A couple of months later, I got a collect phone call from Algeria. I said, "Timothy, I take it that you didn't like the brief," because he went over the wall. He said, "It doesn't really have anything to do with your brief writing or your legal ability, Michael. It is just that I didn't have much confidence in the courts." So he chose another route.

My first reaction was, I didn't believe that he had escaped. I thought they had killed him or something. The level of paranoia was sufficiently higher in 1970 than it is now. I got a copy of the statement that was given to the media by the Weather Underground. The statement was in Leary's handwriting, and I could authenticate it. I had gotten so many calls from the press that we held a press conference to authenticate the fact that he had escaped, apparently with the help of the Weather Underground organization. At the time I thought it was an extraordinary thing.

Timothy Leary was in jail illegally, without any doubt. He had been convicted of having two small roaches in the ash tray of a station wagon that didn't even belong to him. He was clearly convicted for political reasons, because of who he was and what he had said and done. Furthermore, Judge MacMillan in Orange County sentenced Leary and denied Leary bail pending appeal when they knew that case was a loser, because we had a deadpan winner on appeal. Had Tim stayed in jail, we would have gotten him out. And he wouldn't have been in the predicament he later found himself in. But he was clearly in jail illegally.

And the judge had illegally denied Leary bail to keep him from being able to communicate with the public, because Leary was having a pronounced effect on the young at that time. It seemed to me that a coalition between Timothy Leary and a revolutionary organization such as the Weather Underground was a good, progressive marriage.

In 1970, I looked at the youth of America as being the primary force of revolutionary change in this country. And the vast majority of the youth, it seemed to me, rather than being into a political consciousness that helped them to understand the conditions that were getting increasingly worse, as Nixon was becoming stronger and stronger—rather than understanding conditions and doing something about them, it seemed to me that they were deliberately turning their backs and using dope and music to do that.

Well, I love the dope and I love the music but it seemed to me that they were ignoring a very important aspect of life, namely the political situation. And when an individual of the prominence of Leary connects himself with the most prominent underground organization and the only cohesive political force on the Left then, I thought it was a phenomenal thing, a truly great event.

In retrospect, six years later, I think that was true then and I think it is true now. What happened, unfortunately, was that Leary himself was never able to respond politically to the situation. He was not able to discipline himself sufficiently in Algeria to develop a comfortable life there. He was not able to sufficiently discipline himself in Switzerland to develop a comfortable life there. The Swiss were perfectly willing to grant him asylum, despite the fact that John Mitchell himself went over there and told the Swiss, "You know, we are very serious about this. The United States government wants him back." It is a typical example of how stupid Mitchell can be. I mean, to want a problem such as Leary back in your backyard has to be crazy.

But Leary could have stayed in Switzerland and allowed himself to develop politically into a very progressive international force. For reasons that escape me, and for reasons that probably have to do with his sense of himself, he chose to put himself in Afghanistan, which is a country that he knew was controlled in large measure by what was then the Bureau of Narcotics and Dangerous Drug Enforcement, whose illegitimate child is now the DEA.

So when Leary went to Afghanistan, he had to know that he was going to get popped there, but he went anyway. There was some suggestion that he went at the behest or request of Joanna Leary, and some people said that she was an agent. I don't know if she is an agent or not, but she certainly didn't do anybody any good that I can see. Some people say that Dennis Martino set him up for that. Dennis was later killed under suspicious circumstances in Spain.

But anyway, Leary, unless he was totally out of his mind—and there is reason to believe that he may always have been—went to Afghanistan, was busted, put on a plane, and sent back here. And when he came back, he expected, I guess, some type of youthful revolutionary exuberance to free him. When, in fact, while there was a good deal of youthful exuberance, it certainly wasn't directed at freeing him. So Tim found himself languishing in a jail once again.

I still don't think it was justifiable that Leary was in jail. Millions of people in this country, revolutionary and otherwise, have found themselves in the position of being in jail unjustifiably and have been given the opportunity to buy their freedom by selling somebody else's. My experience is that the vast majority of people don't do that, and clearly people of political beliefs and political integrity don't do that. But when Leary felt himself abandoned, then he chose to put himself in a position where he would barter his freedom and his fucked-up life for other people's freedom. And they began.

By "they" I mean he and Joanna. He and Joanna set up George Chula, a lawyer who had tried Tim's case and was an old friend of Tim's in Orange County. Joanna wired herself and persuaded George Chula to give her a little bit of cocaine in a hotel room that she had bugged. They busted George on that. Timothy Leary testified to a grand jury in Orange County that George had brought him hash into the jail. The grand jury in Orange County, which has indicted everybody for anything at the request of the

DA down there, refused to indict George because they found Leary inherently unbelievable. So, fortunately, George didn't take a fall on that charge.

Thereafter Leary testified and was thoroughly debriefed by the FBI and I don't know how many other federal and state agents. He testified before grand juries in Chicago, in San Francisco and possibly other places. He was going to deliver up some big indictments, and he was going to deliver up some lawyers, and he was going to deliver up a whole lot of people. It turned out that he didn't deliver up anybody. I don't believe it is because he didn't make the attempt.

High Times: There are people who say that no one went to jail because of Leary, whatever Leary did. Either he was playing it that way, or he was too unbelievable anyway. But your feeling is that he would have if he could have?

Kennedy: Timothy is one of the most opportunistic scoundrels I have had the dubious pleasure of meeting. And while he may say now that in fact he didn't hurt anybody by his testimony, the other side of that is, if he didn't hurt anybody it wasn't because he didn't try. What he was trying to do was exchange his freedom for other people's. The fact that he didn't succeed in it doesn't cause me to feel that he is any the less guilty of a political crime. And I think he is. And I think he knows it.

And, as I have said, when people have asked me what Timothy Leary is doing now, I've said that I understand he is trying to build a spaceship to go to Venus, and I think the conscientious people in this country should do all they can to help him.

High Times: Tell us about the Brotherhood of Eternal Love acid conspiracy.

Kennedy: The biggest acid bust ever made was the acid bust of the Brotherhood of Eternal Love on the West Coast and in Hawaii. They claimed it was the largest ring in the world, that they were capable of making a million hits a week, and that they had made several hundred million hits and spread them all over the world. To read the indictments, there was enough acid made by the Brotherhood of Eternal Love to turn on everybody on the planet indefinitely.

When they made this massive bust, they only came up with half a dozen people, and they came up with no acid at all, which was always amazing. There is no question that the Brotherhood of Eternal Love was manufacturing acid at some point. There was some question as to who was in the Brotherhood of Eternal Love, or whether it really existed. It certainly never existed in the monolithic and conspiratorial way that the indictment alleged or that the government thought. They were a number of individuals who had a loose connection, and who also had the dubious distinction of associating with Dr. Timothy Leary.

High Times: What exactly was the Brotherhood? Can you explain it?

Kennedy: It was a loose-knit group of individuals, the common denominator of whom was that they all believed in psychedelics, they all believed in hallucinogenics and they all believed that the world would be better if more people took psychedelics. And what they tried to do was to spread as many psychedelic substances as they could around the land. Sort of like Johnny Appleseed.

High Times: In 1973 they indicted the Brotherhood, in a major indictment that was on the cover of the *New York Times* and virtually nowhere else in the media. It was supposed to be the culmination of the Bureau of Narcotics and Dangerous Drugs' operation to crush this movement. What ultimately happened on all those cases?

Kennedy: The DEA never caught the bulk of the individuals they wanted in that case. Of the few they caught, several were acquitted or charges were dismissed. A few pleaded guilty to minor offenses. I think the maximum sentence served in that case was six months. One man went back underground—namely, my client Michael Boyd Randall, after they had rebusted and beaten the shit out of him. I can understand why he would.

High Times: Some of the Brotherhood people themselves described the group as the brotherhood of eternal hoods. Was it a mixed group of people as to their level of idealism and their ethics?

Kennedy: Oh, yes, they were very mixed. And there were a number of people who became quite embittered with others, and that is why so many snitches developed. Because they had no basic political views that they could cling to.

High Times: Yet the government still tries to keep this concept, that there is a brotherhood, actively functioning and responsible for some portion of the drug traffic in this country. They try to keep this concept alive. Is it still alive? And if not, why does the government try to keep it alive?

Kennedy: It is not alive based upon anything that I know of. I think that it, along with the LSD movement, passed in history. It was the end of an era. And not as a result of extraordinary police skills, but because the era happened to end. Individuals moved on to other levels and other things.

It doesn't surprise me that the bureaucrats and the narcotics officers would continue to say that there is out there this public menace, whether they describe it as a brotherhood or what. It is like J. Edgar Hoover going into the Senate, saying that now there are 75 million Communists in this U.S. of A. You got to give me an extra hundred dollars per in order for me to be able to find them. The fact of the matter is that they didn't exist at all. But what he wanted to do was to perpetuate his own bureaucracy.

High Times: In 1974 they tried to dig up the ghost of the Brotherhood?

Kennedy: The Nick Sand trial in San Francisco was an extraordinary case. It was to be the terminal-seminal acid conspiracy case, and they had all the biggies in there. It had everything in the case but acid. It had the only multi-millionaire snitch I knew of in Billy Hitchcock, it had two of the brightest and best acid manufacturers ever, other than Owsley. There were Nick Sand and Tim Scully. They had a brilliant chemist who was also a very straight full professor at Case Western. It had hidden bank accounts in the Bahamas, hidden bank accounts in Switzerland, talk of millions and millions of hits of acid, millions and millions in dollars. Suitcases filled with thousand-dollar bills floating in and out. None of this was evidence. This was all in the recollections of people. And it had Billy Hitchcock coming in with his Gucci agenda.

It also had Leary. Leary had an opportunity—this is when I first knew that he turned snitch—Leary had an opportunity to testify in that case. He was up at Vacaville being deprogrammed. That California medical facility. I think they were trying to find his brain, and if he had any chromosomes left. And Timothy was at a meeting that had been held with Nick Sand and other people. At this meeting there was some talk about Nick Sand becoming the chemist for the Brotherhood. That's what one of the snitches said. There were many of them. As a matter of fact, it turned out everyone was a snitch except for Sand, Scully, and Friedman.

Leary was at that meeting. I talked to Leary about it, and he said that no discussion had ever occurred about Sand being the chemist for the Brotherhood. I asked Leary if he would testify to that fact, and he said he thought he would. "After all, it's the truth," he said, with his eyes glowing.

An hour after I left, the prosecutor came in to see Leary, and they had a several-hour chat. I called Leary's lawyer and asked him if he knew that his client was talking to the government prosecutor. He said he didn't, but he would check into it. Then I got a letter from Leary saying that under the circumstances he didn't think he could help Sand, so he refused to testify in that particular case.

I had a Hell's Angel on the stand, and I was cross-examining to try to convince the jury that he was a liar and that anything that he said couldn't be true. "Now," I said, "now isn't it a fact that you pumped six bullets into the head of your best friend?" He said, "No, that's not true." I said, "What do you mean, that's not true? I have—" and I started to pull out a police report and show it to him, and he said, "It was seven—seven bullets."

The other thing that was difficult about that case was that they charged one conspiracy and they proved fifteen separate unrelated conspiracies. The judge allowed the prosecutor to bring in every piece of extraneous gossip, nasty, negative information about any of these individuals or their associates that could possibly be done. So it was a total trial by character assassination.

High Times: Nevertheless, they didn't get that much from it.

Kennedy: The most that they were able to get was that almost everyone thought that Sand and Scully were remarkably decent people, idealistic.

High Times: What was the sentence that Sand and Scully got?

Kennedy: Scully got twenty years and Sand got fifteen years.

High Times: Where are they now?

Kennedy: They're out on bail pending appeal. The judge put a million dollars bail on them. The Ninth Circuit reversed it.

High Times: The publicity that came out of that trial—I'm thinking of one *Village Voice* article in particular—was all to the effect that this exposed Tim Leary and the psychedelic movement as just sort of snake-oil peddlers. Now I know you have your obvious disagreements with Leary, but what would you say, what's your reaction to that?

Kennedy: There clearly was no evidence that they were peddling snake oil. But the prosecution was arguing that these individuals were exclusively money-oriented. The only person in that case who was exclusively money-oriented was Billy Hitchcock. Billy Hitchcock, "Old Megabucks," came in with all the money, spread the money out so the acid could be manufactured and took far and away the bulk of the money that came back, and not that much money came back. Sand and Scully could both have made fortunes in a variety of ways. Scully invented the biofeedback machine—he could make a million dollars on that alone.

They weren't in it for money. They were in it because they believed that the mental and emotional and psychological expansionist effect of acid was one of the clearest ways to break through what they saw as a complete cultural block lying on us. You can't live in this country and not feel this block. And they made, they said, an acid that was legal. It was called ALD-52. And the interesting thing about ALD-52 . . .

High Times: At no point did the government ever prove that they were manufacturing LSD?

Kennedy: That is right.

High Times: But they got very wiped out on what they did manufacture.

Kennedy: We had evidence to indicate that they had been manufacturing ALD-52. LSD-25 is illegal. ALD-52 hasn't been made illegal, and the only reason they haven't made it illegal is because the narc chemists haven't found it yet, although it was in all the literature. Hofmann isolated it. And it has an acetyl group that is attached to the lysergic acid, which develops the same hallucinogenic effects as LSD-25. But you don't have to go through LSD-25 in the manufacturing process.

When they said that they hadn't made LSD-25 but that they had made ALD-52 I said, well, at some point you had to have had LSD-25 to get to this stage. But they didn't. And they showed me the charts of how it could be done. And Scully, being the archivist, or rat-packer that he is, had something. He dug it up, we analyzed it and on the chromographic scale it showed that in fact it was ALD-52. And that was the only acid in the case. The government didn't have any.

High Times: How exactly was that introduced into court?

Kennedy: Tim Scully was sitting on the stand, and I said, "Well, do you happen to have any ALD-52 with you?" He said, "Yes, I do." I said, "Where did you get it?" He had had it buried at his ranch in Mendocino for years. They examined it. And they performed two tests on it, both of which destroyed the acetyl group. So they came up positive LSD for the trial. We put an expert on the stand to explain that, in their testing processes, they destroyed the acetyl group and they created LSD-25. My argument was that the government manufactured LSD-25.

High Times: But what you needed was a spectroscopic analysis which would be more precise. And they purposely avoided that test?

Kennedy: They refused to do it. We gave them the opportunity.

High Times: I have heard that when Sand was arrested they found some pieces of paper which contained over a hundred formulas for psychedelic drugs unknown to the general public, and many unknown even to psychedelic chemistry researchers. In particular, do you know anything about this? Are these formulas now lost to psychedelic science?

Kennedy: That evidence was confiscated from Nick when he and Judy were busted in Fenton, Missouri. At what they described as the largest clandestine lab in the world. Nick says that the formulas are all in his head. I am sure they probably are. There is a lot in that head.

High Times: It seems that an analysis of the methods of distribution of acid in the Sixties or early Seventies would show that the basic purpose was noncommercial.

Kennedy: Oh, yes.

High Times: A price was put on it to motivate it down the line, and some people certainly made money, but many other people were just kind of moving it around.

Kennedy: Right. That was basically the experience I had with the clients I dealt with. But they weren't in it for money.

High Times: What is the acid-dealing scene like now?

Kennedy: It is almost nonexistent. Not quite nonexistent, but almost nonexistent.

High Times: Acid itself is still around.

Kennedy: Oh, yes. But the acid future has apparently gone down. The bottom has fallen out of the market. It gets around quietly, though.

High Times: You represented the Weather people . . .

Kennedy: I represented some of the Weather people in Chicago around the Chicago convention and after the Days of Rage. And I knew quite well Bernadine Dohrn, who was active in New York as an organizer for the National Lawyers Guild when I first met her. And I met several of the Weather people in Chicago at the time they were in SDS. Thereafter I represented several Weather people who surfaced or were captured in indictments against them in Chicago, Detroit, and San Francisco. And I represented people who have been hauled in front of Weather grand juries in various parts of the country, including Leslie Bacon up in Seattle.

High Times: They haven't captured any Weather people. Why is that?

Kennedy: Well, I think there are two possible explanations. The FBI and the Internal Security Division of the Justice Department are incompetent. And/or the Weather Underground are extremely competent. Probably a little of both.

It seems fairly clear that the Weather Underground organization couldn't sustain six years of underground activity without a very large overground support contingent. I think, in fact, that they get a tremendous amount of support from people in this country. And that, to me, is the primary explanation for their survival. For them to have survived the heavy years of the Nixon administration makes it even more remarkable.

High Times: What do you feel about the direction their politics are going in now?

Kennedy: I always empathized with their actions. They didn't hurt any-body, and the symbolism of their targets was phenomenal, because one of the things that seemed to be particularly oppressing during the Nixon years were these feelings of impotency and cynicism. And with their actions they overcame that in a variety of ways and showed the vulnerability of U.S. imperialism from within. I thought it was an important lesson. But it seemed to me that they lacked the strategy necessary for the long haul.

I thought that the publication of *Prairie Fire* was the real beginning, even though it has its shortcomings. And I noticed in their *Osawatomie* issues that they have begun to criticize some of their shortcomings. I expect to see another manifesto of theirs soon. They are clearly trying to organize a party now. They have an anti-imperialist strategy. They have an understanding of the importance of national liberation and of the libera-tion of women. That seems to be a higher understanding than any other organization around, with the possible exception of the Puerto Rican Socialist Party. They have gotten their theory and practice into a better tandem.

High Times: There's been talk about grand juries on the West Coast going after *Prairie Fire* and *Osawatomie*.

Kennedy: Well, the government gets all the copies of *Prairie Fire* and *Osawatomie* they want. An article appeared that named members of the *Prairie Fire* organizing committee, which is an aboveground support group that distributes *Prairie Fire* around the country and things like that. It was one of the key organizers of the Hard Times Conference in Chicago and one of the members of the July Fourth coalition. And there was a time when, according to press reports, a member of the Oregon Communist Party was in the *Prairie Fire* Organizing Committee. And they tried an old-fashioned 1950's Communist witchhunt scare tactic.

I don't think the government had any intention whatsoever of subpoe-naing *Prairie Fire* people, because they knew exactly what they were going to do, their position of noncollaboration had been clear before. And the govern-ment saw that by subpoenaing them they would give *Prairie Fire*'s organizers an opportunity to organize further and give them an additional forum.

The nearest thing to subpoenas in terms of the Weather Underground organization recently was the attempt to subpoena the filmmakers in Los Angeles who filmed the Weather people. And the subpoenas were not only withdrawn, but two other things happened. The Hollywood community, going against the example of their fear and trepidation when they ran and even snitched on one another in the fifties, came out very strongly in support of this film and their right to make it. The other thing was that the Assistant U.S. Attorney who issued the subpoenas was fired, because he had overstepped his political bounds. The government doesn't want to take the Weather Underground to the grand jury forum. They have been beaten in that regard.

High Times: So are they pretty much helpless, or are there new weapons they are developing? What do you think the next stage of that is going to be?

Kennedy: I think the machinery of the state is never helpless, particularly in a state that's as highly organized as our state is. But I don't think that people are without the will and the understanding to fight. The victory of the Vietnamese people is a great lesson. So are the national liberation struggles in Mozambique and Angola. These are lessons of two types. One is that U.S. imperialism is not undefeatable. And secondly that people are not without the ability to determine their own fate.

High Times: People on the East Coast have a hard time getting a fix on what seems to be a whole new underground development in San Francisco, the New World Liberation Front.

Kennedy: It is hard to get a fix on that on the West Coast. It is probably hard to get a fix on it even if you are in the organization.

High Times: What do you think of that? Do we take them seriously as a revolutionary organization?

Kennedy: I think groups such as the SLA and the NWLF are not entirely the red guerrilla army—and not entirely aberration. But I think they can't go very far politically, primarily because they are operating on what seems to me to be the theory of Regis Debray: a foco theory of politics. That is, you can create a revolution by having a small band of armed guerrillas through exemplary action do particular things and then have the whole body politic, the working class, rise up and throw out the bourgeoisie. I don't think that's the way it happens at all, particularly in a society as privileged and alienated and split as ours.

I think we have to take them seriously because I think they are dedicated, and I think that they are trying in their own way to bring about change and to heighten people's political consciousness. But in fact what I think they are accomplishing is to put themselves into a dead-end track, into a position where they become further alienated from their constituency, which has to be the people of this country, working class people and blacks, women, native Americans, Puerto Ricans, Mexican Americans.

By the way, I think the Weather Underground was running that same risk. Before *Prairie Fire* and before some of the statements that have come out in Osawatomie, which show that they are not going to go down that dead-end road. They are in fact going to develop a Marxist party.

High Times: You were involved in the whole controversy over the SLA, the Jack Scott involvement. What can you tell us about that?

Kennedy: Well, it is true that I represented Jack Scott and Micki Scott, although I don't represent them any longer. While they were underground and being chased by what seemed to be virtually every cop in the country, they called me and asked me whether or not I would meet with them. And I told them that I would, and I did meet with them. They said that they wanted to turn themselves in, that they were innocent of any wrongdoing. They wanted to come back and fight, and if that fight meant going to jail for refusing to collaborate with the grand jury or for harboring Patty Hearst or whatever, they wanted an opportunity to fight it.

The thing that was worrying them most was that massacre of the SLA people in Los Angeles because there was a variety of ways they could have gotten those young people out of that house without having to kill them. Jack and Micki were rightfully terrified that they wouldn't be allowed to surface, that they would be killed also, because for all the government knew, they were members of the SLA.

So when they called, I arranged to meet with them, and we agreed that they would surface. I said the safest way to surface is to surface right in the middle of the media. So we organized a press conference in San Francisco, and with the help of some friends in San Francisco and Cecil Williams at the Glide Memorial Church, we were able to surface them right under the noses of the FBI, much to the FBI's embarrassment.

And after they were surfaced, the truth, I think, came out. So even if they could have made a harboring case against Jack or Micki in Harrisburg for harboring Patty Hearst, the government knew damn well that the case had no prosecutorial romance to it. They couldn't win it.

There are two great examples of why they couldn't win it. One is Poindexter, who harbored Angela Davis. They caught them red-handed, and the jury still walked Poindexter out. Stringfellow harbored Dan Berrigan, and they couldn't make a case against him. Because it is very difficult in this country for the government to persuade a jury, unless the jury is completely reactionary, that an individual who does nothing more than give human comfort—I am not talking about collateral criminal activity, but comfort and care to another human being—that such a person should be jailed.

That proved to be a correct strategy, and Jack and Micki were not indicted. They were called before a grand jury and they refused to cooperate. And then, while the government was trying to figure out what it was going to do with their refusal to cooperate, Patty Hearst was captured on the West Coast, and that changed all the odds significantly.

High Times: Did Jack and Micki make a mistake if they, as it seems, collaborated with *Rolling Stone*?

Kennedy: It is hard for me to figure out whether or not that was a mistake. I think it probably was. The primary mistake that Jack and Micki made was to engage themselves on the press or media level, rather than on a political level. They apparently found the spotlight irresistible, because one of the first things they asked me to do was to introduce them to some media people. I said, "I will be glad to do that, but it seems to me that you would be better off going back to Oregon and engaging yourself in political roots so that you can have a defense organization." But I introduced them to David Weir and Howard Kohn. I also introduced them to a stringer from *the New York Times*. And to another writer, David Harris.

Ultimately there was an agreement that Jack was going to do a book, and that Howard Kohn and David Weir were going to ghost. I had nothing to do with that at all. I did handle some of the negotiations to sell the book in New York, which fell through for a variety of reasons. We then went on a trip, Mrs. Kennedy and I, to the People's Republic of China. And when we came back, this *Rolling Stone* piece had already been written.

According to *Rolling Stone,* Scott was to get some money. He didn't get enough. Then he got very upset and he wanted to back out of the project. *Rolling Stone* issued a check to him for the amount of money that had been agreed on. Jack refused to accept the check. He called me and told me to fight it and stop the piece, that he was going to come out and say that I had introduced Kohn and Weir to him as my legal investigators. He knew that I knew Howard and David quite well, and that I also knew a lot of people at *Rolling Stone* and maybe I could kill the article.

I told him that in my view the article was ill-advised and that I would talk to Howard and David about it. But under no circumstance was I going to cave in to his bullshit threat, because he knew that it wasn't true. They were not my legal investigators, had not been introduced to him as such. They were introduced to him as members of the press, because that is who he was interested in meeting.

So the article appeared, and the next day on the front page of the *Examiner* there appeared this article in which Scott accused me of breach of faith and breach of confidence and claimed that Kohn and Weir were my investigators. That was on the front page. Scott subsequently retracted that statement and apologized for it. The retraction was on page 32, buried in the corner. And I had no further contact with Jack or Micki Scott.

High Times: How do you feel about what happened to Patty? The verdict?

Kennedy: I haven't figured out what's happened to her yet. I know that she's been kidnapped at least twice. It seems to me that she's having more difficulty getting rid of her second set of kidnappers than she had with the first set. I think she probably liked the SLA better than she likes her present kidnappers—namely her parents and the FBI.

She's clearly become a snitch, and I think the strategy that Lennie Weinglass used for Bill and Emily Harris was an intelligent one, because there's little doubt in my mind that the government was going to sandbag the Harrises with Patty.

I think she's a very unfortunate person, and I hope that she is able to survive this experience and that she's able to extricate herself from the most recent kidnapping and avoid further kidnappings for the rest of her life.

High Times: Do you see a parallel between her and Leary?

Kennedy: I think there is one. When an individual who is not rooted politically finds himself or herself in harm's way, they don't have the ability to respond in a principled political fashion. So they respond in an opportunistic fashion. She's trying to buy her best deal by selling other people. Leary tried to buy his best deal by selling other people.

High Times: How would you have defended Patty?

Kennedy: It's always difficult for any lawyer to judge another lawyer. But from what I know, you never put a defendant on the stand when you know the defendant is going to have to take the Fifth Amendment in front of the jury, because that seems to me to be a devastating attack on your own client's credibility. F. Lee Bailey is a very reactionary, very right-wing guy. He was clearly in a position of wanting the Hearst and FBI forces to prevail, and he saw the situation of his client, I think, in line with the Hearsts and the FBI.

High Times: Didn't you say you wouldn't take the Hearsts' money? Were you approached by Mrs. Hearst?

Kennedy: No. After I had surfaced Jack and Micki Scott, Mr. Hearst came in. He said, "Call me 'Randy.' " He asked whether or not he could retain me so that we could have an attorney-client privilege. I told him no, I wasn't interested in being retained by him, nor was I interested in having any privilege.

High Times: What's to become of Abbie Hoffman? What is his legal situation if he comes back? Is the statute of limitations suspended when someone is a fugitive?

Kennedy: Yes. Basically, the statute of limitations would not help Abbie because the statute of limitations on a New York State crime would not run out while Abbie is a fugitive from the state. He fell victim to the Rockefeller laws in New York, as well as falling victim to his own mistake in judgment.

High Times: What mistake was that?

Kennedy: He was getting himself into a position with a whole lot of cops where he could be entrapped into a coke sale. He ended up spending some time with some very strange people. To put himself into that position was a mistake. But to face fifteen years to life, under the Rockefeller law, to face going to Attica, where he probably would have been killed, causes one to understand why he split.

I think that the times have changed a little bit. I also think the Rockefeller laws have failed in their purpose. Their avowed purpose, of course, was to stop drug traffic, but I don't see how you can stop drug traffic when the bulk of the drug traffic Is being done by cops anyway.

The first thing that I saw happen with reference to the Rockefeller laws was that the drug traffic in Jersey got a real shot in the arm. Because the bulk of the dealers went across the river. But since that time the impact has basically failed. That is, they have not stopped traffic in heavy drugs, and the reason they haven't stopped traffic in heroin, which is the heaviest drug, is because they don't want to stop heroin traffic. They want to continue it, particularly in Harlem, because it's the greatest opportunity to keep what is one of the most potentially insurrectionist areas of our country, namely Harlem or the South Bronx, from blowing up. In other words, they keep it from blowing up by poisoning the minds of the young people with all the smack they can possibly keep on the street.

High Times: Is there any way left to attack the Rockefeller laws, aside from getting them repealed?

Kennedy: The bulk of the legal strategies have been tried. Dope laws are predominantly a political and not a legal problem, and until the political situation has changed, the dope laws are going to continue to be a vehicle for a lot of very aggressive, authoritarian-type individuals to continue to lord it over other people.

High Times: Getting back to Abbie, would you think things have changed enough so that you would advise him, were he to ask your advice, to turn himself in?

Kennedy: I would advise Abbie, if I had the opportunity, to try to understand himself, his desires and his goals, the conditions he finds himself in now being underground and the conditions that exist in the state of New York as carefully as he can. Were he to make the decision to return, I would help him out.

The one thing that has not been tried completely in Abbie's case, although Gerry Lefcourt did a great job at the hearings in Abbie's absence, was the illegal means they employed to get Abbie. With the disclosures that have come out about the illegal activities of the CIA, the FBI, alcohol, firearms and tobacco, the New York police bosses and the rest of them, it is almost impossible for there not to have been very heavy criminal activity perpetrated against Abbie that could be used in his defense. That opportunity has not presented itself. His presence will present that opportunity.

If he's busted in an underground situation, the chances of his getting bail are very poor, whereas if he voluntarily surrenders himself, his chances of getting bail are greater. Were he to turn himself in in a state with more progressive laws—California or Oregon, for example—and try to raise some of these political questions in his extradition flight, that might be a good view. Or, in fact, he may stay underground and become a really viable, political, progressive force.

I view Abbie as a highly visible individual. Invisibility seems inconsistent with his character. I would not be surprised if he surfaced. It's hard to figure out what's going on with the interviews.

High Times: As for the Weather Underground, you obviously would help if they turned themselves in. But they seem to be pleased with what they're doing. Do you foresee them surfacing?

Kennedy: My guess is pure speculation. But if in fact they're moving in a direction that seems to be more broadly based than they have in the past, which I think is a correct direction for them to be going, their leadership is going to have to become more visible, and that could mean that individuals will surface. But I have no idea. Maybe that leadership would develop elsewhere. But certainly there's going to have to be visible leadership to form a Marxist-Leninist party.

High Times: Some cynics have said that the term "radical lawyer" is a contradiction in terms itself.

Kennedy: It is. It is a contradiction.

High Times: Do you ever have to turn down clients? If so, how many and why? Is there anyone that you wouldn't defend, say, Charles Manson?

Kennedy: Well, there's nobody individually that I wouldn't defend, because it would depend on the crime. And the only crime that I have refused to defend is rape. And the reason for that is that I couldn't in good conscience do to the prosecuting witness in a rape case what the law basically requires be done to defend the individual. And that is to attack her reputation, her chastity and all the rest of that crap. You basically have to destroy her and make her look like a sex maniac.

To put a woman in the context of having to justify her credibility by showing that she may or may not have ever slept with anyone else is complete bullshit. Because a woman could have had sex with every person in the world and still be raped. A woman could be a prostitute and still be raped. So it is a completely phony defense, and I won't participate.

High Times: How about Manson?

Kennedy: Manson sent an inquiry to us in San Francisco as to whether or not we would come interview him before his trial. And I thought about it a lot. It was primarily an academic exercise, because the fact of the matter was that we were too busy at the time to be able to take a case of that magnitude.

Politically I saw that case in part as an attack on our culture. And I had no qualms about defending against that. Also, there was no way in which I could understand, let alone justify, the crimes he was accused and found guilty of. I would take a case such as that only if there were no one else to represent him. I certainly wouldn't let the state take it by default. Fortunately, it didn't get to that point.

High Times: What do you think should be society's proper disposition of such a person if everything that was said was true? Should such a person be on death row?

Kennedy: No. I don't think there should even be a death row. I don't think there should be a death penalty. We lack the ability to be able to solve a problem such as Manson. We lack the ability because we are too damn busy. The reactionaries are too busy making money, robbing other people and trying to get us on the moon to be able to concentrate on anything such as human problems.

If we focus on that kind of a problem, we can solve it. The answer lies in undercutting the conditions that create a Manson, even when you aren't able to successfully undercut all those conditions. Because in China, the People's Republic of China, and in Cuba they still have some crimes; certainly less than we have here. But what they have done is changed the conditions so drastically that the reasons underlying criminal activity don't exist. But when a crime does occur, they concentrate on rehabilitation and re-education, and not on punishment. Because punishment does not accomplish a thing.

High Times: You know that many doctors are upset by socialized medicine. As a lawyer, how do you feel about socialized law?

Kennedy: Well, it has to be better than capitalized law. I've seen two legal systems in socialist countries. One in the People's Republic of China and the other in Cuba. Each is substantially different and each substantially better than ours. In China, lawyers have essentially been abolished. The bulk of the problems that occur are defined as political, social, cultural, economic, or educative problems. And when a contradiction occurs among the people, or between two people, rather than bring a lawyer in, they attempt to bring the two people together to try to work it out themselves. And the law in China basically *requires* that these individuals come together and try to work it out.

A typical case would be a divorce, and we had the opportunity to follow one while we were in Peking. In the United States what happens is that the husband and the wife have a disagreement, they agree that they are going to disagree. One goes and hires a lawyer and the other goes and hires a lawyer. It is to the lawyer's advantage to perpetuate the contradiction between the two rather than to solve it, because the longer it can be drawn out, the more of the estate the lawyer can get in each case.

In China what happens is that the lawyers are kept out and the vicious, self-perpetuating bureaucratic cycle is removed, because the money ingredient is removed. So in China the couple is brought together, they are counseled. Each one belongs to a work unit as well as a living unit that is a collectivized situation. If they can't solve it themselves, their living units and their working units go to work on the problem. And 90 percent of them are solved, and there is no need for a lawyer.

In Cuba there is a form of socialized law that is probably much more in tune with the concept of socialized medicine that upsets doctors so much. And the reason that doctors get upset by socialized medicine is that not only will it work better and will people get better health care, but the doctors will get less money. In Cuba there are collectives of lawyers that might consist of five, ten, fifteen lawyers. The collective is paid by the state so much money per month, per year. They divide the money among the lawyers based upon the work that the individual lawyers do. No lawyer can get a fee in excess of the equivalent of about $500. And no lawyer gets a fee less than what is effectively $250 a case. So the economic incentive, the capitalist incentive is, in fact, removed.

And the argument of the United States lawyer is that this would take away what is really motivating the lawyers in this country. That is, if you don't pay him, he is not going to work. The trouble is that most people ire this country can't afford to hire a lawyer anyway. So that under our system the vast majority of people are deprived of the legal system. So socialized law in one form or another is a very good thing. As I said before, the ultimate test of a lawyer to me is how hard that lawyer works at abolishing the need for his or her services.

High Times: Do you believe that the red star should be flying over Washington?

Kennedy: It may be a blue star or a white star. The flag of the People's Republic of North America, whatever it becomes someday. There will be a flag that people decide on. And it will undoubtedly bear some resemblance to the history of those people and their aspirations. I don't know what that will be.

I think, in fact, that a system where people work together in a communist way is inevitable. I also think that it is going to take longer to come about in this country than any other country in the world. It is going to come about more rapidly, for example, in South Africa, because the blacks are going to kick the shit out of the whites there and see that it happens. Here it is going to take a substantially longer period of time, but it will happen.

And the way in which I see a communist society is in terms of competition. In a capitalist society, basically what we are taught is that we are in a hierarchical situation, and that we are all on a ladder and the ultimate goal is to get to the top of the ladder. And there are some people on rungs above you and some people on rungs below you. And the way in which you can best live your life is to be constantly grabbing at the legs of the people on the rung above you in order to pull them down so you can get ahead of them and simultaneously stomping on the toes of the people below you who are trying to climb up the ladder.

In a communist society, the situation is much more human because it is the horizontal concept. And, in fact, individuals can be interlocked in terms of holding hands or locked arms and they are all moving together. And you compete with the external contradictions, and you compete against nature, and you compete in terms of sports and other activities and friendship with other people.

When you stop defining yourself in terms of dollars and cents and start defining yourself in terms of human worth, then you are a whole lot better off. The biggest crime in the communist countries is to be nonproductive.

High Times: Do you think that should be a crime?

Kennedy: Absolutely. Because in this country, the greatest reward in this country is, you know, getting into a position where you can do nothing. That means that you are really high class in the U.S.

High Times: What about dope laws in Russia? We've heard of huge busts of LSD and occasionally hashish and marijuana in Russia.

Kennedy: I am more familiar with China and Cuba, but somewhat familiar with the Soviet Union. What they have done is make it almost impossible for anyone to make a profit off of dope.

High Times: In Russia?

Kennedy: In Russia, in China, and in Cuba. What happens, though, is that occasionally there are individuals who want to make a profit. And black-market stuff is available to almost any chemical outlet, any chemist, or any neighborhood pharmacist.

You see marijuana growing in China. They use it to make rope. They also use it in acupuncture. We walked into a hospital in China and took a big whiff and I smelled dope. I definitely smelled killer weed. There was this old gentleman who had bad arthritic conditions in both knees. He had the acupuncture needles going into both knees, and on the end of each knee was cannabis wrapped tightly up on the end. It was lit and the essence of the cannabis the THC works its way right down the needle into the muscle.

In Cuba we had a meeting with a member of the Supreme Court and we were asking him some questions about the dope problem in Cuba. He said, "This was quite a problem at one time. At one time some of the people on the island were very proud that we had the best marijuana in the world. Now we have less of a problem. We are accused of being an underdeveloped country. In some respects that is true. Our criminals are underdeveloped."

High Times: Do you think there is a drug abuse problem in America? And if there is, what should be done about it?

Kennedy: There is a drug abuse problem in America, and I think the problem is primarily fostered by the Drug Enforcement people themselves. The abuse comes when drugs are sold to individuals in order to keep them from finding themselves, from being something better, the deliberate, conscious trafficking in heroin by narcotics officers, by the government in Harlem, the South Bronx, in Detroit, Chicago, most of our major urban areas, particularly where there are substantial minority populations. That is a distinct drug abuse problem. I don't think people smoking flowers or whatever are particular problems.

High Times: There is an organization now called Youth International Party. Do you think that youth should have their own political party in national politics?

Kennedy: I think it would certainly make more sense to have a party that was created upon some common political experiences, such as age group, than upon the arbitrary and mostly specious distinctions that exist between the Democratic and Republican parties. If there were, for example, a party of young people, a party of middle-aged people and a party of older people, and if all three had basically equal abilities in terms of the election of leaders, the creation of the different social institutions and structures that exist, that would be a substantially fairer and more egalitarian system than what we now have. If we are going to continue to let capitalism play itself out without trying to interfere with it in some revolutionary way, then it seems to me about the only thing we can do is to try to organize lobby-type organizations for those groups that seem to be representing the most progressive forces.

Young people ought to be able to vote from the time they are eight, ten, as soon as they can crawl to the polls. They are human beings. To arbitrarily deprive them of the vote because they can't satisfy an adult that they can follow orders until they are eighteen is completely arbitrary. They are smarter when they are younger because they haven't yet been fed all that conditioning. It is the conditioning, it is not the intellect.

High Times #24, August 1977

HUNTER S. THOMPSON

The Good Doctor Tells All . . . About Carter, Cocaine,
Adrenaline, and the Birth of Gonzo Journalism

RON ROSENBAUM

SEPTEMBER 1977

THE FIRST TIME I met Hunter S. Thompson was back in 1970, at the America's Cup yacht race where Hunter had chartered a huge power yacht and was preparing to sail it full steam right into the middle of the race course. (This was shortly after his spectacular but unsuccessful run for the office of the sheriff of Aspen, Colorado, on a mescaline-eating "Capitalist Freak Power" ticket.) When I arrived on board the huge yacht, I found Thompson ensconced on the command deck, munching on a handful of psilocybin pills and regarding the consternation of the snooty Newport sailing establishment with amusement.

We never did manage to cross the path of the cup contenders and *Scanlon's* magazine went bankrupt before Hunter wrote up the whole fiasco, but I did learn one thing: this is a guy who understands the importance of perspective. He rode with the Hell's Angels—and got himself a nasty beating in the process of getting a unique perspective on them. He loaded his car, his bloodstream and his brain cells full of dangerous drugs to cover a conference of drug-busting D.A's and turned that experience into *Fear and Loathing in Las Vegas*, a brilliant exploration of the dark side of the drug scene at the peak of Nixon's power.

When he covered the 1972 presidential campaign as national affairs editor for *Rolling Stone,* Thompson's special dead-line-and-drug-crazed "Gonzo" journalism—his own patented mix of paranoia, nightmare, recklessness and black humor—would fill nervous secret service agents with fear and loathing on the campaign trail. Ever since then, Thompson's become a kind of national character with millions of people following the exploits of "Uncle Duke," in the "Doonesbury" comic strip.

This year too, Thompson had another very special but very different perspective: he's widely reported to have become close to Jimmy Carter and to Carter's inner circle from the time back in 1974 when he heard Carter's now-famous Law Day speech. But curiously, there have been more articles speculating about Thompson—his relations with Jimmy Carter and Jann Wenner—this year than by him. He's never put his own role into perspective until now.

High Times: How have your attitudes toward politics changed since you wrote about the '72 presidential election in *Fear and Loathing on the Campaign Trail*?

Thompson: Well, I think the feeling that I've developed since '72 is that an ideological attachment to the presidency or the president is very dangerous. I think the president should be a businessman; probably he should be hired. It started with Kennedy, where you got sort of a personal attachment to the president, and it was very important that he agree with you and you agree with him and you knew he was on your side. I no longer give a fuck if the president's on my side, as long as he leaves me alone or doesn't send me off to any wars or have me busted. The president should take care of business, mind the fucking store and leave people alone.

High Times: So you developed a tired-of-fighting-the-White-House theory?

Thompson: I think I've lost my sense that it's a life or death matter whether someone is elected to this, that or whatever. Maybe it's losing faith in ideology or politicians—or maybe both. Carter, I think, is an egomaniac, which is good because he has a hideous example of what could happen if he fucks up. I wouldn't want to follow Nixon's act, and Carter doesn't *either*. He has a whole chain of ugly precedents to make him careful—Watergate, Vietnam, the Bay of Pigs—and I think he's very aware that even the smallest blunder on his part could mushroom into something that would queer his image forever in the next generation's history texts . . . if there *is* a next generation.

I don't think it matters much to Carter whether he's perceived as a "liberal" or a "conservative," but it *does* matter to him that he's perceived—by the voters today and by historians tomorrow—as a successful president. He didn't run this weird Horatio Alger trip from Plains, Georgia, to the White House, only to get there and find himself hamstrung by a bunch of hacks and fixers in the Congress. Which is exactly what's beginning to happen now, and those people are making a very serious mistake if they assume they're dealing with just another political shyster, instead of the zealot he really is. Jimmy Carter is a *true believer,* and people like that are *not* the ones you want to cross by accident.

I'm not saying this in defense of the man, but only to emphasize that anybody in Congress or anywhere else who plans to cross Jimmy Carter should take pains to understand the real nature of the beast they intend to cross. He's on a very different wavelength than most people in Washington. That's one of the main reasons he's president, and also one of the first things I noticed when I met him down in Georgia in 1974—a total disdain for political definition or conventional ideologies.

His concept of populist politics is such a strange mix of total pragmatism and almost religious idealism that every once in a while—to me at least, and especially when I listen to some of the tapes of conversations I had with him in 1974 and '75—that he sounds like a borderline anarchist . . . which is probably why he interested me from the very beginning; and why he still does, for that matter. Jimmy Carter is a genuine original. Or at least he was before he got elected. God only knows what he is now, or what he might turn into when he feels he's being crossed—by Congress, the Kremlin, Standard Oil or anything else. He won't keep any enemies list on paper, but only because he doesn't have to; he has a memory like a computerized elephant.

High Times: Did you ever have any ideology in the sense of being a liberal, a conservative . . . or were you an anarchist all along?

Thompson: I've always considered myself basically an anarchist, at least in the abstract, but every once in a while you have to come out of the closet and deal with reality. I am interested in politics, but not as ideology, simply as an art of self-defense—that's what I learned in Chicago. I realized that you couldn't afford to turn your back on the bastards because that's what they would do—run amok and beat the shit out of you—and they had the power to do it. When I feel it's necessary to get back into politics, I'll do it, either writing about it or participating in it. But as long as it's not necessary, there are a lot of better ways to spend your time. Buy an opium den in Singapore, or a brothel somewhere in Maine; become a hired killer in Rhodesia or some kind of human Judas Goat in the Golden Triangle. Yeah, a soldier of fortune, a professional geek who'll do anything for money.

High Times: You've received a lot of flak for your enthusiasm about Jimmy Carter's Law Day speech in Athens, Georgia. Do you still like Carter?

Thompson: Compared to most other politicians, I do still like Carter. Whether I agree with him on everything, that's another thing entirely. He'd put me in jail in an instant if he saw me snorting coke in front of him. He would not, however, follow me into the bathroom and try to catch me snorting it. It's little things like that.

High Times: In that Law Day speech, Carter quoted Bob Dylan. Do you really think Carter cares about Bob Dylan's music the way we do?

Thompson: I listened to Bob Dylan records in his house, but that was mainly because his sons had them. I don't think he goes upstairs to the bedroom at night, reads the Bible in Spanish while listening to *Highway 61*.

High Times: Why haven't you written anything about Carter and the '76 campaign trail?

Thompson: I was going to write a book on the '76 campaign, but even at the time I was doing research, I started to get nervous about it. I knew if I did another book on the campaign, I'd somehow be trapped.

I was the most obvious journalist—coming off my book on the 1972 campaign—to inherit Teddy White's role as a big-selling chronicler of presidential campaigns. I would have been locked into national politics as a way of life, not to mention as a primary source of income. . . . And there's no way you can play that kind of Washington Wizard role from a base in Woody Creek, Colorado. I'd have had to move to Washington, or at least to New York . . . and, Jesus, life is too short for that kind of volunteer agony. I've put a lot of work into living out here where I do and still making a living, and I don't want to give it up unless I absolutely have to. I moved to Washington for a year in 1972, and it was a nightmare.

Yeah, there was a definite temptation to write another campaign book—especially for a vast amount of money in advance—but even while I was looking at all that money, I *knew* it would be a terminal mistake. It wasn't until I actually began covering the campaign that I had to confront the reality of what I was getting into. I hadn't been in New Hampshire two days when I knew for certain that I just couldn't make it. I was seeing my footprints everywhere I went. All the things that were of interest last time—even the small things, the esoteric little details of a presidential campaign—seemed like jibberish the second time around. Plus, I lost what looks more and more like a tremendous advantage of anonymity. That was annoying, because in '72 I could stand against a wall some-where—and I'd select some pretty weird walls to stand against—and nobody knew who I was. But in '76, Jesus, at press conferences, I had to sign more autographs than the candidates. Through some strange process, I came from the '72 campaign an unknown reporter, a vagrant journalist, to a sort of media figure in the '76 campaign. It started getting so uncomfortable and made it so hard to work that even the alleged or apparent access that I had to this weird peanut farmer from Georgia became a disadvantage.

High Times: You became a public figure?

Thompson: Thanks to our friend Trudeau.

High Times: Did Garry Trudeau consult you before he started including you as the Uncle Duke character in "Doonesbury"?

Thompson: No, I never saw him; I never talked to him. It was a hot, nearly blazing day in Washington, and I was coming down the steps of the Supreme Court looking for somebody, Carl Wagner or somebody like that. I'd been inside in the press section, and then all of a sudden I saw a crowd of people and I heard them saying, "Uncle Duke." I heard the words *Duke, Uncle;* it didn't seem to make any sense. I looked around, and I recognized people who were total strangers pointing at me and laughing. I had no idea what the fuck they were talking about. I had gotten out of the habit of reading funnies when I started reading the *Times.* I had no idea what this outburst meant. It was a weird experience, and as it happened I was sort of by myself up there on the stairs, and I thought: What in the fuck madness is going on? Why am I being mocked by a gang of strangers and friends on the steps of the Supreme Court? Then I must have asked someone, and they told me that Uncle Duke had appeared in the *Post* that morning.

High Times: So all this public notoriety was a burden in trying to return to the campaign?

Thompson: It was impossible because there was no way for me to stay anonymous, to carry on with what I consider my normal behavior, which is usually—in terms of a campaign—either illegal or dangerous or both. . . . It was generally assumed that I was guilty—which I was.

High Times: So eventually you found that refuge in a kind of band of brothers?

Thompson: What? No, I have never had much faith in concepts like "a band of brothers"—especially in politics. What we're talking about here is a new generation of highly competent professional political operatives and also a new generation of hot-rod political journalists who are extremely serious and competitive during the day, but who happened to share a few dark and questionable tastes that could only be mutually indulged late at night, in absolute privacy. . . .

Because no presidential candidate even *wants to know,* much less have to explain at a press conference, why rumors abound that many of his speech writers, strategists and key advance men are seen almost nightly—and sometimes for nine or ten nights in a row—frequenting any of the two or three motel rooms in the vortex of every primary campaign that are known to be "dope dens," "orgy pads," and "places of deep intrigue."

They simply don't want to hear these things, regardless of how true they may be—and in 1976 they usually were, although not in the sense that we were running a movable dope orgy, right in the bowels of a presidential campaign—but it was true that for the first time, there was a sort of midnight drug underground that included a few ranking staff people, as well as local workers and volunteers, from almost every democratic candidate's staff, along with some of the most serious, blue-chip press people . . . and it was also true that some of the most intelligent and occasionally merciless conversations of the whole campaign took place in these so-called dope dens.

Hell, it was a fantastic luxury to be able to get together at night with a few bottles of Wild Turkey or Chivas Regal and a big tape deck with portable speakers playing Buffett or Jerry Jeff or The Amazing Rhythm Aces . . . yeah, and also a bag of ripe Colombian tops and a gram or two of the powder; and to feel relaxed enough with each other, after suffering through all that daytime public bullshit, to just hang out and talk honestly about what was *really* happening in the campaign. . . . You now, like which candidate was fatally desperate for money, which one had told the most ridiculous lie that day, who was honest and who wasn't.

In a lot of ways it was the best part of the campaign, the kind of thing I'd only be able to do with a very few people in 1972 and '68. But in '76 we were able—because there were enough of us—to establish a sort of midnight-to-dawn truce that transcended all the daytime headline jibberish, and I think it helped all of us to get a better grip on what we were really doing.

I could illustrate this point a lot better by getting into names and specific situations, but I can't do that now for the same reason I couldn't write about it during the campaign. We all understand that, and the very few times I even hinted at this midnight underground, I did it in code phrases—like "tapping the glass."

High Times: Tapping the glass. I wonder if you could explain that?

Thompson: Well, that's one of those apparently meaningless code phrases that I use in almost everything I write. It's a kind of lame effort to bridge the gap between what I know and what I can write without hurting my friends—sort of working on two or three levels at the same time.

High Times: So if you go back and read your stories, a scene where you talk about "tapping the glass" with Carter campaign staffer "X" . . .

Thompson: Right. That means chopping up rocks of cocaine on a glass coffee table or some mirror we jerked off the wall for that purpose—but not necessarily with one of Carter's people. The whole point of this wretched confession is that there were so many people tapping the glass in the '76 campaign that you never knew who might turn up at one of those midnight sessions. They were dangerously nonpartisan. On any given night you would meet Udall and Shriver staffers, along with people from the Birch Bayh and Fred Harris campaigns. Even George Wallace was represented from time to time; and, of course, there was always the hard corps of press dopers.

High Times: That's amazing. You were covering this media-saturated presidential campaign during the day, then snorting coke at night with all those hotshot politicos?

Thompson: They weren't very hotshot then.

High Times: OK. But since we're talking about drug use during the '76 campaign, it's obvious we're talking about people who are now in the White House, right?

Thompson: Well . . . some of them, yes. But let's get a grip on ourselves here. We don't want to cause a national panic by saying that a gang of closet coke freaks are running the country—although that would probably be the case, no matter who had won the election.

High Times: Times are definitely changing, eh? But since Carter *won* the election, let's focus on him for a moment.

Thompson: Well, why not? Let's see how thin a wire we can walk here, without getting ourselves locked up . . . Indeed, and meanwhile let's rent a big villa in the mountains of Argentina, just in case my old friend Jimmy is as mean as I always said he was. Anyway, yeah, we're talking about at least a few people in the White House inner circle; not Cy and Ziggy and that crowd, the professional heavies who would have gone to work for anybody—Carter, Humphrey, Brown. Shit, they'd even work for me, if I'd won the election.

High Times: The inner circle of Carter's people are serious drug users?

Thompson: Wait a minute, I didn't say that. For one thing, a term like serious users has a very weird and menacing connotation; and, for another, we were talking about a *few people* from almost *everybody's* staff. Across the board. . . . Not junkies or freaks, but people who were just as comfortable with drugs like weed, booze, or coke as *we* are—and we're not weird, are we? Hell no, we're just overworked professionals who need to relax now and then, have a bit of the whoop and the giggle, right?

High Times: Weren't they nervous, or were you nervous, when you first started doing coke together?

Thompson: Well. I suppose I should have expected the same kind of difference between, say, the '72 and '76 campaigns as I saw between '68 and '72. When I went to New Hampshire in '68 I was a genuine unknown. I was the only person except for Bill Cardozo who would smoke weed, ever. I mean in the press. In '72 it was a revolution in that sense, and people in the press openly smoked hash and did coke. So I should have expected it in '76, but I hadn't really thought of it. It stunned me a little bit in '76 that coke was as common as weed had been in '72 and almost right out in the open, used in a very cavalier fashion. As I say, in 1972 it was a fairly obvious consistent use of the weed by McGovern's people, in '68 it was McCarthy, but this time it was across the board.

High Times: In a way, what you're saying is that it was a kind of truth-telling substrata of drug users, and that's why you couldn't write stories about it.

Thompson: Yes, for the first time I was really faced with the problem of knowing way too much.

High Times: Was this a good or a bad thing?

Thompson: I think it was good. It allowed people who would never under the circumstances have been able to sit down, get stoned and talk honestly about whether they should even be working there.

High Times: People are always asking how did you get away with it. Why aren't you in jail with all the stuff you write about drugs on the campaign trail? Do you feel that the secret service was specifically tailing you after you started writing these articles about all the dope you had taken?

Thompson: No. I made my peace with the secret service early in '72 when I went to a party in the Biltmore Hotel here in New York after McGovern's primary victory, and there were about ten agents in a room. Three of them were obviously passing a joint around. The look on their faces when I walked in there . . . all of them turning to look when I walked in . . .it was a wonderful moment of confrontation. I didn't want to be there, they didn't want me in there. Immediately they just crushed the joint and tried to ignore it. But the room was obviously full of marijuana smoke.

High Times: And everybody knew that you knew.

Thompson: Oh yeah, of course. But I decided not to write about it—at least not right away.

High Times: Was there ever any kind of trouble with the secret service after that?

Thompson: No trouble at all, except when they tried to bar me from the White House during the impeachment thing. I called the guards Nazi cocksuckers or something, and in order to get in the White House I had to promise not to call anybody Nazi cocksuckers. I just waved my hand at the White House itself, you know, with Haldeman inside. I kind of got off that hook. And then I promised not to call anyone Nazi cocksuckers, and they let me in.

High Times: Some of your fans wonder if you ever make up some of the bizarre incidents you describe. You've said that all the outrageous drugs you did and things you did in your Las Vegas book were true, except the notorious incident where you supposedly paralyzed yourself with adrenochrome extract from live human adrenal glands.

Thompson: If I admitted that it was true, it was tantamount to admitting that I was a first-degree murderer of the foulest sort, that somebody would kill a child in order to suck out the adrenaline.

High Times: But in the book you didn't say that you killed the kid. You just said that you got it.

Thompson: That's right. I said that my attorney had gotten it from a client of his. What I was doing was taking what you normally feel from shooting adrenaline into the realm of the extremely weird.

High Times: Have you ever had that feeling? Shooting adrenaline?

Thompson: Oh, yes. Whenever it was necessary. Sometimes nothing else works. When you really have to stay up for the fifth day and fifth night . . . and nothing will work, not even black beauties. Then you shoot adrenaline. But you have to be very careful with it. First, don't ever shoot it into a vein. That's doom. But even then, you've got to be very careful because you can drive yourself completely berserk, and I'm sure it would be just the way I described it in Las Vegas.

High Times: I always thought you were talking in metaphorical terms when you said, "I like to work on the adrenaline."

Thompson: Yeah, but usually my own. I'm really an adrenaline junkie; I never get anything done without the pressure of some impossible deadline.

High Times: How would you describe the adrenaline high?

Thompson: At its best it's one of the most functional of all the speed sort of drugs in that it has almost no rush unless you overdo it, and almost no crash. I never considered speed fun. I use speed as fuel, a necessary evil. Adrenaline is much smoother and much more dangerous if you fuck up. I fucked up one time in a motel in Austin, Texas. I was very careless, and I just whacked the needle into my leg without thinking. I'd forgotten the vein thing, and after I pulled the little spike out, I noticed something was wrong. In the bathroom the tile was white, the curtain was white—but in the corner of my eye in the mirror I looked down and saw a hell of a lot of red. Here was this little tiny puncture, like a leak in a high-powered hose. . . . You could barely see the stream. It was going straight from my leg and hitting the shower curtain at about, thigh level, and the whole bottom of the curtain was turning red.

I thought, oh Jesus Christ, what now? And I just went in and lay down on the bed and told the people in the room to get out without telling them why; then I waited twenty minutes and all I could think of was these horrible Janis Joplin stories: you know, ODing in a motel . . . Jim Morrison . . . Jimi Hendrix . . . needles. And I thought, oh fuck, what a sloppy way to go—I was embarrassed by it. But after twenty minutes nothing happened. Then I really began to get nervous and I thought, oh God, it's going to come all at once. It's a delayed thing, like those acid flashbacks they've been promising all these years.

High Times: When are we going to have them?

Thompson: I've been waiting for a long time.

High Times: Once I asked a friend of yours why you are so attracted to Carter, and this guy says, well, Carter's basically in a lot of ways a conservative good old boy and so is Hunter. Do you think that's true in some ways, or that you're a good old boy that's gone weird?

Thompson: That sounds better. Good old boy gone weird. That's a good line anyway I wouldn't deny that; I would just as soon admit it.

High Times: You had a fairly straight upbringing in Louisville, Kentucky, didn't you?

Thompson: Well, I was a juvenile delinquent, but a straight juvenile delinquent. The kind that wore white bucks, buttoned-down Oxford cloth shirts, suits. It was a good cover to use to rob crowded liquor stores. I discovered then that it helps to have a cover. If you act as weird as you are, something terrible is bound to happen to you, if you're as weird as I am. I mean if I looked like I thought, I wouldn't be on the streets for very long.

High Times: Were you ever busted?

Thompson: Yeah, repeatedly. I learned about jails a lot earlier than most people. On about ages fifteen through eighteen I was in and out of jails continually. Usually for buying booze under age or for throwing fifty-five–gallon oil drums through filling station windows—you know, those big plate glass windows. And then I was expelled from school once—for rape, I think. I wasn't guilty, but what the hell. We were in the habit of stealing five or six cases of beer on weekends to drink. That night was the Friday night after my expulsion. We did our normal run and stole about five or six cases. We took one of them and put it on the superintendent of schools' lawn at one o'clock in the morning and very carefully put twenty whole bottles right through every pane in the front of his house. We heard them exploding inside, and they must have gone mad—you hear them in the bedrooms, in the living room, every window was broken. I mean, what kind of thugs would do that? Twenty-four hand beer bottle grenades . . . to wake up and hear the whole house exploding! Which window is going to be hit next? We deliberately took about ten minutes to put them through there because we knew they'd never get the cops there in ten minutes.

High Times: Makes you feel someone's out to get you. Twenty-four bottles of beer, that's heavy. So you were into overkill when making statements?

Thompson: That wasn't overkill. It was massive retaliation, the court of final resort. I was expelled for something I hadn't done or even thought about doing.

High Times: What is your favorite drug experience?

Thompson: Well, there are very few things that can really beat driving around the Bay Area on a good summer night—big motorcycle, head full of acid—wearing nothing but a T-shirt and a pair of shorts and getting on that Highway 1 going 120 miles an hour. That's a rush of every kind—head, hands—it's everything put in a bundle. Because first of all, it's a rush, and also it's maintaining control and see how far I can go, how weird I can get and still survive, even though I'm seeing rats in front of me instead of cops. Rats with guns on . . .

High Times: How do you handle something like that?

Thompson: I never know. It's interesting, always a different way. Mainly it's figuring out real fast whom you are dealing with, and what their rules are. One of the few times I ever got in trouble, I wasn't drunk or pumped up. I had a loaded .44 magnum in the glove compartment, a bottle of Wild Turkey open on the seat beside me, and I said, well, this is a good time to try that advice a hippie lawyer gave me once—to pull down the window just a crack and stick out my driver's license. So I started to do that. I was just getting it out, when all of a sudden the door on the other side opened. I looked around, and here was a flashlight glaring right in my face, and right beside the flashlight was a big, dirty .57 magnum pointed at me. They didn't give a fuck about my license. They jerked me out of the car and pushed me up against the side. I said something about my constitutional rights, and they said, "Well, sue us" or something and kicked my legs. So I gave it up and eventually I paid a $35 fine, because it's easier than arguing. I had just bought the car. It was a Saab. The night before I had pushed my English Ford off a cliff in Big Sur, 400 feet down to the ocean, to get even with the bastard for all the trouble it caused me. We filled it with gasoline and set it on fire just before it went over the edge.

Ever since then I have made it a point to be polite to the California Highway Patrol. I have a National Rifle Association sticker on the back window of my car, so that any cop on the driver's side has to pass that and see it. I used to carry a police badge in a wallet, and that helped a lot.

High Times: I reread *Fear and Loathing in Las Vegas* last summer. I loved it, but I felt it was really a sad book filled with regret for the passing of the San Francisco scene.

Thompson: No, not really. But I think almost any kind of humor I like always has a touch of melancholy or weirdness in it. I seem to be alone, for instance, in considering Joseph Conrad one of history's great humorists.

High Times: Were you also down on the drug experience in that book?

Thompson: No. I kind of assumed that this was sort of a last fling; that Nixon and Mitchell and all those people would make it very soon impossible for anybody to behave that way and get away with it. It wouldn't be a matter of a small fine. Your head would be cut off.

High Times: So it's a real exploration of terminal paranoia.

Thompson: Well . . . It was kind of a weird celebration for an era that I figured was ending.

High Times: Maybe you can tell us the true story of the birth of Gonzo journalism. It was the Kentucky Derby story you did for *Scanlon's* magazine in 1969, right?

Thompson: I guess it's important to take it all the way back to having dinner in Aspen with Jim Salter, a novelist who had sort of a continental style. It was one of those long European dinners with lots of wine, and Salter said something like, "Well, the Derby's coming up. Aren't you going to be there?" And I thought, well, I'll be damned. That's a good idea.

I was working at the time for Warren Hinkle at *Scanlon's* magazine. So I immediately called Hinkle and said, "I have a wonderful idea, we must do the derby. It's the greatest spectacle the country can produce." It was 3:30 in the morning or something like that, but Hinkle got right into it. By that time I'd learned to hate photographers; I still do. I can't stand to work with them. So I said we've got to get an illustrator for this, and I had Pat Oliphant in mind. Hinkle said fine, you know, do it.

In an hour's time the whole thing was settled. Oliphant wasn't available, but Ralph Steadman was coming over on his first trip to the U.S. and it was all set up that I would go to Louisville and do the advance work, and Ralph would meet me there later.

I think I took off the next day. The whole thing took less than twenty-four hours. I got there and of course found that the place was jammed, there were no rooms and it was out of the question to get a press pass. The deadline had been three months earlier. It took me about two days to get two whole press kits. I'm not sure exactly how I did it. I traded off the outrage, which was so gross, that somebody from a thing called *Scanlon,* which we told them was an Irish magazine famous all over the world, was sending a famous European artist to illustrate the derby for the British Museum, weird stuff like that. They agreed to give me two of everything except passes to the clubhouse and the drunk tank—I mean the blue-blood drunk tank at the center of the clubhouse. That's where Goldwater and all the movie stars and those people sit. The best seats in the house. They wouldn't give us those. So I think we stole those.

In any case, we got total access to everything, including a heavy can of mace . . . Now this is bad, this is ugly. The press box is on the roof, directly over the governor's box. And I had this can of mace, I'm not sure why . . . maybe for arguments; mace is a very efficient way of ending arguments. So I'd been fondling the can in my pocket, but we couldn't find any use for it—nobody threatened me. I was kind of restless. Then just before the derby started we were standing in the front row of the press box, up on the roof, and just for the hell of it I blasted the thing about three times about 100 feet straight down to the governor's box. Then I grabbed Ralph and said let's get out of here. Nobody maces the governor in the press box. It's not done. It's out of the question. I have no idea what the hell went on in the box when the stuff hit because we took off. That was sort of the end of the story.

About two days later, Ralph had all the drawings done, and I stayed on to write the story, but I couldn't get much done. That goddamned Kent State thing happened the Monday after the derby; that was all I could think of for a while. So I finally flew up to New York, and that's when the real fear started. Most of the magazine was either printed or on the press out in San Francisco—except for my story, which was the lead story, which was also the cover story, and I was having at the time what felt to me like a terminal writer's block, whatever the hell that means.

I would lie in the bathtub at this weird hotel. I had a suite with everything I wanted—except I couldn't leave. After three days of not writing more than two pages, this kind of anxiety/depression syndrome builds up, and it really locks you up. They were sending copy boys and copy girls and people down every hour to see what I had done, and the pressure began to silently build like a dog whistle kind of scream, you know. You couldn't hear it but it was everywhere.

After the third day of that horrible lockup, I'd lie in the tub for three hours in the morning drinking White Horse scotch out of the bottle—just lying in the tub, feeling like, "Well, I got away with it for a while, but this time I've pushed it too far." But there was no alternative; something had to go in.

Finally I just began to tear the pages out of my notebooks since I write constantly in the notebooks and draw things, and they were legible. But they were hard to fit in the telecopier. We began to send just torn pages. When I first sent one down with the copy boy, I thought the phone was going to ring any minute, with some torrent of abuse from whoever was editing the thing in the New York office. I just sort of sat back and watched TV.

I was waiting for the shit to hit the fan. . . . But almost immediately the copy boy was back and wanted more. And I thought, "Ah, ha, what's this?" Here's the light at the end of the tunnel. Maybe they're crazy, but why worry? I think I actually called Hinkle in San Francisco and asked him if he wanted any more pages and he said, "Oh, yeah. It's wonderful stuff . . . wonderful." So I just began to tear the fucking things out. And sometimes I would have to write handwritten inserts—I just gave up on the typewriter—sending page after page right out of the notebook, and of course Hinkle was happy as twelve dogs. But I was full of grief, and shame; I thought this was the end, it was the worst hole I had ever gotten into. And I always had been almost pretty good about making deadlines—scaring people to death, but making them. This time I made it, but in what I considered the foulest and cheapest way, like Oakland's unclean touchdown against Miami—off balance. . . they did it all wrong . . . six seconds to go . . . but it worked.

They printed it word for word, even with the pauses, thoughts, and jagged stuff like that. And I felt nice that I hadn't sunk the magazine by failing to get the story done right, and I slunk back to Colorado and said oh fuck, when it comes out I'm going to take a tremendous beating from a lot of people.

But exactly the opposite happened. Just as soon as the thing came out, I started getting calls and letters. People were calling it a tremendous breakthrough in journalism, a stroke of genius. And I thought, *What in the shit?*

One of the letters came from Bill Cardozo, who was the editor of the *Boston Globe Sunday Magazine* at the time. I'd heard him use the word *Gonzo* when I covered the New Hampshire primary in '68 with him. It meant sort of "crazy," "off-the-wall"—a phrase that I always associate with Oakland. But Cardozo said something like, "Forget all the shit you've been writing, this is it; this is pure Gonzo. If this is a start, keep rolling." Gonzo. Yeah, of course. That's what I was doing all the time. Of course, I might be crazy.

High Times: Is it sheer intelligence?

Thompson: Well, it's more than that . . . Let's not forget now I've had at least ten years of paying dues. I know I have some talent, whatever that means. Some people are good at money and some people are good at basketball. I can use words to my advantage, which is a great trick to have.

High Times: Are there some things in your notebooks you can't put in your stories?

Thompson: All the best stories are unwritten. More and more I find that I can't tell the whole truth about events. I have one book I'd like to write, and the rest will have to be done to pay the fucking rent. That'll be the one where there'll be no question if anybody's lying. Well, there will be some question, but the truth is usually a lot weirder than anything you can make up. I'll make sure that it dooms as many people as possible—an absolutely true account, including my own disaster and disappearances. To hell with the American Dream. Let's write it off as a suicide.

WHO TURNED ON WHOM

From Dr. Albert Hofmann to You—
How Western Civilization Got High Again, One Head at a Time

PETER STAFFORD AND BRUCE EISNER

OCTOBER 1977

LSD CREATES IN ITS takers a sort of instant messianism, an urge to turn on friends, relatives, acquaintances, and perfect strangers. Marijuana, too, is a sort of friendship ambassador from the vegetable kingdom, telling us to declare peace on the world. And during the Forties and Fifties, as acid and grass slowly spread from among an enlightened few to the electrified many, the genealogy of turn-ons began to read like a *Who's Who* in the scientific, political, and cultural worlds. There were artists and writers like Aldous Huxley, Jack Kerouac, Ken Kesey, Salvador Dali, and R. Crumb; actors like Robert Mitchum, James Coburn, Gary Grant, Peter Fonda, and David Carradine; scientists like Stanislav Grof, John Lilly, Claudio Naranjo, and Albert Hofmann; media moguls Walt Disney and Henry Luce; top political figures John and Robert Kennedy. All took the magical mystery tour and returned to pick up their friends.

It started during World War II. The scene was the New Products Laboratory of Sandoz Pharmaceuticals in Basel, Switzerland, in a building now dwarfed by the massive Sandoz tower that dominates the skyline.

On April 16, 1943, the chemist Albert Hofmann, who had concocted a new molecule five years earlier while searching for a uterine constrictor, decided to test it again on birds, who had previously displayed no reaction. By accident, Hofmann absorbed a minute quantity of the chemical through his skin. The agent involved, LSD-25, turned out to be such a potent psychedelic that it had to be weighed out in millionths of a gram. If the substance can be seen with the naked eye, it is a very large dose. By comparison, mescaline must be taken in amounts of 3,000 to 4,000 times the weight to produce a turn-on of a similar scope.

Hofmann's second trip, on April 19 of that year, confirmed that LSD-25 had been the precipitating psychoactive agent three days earlier. Though dramatic, the trip was hardly the first time that psychedelics had influenced civilization's collective psyche.

Marijuana use, of course, extends back into prehistory. It was heartily recommended in the earliest book of Chinese herbal medicine, which had influenced much of the East by the time of our earliest documentations, and, as tradition has it, was carried to the West by Hasan-i-Sabbah ("the Old Man of the Mountain") in about 1090 A.D. Its earliest use as a recreational drug coincided with its introduction into Western medicine—since Joseph Moreau de Tours, who acquired it in Algeria and saw its medical possibilities, also brought it to the attention of the poet Théophile Gautier.

Gautier was something of a dandy in France in the 1840s, and he founded *Le Club des Haschischins*. Members were administered *Cannabis indica* in the form of a potent greenish jam, and many published extravagant praises of their vision-filled trips. (De Tours first noticed he was affected when he discovered himself fencing with a banana.) Recreational usage in the United States, however, didn't really catch on until the Twenties, when Mexican laborers and blacks brought it up along the Mississippi from Louisiana and into Harlem and other parts of the country.

The prohibition of alcohol in the U.S. spurred pot's further spread. But for the most part, it remained an activity of the lower-class black and Chicano subcultures, jazz musicians, Bohemian artists, and other assorted members of the creative professions. Meanwhile, an antimarijuana scare campaign carried on by the Federal Bureau of Narcotics effectively stemmed the pot tide. Weed perforce remained an underground sacrament until the beatniks began to turn on. Pot became as essential to the Beat movement as poetry, Zen Buddhism, espresso coffeehouses, and pounding on a bongo.

When it comes to explaining how the Beats caused us to see beyond what Allen Ginsberg called "the clouds of literal consciousness" that shrouded the Fifties, we must again note that many of those most centrally involved—such as Jack Kerouac—themselves "turned on" relatively infrequently. Oh, it is true that Jack smoked a lot of pot, particularly while writing *Dr. Sax* down in Mexico (much to the annoyance of William Burroughs, who objected that it excessively smoked up the room). But

Kerouac and John Clellon Holmes, perhaps the major publicists of this "go" generation of the late Forties and Fifties, personally tried little of the major psychedelics.

When it came to dope, Kerouac and Holmes were largely outsiders with their noses pressed against the window, recording the activities of Ginsberg, Neal Cassady, Gregory Corso, Lew Welch, Gary Snyder, and Herbert Huncke. These were people who gulped down psychedelics whenever given the chance. Snyder, for example, became the hero of Kerouac's *Dharma Bums* after seeing the value of psychedelics while a student at Reed College in Portland, Oregon. This group's experiences of fairly continual dope use as recorded, were to entice an entire upcoming generation.

But we are getting ahead of our story. After he made his initial studies of the properties of lysergic acid in 1043, Hofmann turned on Werner Stoll, his lab collaborator's son, and Stoll turned on his patients—sixteen schizophrenics and twenty "normals." The results of this experiment were reported in 1947 in the Swiss Journal of Neurology. From here on this psychedelic message quickly spread.

The decade following Stall's initial report saw LSD enter the heads of psychiatric patients, volunteers and, of course, psychotherapists. In 1949 the molecule came to America via psychologist Max Rinkle. A few years later in Canada, a group of psychologists and related workers headed by Drs. Humphry Osmond and Abram Hoffer began giving it to alcoholics in the hopes of sobering them through artificial d.t.'s. Instead, many saw the light, and *psychedelic* was born as a word and perhaps a philosophical concept as well.

Most of the early work with LSD was done with small doses—often only 30 to 50 micrograms and rarely over 100. Hofmann's opinion is that 250 micrograms is about the maximum dosage, and he felt his initial experience on that amount was an overdose. Large single-shot doses were first suggested by Al Hubbard, a former Canadian uranium salesman, considered a wild man by his associates in alcoholic therapy.

In the late Fifties in Los Angeles, a number of psychologists began to administer LSD to patients for therapeutic purposes. Via this process they managed to turn on such popular figures as TV comedian Steve Allen, the first to announce his turn-on on television. Gary Grant credited LSD with enabling him to become a parent for the first time. One fascinating record from this period is *My Self and I,* by Constance Newland, the Thelma Moss of recent Kirlian and psychotronic fame. By about 1957, according to the writer Chester Anderson, a substantial LSD leak led from the Sandoz plant in Hanover, New Jersey, to Manhattan's East Village. Peyote, pot, and eventually LSD were the main condiments used by the Beats to turn on—and they were also among the most active proselytizers. But word passed quickly of other possibilities for mind expansion. Alan Watts described this type of experience as "instant satori" in his 1959 book *This Is It.* Ginsberg and Burroughs soon were bringing back additional tales relating to the yagé intoxication of South America. Though there was much about their reports and those of others indicating unpleasant effects, a search for mind alteration was clearly part of the ethos, and many were turned on in the process.

The Chilean psychologist Claudio Naranjo acquired yagé after deciding he wanted to go into country where "people ate people." He says he knew he couldn't learn the languages he would encounter, so he brought along a Polaroid camera and some acid, which he dropped onto drawings he had made of stars, moons, and the sun. He would tell the natives that he was a medicine man and that they should meditate upon the heavenly bodies after swallowing the "medicine" appearing on the drawings. Then he paddled away in his canoe as quickly as possible, not knowing what the effects would be. Later, however, the natives indicated they were impressed and grateful—and gave him lots of yagé. Naranjo was the first to try MDA after its discoverer, Gordon Alles, and he also gave the first scientific report on ibogaine, after hearing accounts by African natives of their rituals and experiences.

Then in May of 1957, Wall Street banker R. Gordon Wasson published his account of being one of the first two white men to be "bemushroomed." *Life* magazine gave Wesson's story a full color spread as part three of a "Great Adventures" series. This was to lead to Albert Hofmann's synthesis of psilocybin and psilocin, the primary active substances in the Mexican psychedelic fungi. Hundreds would travel to Oaxaca, Mexico, in search of magic mushrooms and/or Maria Sabina, the *curandera* who had conducted Wasson on his remarkable nighttime journey. Budd Schulberg, author of

What Makes Sammy Run? was one of these seekers, as was Jeremy Sandford, who wrote *In Search of the Magic Mushroom.* By the late Fifties, Sandoz was sending samples of these synthetics out to investigators. One of them was Sabina, who reported that "the spirit of the mushroom is in the pill."

A significant event of the early Sixties occurred when a seeker named Timothy Leary tripped out poolside in Cuernavaca, near Mexico City. His rational, symbolic mind took a vacation, and he resolved to dedicate the rest of his life to studying this new instrument. Having just been appointed to a lectureship in psychology at Harvard, Leary took it upon himself to initiate research into this with his graduate students. Thus was born the Harvard Psilocybin Project—which rapidly turned on hundreds of creative individuals, religious figures, convicts, psychologists, and graduate students. Leary also turned Allen Ginsberg on to psilocybin, whereupon Ginsberg immediately tried to phone Jack Kennedy, Kerouac, and Nikita Khrushchev (his three favorite Ks) to tell them about it.

In 1960 Dr John Beresford wrote Sandoz from New York and explained that he was interested in investigating LSD-25's possible effects on amoebas. Back by return mail came a gram labeled "pharmaceutically pure" and a bill for $285. Before the year was out, Beresford, Jean Houston, and Michael Corner had established an LSD research center, the Agora Scientific Trust. Much of the turning on they performed is described in *The Varieties of Psychedelic Experience.*

Eventually the gram Beresford bought was split up with an associate, Michael Hollingshead, who conveyed part of it to Harvard, where he turned on dozens of scientists and volunteers. He stayed for a while with Leary at a house that was the site of many psylocybin turn-ons. Despite this, many were afraid of LSD. One of those declaring himself most uninterested was Timothy L. By 1962, jazz musician Maynard Ferguson and his wife Flo were obviously having such a good time on it that Hollingshead finally was able to convince Leary to try a spoonful from his LSD-25 mayonnaise jar.

In addition to Leary, Hollingshead turned on Paul Krassner, Richard Alpert, Art Kleps, Ralph Metzner, Donovan Leitch, Keith Richard, the Yardbirds, and others of early English rock scene, from a center he established in London (having been sent there for that purpose by Leary). Though

Leary claims to have turned on very few people personally, he and some thirty graduate students, young professors and theologians were, in his words:

> . . . thinking far-out history thoughts at Harvard . . . believing it was a time (after the shallow, nostalgic Fifties) for far-out visions. . . . With . . . scientific concepts as suggestive text and with LSD as instrumental sacrament and with prayers for grace, we began to write and to talk publicly about the possibility of a new philosophy, a new individual scientific theology.

Soon Harvard Square became the center of the "psychedelic revolution," with consequences well known. After being forced out of Harvard, Leary, Alpert (now Baba Ram Dass) and their associates decided it was time for the psychedelic movement to go public and established their International Federation for Internal Freedom (IFIF). In 1964 IFIF even opened a pilot LSD-training center in Zihuatanejo, Mexico, and the following summer offered a week at this resort for $200. They received over 1,500 applications.

Acid has appeared in many forms, but one of the strangest was one that Alpert went down to retrieve after he and Leary had been thrown out of their resort hotel in Zihuatanejo. To bring it through Customs, Alpert put it in a shaving lotion bottle. At the airport, his luggage was thrown up on the rack and fell off. He thought that the bottle might have broken, but didn't dare check until speeding from the airport in a taxi. Sure enough, the suit the LSD had been wrapped up in was all wet. One idea was to cut the suit up into squares like fabric samples; instead, it was just hung on the wall, where anyone who wanted to turn on could suck on it. (A seersucker suit, as it were).

After Zihuatanejo, this hearty band of experimenters set out for the British West Indies seeking island sanctuary. Discouraged, they returned to the U.S., and at the invitation of Peggy and William Hitchcock—heirs to the Mellon banking fortune—established a longer-lasting psychedelic vortex in Millbrook, New York. From here emanated the Psychedelic Review, early light shows carried to New York City and other messages transmitted via pilgrims who had made the trek to visit the Castalia Foundation and the League for Spiritual Discovery, the slightly altered names for IFIF. The high visibility of such activities dismayed more conservative investigators, but nonetheless drew much media attention leading to the mass turn-ons of the mid-Sixties.

In the spring of 1963, according to Beresford, Bobby Kennedy was known to be taking LSD or psilocybin and providing psychedelic entertainment for foreign dignitaries in a fashionable New York apartment. JFK reportedly smoked pot in the White House with Judith Campbell Exner. By this time, Eric Loeb ran a store with window displays on East Ninth Street in Manhattan, where he legally sold peyote buds from Arizona, mescaline, harmaline, and ibogaine. And the Englishman Gerald Heard had by now turned on the publisher of *Time* and *Life*, Henry Luce, and his wife, the vivacious playwright Clare Booth Luce.

Even more public and outrageous than the psychedelic circuses and celebrations of the Leary clique and upper-class New York society were the antics of Ken Kesey. Kesey, oddly enough, was turned on by the U.S. Army, which along with the CIA had been conducting its own turn-ons from the early Fifties onward. Of course, these turn-ons were given many times without preparation—yet many, such as Kesey, had good trips despite the lack of structure, and this may have inspired Kesey's Merry Pranksters to create their Electric Kool-Aid Acid Test, the namesake of a Tom Wolfe book. The test turned on many who had little advance knowledge, from the Fillmore ballroom to a Watts church. Wavy Gravy, former nightclub comedian Hugh Romney and one of the Pranksters, denied that he put the acid in the punch on these occasions.

Jerry Garcia could be considered another Army turn-on. The lead guitarist for the Grateful Dead, a notorious peyote-gulper in his early Berkeley coffeehouse days, Garcia recounts what caused him to gain the moniker "Captain Trips":

[In] '60, '61, '62, I guess, or '63, the government was running a series of drug tests over at Stanford, and Hunter [the Dead's lyricist] was one of the participants of these. They gave him mescaline and psilocybin and LSD and a whole bunch of others and put him in a little white room and watched him. And there were other people on the scene who were into that. Kesey. And as soon as these people had had those drugs they were immediately trying to get them, trying to find some way to cop 'em or anything, but there was no illicit drug market then like there is now.

The acid tests beginning in mid-decade were something entirely new. Instead of the turn-on being spread from friend to friend, communal conversions were now the order of the day and a new term was introduced into the language—"freaking freely." The first real "gathering of the tribes" occurred on October 16, 1966, the day when California became the first state to ban LSD. This was the earliest of what might properly be called the "Human Be-ins," and was celebrated by thousands on both coasts. A wave of media publicity about the gentleness of this mass turn-on resulted in an even larger gathering in San Francisco's Golden Gate Park in January 1967. An estimated 10,000 turned on while listening to Leary, Ginsberg, Lenore Kandel, McClure and many others praise the psychedelic revolution, accompanied by rock bands from San Francisco, such as Big Brother and the Holding Company, the Grateful Dead, and the Jefferson Airplane. Augustus Owsley Stanley III, already known by his middle name as a great acid maker, dropped by parachute into the crowd. Longhairs sporting flowers blew bubbles in the grass. By the time the beautiful, vibrant day, was over, everyone knew that San Francisco would soon celebrate a "Summer of Love."

The likes of Janis Joplin, Steve Miller, Neil Young, Stephen Stills, Jorma Kaukonen, Paul Kantner, Grace Slick, Country Joe McDonald and others formed a loose-knit "family" of turned-on rock stars on the West Coast. Chester Anderson has referred to such groups as Sturgeonesque "homo-gestalts" in *Crawdaddy*, the earliest rock magazine. Anderson partially explained why these San Francisco musicians and other acid-rockers such as the Stones, the Beatles, the Mothers, and the Doors, not to mention hundreds of other bands of similar odd fellows, were such an encouragement to the turn-on:

Rock is a legitimate avant-garde art form, with deep roots in the music of the past (especially the baroque and before), great vitality and vast potential for growth and development, adaptation, experiment, etc.

Its effects on the younger generation, especially those effects most deplored by type-heads, have all been essentially good and healthy so far.

With rock's heavy profit orientation today, these principles may sound a bit high-flown, optimistic and idealistic. Yet in the mid-Sixties, millions thought of the Beatles almost as gods (or at least as the four evangelists), and for months after *Sgt. Pepper's Lonely Hearts Club Band* became available, people argued endlessly about the secret meaning of "Lucy in the Sky with Diamonds."

LSD-25 made its debut in rock in 1962 in a single by the Gamblers. By 1965, Eric Burden and the Animals were crooning their love song, "To Sandoz"; the Stones were singing about how "Something Happened To Me Yesterday"; the Byrds were harmonizing about how they were "Eight Miles High," and the Beatles had long been advising everyone to "Turn off your mind, relax and float downstream. This is not dying . . ."

Ginsberg says he was turned on to pot by Al Aronowitz, a pop-rock writer for the *New York Post* who also performed the same service for Bob Dylan. Ginsberg mentions that the Beatles were turned on by Dylan when their planes once crossed at JFK airport. He asked whether they wanted to turn on, and they were hesitant. Finally, Ringo said he'd try it. They went behind a hangar, and after returning to the others, Ringo was asked what he thought of it. He was smiling so much, the others decided to try it too.

In retrospect, it may seem a strange quirk that the Beatles were turned on to acid by their dentist—the "Dr. Robert" of an early song—who over dinner slipped it into Paul's and John's coffees. "He didn't know what it was," one explained later. "We didn't ask for it, but later we did say 'thank you.' " Jimi Hendrix was another first turned on in England. He responded by putting "Purple Haze" at the top of the charts. In *Film About Hendrix*, we see his acid taster, who followed Jimi wherever he went and checked out his tabs to see how good they were before he tried them. According to many stories, Owsley made a double-strength, special batch of acid for him, and Jimi once ate a handful of these tabs before going on stage.

We haven't said anything about the role played by the Fugs, Steppenwolf, Pearls Before Swine, H. P. Lovecraft, Peter Walker, the Seeds, Quicksilver

Messenger Service, the Strawberry Alarm Clock, Arthur Brown, the Lovin' Spoonful and the Beach Boys, but these and hundreds of other groups all contributed enormously to the turning-on of the world.

Grace Slick likes to tell the story of how she and Abbie Hoffman were invited to a party for Tricia Nixon which Richard Nixon attended. They planned to dose Tricky Dick with some of Owsley's best, contained beneath her fingernail, before they were stopped at the door by security.

Hoffman relates his version of becoming another of the Army's turn-ons:

Aldous Huxley had told me about LSD back in 1957. And I *tried* to get it in 1959. I stood in line at a clinic in San Francisco, after Herb Caen had run an announcement in the *Chronicle* that if anybody wanted to take a new experimental drug called LSD-25, he would be paid $150 for his effort. Jesus, that emptied Berkeley! I got up about six in the morning, but I was about 1,500 in line so . . . I didn't get it until 1965. The acid was supplied by the United States Army. My roommate from college was an Army psychologist . . .

By the last half of the sixties, the psychedelic message was appearing almost everywhere, even if the lettering was somewhat difficult to read. The first Psychedelic Shop debuted in San Francisco, along with the *Oracle*, a newspaper that centered on psychedelics, showed up irregularly and ushered in for a short while the use of a split-font color technique that produced almost Day-Glo graphics. Both were quickly imitated by other shops and newspapers sprouting up to speak to new psychedelic consumers.

In Manhattan there was the *East Village Other,* started by Walter Bowart, now publisher of Omen Press, and John Wilcock, a British journalist. *Yarrowstalks* came from Philadelphia, the *Great Speckled Bird* from Atlanta, the *Astral Projection* from New Mexico, the *Kaleidoscope* from Milwaukee, the *Seed from Chicago,* the *Georgia Straight* from Vancouver, British Columbia, and the *Nola Express* from New Orleans, to name only a few. In L.A., the psychedelic message was conveyed by the *Free Press,* started by Art Kunkin at Pandora's Box on the Sunset Strip. Los Angeles also had its own *Oracle,* trying to reach the standards already set in San Francisco. Beyond this, a variety of "Communication Company" memos were issued sporadically in New York by Jimmy Fouratt and in San Francisco by Chester Anderson, the author of *The Butterfly Kid.*

All of these updating communiqués were members of the rapidly growing Underground Press Syndicate (UPS). They freely allowed the reprinting of psychedelic-encouraging material, such as this widely-quoted statement from Ginsberg:

> Abruptly then, I will make a first proposal—on one level symbolic, but to be taken as literally as possible, it may shock some and delight others—that everybody who hears my voice, directly or indirectly, try the chemical LSD at least once, every man, woman and child American in good health over the age of 14—that, if necessary, we have a mass emotional nervous breakdown in these states once and for all, that we see bankers laughing in their revolving doors with strange staring eyes . . . I propose, then, that everybody including the president and his and our vast hordes of generals, executives, judges and legislators of these states go to nature, find a kindly teacher or Indian peyote chief or guru guide and assay their consciousness with LSD . . .

The surprising thing in the situation at this time was that so few, in the wider perspective, were very curious. A dean at Columbia spoke of this once when he suggested at a faculty meeting that the university not graduate any senior who hadn't at least smoked some grass. Students who hadn't toked up by the late sixties, he said, showed such little interest in the real world that they could never be a credit to the institution.

Hollywood also was on the psychedelic bandwagon, using the turn-on as a central theme in wide-screen technicolor production. Peter Fonda was featured in *The Trip,* a Hollywood version of the psychedelic experience. It was reported at the time that Fonda would smoke grass on the patio of his Hollywood Hills home while police helicopters buzzed by periodically.

The namesake for *I Love You, Alice B. Toklas* was Gertrude Stein's author-lover, who had a notorious recipe for hash brownies. We can only speculate whether the film's star, Peter Sellers, partook. But Lew Gottlieb, the psychedelic guru in the movie, definitely did. Gottlieb started Morning Star, a communal farm in Sonoma County, California, and he was also one of the Limeliters. Other psychedelic films included *The President's Analyst*, starring a dapper and possibly turned-on James Coburn; and that tour de force of psychedelic animation, *Yellow Submarine*, which blended turn-on movement with the Beatles' music.

By the time the Beatles had gotten themselves decked out in Sgt. Pepper costumes, however, the country was also being turned on by a new kind of film, which Gene Youngblood would call the "expanded cinema." This genre was typified by Jordan Belson's *Re-Entry, Samadhi,* and *Momentum.* Other filmmakers, including Jean Mayo and Francis Lee, tried to convey an impression of their own psychedelic experiences.

Psychedelic cinema was being projected on the walls and screens of light-show emporiums such as The Electric Circus in New York's Lower East Side, the Avalon, Fillmore and Family Dog in San Francisco, the Kaleidoscope and Shrine Auditorium in L.A. and in dozens of rock venues across the land. The ultimate rock-acid rush was Woodstock and the hundreds of festivals it begat.

Until 1960, according to Hofmann, the world supplies of ergot, the necessary precursor to the manufacture of LSD-25, were extremely limited. Peyote was available, but not to any great extent. Yagé, DMT, psilocybin, MDA, STP, MMDA, and ibogaine were all but unknown. But then, as Humphry Osmond put it, somebody discovered how ergot could be grown in churns. Now the ball really had begun to roll.

The discovery of how to mass cultivate ergot on *Claviceps paspali* was made in the Farmitalia labs in Milan, Italy. Before long, Farmitalia was offering LSD-25 at $10,000 a kilo, enough for eight million 250-microgram experiences. Then Spofa Pharmaceuticals in Czechoslovakia began manufacture, providing a high-quality product which became available to anyone in Prague who wished to try the experience under medical supervision. Communist party leader Alexander Dubcek and most of the city's artistic community took advantage of the offer, which many claim led to the

"Prague Spring" of 1968 that ended in a Soviet invasion. Spofa, however, continued to supply the drug until just very recently.

In the early sixties, nearly all the LSD ingested came from these pharmaceutical sources. When Sandoz recalled LSD after the heavy scare campaign of 1966, most users became dependent upon underground supply. This had remained fairly amateurish and small until the advent of Augustus Owsley Stanley III, grandson of a Kentucky senator.

Owsley came to the making of acid in 1961 after collaborating with one of the earliest manufacturers. Soon he was in business for himself in a makeshift laboratory behind a vacant store in Berkeley, California. His acid varied from early white capsules to what became known as "Owsley tabs," blue at first, but later—when cheap imitations hit the market—in other colors. Some were stamped with the figure of Batman or Robin, bearing such names as "Midnight Hour," "White Lightning," or "Monterey Purple."

Owsley got into the game due to his inability to procure pharmaceutical LSD-25, and within five years it had made him a millionaire. But he was put out of business following his bust in December 1967 at his Orinda tabbing center. His apprentice, Tim Scully, carried on in association with Nicholas Sand, prolific Brooklyn alchemist. Together they put out most of the fabled "Sunshine" acid.

Sunshine was the second acid to gain a large distribution—world-wide, as a matter of fact. The main source of these orange, crumbly tablets was Laguna Beach, a beautiful art colony on the coast of California. A "clean" scene developed there in the mid-Sixties, with many taking Sandoz on the picturesque sands. Here was where Timothy Leary stayed after touring communes of the southwestern United States, the sites of many religious turn-ons.

By 1969, five years after this town's first head shop was established, large amounts of Sunshine began to be pumped to an acid-hungry population by a group called The Brotherhood of Eternal Love. Actually, the Brotherhood had started several years earlier as a religious group. But as dealing became big business, new faces emerged. Brotherhood members made large fortunes from the import of Afghanistan hash, selling it from a center on a small street called Woodland Drive. The Brotherhood house burned down after a hookah filled with the best "primo" tipped over. Brotherhood members and Afghani royalty escaped the flames.

In the Sunshine field, Nick Sand and Timothy Scully were the original suppliers, claiming to have produced the "improved" acid homologue ALD-52. By the turn of the decade, some 35 million doses of LSD—brown from oxidation and decomposition—had come via the European lab of Ronald Stark, presently a fugitive. The largest amount of this appeared on the West Coast late in 1970 (hence the designation "Christmas acid"). Leary, at this point, remarked, "The challenge to the dealer is not only must his product be pure and spiritual but he himself must reflect the human light he represents. Therefore, never buy dope, never purchase sacrament from a person that hasn't got the qualities that you aspire for."

HEROIN, OLD AGE, RHYTHM AND BLUES

An Interview with Keith Richards

JANUARY 1978

KEITH RICHARDS HAS BEEN the Rolling Stones' lead guitarist for the last 15 years and one of rock's leading crusaders and criminals. His most recent brush with the law came in Toronto six months ago, when he was arrested for possession of heroin with intent to sell.

High Times reached him at his new house in Westchester County, sixty minutes outside of Manhattan. Getting the interview became complicated when the president of Rolling Stones Records, Earl McGrath, tried to persuade Keith not to talk with us because it would have an adverse effect on his court case. Keith thought that was a bit soft.

High Times: Do you feel that it was your destiny to be a musician?

Richards: Well, when I used to pose in front of the mirror at 'ome, I was hopeful. The only thing I was lacking was a bit of bread to buy an instrument. But I got the moves off first, and I got the guitar later.

High Times: Is music magic to you?

Richards: In the way that *magic* is a word for something that is power that we don't fully understand and can enable things to happen. I mean, nobody really understands about the effect that certain rhythms have on people, but our bodies beat. We're only alive because the heartbeat keeps going all the time. And also certain sounds can kill. It's a speciality of the French for some reason. The French are working with huge great speakers which blow down houses and kill laboratory technicians with one solitary blast. I mean, the trumpets of Jericho and all that.

I've seen people physically throw up from feedback in the studio. It's so loud it started their stomach walls flapping. That's the most obvious aspect of it. But on another level, if you go to Africa or Jamaica, you see people living to that rhythm. They eat, talk, walk, fuck, sleep, do everything to that rhythm. It's magic in that it's an unexplored area. Why, for instance—zoom in 'ere—should rock and roll music suddenly appear in the mid-fifties, catch hold and just get bigger and bigger and show no signs of abating?

High Times: Brian Jones was the leader, then Mick became the leader, but now there's a feeling that, musically, you're the leader of the Rolling Stones.

Richards: I guess it takes a long time. . . . I mean, I'm basically doing the same thing now as I always have done. I run around trying to communicate with the rest of them, because Charlie's sitting down and Bill's over there and I'm more free, and I give them the tempo because early on I evolved a certain style of playing that is fairly basic. I know that I can give what's needed to Charlie and Bill and Ronnie to keep the thing together.

High Times: And to Mick?

Richards: I hope Mick should get the whole thing. I'm trying to keep all the separate things together so that by the time it gets to the front of the stage and out into the audience, it's jelled together.

High Times: Is the guitar an instrument you can get further and further into?

Richards: I think most guitar players feel that they're always still learning. Nobody ever feels that they've reached anywhere near covering the whole thing. It's still coming up with surprises. Although that's not the most important thing to me.

It's never been a function in our band to do one thing or another. We're all doing all of it, you know. That's what happens and that's what interests me about it, it's not who's playing virtuoso. I'm interested in what people can do in terms of an overall sound and the intensity of it that can be done on that level. I mean, five people produce one thing out of five separate things going on. After all, what's the point of dissecting everything and putting parts under a microscope and ignoring the rest?

High Times: Do you get very high off the response to your records when they're particularly effective in some way?

Richards: Yeah, sometimes, you try to, but it's not always that immediate. You put a record out, and then you get the feeling everybody's disappointed with it. Then two years later you bring another record out, and you suddenly realize that they're all holding this other record up and saying, "If only it was as good as this one." And I know it's not because we're ahead of our time, because that's not ever what we're trying to do.

It's not avant-garde, no, that's not it. It's just that when you've been around as long as we have, people have got their own fixed idea of what they want from the Stones, and it's never anything new. Even though they do really want it, they still compare it with this big moment in the back seat of a car fifteen years ago, and it was never as good as then. There's so much nostalgia connected with it that you can't possibly fight, so you have to sometimes let the record seep into their lives, let them have a good time with it first.

A lot of the time with records it's the experiences that people have been through while that record's been playing that makes it special to them. "It's our song, darling." That sort of shit. And the longer you've been around the harder it is to fight that one, 'cos you got so much other stuff which is somebody else's song, darling. And although they're interested and they'll buy the new record, it doesn't mean as much to them as the one they heard that magical night when they screwed fifteen chicks.

High Times: Do you think of songs as short stories?

Richards : Some of them. I mean, things like "Hand of Fate" particularly, we got into a story. Others are just connections, almost stream of consciousness. One line doesn't really connect to what's gone before. People say they write songs, but in a way you're more the medium. I feel like all the songs in the world are just floating around; it's just a matter of an antenna, of whatever you pick up.

So many uncanny things have happened. A whole song just appears from nowhere in five minutes, the whole structure, and you haven't worked at all. You're playing and you're bored stiff and nothing's happening, oh dear, and you go out and 'ave a joint or something and *euhuh!* There it is. It's just like somebody tuned in the radio and you've picked it up.

Some people equate good work with being difficult to do, but a lot of the time it's the easiest thing. It just sort of flashes by you so quick that people virtually tell you. You didn't even see it yourself. "Satisfaction" was the biggest hit we've ever had, and it just came *boing bang crash,* and it was on tape before I felt it.

High Times: It's obvious that everyone's life is very much involved at this point, with drugs and increasingly so, and it's not going to get less . . .

Richards: Oh, no way, no.

High Times: It's something that people have to talk about, it's something we need to know more about. Do you have any advice you could give people who read *High Times* about the drug situation, generally speaking, in America?

Richards: I don't think I'm in any position to give any advice, as such, but maybe just by talking about it we can make things a bit clearer. It's interesting that they're lightening up on the marijuana laws slowly, and it's accelerating. I mean since I've come to the states, New York is decriminalized, and once that sort of thing happens it snowballs. Already you hear talk of a commission looking into cocaine to give that a different status.

In a way I feel it's all a bit of a game because there's all this flimflam about decriminalization, which isn't legalization, and eventually what it comes down to is money anyway. If they can figure out a way of taking it over and making bread out of it, it'll be legal. The only reason methadone's such a big deal in America is because a lot of people are making millions on it.

High Times: But why can't they find a way at this point to make money out of grass and cocaine?

Richards: Because I think they realize that even if they sell twenty filtered Acapulco golds, real grass heads will still be buying their stash from the man who comes over the border with it under the floorboards of his truck. If you want good tobacco, you don't buy Newports or Marlboros. You go to some little tobacco stall and choose your tobacco.

High Times: Then you think because of the quality differences, marijuana is a very hard thing to merchandise?

Richards: 'Oo knows? Let's just say that I can't see myself, or anybody that I know, preferring to buy a packet of prerolled marijuana cigarettes when I know that it's going to be grade C.

High Times: But doesn't it seem more and more necessary to recognize that the human being is a chemical machine?

Richards: Yes. I think that what we can really say is that anybody interested in drugs and wanting to take anything ought first to find out as much as they can about what it is that they're taking, what it is that it does to them, in order that they can compensate as much as necessary for what it is they're introducing into their systems. Even with grass, so many people don't take the simplest precautions.

I think that, personally, it's purely a matter of the person concerned. I mean, it's like a good blowjob. You know, in some states that's still illegal. It's just a matter of how far people are prepared to put up with so-called authorities prying into their lives. If they really don't want to accept it, then they'll do something about it because there'll be no way they can enforce it.

The other way, I think, is from the government. They ought to do a lot more about educating people about drugs, rather than just trying to scare people by keeping them in the dark about everything, including possible ways of getting off really heavy drugs, because it can be done perfectly painlessly. That isn't the main problem. As they'll all say, disintoxication is 5 percent of the battle; 95 percent is keeping them off anything when you send them back. But 'ow do you know when all you're doing is keeping them on methadone all the time? You don't give them a chance that way.

High Times: Do you think alcohol addiction is as hard to kick as drug addiction?

Richards: Yes. I think so. All these things are very individual. One drug'll have a different effect on one person than on someone else. I can booze for weeks and months and get lushed every night, and then, because I have a change of environment or whatever, I can stop and just not miss it. I just can't stop smoking cigarettes for the life of me. I'm as addicted to that as the biggest junkie is addicted to heroin. But then, millions of us are. That's something else.

Booze is something that I can take or leave, but it's a poison. I do feel there's that double standard that we all talk about. I consider booze to be far more harmful than any other available drug, far more damaging to the body, to the mind, to the person's attitude. The way some people change on it is amazing, and then, goddamit, every morning when you wake up you've got a cold turkey whether you like it or not. You know, just because it's called "the hangover" . . . It seems to me to be the most uneconomical and inconvenient high you could possibly have, 'cos every morning you've got to pay for it. I mean, even a junkie doesn't have to do that unless he decides to stop or runs out of stuff, but even if you've got bottles of booze in the morning, you've still got a hangover. And it just seems so vague putting yourself through those constant incredible changes. That's what I think really does you with booze.

High Times: Do you pay a lot of attention to taking care of yourself physically, considering the amount of work you do?

Richards: I don't pay that much attention to it, just because I've never had to. I'm very lucky in that everything's always functioned perfectly, even under the most incredible strains and amounts of chemicals. But I think a lot of it is to do with a solid consciousness of it in a regulatory system that serves me. I never take too much of anything. I don't go out for a big rush or complete obliteration. I sometimes find that I've been up five days, and I'll collapse and just fall asleep. But that's about the only thing that I do to myself, and I only do that because I find that I'm capable of doing it.

High Times: Have you read William Burroughs' statement in *Junky:* "I think I am in better health now as a result of using junk at intervals than I would have been if I had never been an addict"?

Richards: Yeah, I agree with that. Actually, I once took that apomorphine cure that Burroughs swears by. Dr. Dent was dead, but his assistant, whom he trained, this lovely old dear called Smitty, who's like mother hen, still runs the clinic. I had her down to my place for five days, and she just sort of comes in and says, "Here's your shot, dear, there's a good boy." Or, "You've been a naughty boy, you've taken something, yes you have, I can tell." But it's a pretty medieval cure. You just vomit all the time.

High Times: What's the new cure they're working on in London at the moment?

Richards: There's a Dr. Paterson who's been working on an electro-acupuncture cure that she's developed from a colleague in Hong Kong. Her husband was a Fleet Street journalist, a real hustler, so he figured they could market it. It's a little box about six inches by two inches with two wires coming out, one on each side. You plug one of these wires into each ear and they put out a beat that you can regulate yourself. As long as the beat is going on, you don't feel any pain. I had Dr. Paterson and her husband flown over from England, and they stayed with me during the cure. I kept this thing plugged in for two-and-a-half days. Anita and I did it together. You wake up in the morning and you feel all right. You can read a book, have a cup of tea. Things you could normally never do on first days getting off.

High Times: We live in a time where so much could be done medically to the system. With the correct medical information or supervision, we could take drugs all the time.

Richards: Look at the astronauts. I mean, they're completely chemically regulated from the minute they start that thing until they come down. I think the sooner they realize that, they're gonna have to take notice of it and they start learning and they start teaching people more about certain things—I don't think any drug is harmful in itself. All of them have their uses and their good sides, so it's the abuse of them and the fact that, because of their so-called illegality, one has to get them from dubious sources, so you never know what you're actually getting. Maybe you're getting what you're after, but it's mixed with strychnine, which has happened to several people I know.

High Times: Have you ever been in a dangerous situation with drugs?

Richards: No. I don't know if I've been extremely lucky or if it's that subconscious regulatory thing I've gotten, because I'm not extremely careful, but I've never turned blue in somebody else's bathroom. I consider that the height of bad manners. I've 'ad so many people do it to me and it's really not on, as far as drug etiquette goes, to turn blue in somebody else's John. You suddenly realize that somebody's been in there for like an hour and you 'aven't 'eard a sound, and I think it's such a drag, because I think it's a drag when people do it to me, thumping on the door: "Are you all right?" "Yeah! I'm having a fucking crap!"

But people do do it. I mean, if somebody's been in the John for hours and hours I'll do it, and I know 'ow annoying it is when I hear the voice comin' out: "Yeah, I'm all right!" But sometimes I'm glad I've done it, because we've knocked the door down and there's somebody going into the last stages of the colors of the rainbow and that's really a drag. The ambulance comes and . . . clear everything up. Because you can't pretend 'e's just fallen ill or something.

High Times: Rock is like drugs in a way, because people listen to it to cure their pain. Rock music makes you feel good, brings you out of yourself under any circumstances at all.

Richards: It will do that for you in a way. Maybe why drugs are so associated with rock music is that the people who actually create the music no longer get that feeling from rock unless they're actually playing it. I mean, they can't put a record on and just feel good anymore because it's just so much to do with part of their business. So you turn to other things to make yourself feel good. It's a theory *[laughing]* . . . I don't know. That's my excuse, anyway.

High Times: But in a way, you're addicted to the guitar, right?

Richards: Yeah. There's another thing. Now maybe it's because rock and roll's such a tight formula. The most important thing is, because the formula is so strict, it's the variations that come about within this format that are the things people turn onto. Because it's the same old thing again, but there's one or two slightly different ways of doing things that make one record stand out different from another. And it's when you're into it to that degree of trying to find . . .

High Times: How much do you think you keep being successful because you work so hard?

Richards: I think it's probably got more to do with it than even we realize, because it's very easy to be lazy when you don't have to work. I've found it's very dangerous for me to be lazy. I develop lots of nasty habits, which are not good for me, whereas if I keep working—and in a way it's just like a compulsion—I'll keep myself together. The minute I relax and let it go, I just sort of drift. I can drift into anything. I'm fair game!

High Times: Well, I know Mick is, but are the rest of the members of the band into working like that?

Richards: Yeah. Charlie loves to be at home, but that's his own little battle, 'cos he also likes to work. If Charlie could find a way of being on the road every night, but also being at home, he'd do it. Ronnie lives for nothing but playing, and that's the way Mick and I have always been. What we've got to push for now is a way to work regularly and to work a lot more varied venues in a lot more varied places, to get off the old warpath.

For instance, if they lay an American tour on us tomorrow, I can name 90 percent of the cities we're gonna go to. Rock and roll tours don't go to Wyoming, Idaho, Montana, North or South Dakota. They don't exist as far as rock and roll's concerned. But it can't be that people in there are not interested. They've got radio stations, and the same records are number one. It comes down to the agents and promoters who are totally into country music in those areas. So the only people who go there are country musicians.

It's amazing to me that in America, in this day and age, they can still keep these very rigid separate circuits. They are slowly breaking down, but I remember ten or twelve years ago in America the black circuit was just totally separate. But the amazing one is the country music one, which is *still* rigidly separated from anything else. And for music which is in lots of ways so similar . . . when you come down to the basis of it and trace where it all comes from, one of the major influences on rock is white country music. That's 50 percent of it. The other 50 percent is black music. And the fact that those two just . . . . it's apartheid, you know, so they're not white, they're rednecks.

High Times: Have you thought at all about doing a concert tour like Dylan's Rolling Thunder? Is it totally impossible for you to do that still?

Richards: No. I think that's the way things have really gotta go. I can't see going around forever playing bigger and bigger baseball parks and super-domes. I think audiences have gone about as far as you can go with it. In fact, I think a lot of people probably don't go because they just can't stand to go to those places.

High Times: When you get off these exhausting tours, what do you do?

Richards: Aaaahhh, that is the weirdest time. Yeah.

High Times: It must be a real difficult transition.

Richards: That's my problem period. If I don't find something to do right away, that's when I've found that I've been getting incredibly lazy, but also incredibly restless because you're so used to being hyper every day, and suddenly you've got nothing to do and you think "aaah . . . nothing to do, great!" And you sit back for five minutes and then you say "Phew!" You've got nowhere to go, and you walk around the room ten times and it's . . . it's . . . WEIRD!

High Times: Do you hang around with each other or does the group completely separate?

Richards: These days everybody just fragments too, so suddenly you're alone from all these people who you've been incredibly close to for two or three months. Sometimes Ronnie and I are with each other for five or six days on the trot. Other people have been to sleep six times and we've seen six dawns. You can't even remember the last time you slept because you've got this memory . . .

It's funny, you know, when you sleep everything is so neatly put into compartments of that day and that day, and I did that on that day, but if you stay up for five or six days the memory goes back into one long period with no breaks at all, and days don't mean anything anymore. You just remember people or specific events.

High Times: If you all keep in good shape, do you think you have another fifteen years?

Richards: Oh yeah. I hope so. There's no way to tell. We know a lot of the old black boys have kept going forever. A lot of the old roots boys, the old blues players, and as far as we're concerned they're virtually playing the same thing. They kept going till the day they dropped. They still are. B. B. King's close to sixty. Jimmy Reed died last year, and he was going to the end. Chuck Berry's still going. Muddy Waters just had one of his biggest albums ever. Howling Wolf kept going to the very end. Sleepy John just died last month; he was preparing to go on a European tour. . . . I mean, Elvis was the one that I would have said, but he happened to have went early.

It's a physical thing. There's no denying that there's a high fatality rate in rock and roll. Up until the middle Sixties the most obvious method of rock and roll death was chartered planes. Since then drugs have taken their toll, but all of the people that I 'ave known that 'ave died from so-called drug overdoses 'ave all been people that've 'ad some fairly serious physical weakness somewhere.

Brian was the only one amongst us who would ever get ill. He was the only one of us who missed some gigs because of health, and this was before he was involved with any drug at all, and a couple of other guys I've known that have died from overdoses weren't particularly strong physically, and they probably went a lot quicker because of the fact that they were on drugs. But they're not people who you would have said would have lasted forever anyway. Meaning, I guess, that a lot of the time drugs just accelerated what's going to happen anyway.

High Times: At this point do you believe anything's going to get better, or do you think the Stones might not be able to continue doing what they've been doing?

Richards: I can't see any real obstacles in the way as long as the Stones don't just sit on their asses, as long as we try and do things that we think are beneficial for all concerned.

High Times: So you don't worry about members of the group getting fucked up?

Richards: No, not now . . .

High Times: I mean, you've survived so much.

Richards: Exactly. The thing is that whatever's happened, nobody's ever felt alone. If anything's happened, somebody's always rallied around, and not just the Stones. Friends, other bands, other musicians and just other people generally, people not connected with the music business, just friends and people we don't even know, but you find they've been taking an interest in you. We all feel that as long as you don't feel isolated and completely cut off from everything, you're okay.

I feel very hopeful about the future. I find it all very enjoyable with a few peak surprises thrown in. Even being busted . . . it's no pleasure, but it certainly isn't boring. And I think boring is the worst thing of all, you know, anything but boring. At least it keeps you active.

High Times: Do you ever get worried that they'll finally get you?

Richards: Well, if they haven't done it by now, no. It must be fairly obvious to everybody now that they've 'ad a go with trying. If they try again, I don't see any real way they can get away with it just because they have been trying to get me and it never works that way.

WHY I LOVE TO LIVE *FAST*

ANDY WARHOL

MAY 1978

FIRST OF ALL, IT'S best to be born fast, because it hurts, and it's best to die fast, because it hurts, but I think if you were born and died within that minute, that would be the best life, because the priest says that way you're guaranteed to go to heaven. He says you're born to die. "Born to die"—you could write a song about it.

I know I love to live fast because all my favorite things are the fastest— the new Polaroid Super 8 movie camera, the Roy Rogers Family-Style Restaurants, pushbutton telephones, Xerox machines, my Konica cameras and Sony tape recorders, the Concorde, drive-in movies (because you can go in your pajamas). And my favorite person is Tom Seaver, because he pitches the fast ball and he gave me the fast bat I'm holding in this picture taken by the fastest photographer in America.

Ever since I was a kid I've wanted to live as fast as I could, so I always try to find ways to do things faster: I like to sleep fast, that's when you just snooze, and I like to love fast, that's when you have a one-night affair (but remember, a fast person can never have any kind of relationship with a slow person). And I really like Swanson's TV dinners when you have friends over, because there are no greasy dishes to think about afterwards. When I get up in the morning, it doesn't take me any time to get ready for work because I wear the same thing every day. So uniforms are great, and the fastest uniform today is the jumpsuit: you just jump in it, jump out the door, and jump to work.

Some people complain that you should have slow sex—like in India I heard that it takes fourteen hours—but then they have all these problems with, what do they call it, premature ejaculation? See, I always thought that was the best kind. You should never even get it in before you come. I mean, you might be able to get to the point where you just shoot it inside your pants, thinking about it, and that would be the best.

Frankly, in my opinion, there's nothing it's good to do slow, so the only thing is, how to live fast if you live slow? I don't know anyone who takes amphetamines anymore, but you could hang around with girls who take diet pills, because they'll get you nervous and jittery and that makes you go fast. But what really makes you go fast is if you knit: you never can stop once you get started, and it teaches you that it's best to keep doing something all the time because that way you live faster and faster. I paint faster now, because I use a sponge, and I make movies faster, but I think new movies will be even faster, like only half an hour. I mean, for me time goes by so fast I find myself asking everybody on Friday if it's still Monday.

Funnily enough, America isn't the fastest country. They live faster in Japan, but the Japanese are such completely different people you can't make any comparisons. And, anyway, fast Americans are the most glamorous people: they do more, see more, learn more, and get more money because they get fast money. I love to live fast, because then you don't have to think about anything. For example, writing this took me four minutes—which is the time it takes to eat a Big Mac—so I did it in my lunch minutes, and I was glad because, instead of just eating and talking to the kids in the office about my problems, I was eating and writing an article for *High Times*, so I got more done and made more money and felt better faster. And that's what we're here for, isn't it?

I WISH I HAD INVENTED SEX

Debbie "Blondie" Harry

October 1978

WELL, UH, *HIGH TIMES* called me and said they were dedicating this issue to sex or some such and that I should write some such. Since sex is one of the main activities people get high for, and since I have been asked "how does it feel to be a sex symbol?" about a thousand million times in the last six months, it all seems very natural, and after all nature is gonna win no matter what all you suckers do.

Sex sells more magazines, books, movies, records, etc., than anything else. Only violence runs a close second, with flying saucers and drugs tied for third. I wish I had invented sex.

"So tell us how it feels to be a sex symbol, Debbie."

"Well Johnny . . . uh, why don't you go fuck yourself with a double water-spurting pulsating, rubber, moterized, body-temperature dildo— then and only then will you know the truth, the answer you have sought."

The real truth is that I learned about sex at the zoo. As a cute but clumsy four year old, I was taken to the Central Park zoo by my mom. We stood peacefully watching the bears while they sat and scratched themselves, when out of the blue came superjerk in his weather-beat-in raincoat (à la Columbo) flashing his worn-out privates. My mom was pissed off. I couldn't have cared less, except he seemed to have three of 'em and I couldn't get much of an explanation from my mom.

Years later I discovered that the male of the species is equipped with nuts and that these in fact were what I had mistaken for two extra wangs.

My only sex-related problem is the unexpected biological urge at the most inappropriate time, e.g., lines at the supermarket or crowded buses and elevators. And if I can be completely open with all of you perverts, the supermarket is the place for a turn-on. I can't say exactly what it is that turns me on: the bright lights, the Muzak, the smells of the deli department floating around the aisles or the bloodied uniforms of stiff white-duck material. I don't know, I don't know. And it doesn't cost twenty-five cents to get in!

Pinball is sex. The flashing lights, the tensions, the façade, the score, the climax and the anticlimax, and after all, as the pros say, "All you need is one good ball."

Game shows on TV are sex—big orgasms as we see what's in the box! Everyone knows rock 'n' roll is sex.

Just sex is not really sex because it's private and you're not supposed to think about it. Better you should go beat one of your friends to death with a meat ax. That would be much less perverse.

I can only think of one market where sex has not been totally exploited: furniture. We use furniture most in connection with active and passive sex.

I got a couch
Shaped like a penis
I just hope
It don't come between us.

Well, when Wayne County saw this couch of mine, he was fit to be filled with "Crocodile Tears." (The Mumps.) I couldn't blame him, after all those years of searching the 42nd Street and Village sex shops for battery-powered cock rings and padded toilet seats, the poor thing was exhausted. I am surprised that there isn't more furniture like those tables in Clockwork Orange or even more bidets like in Europe.

I really did have a couch shaped like a penis, only it made one of my chairs pregnant, and I threw them both the fuck out.

So that's my report. Don't believe everything you read, however, especially things related to rock 'n' roll, since no one in the business can read or write, especially rock 'n' roll writers and/or musicians. And remember, boys, if you're tired of shaving, get laid more, so your hormones come out of your cock instead of your face.

Love and X,

—Debbie "Blondie" Harry

High Times

June '77

$1.75

Captain Crunch:
King of the
Phone Phreaks

ALBERT
GOLDMAN
EATS HASH

MURDER AT
ELAINE'S
Original
Mystery Serial

DOPE
MANNERS
Were You Raised
in a Barn?

Guide to
Psychedelic Cacti

Furry Freak Bros.
Look-Alike Contest

Swimsuits for
the Nude Beach

YIPPIE
DANA BEAL
On Not Having
Nixon to
Kick Around

BLONDIE
The Marilyn
Monroe
of Punk
Rock

High Times #22, June 1977

KEROUAC

An Historic Memoir of America's Greatest Existentialist

WILLIAM S. BURROUGHS

MARCH 1979

KEROUAC WAS A WRITER. That is, he *wrote*. Many people who call themselves writers and have their names on books are not writers and they can't write—the difference being, a bullfighter who fights a bull is different from a bullshitter who makes passes with no bull there. The writer has been there or he can't write about it. And going there he risks being gored. By that I mean what the Germans aptly call the Time Ghost—for example, such a fragile ghost world as Fitzgerald's Jazz Age—all the sad young men, firefly evenings, winter dreams, fragile, fragile like his picture taken in his twenty-third year—Fitzgerald, poet of the Jazz Age. He went there and wrote it and brought it back for a generation—he wrote the Jazz Age. A whole migrant generation arose from *On the Road to Mexico,* Tangier, Afghanistan, India.

What are writers, and I will confine the use of this term to writers of novels, trying to do? They are trying to create a universe in which they have lived or where they would like to live. To write it they must go there and submit to conditions which they may not have bargained for. Sometimes, as in the case of Fitzgerald and Kerouac, the effect produced by a writer is immediate, as if a generation were waiting to be written. In other cases there may be a time lag. Science fiction has a way of coming true. In any case, by writing a universe the writer makes such a universe *possible*.

To what extent writers can, actually do, or how useful it is for their craft to act out their writing in so-called real life, is an open question. That is, depending which way you come on it—like are you making your universe more like the real universe or are you pulling the real into yours? *Winner Take Nothing*. For example, Hemingway's determination to act out the least interesting aspects of his own writing and to actually *be* his character was, I feel, unfortunate for his writing. Quite simply, if a writer insists on being able to do and do well what his characters do, he limits the range of his characters. However, writers profit from doing something even when done badly; as I was for one short week—brings on my ulcers to think about it—a very bad assistant pickpocket. I decided that a week was enough and I didn't have the touch, really.

Walking around the wilderness of outer Brooklyn with the Sailor after a mooch (as he called a drunk) came up on us at the end of Flatbush: "They'll beat the shit out of us . . . you have to expect that . . ." I shuddered and didn't want to expect that and decided right there that I was going to turn in my copy of the *Times*—the one I used to cover him when he put the hand out. We always used the same copy—he said people would try to read it and get confused when it was a month old, and this would like keep them from seeing us. He was quite a philosopher, the Sailor was . . . but a week was enough before I got what I "had to expect". . . .

"Here comes one . . . yellow lights too . . ." We huddle in a vacant lot . . . speaking for myself at least, who can always see what I look like from outside, I look like a frightened commuter clutching his briefcase as Hell's Angels roar past.

Now if this might seem a cowardly way of cowering in a vacant lot when I should have given myself the experience of getting worked over by the skinny short cop with the acne-scarred face who looks out of that prowl car his eyes brown and burning in his head, well, the Sailor wouldn't have liked that and neither would a White Hunter like a client there to get himself mauled by a lion. Fitzgerald said once, to Hemingway, "Rich people are different from you and me."

"Yes . . . they have more money." And writers are different from you and me. They write. You don't bring back a story if you get yourself killed. So a writer need not be ashamed to hide in a vacant lot or a corner of the room for a few minutes. He is there as a writer and not as a character. There is nothing more elusive than a writer's main character, the character that is assumed by the reader to be the writer himself, no less, actually doing the things he writes about. But this main character is simply a point of view interposed by the writer. The main character then becomes in fact another character in the book, but usually the most difficult to see, because he is mistaken for the writer himself. He is the writer's observer and often very uneasy in this role and at a loss to account for his presence. He is an object of suspicion to the world of nonwriters unless he manages to write them into his road.

Kerouac says in *Vanity of Duluoz:* "I am not 'I am' but just a spy in someone's body pretending these sandlot games kids in the cow field near St. Rita's Church . . ." Jack Kerouac knew about writing when I first met him in 1944. He was twenty-one; already he had written a million words and was completely dedicated to his chosen trade. It was Kerouac who kept telling me I should write and call the book I wrote *Naked Lunch.* I had never written anything after high school and did not think of myself as a writer and I told him so. "I got no talent for writing . . ." I had tried a few times, a page maybe. Reading it over always gave me a feeling of fatigue and disgust and aversion towards this form of activity, such as a laboratory rat must experience when he chooses the wrong path and gets a sharp reprimand from a needle in his displeasure centers. Jack insisted quietly that I did have talent for writing and that I would write a book called *Naked Lunch.* To which I replied, "I don't want to hear anything literary."

Trying to remember just where and when this was said is like trying to remember a jumble of old films. The 1940s seem centuries away. I see a bar on 116th Street here and a piece five years later in another century; a sailor at the bar who reeled over on the cue of *Naked Lunch* and accused us—I think Allen Ginsberg was there and John Kingsland—of making a sneering reference to the Swiss Navy. Kerouac was good in these situations since he was basically unhostile. Or was it in New Orleans or Algiers to be more precise, where I lived in a frame house by the river, or was it later in Mexico by the lake in Chapultepec Park . . . there's an island there where thousands of vultures roost apathetically. I was shocked at this sight since I had always admired their aerial teamwork, some skimming a few feet off the ground, others wheeling way up, little black specks in the sky—and when they spot food they pour down in a black funnel—we are sitting on the edge of the lake with tacos and bottles of beer . . . "*Naked Lunch* is the only title" . . . I pointed to the vultures.

"They've given up, like old men in St. Petersburg, Florida . . . go out and hustle some carrion you lazy buzzards!" Whipping out my pearl-handled .45 I killed six of them in showers of black feathers.

Black wood table in the booth rum and Coca Cola Hong Kong Blues on the juke box no that was another bar on 42nd Street.

The other vultures took to the sky . . . I would act these out with Jack, and quite a few of the scenes that later appeared in *Naked Lunch* arose from these acts. I remember we were in the University Club, of which I was a member, and a spastic member on a crutch got in the elevator and we got the idea of tripping him and taking his crutch away and mimicking his twitches. When Jack came to Tangier in 1957 I had decided to take his title and much of the book was already written.

In fact during all the years I knew Kerouac I can't remember ever seeing him really angry or hostile. It was the sort of smile he gave in reply to my demurrers, in a way you get from a priest who knows you will come to Jesus sooner or later—you can't walk out on the Shakespeare Squadron, Bill. Now as a very young child I had wanted to be a writer. At the age of nine I wrote something called the *Autobiography of a Wolf*. This early literary essay was so strongly influenced as to smell of plagiarism of a little book I had just read called the *Biography of a Grizzly Bear*. There were various vicissitudes including the loss of his beloved mate . . . in the end this poor old bear slouches into a valley he knows is full of poison gases, about to die . . . I can see the picture now, it's all in sepia, the valley full of nitrous yellow fumes and the bear walking in like a resigned criminal to the gas chamber. Now I had to give my wolf a different twist, so saddened by the loss of his entire family he encounters a grizzly bear who kills him and eats him. Later there was something called *Carl Cranbury in Egypt* that never got off the ground really . . . a knife glinted in the dark alley. With lightning speed Carl V. Cranbury reached for the blue steel automatic under his left arm . . . frozen forever an inch from his blue steel automatic . . . These were written out painfully in longhand with great attention to the script—the actual process of writing became so painful that I couldn't do anything more for Carl Cranbury as the Dark Ages descended—the years in which I wanted to be anything else but a writer. A private detective, a bartender, a criminal . . . I failed miserably at all these callings, but a writer is not concerned about success or failure, but simply about observation and recall. At the time I was not gathering material for a book. I simply was not doing anything well enough to make a living at it. In this respect Kerouac did better than I did. He didn't like it but he did it—work on railroads and in factories. My record time on a factory job was four weeks. And I had the distinction to be actually *fired* from a defense plant during the war.

Perhaps Kerouac did better because he saw his work interludes simply as a means to buy time to write in. Tell me how many books a writer has written . . . we can assume usually ten times that amount shelved or thrown away . . . and I will tell you how he spends his time. Any writer spends a good deal of his time alone, writing. And that is how I remember Kerouac—as a writer talking about writing or sitting in a quiet corner with a notebook, writing in longhand. He was also very fast on the typewriter. You felt that he was writing all the time; that writing was the only thing he thought about. He never wanted to be anything else.

If I seem to be talking more about myself than about Kerouac, it is because I am trying to say something about the trade of writing and also something about the particular role that Kerouac played in my lifescript. I had given up as a child on writing, perhaps unable to face what every writer must: all the bad writing he will have to do before he does any good writing. It would be an interesting exercise to collect all the worst writing of any writer—which simply shows the pressure that writers are under to write badly, that is, not to write. This pressure is of course in part simply the writer's own conditioning since childhood to think (in my case) white Protestant American or (in Kerouac's case) to think French-Canadian Catholic. There are many other pressures from well-established pressure groups in big business and the mass media. Writers are potentially very powerful indeed. They write the script for the reality film. Kerouac opened a million coffee bars and sold a million Levi's to both sexes. Woodstock rises from his pages. Now if writers could get together into a real tight union, we'd have the world right by the words. We could write our own universes, and they would all be as real as a coffee bar or a pair of Levi's or a prom in the Jazz Age. Writers could take over the reality studio. So they must not be allowed to find out that they can make it happen. Kerouac understood this long before I did. "Life is a dream," he said.

"My birth records, my family's birth records and recorded origins, my athletic records in the newspaper clippings I have, my own notebooks and published books are not real at all, my own dreams are not dreams at all but products of my waking imagination . . ." This is then the writer's world—the dream made for a moment actual on paper you can almost touch in the end of *The Great Gatsby* and *On the Road*. Not that I am comparing the two works, but both express a dream that was taken up by a generation.

Life is a dream in which the same person may appear various times in different roles. Years before I met Kerouac, a friend from high school and college, Kells Elvins, told me repeatedly that I should write and was not suited to do anything else. When I was doing graduate work at Harvard in 1938 we wrote a story in collaboration, entitled "Twilight's Last Gleamings," which I used many years later almost verbatim in Nova Express. We acted the parts out sitting on a side porch of the white frame house we had rented together and this was the birthplace of Doctor Benway . . . "Are you all alright?" he shouted, seating himself in the first lifeboat among the women; "I'm the doctor . . ."

Years later in Tangier, Kells told me the truth: "I know I am dead and you are too . . ." Writers are all dead and all writing is posthumous. We are really from beyond the tomb and no commissions . . . all this I am writing just as I think of it according to Kerouac's own manner of writing . . . he says the first version is always the best.

In 1945 or thereabouts, Kerouac and I collaborated on a novel that was never published, and it is in fact difficult to remember what it was about; the manuscript has been lost. Some of the material covered in this lost opus was later used by Jack in *The Town and the City* and *Vanity of Duluoz*. At the point the anonymous gray main character William Lee was taking shape. Lee who is there just so long and long enough to see and hear what he needs to see and hear for some scene or character he will use twenty to thirty years later in writing. No he wasn't there as a private detective, a bartender, a cotton farmer, a lush worker, an exterminator; he was there in his capacity as a writer. I did not know that until later. Kerouac it seems was born knowing. And he told me what I knew already, which is the only thing you can tell anybody. Sooner or later you can't walk out on the tender criminal. A very young child wanted something called the autobiographical recall. A little book just did better than I did. Unreplied an inch from his blue steel automatic . . . I can't remember writing became so painful hostile sort of smile. Writers are to write in. Tell me how many books for the reality film. Writers could get together in writing and that is how I remember we could sitting in a quiet corner all be real as a coffee bar. Fast on the typewriter, writers could take over the time. Perhaps unable to face published books are not real at all.

I am speaking of the role Kerouac played in my script, and the role I played in his can be inferred from the enigmatically pompous Hubbard Bull Lee portrayals which readily adapt themselves to the scenes between Carl and Doctor Benway in *Naked Lunch*. Kerouac may have felt that I did not include him in my cast of characters, but he is of course the anonymous William Lee as defined in our collaboration—a spy in someone else's body where nobody knows who is spying on whom. Sitting on a side porch he was there in his capacity as a writer and this was the birthplace Kerouac it seems was born knowing . . . the only thing you can tell. On the tender criminal a young painful smile. . . . (Unreplied. Posthumous.) This I am writing just as I remember writing the first coffee bar. Fast on the typewriter. Years before I met Kerouac a character William Lee was taking shape told me repeatedly that I should write enough to see and hear what he was doing, collaboration entitled Twilight's Last White frame. Doctor Benway told me what I knew already.

"Are you all alright? Sooner or later you can't walk."

"I'm the doctor . . ."

Child wanted something called years later in Tangier. Kells told me book just did better than I did . . . "I know I am dead and you are too . . ." Kerouac and I are not real at all. The only real thing about a writer is what he has written and not his so-called life.

And we will all die and the stars will go out one after another. . . .

THE SECRET LIFE
OF WALTER DISNEY

The Weird, Weird Ways of the Führer of Fun

J. HOBERMAN

APRIL 1979

"I don't like depressing pictures. I don't like pestholes. I don't like pictures that are dirty. I don't ever go out and pay money for studies in abnormality. I don't have depressed moods and I don't want to have any. I'm happy, just very, very happy."

—Walt Disney

"I'll let down my trousers and shit stories on them, stories . . ,"
—Samuel Beckett, *The Unnameable*

ONE OF THE THINGS about life that used to bug Walt Disney was death. He hated the idea of it. "Dad never goes to a funeral if he can help it," daughter Diane once revealed. "If he has to go to one, it plunges him into a reverie which lasts for hours after he's home." Obviously Walt was figuring something out. "I don't want a funeral. I want people to remember me alive," he'd say. Accordingly, when Disney died in December 1966 his funeral service wasn't announced until after it was over. No details, including disposition of the body, were ever released. All that the *Los Angeles Times* was able to discover was that the "secret rites" had been conducted at Forest Lawn Cemetery—a theme park with a "Mausoleum of Freedom" for dead soldiers and a "Babyland" for stillborn infants.

It's not nice to kill off Santa Claus, so most cynics figured that the decision to downplay Disney's funeral was simply good business. Romantics believed that Disney, with a late interest in cryogenics, had had himself frozen like a TV dinner to sleep on a cushion of liquid nitrogen until some Prince Charming appeared with a cure for the big C. Meanwhile Disney's corporate heirs continued to act as though their master were still alive. By reverently and continually quoting his missives—always in the present-tense "Walt says. . . "—they fed the rumors that Disney had left them with a twenty-year master plan in the form of filmed (why not holographed?) messages, a new one screened at each yearly board meeting.

Walt Disney never learned to draw Donald Duck or Pluto, or to duplicate the famous signature that emblazoned every one of his products, but his insight into the American collective unconscious was nothing short of mystical. It was Walt who spotted little Annette Funicello dancing in the Burbank Starlight Bowl and knew she'd be the sex star of *The Mickey Mouse Club*; it was Walt who coined the phrase "zip a dee doo dah," which, once set to music, would win an Oscar for *Song of the South* (1946). Disney had the system beat: He copped an Emmy by televising an hour-long promo for an upcoming theatrical release; he maintained a separate firm that licensed the use of his name back to Walt Disney Productions. In the end, the culture machine that Walt built and left behind was so perfect that, like his android Abraham Lincoln, it could walk and talk without the benefit of a brain.

When cornered, Disney spokespersons will admit that today it is only "the merchandizing and publicity" that keep the original Disney characters alive. But they argue that "there is no corporation in the world that wouldn't love to be associated with our family appeal," and it's true. Doubtless, Richard Nixon was hoping that a little Disneydust would rub off on him—and not be mistaken for dandruff—when he launched "Operation Candor" in the fall of 1973 by declaring, "I am not a crook" at a Disney World press conference. During the Vietnam War, the Laotian general Vang Pao used to parade with his troops while dressed in the Zorro suit presented to him on a trip to the Magic Kingdom.

In Chile, the Disney mythos became an emblem of the country's native fascism. While the CIA organized, funded and armed opposition to the Allende government, Donald Duck used his comic strip to exhort his fellow funny animals to overthrow the revolutionaries and "restore the king," and a March 1975 article in the *New York Times*, titled "How Life Survives in a Chilean Slum," reported that "after the coup the president of the neighborhood council ripped down the socialist calendars and slogans that hung on the walls of his two-room wooden shack. In their place he put up some posters of Mickey Mouse and Donald Duck."

Pushing everything from birth control in Costa Rica to chewing gum in Czechoslovakia, Disney's characters are clearly the closest thing that the United States has to an official culture. Indeed, the man who succeeded in grafting a pair of mouse ears on the globe can justifiably be called the greatest artist that America has ever produced. At least since J. Hector St. John de Crèvecoeur.

For a man as intense as Disney in his desire to control his environment," critic Richard Schickel once observed, "animation was the perfect medium psychologically." The quintessential Disney shot occurs at the end of *Song of the South* as photographic reality melts into an idealized cartoon-land. Yet, there was a brief time in Disney's career when he used the cartoon not to supplant reality but to unmask it. In the first few heady days of Mickey Mouse (when Disney and his alter ego were still skinny, sharp-faced, somewhat sadistic fellows) the ex-farm-boy cartoonist gave vent to his suspicion that the world was nothing but one huge and bloody barnyard, full of dirt, violence, and exploitation. In *Plane Crazy* (1928) Mickey powered his jerry-built airship with a rubber band made out of a dachshund. In *Steamboat Willie* (1928) the mouse turned a bunch of pigs, goats, and cows into musical instruments. Anticipating the Disney "True-Life Adventures" of the 1950s, Mickey banged, twisted, and tweaked their bodies, to produce a rendition of "Turkey in the Straw." But soon, Walt repressed such monsters from his/Mickey's id. Enormous success made the team dully respectable. Around the time that Walt took up polo, the nouveau bourgeois Mickey became the first mouse in the history of the universe to own a pet dog.

Although Disney's temper tantrums might be likened to those of Donald Duck, his later cartoons were only intermittently autobiographical. He satirized his love of animals by appearing in caricature as the matador in *Ferdinand the Bull* (1938) and probably identified with the heroine of *Cinderella* (1950), who spent her days sewing little caps for birds and pants for mice. In 1953 he made the coyly confessional *Ben and Me,* which attributed Benjamin Franklin's success to the friendship of another clever mouse. Disney's erotic kinks and miscellaneous obsessions can be found sprinkled throughout his work, but only once did he give full rein to the darkest drives of his complex personality.

In *Pinocchio* (1940), the masterpiece whose theme song "When You Wish upon a Star" would become the national anthem of Disneyland, Walt brooded over the nature of his art. Was he a kindly Geppetto, maker of toy marionettes? Or a greedy Stromboli, exploiting his puppets on the stage? The glamorous Blue Fairy who animated Pinocchio with the gift of life? Or the cruel proprietor of Pleasure Island, the amusement park where little boys are transformed into braying donkies? Perhaps he was Pinocchio himself—a wooden antihero who disappoints his "father," suffers all manner of abuse and humiliation, and must finally journey into the belly of a whale to win his Papa's approval and join the human race.

Such might have been the stuff of Disney's childhood fantasies. His father, Elias Disney, was a hard man, as free with his whippings as he was tight with his money. When grown-up Walt became rich he bought himself all the toys and candy he felt denied as a child—scouring the world for doll furniture, constructing an elaborate electric train set around his house, installing a giant soda fountain in his living room. Young Disney lived on a farm, but when he was nine Elias bought a paper route in Kansas City. For the next six years dutiful Walt got up each morning at three-thirty, delivering his father's papers for no more pay than bed and board. The rest of his life Disney suffered from a recurring nightmare that he had missed a customer along the route. His daughter recounted that "he wakes up sweating and thinking, 'I'll have to hurry and get back and leave a paper before Dad finds out that I didn't.' "

Disney had good reason to hate his parents (with whom he had little to do once he became successful) and his childhood as well. His almost petulant insistence that his films and amusement parks were intended for adults at least as much as for children supports the hunch once voiced by the littlest mouseketeer, Karen Pendleton, that Uncle Walt really "didn't like kids very much." Kenneth Anger, the author of *Hollywood Babylon*, maintains that Disney, who had once been an inveterate practical joker, used to "open a small, rounded door in the wall—a fairytale door that creaked—and take his guests down a winding staircase into a dungeon filled with racks and Iron Maidens scaled to the size of a five year old. "Now this is how I really feel about the little bastards," he'd say, and puff on his cigar.

One of Walt's major improvements on nature would be to eliminate the biological link between parent and child. Thus, Pinocchio has no mother, Snow White and Cinderella are the victims of evil stepparents, Bambi's momma gets killed, and Dumbo is forcibly separated from his mother. "I believe that every conception is immaculate," he told a staff member, and he opened *Dumbo* (1941) with a squadron of storks flying over Florida to "deliver" the babies of expectant circus animals. In the Disney comic books of the 1950s, families like the Ducks of Duckburg were linked in a curious uncle-to-nephew or (less frequently, as Duckburg and environs were primarily male) aunt-to-niece formation. One suspects that Disney did not consider the absence of genital sexuality to be any great loss. With the warmth of a computer print-out he once explained his motivation for marriage: "I realized that I'd need a new roommate, so I proposed to Lilly." Late in his life he was quoted as saying, "Girls bored me—they still do," and "I love Mickey Mouse more than any woman I ever met."

The most suggestive sequence in the entire Disney oeuvre occurs in *Melody Time* (1948) when Slue Foot Sue kisses Pecos Bill and his six-guns spontaneously shoot their load, but Ward Kimball, the animator on that scene, claims that Disney actually missed the innuendo. "You could never tell Walt a dirty joke," he recalled. Yet, the Disney cosmos was not entirely devoid of eroticism. As Richard Schickel delicately put it: "Disney's interest in the posterior was a constant in all his films. Rarely were we spared views of sweet little animal backsides twitching provocatively as their owners bent to some task." The most famous of the many examples of this fetish is found at the climax of the "Pastoral Symphony" in *Fantasia* (1940)—the sequence of which Disney is supposed to have exclaimed, "Gee! This'll make Beethoven!"—when two cupids draw a curtain over the mating dance of the centaurs and in doing so bring together their adorable butts to form a single palpitating heart.

Disney's anal-eroticism carried over into a propensity for bathroom humor. This was usually edited out of his films, but it's said that at least one squeamish writer quit the studio because flirtatious Walt kept slipping toilet jokes into her scripts. In an early TV special, Walt's Christmas gift for America turned out to be a cartoon about a little boy who is unable to keep the back flap of his Dr. Dentons snapped and is presented by Santa with a tiny chamber pot. "He could talk about turds for thirty minutes without pausing for breath," Kimball remembers. "One time Walt was late for a screening. He apologized by saying, 'I was taking a shit.' He'd often talk about turds. He'd talk about how big and juicy and light brown turds were when you're a baby and how as you get older they get blacker and harder, and all that stuff. He'd go on and on and you kind of looked at him and wondered, when is he going to get to the punch line? There wasn't any."

Obviously Walt was able to channel some of his fascination with feces into adult concerns. One of his favorite koans was "Dollars are like fertilizer—they make things grow." He exhibited in abundance the three cardinal traits of obstinacy, parsimony, and orderliness by which Dr. Freud defined the anal personality. Perhaps this disposition was fanned by the numerous spankings Disney received at his father's hands; perhaps it was related to the fact, dutifully recorded by daughter Diane, that grandma Disney used to reward little Walt with candy laxatives. In any case, Disney's childhood anxiety over controlling his bowels became, in Schickel's phrase, a "lifelong rage to order, control and keep clean any environment he inhabited . . . He just couldn't abide a mess."

When the Nazi film maker Leni Riefenstahl visited Hollywood in 1938, Disney was the only industry notable who greeted her publicly. Had he been smitten by the vision of totality that she had so adroitly presented in her pseudo-documentary *Triumph of the Will* (1934)—as controlled an artifice as any of his cartoons? For, although not everyone is as blunt as Kenneth Anger (who told an interviewer that "Walt Disney was the Hitler of children! He killed their imaginations by programming them with his saccharine prefab fantasies!"), it has more than once been observed that the mania for cleanliness, control, and order was a trait that Uncle Walt happened to share with the Nazi dictator.

Of course, Disney only indulged in the *fantasy* of mass murder, and just once at that. Under the pressure of World War II, but acting as a private citizen, he dreamed up *Victory Through Air Power* (1943), a long-since-suppressed feature-length cartoon that ended with the triumphant obliteration of Tokyo. Apparently the film displayed an alienation worthy of Riefenstahl's. A contemporary film reviewer cited the absence of "suffering and dying enemy civilians" underneath its animated explosions and called it "a gay dream of holocaust" that reduced war to a "morally simple [matter] of machine-eat-machine."

But whatever else Walt and Hitler had in common, the Führer (unlike his buddy Benito Mussolini) was not a fan of "Michael Maus." Evidently no mouse could be clean enough for Hitler. He termed Mickey "the most miserable ideal ever revealed" and unsuccessfully attempted to have it banned from his Reich. Hitler's failure to get rid of Mickey may explain the megalomaniac undercurrent in Disney's response to this attack on his alter ego. In a ghost-written magazine article of the mid 1930s he complained that "Mr. A. Hitler, the Nazi old thing, says Mickey's silly. Imagine that! Well, Mickey is going to save Mr. A. Hitler from drowning one day. Just wait and see if he doesn't. Then won't Mr. A. Hitler be ashamed!"

However, by the time he made *The New Spirit* (1942), the first of the government-sponsored propaganda and training films that virtually subsidized the Disney studio during World War II, Walt did decide to let the "Nazi old thing" drown. He demonstrated his distaste by showing the swastika "flushed away in a vortex of dark, swirling water." The next year saw *Education or Death* (with Hitler playing Prince Charming to Hermann Goering's mountainous Sleeping Beauty) and Disney's greatest piece of agitprop, *Donald in Nutzi Land*. Also known as *Der Führer's Face*, the cartoon won an Oscar, while Spike Jones's recording of the soundtrack sold a million and a half copies. In a dour comment on the mock flatulence of the song's chorus, Richard Schickel remarked, "Even in wartime [the Disney studio] found a way to state its belief in the location—the seat as it were—of human emotions."

What's particularly interesting about *Der Führer's Face* is Disney's visualization of "Nutzi Land." Donald's room is plastered with swastika wallpaper, he sleeps in swastika pajamas between swastika sheets, his alarm clock keeps time with swastika numerals. It's as though the Disney artists were rehashing the 2,000 Snow White products that helped pull the toy industry through the recession of 1937. Even nature is not immune to the totality of "Nutzi Land." Outside Donald's window we see that trees and hedges have been shaped into swastikas. Such an improvement may never have occurred to Hitler, but a decade or so later the bushes of Disneyland would be carefully trimmed to resemble Mickey, Donald, and Dumbo.

When Disneyland opened in 1955 it was with one inescapable stipulation. Before being born again within the confines of the Magic Kingdom, each guest had to pass through an idealized version of the Marceline, Missouri Main Street where Walt believed he'd spent his happiest years. "To the people in Marceline, I'm like God," Disney used to say.

Gustave Flaubert's crack that "life is so horrible one can only bear it by avoiding it, by living in the world of art" might have served Disney as his lifelong motto. His very first cartoons reversed the formula of the Fleischer Brothers' popular *Out of the Inkwell* series. While the latter brought its star, Koko the clown, off the drawing board and into photographic reality, Disney's *Alice in Cartoonland* locked a real child into an animated universe. Then Disney himself, in a manner of speaking, became Alice, as the voice and alter ego of the fabulous Mickey Mouse, and the success of this mutant creature—hailed by Sergei Eisenstein as "America's most original contribution to world culture"—enabled him to dream of someday building Cartoonland in steel and concrete.

In Disneyland, above the firehouse on Main Street where Disney creatures with air-conditioned, encephalitic heads amble among the crowds like the sacred cattle of Calcutta, Walt furnished a little apartment for himself. By night, in his bathrobe, he roamed through "the happiest place on earth" alone. They say that when the Reverend Billy Graham came to bless his fellow wizard's "fantasy," Walt exploded, "Fantasy? The Fantasy is out there . . . outside the gates!" But in Anaheim, "outside" wasn't far enough away. You could stand in the parking lot and see the fast-food stops and motels encrusted like neon barnacles on the Disney ship of state. When Walt reconstructed his World in Florida he purchased a forty-square-mile tract to more perfectly insulate it.

In Walt Disney World the security guards don't wear uniforms but "costumes." Employees aren't hired, they're "cast" and programmed with fewer responses than the android birds of the Enchanted Tiki Room. Tie clips, hair ribbons, deodorants, and sometimes even names are subject to company approval. All employees are graduates of the University of Walt Disney, where they have studied Walt Disney Traditions One and Two and learned, in the words of one campus directive, "to enjoy thinking our way." The World, as it's called, controls its own sewage and utility systems, writes its own building codes, appoints its own judges, maintains its own police force and—so it claims—harbors the planet's fifth largest fleet of submarines.

Everything—from the udderless robot hippos of the Jungle Cruise, to the people mover in Tomorrowland, to the Muzak rendition of "Someday My Prince Will Come" that wafts through the lobby of the Polynesian Village hotel—is controlled from a subterranean computer center. So too is the "Automatic Monitoring and Control System," which keeps every inch of the World under constant video surveillance. Tomorrowland (really Todayland) to the contrary, the future, as George Allen used to say, is now. Apologists for the World claim that "with computers and statistics it's easy to prove what's art," that the World has been "designed to satisfy the existing imaginations of tens of millions of men, women, and children," even that one can no longer tell the World from reality! When Walt died he was drawing up plans for a city—cash free, climate controlled, vacuum cleaned—a space-age pyramid of Cheops where 20,000 or so lucky Alices could live inside his Magic Kingdom for the rest of their lives.

A SHORT HISTORY OF THE DEVIL

Shedding a Little Light on the Prince of Darkness

GLENN O'BRIEN

MAY 1979

THE DEVIL AS HE is known today comes out of the Judeo-Christian tradition. Not that he's a Jew or a Christian, or even their "Opposites." But that's where he was first spotted. He was developed and marketed by Indeo-Christians in much the same way that they first handled today's God. Before Judeo-Christianity covered the globe, the divinity market was rife with small-time operators, gods who specialized, doing a great job in a modest sphere.

Though they were gods, they weren't strictly "good" or "bad." They were generally a mixture of both. That made them interesting. When they were good, they were very, very good. But when they were bad, head for the caves. At any rate, heaven was not exclusive turf, not virgin either. There was still room for expansion and profit. It was still possible for a new operator to move in and carve out a piece of the action.

Polytheism was everywhere. But that doesn't mean that there was no idea of One God. Almost everywhere the gods were, there was the idea of One God, an ultimate deity. But this God was regarded as so abstract, unknowable and even irrelevant to our petty learning problems as to require some divine intermediaries who themselves had to answer to some higher logic.

Anyway, as time went by and planets got more crowded and civs bumped into and often destroyed one another, heaven tended to get mixed up a lot. Gods got into deadly competition. There was war in heaven.

Chaos. It was the perfect opportunity for someone to move in and organize things. Basically, what Judeo-Christianity did was organize heaven as a conglomerate. One by one the old deities' individual territories were taken over by the One God Syndicate. Sometimes the old gods were allowed to stay on and run their old territory, but they were demoted to sainthood and honored only in the measure of their devotion to the Boss. As long as they were good.

If they were bad, of course, they would become devils. For as soon as there was only one God there had to be a Devil to blame all the mistakes on.

But the odd thing is that the Devil really doesn't have much of a history. He seems almost a conglomerate invention.

The Jews are not really into the Devil, unless he's personified.

And by checking our biblical sources we find that the Devil isn't really the horror we think of until sometime after Christ.

The greatness of the true form of the Jewish religion was that its One God delivered man from the confusion of the gods. This form of religion probably occurs naturally when men have forgotten that, as Blake put it, "all deities reside within the human breast."

Old-Time Jewish Prophets, at their best, and later Jesus & Company, humanized the heavens. But at worst their organizations reinstilled a reign of terror. Often with the help of the opposition. When God took over the gods, room was made for some old-timers in the new organization. But the others were put in the pits. Their old ways didn't fit. Some were worked in. Norse gods got Santa Claus jobs celebrating Jesus' birthday. But others were pegged as devils and had to hide for their lives.

It wasn't always that way. You're hard pressed to find a read Devil in the Old Testament. Usually the villains are men, and sometimes God himself seems less than nice.

The only Old Testament passage dealing with Satan as a personality occurs in the highly theatrical Book of Job. The Sons of God go to see the Lord, and who shows up but Satan. The Lord is surprised to see Satan and says, "Whence comest thou?" or, "Where did you come from?" Satan says, "From going to and fro in the earth, and from walking up and down in it" or, "I've been around." So they've never seen each other before, right?

The first thing God says is: "Hast thou considered my servant Job, that there is none like him in the earth, a perfect and an upright man, one that feareth God, and escheweth Evil?" A great opening line, no? God is tempting Satan, showing off, but not only that, he's doing it with someone who is on his side as bait, someone who loves him. A pretty mean trick for a pal!

Satan picks up on this and says "Hast thou not made an hedge about him, and about his house, and about all that he hath, and he will curse thee to thy face." Or: "You set the guy up and now he's doing great. He hasn't got a problem in the world. But a couple of setbacks and he'll want out."

God is miffed and winds up ranting that Job is in his power and Satan had better keep hands off. If this was a sincere statement, God must have been pretty naïve—sounds more like a little reverse psychology.

So anyway, Job is sitting around one day, partying and feasting and drinking wine, when all of a sudden it's Hell-zapoppin. First the Sabeans fall on the oxen and asses, rip them off, and slay the servants. Then the Fire of God falls from heaven, barbecuing the sheep and the shepherds. Then the Chaldeans fall upon the camels and, yea, carry them away, knifing the camel drivers. And then Job's sons and daughters are partying at the home of the eldest at the home of the eldest when—zap—it gets hit with a twister and Job is deprogenated.

Now all this time we don't know who's doing this shit. Then Satan shows up at God's place again.

"Where you been?"

"Around."

"Did you check out Job? There is none like him in the earth, a perfect and an upright man, one that feareth God and eschewth evil. He's still in my corner, although thou movedst me against him, to destroy him without cause."

Check it out: It wasn't Satan who hit Job. It was his pal God! Just because Satan dared him. But Satan remains cool.

"Skin for skin, yeah. But a man'll give up anything for his life. Mess up his face and he'll curse yours."

God had got to get in a hip last word. He says, "Okay, do anything you want with him. Just don't kill him."

Satan gives Job a real case of boils. That's all. But Job's wife has just about had it and says, "Whatdya think of God now?" Job calls her a dim-bulb and snaps, "Whatdya expect? Something for nothing?"

Job's friends soon catch wind of what's gone down. They drop in and hang out for seven days and nights trying to cheer him up. "Hey Job, don't make it bad." "Hey, Job, did you hear the one about the wandering herdsman."

Nothing works. Job gets more and more pissed. And on the seventh day he starts to curse, and he curses all and everything, but he's careful not to mention Mr. G directly. It is a great curse, yet Job's friends don't buy it.

Eliphaz the Temanite really socks it to him, saying, "Everything's been rosy, and you were great. You helped everybody with their troubles and always talked things up, pushed courage. Now look at you, you wretch. Your personal shit hits the fan and you go pussy. You don't hit the shit for nothing, Jack. You must have done something to deserve all this. I was going through the same thing. I was out of it one night, I had a real paranoia attack, and this thing came at me, made my hair stand up. I heard this voice sayin' 'Who do you think you are? God? Bigger than the big guy? He don't need anybody. He even fires angels. But these human slime, they are destroyed from morning to evening: they perish forever without regarding it.'"

But Job has had enough advice and begs God to off him. He tells off his friends for chapters on end and gets hotter and hotter on death's case. Finally he says that he ain't worried 'cause he knows he'll see God in the flesh. Still he doesn't stop kvetching, and loudly regrets that he got involved in all this in the first place.

Finally God gets sick of all the talk and shows up in a whirlwind. He tells Job to put his pants on because he's going to ask him a few questions. God doesn't really expect any answers—He's asking the all-time great rhetorical questions, like: "Where were you when I made the sea, stars, earth, etc.?" In other words, He makes Job feel pretty small, by taking credit for absolutely everything and listing hundreds of his immense accomplishments.

Then He says, "So what have *you* got to say? "Job says the right thing, which is nothing. Again the Lord tells Job to put on his pants, He's going to ask him some more questions, which turn out be more unanswerable kickers; and then God winds up the whole spiel by comparing himself with the elephant and the whale in terms of vulnerability. This really gets to Job, who finally admits that God is everything and he is nothing.

God agrees but by this point is a bit pissed at Job's pals. He orders them to deliver seven head of beef and seven head of sheep for a divine din-din, which they do.

After that, Job gets twice as rich as he was before and lives happily to the age of 140.

Satan, however, seems to have completely lost interest in the case after having given Job boils.

This is really Satan's only character appearance in the Old Testament. His name is tossed around, but mainly as a tempter, a deceiver, the opposition.

(The Serpent who gets Eve to bite the forbidden fruit of the knowledge of Good and Evil in Genesis is identified as the subtlest of the beasts of the field, invented by, that's right, God. The Serpent is not identified with Satan until the Apocalypse, written hundreds of years after Christ.)

In the New Testament, Satan is seen as more of an independent. He is "the prince of demons" (Matthew), "the wicked being" (John), "the tempter" (Matthew), and "the prince or ruler of the world" (John).

But even in the New Testament, Satan makes only one appearance, that being his temptation of Christ (Matthew, Luke). But his character here is developed very little. Satan, especially in Luke, is the voice or spirit of temptation.

In Matthew, Satan is described as having angels in his power. But the identity of Satan's followers remains shrouded. Sometimes it would seem that they were the rulers of the world, or ever-greater beings; sometimes they are the illnesses that afflict the most insignificant persons. Jesus heals the sick by casting out evil spirits with his word. But the real evil in the Bible, the real opposition to Jesus, is made up of men.

The New Testament was written and rewritten during the several hundred years of religious revolution. Satan, as he appears in the New Testament, particularly in his most glamorous moments in the last written book of the Christian canon, Revelations, probably owes much less to the Jews or the original followers of Jesus than to the influence of Mani, the Babylonian prophet of Manichaeism, who lived about two hundred years after Christ.

Mani incorporated many of the principles of Judaism and Christianity into the Zoroastrian dualism of Persia, founding a religion that resembled

Christianity, but with an extremist extension of the concept of Good and Evil. Mani and his followers did not believe in a spiritual and a physical distinction between good and evil. All existence was seen as a struggle between Light, or good, and Darkness, or evil. The soul was good. The body was bad.

Before Mani the ancient religion of the Persians worshiped dual gods of light and darkness, Ormuzd and Ahriman, and each ruled every extension of their principle. But the real religious practice concerned the intermediary between these absolute and necessary dual gods—Mithras, the god on Intelligence. He ain't been seen in a while.

With the grown evil, or confusion, in the days when Christianity was competing head to head with Rome's state paganism and with Manichaeism, it seems that a stronger bogeyman was required. So the New Testament Satan's part was beefed up to compete with Mani's Ahrimanic Satan and the other divine heavies who were doing a fair job of explaining the idiocy that was pandemic.

Somehow, Christianity beefed up with a more powerful and horrifying devil was more appealing to Europeans. Zoroastrianism is a roots Aryan religion, so who knows. If you're gonna have to explain fire worship, a prince of darkness comes in handy. Anyway, the Christianity that won over the entire white race, and then a lot of others at sword point, was a militant organization at war with the Devil.

So, okay. Maybe it's true. Maybe God is all stars and the Devil is all black holes. But the whole point is, this kind of thinking often leads to inhuman extremes in deities both good and bad.

Which is why D.H. Lawrence thought Revelations was the lousiest book in the Bible.

In Revelations, the Devil, Satan, is identified with the old Serpent who first tempted Eve; and history is portrayed as a war in heaven between the angel Michael, and his forces of good, and Satan, and his forces of evil. Satan's m.o. is deception. And his powers of deception make him a mighty force on earth; and he builds up this organization called Babylon, which takes over almost the whole earth.

But then this angel comes and announces the fall of Babylon, and "the merchants of the earth shall weep and mourn over her; for no man buyeth their merchandise any more."

Satan starts a war against God, gets a thousand years in the Pit, is let out for a bit, and then gets sent up permanently to Lake Brimstone. Wherever that is. Probably Akron.

YAGÉ

The Vine that Speaks

<small>ANDREW WEIL</small>

<small>AUGUST 1979</small>

EVERY SATURDAY IN A remote region of south-western Colombia, sick people make their way to a hut in a jungle clearing. The hut is a two- to three- hour walk over a rough trail from a little port town called Mayay-oque on the River Caquetá, a tributary of the Amazon. Some of the people are very sick with high fevers, infections, and chronic diseases that have not responded to medical treatment. The goal of their pilgrimage is an Ingano Indian witch doctor named Luis Nutumbahoy. He is a *yagero,* a man skilled in the use of *yagé* (yah-HAY), the powerful psychedelic drink of the Amazon, and every Saturday he cooks up a batch of it to use in curing ceremonies.

I have been interested in yagé for years and have visited a number of yageros in the western Amazon. Last January, on the recommendation of a Colombian friend, I made the long and difficult trip to see don Luis and his ceremony.

To get there I flew from Bogotá to Florencia, capital of the Caquetá Territory, a large province of Colombia mostly consisting of steamy jungles and large rivers. In recent years, intense colonization has resulted in ugly clear-cutting of the jungle and the growth of rowdy frontier towns noted for their violence. At the moment, the Caquetá is officially considered a war zone because of guerrilla activity, principally of the FARC, the Colombian Armed Revolutionary Forces. In my travels from Florencia to Mayoyoque by bus and boat I was stopped frequently by soldiers, asked for identifica-tion and sometimes searched for weapons. Considerable drug traffic comes through the territory as well, mostly cocaine shipped by river from Peru.

Last January it was hard to get around the Caquetá because it was the middle of an unusually hot "summer," a period of drought and high temperatures that had dried up the territory, making river travel uncertain and causing spontaneous forest fires that filled the skies with smoke and turned the sun an ominous copper color.

I took an uncomfortable bus from Florencia to a port called Curillo on the River Caquetá, then caught a motorized canoe downstream to Mayoyoque. Mayoyoque is in a lawless zone with no police or authorities. The town has seen a number of murders in the past months, and I was not eager to stay there long. The morning after my arrival I set out on the trail to don Luis' house.

The first part of the trail led through blackened, devastated fields, recently burned for new growing and grazing land. Then the forest began, dark and lush despite the lack of rain. I saw many kinds of mushrooms on the ground and on dead logs. There were some spectacular flowers, one a giant red bloom from a tree called *palo de cruz*. Parrots sang in the trees. I crossed deep ravines on crude log bridges. Normally, these ravines are roaring torrents on their way to Caquetá. Now they were still, with a few disappearing muddy pools.

My companions on this trip were Diego Leon Giraldo, a well-known Colombian film maker who had visited don Luis before to make a documentary movie about yagé; his wife, Silvia Patino, a professional photographer; and Carlos Rangel, an Indian guide who knows the territory well.

In late morning we emerged into a sunny clearing with a large palm-thatched house. Luis came out to greet us. He is a fifty-year-old, small, active man with an unusual face that sometimes appears very old, then changes into the face of a young child. His wife and children were there, and they showed us inside to the cool part of the house. Hammocks were strung up, the air smelled of woodsmoke from a kitchen fire, and a noisy parrot strolled about the rafters. Chickens paraded inside the house. Outside was an arrogant rooster that I grew to hate during the week I stayed there, also a family of ducks, some scrawny dogs and a few pigs.

The Inganos are descendants of ancient Incas who migrated north. Some of them live in villages in the mountains near the Ecuadorian border, but most are spread out through the hot lowlands along or near rivers. Like don Luis, most of them live in houses in isolated clearings in the jungle. They hunt, fish and grow a few staples like yuca (tapioca root). They sometimes wear colorful costumes, and they use a number of drug plants, especially yagé, which they call *huasca* in their own dialect.

Yagé is a gigantic liana, a woody vine that climbs up the huge trees of the jungle. In many parts of the Amazon it is a rare plant and some Indians have to make long journeys to collect it. But Luis had many wild yagé vines within walking distance of his house. Some of them were the biggest I have seen, with heavy trunks six inches in diameter, so tall that I could not make out the leaves at the top.

Among the Inganos of this region, yagé is a sacred plant, used only in cer-emonies for specific purposes such as healing and divining. There are certain taboos around it. For example, women are not allowed to see the living vines or their preparation, although they may consume the drink. If a woman sets eyes on a living yagé, that vine is useless and cannot be prepared.

On the day after my arrival Luis cooked up a batch of yagé for me to drink. He began by felling a giant tree with a vine coiled about it, then hacked the yagé into eight-inch lengths with a machete. He carried these back to a small ramada about about five minutes from the house. The ramada is only used for cooking yagé, and no women are allowed near it. Luis half filled a large fire-blackened cauldron with about two gallons of water from a nearby water hole. He added about a quart of finished yagé from his last batch, cooked the previous Saturday. Then he brought fire from his kitchen and kindled a blaze underneath the pot, arranging long pieces of wood so that he could push them in and keep the fire going.

Next he sat down on a log and began to smash the pieces of yagé with a heavy stick. He beat each one until it split apart, exposing the inner fibers. When Luis finished this operation, he stood up, went to a post sup-porting one edge of the ramada and unfastened a net bag. From the inside he extracted handfuls of fresh green leaves. He called these *chagrapango* and said they were the other ingredient that went into his version of yagé.

Each yagéro has his own recipe for the drink, and some use various additives, including toxic plants like datura. In the western Amazon the basic mixture is simply trunks of yagé and leaves of chagrapanga. The botanical name of yagé is *Banisteriopsis caapi* and it owes its hallucinogenic power to two chemicals called harmine and harmaline. Chagrapanga is a related plant, *Banisteriopsis rusbyana*, also a woody vine, whose leaves are rich in DMT, dimethyltryptamine. Luis says that these leaves "brighten the visions" caused by yagé, that with yagé alone "you will get intoxicated but not see anything; chagrapanga shows you pictures."

He put two large handfuls of these leaves into the pot and adjusted the fire to bring the water to a boil. I wanted to see the chagrapanga vine because I had never met *Banisteriopsis rusbyana* in the wild, but Luis said the plants were scarce, and he had gone a long way through the jungle to collect these leaves.

When the water came to a boil, Luis added the smashed yagé, two big bundles of it. He stirred the mixture with a stick, adjusted the fire till it was simmering, then sat back to wait. He told me it was important not to make the fire too high or the liquid would cook down too fast without extracting the power of the yagé.

The cooking took thee hours. It was a scorching day, and the fire made things even hotter, but it was not unpleasant to lounge in the ramada, watching the cauldron bubble, stirring the brew occasionally. When it was done, Luis unhooked the pot from its support and poured the liquid into two containers fashioned from the sheaths of flowers of palm trees, discarding the spent yagé. He covered the two containers with fresh banana leaves. Then he repeated the process from the start, with water, chagrapanga and yagé, and cooked this second batch for the same amount of time.

When the second batch was done, it was late afternoon, Luis combined the liquids from the two cookings and put them back in the pot. He then boiled the mixture down for an hour more to concentrate it. The finished product was muddy brown. When it was cool, Luis poured it into two containers: a large glass jug that had once held whiskey, and a plastic motor-oil bottle. These he carried up to the house, ready for use.

You never drink yagé until dark. And you are not supposed to eat anything after noon on the day you are going to drink it. I had not eaten since breakfast. Expectantly, I waited for sunset and for the heat to subside, watching the animals hunt for food around the house. As it got dark Luis made things ready inside. He arranged some objects on a little altar, lit candles, got out cups and poured himself a few shots of *aguardiente*, the fiery anise-flavored cane whiskey that Colombians love. Luis says that aguardiente increases the effect of the yagé and also kills its bitter taste.

Luis' brother-in-law, named Jorge, had come by to help. It was the middle of the week, not a regular yagé Saturday, and no sick people had come. Only Luis, Jorge and I were going to drink. Jorge prepared a large bowl of water with several aromatic leaves and barks. He called the mixture *fresca* and said it would be used in the ceremony.

Unhurriedly, Luis poured out a portion of his brew into a large gourd. He set this down and began chanting over it: a strange, half-whispered chant, interrupted by puffs of breath. He took down from the wall a kind of noisemaker of bunched, dried palm leaves and rattled it over the bowl of yagé while keeping up his quiet song. This blessing ritual lasted ten minutes. Then Luis dipped out a four-ounce coffee cup of the brown liquid, raised it to his lips and drained it down, chasing it with a quick shot of aguardiente. He then dipped out a cup for me.

I followed Luis' example and drained the cup quickly. The yagé tasted bitter, rusty and unpleasant, though not as bad as peyote. It was not very hard to get the first dose down. Since I did not care for aguardiente, I sucked on a slice of lime instead.

After Jorge drank his cup, Luis settled into a hammock and was quiet. Jorge lay down in another hammock. I was lying on a bench. It was dark except for a few candles, and the night was still hot. We listened to the jungle noises and watched some spectacular fireflies, which the children trapped and put into a jar.

I had taken yagé once before in the mountains of Putumayo Territory southwest of here. But that drink contained datura and other additives and was violently intoxicating. I lost all power of movement, experienced complete physical and mental chaos and received no help from the yagéro, who did nothing at all after a few minutes of chanting before pouring out the dose. My mind ran back to that adventure of a few years before. I was apprehensive, waiting to see what would happen.

In about fifteen minutes I began to feel uncomfortable heaviness in my stomach. It intensified over the next ten minutes, till I had to roll around in search of better positions. Eventually I got up and walked outside the hut to vomit.

Vomiting is the first stage of the effect of yagé. It is not fun, and I say that as someone who likes to vomit in certain circumstances. I held on to a small tree and brought up a small quantity of intensely bitter liquid with wrenching spasms. Yagé tastes much worse on the way up than on the way down—so bad that it left me shuddering for a few seconds. But I felt much better immediately after, and as I straightened up I noticed the stars for the first time. It was a beautiful night with a new moon over the dark forest. I felt high, not the chaotic acceleration of datura-adulterated yagé, but a calm, floating, detached feeling. Breathing deeply I headed back into the candle-lit hut. Luis was still sitting in the hammock, with a serious expression, and Jorge was still lying down.

After a few more minutes I had to answer another call of nature. The second action of yagé is to purge the intestines. The effect is spectacular and painless. When I went back in, Luis asked me if it had been "a good purge." I told him yes. Eventually, he and Jorge also made trips to the jungle. I lay down on my stomach, feeling very disconnected from my body and the external world. I was in a dreamy, trancelike state, not at all speeded. When I closed my eyes I began to see things: plants mostly, what looked like rows of sugarcane against a black background. I felt as if I were floating in a velvety liquid. The plants became undersea plants, waving in a gentle current.

My visions were interrupted by an unwelcome sensation in my stomach, and I shuffled out into the night to my tree for another episode of vomiting, worse than the last. There followed several further walks into the fringes of the jungle with diarrhea. Yagé cleans you out thoroughly from both ends, and that is probably one reason why it helps sick people. It has been shown to be an effective treatment for amebic dysentery, for example. Anyway, in a short time there was nothing left inside to come out.

Back in the house Luis poured me another cup of the bitter brew. This time it was hard to get down. The association of the taste with the terrible vomiting was too strong. But I did swallow it.

Now Luis began chanting in earnest. A yagéro's chant is his most precious possession. It comes to him in dreams and stays with him all his life. Until a man receives his chant from the spirit of the vine, he cannot conduct ceremonies. Luis's chant was strangely hypnotic, a mixture of sounds, tunes and words. There were Spanish words, Ingano words and words of a sort I had never heard before. I asked him what one particular word meant. "It is yagé speaking," he answered. "It doesn't mean; it is yagé speaking." He resumed the chant. At times the sounds turned into the grunts and snorts of a big cat, and his face assumed an animal expression. He looked up and grinned at me. "I can be a jaguar when I want to," he said.

I vomited a few more times, then came in and collapsed on the bench. Luis went out to vomit, too, but I could barely hear a break in his chanting. From now on he chanted nonstop and would go on until dawn. At times it was quiet, at times loud, always fascinating and powerful. Under its influence my visions of plants became more elaborate with huge forest trees and vines. But all was calm and peaceful: a world of plants with no animals.

Luis told me later that yagé visions come in stages with practice and increasing dosages. First come patterns, then plants, then animals, then fantastic architecture and cities. If you are fortunate, you see jaguars. Though he had been no farther from his home than Mayoyoque, Luis says that under yagé he has left his body and visited distant towns and cities, including Florencea and Bogotá. In the visions he sees the causes of illnesses and the cures. He sees what plants a sick person should take or what pills if plants are not strong enough for a particular illness. People consult him about missing persons, too, bringing photographs if they have them, and in the visions Luis discovers their whereabouts. Recently he saw one missing relative in the army in Bogotá.

I saw only plants, after two cups of yagé except for a brief period of suspension bridges. These looked like the beginnings of fantastic architecture but did not progress to cities. And I saw no animals. Luis wanted me to drink more of his brew, but I could not. My body rebelled at the thought of consuming more. In the course of the evening Luis drank nine cups of the stuff. Each one sent him to the jungle for further purging, but his animated chanting continued without pause. With each cup he became more energetic. Finally, Jorge helped him into a heavy necklace of jaguar teeth and a fantastic headdress of parrot feathers. Then, palm-leaf rattles in his hands, Luis began a stomping, turning dance around the house, all the while uttering the sounds of yagé.

After a time he sat down and had me sit in front of him. He chanted over me, shaking the palm-leaf rattles loudly over my head, and finally he took a big mouthful of fresca and sprayed it all over me. It felt wonderfully cool and revived me from the dreamy trance with overtones of nausea. Jorge explained that fresca brings you down if you are too high and calms you if you are having anxiety. All you have to do is sip some. I took a little because I was thirsty, but I felt no anxiety. I just wanted to stay curled up on my bench, float among the visionary plants and listen to Luis' sounds.

As the night wore on, Luis kept up his dancing. From time to time he would pick up a harmonica and turn into a one-man band. He would dance out the door and we would hear him chanting and singing off into the jungle, circling the house, disappearing into the night. Then he would burst through the doorway in an explosion of feathers and palm leaves, growling like a jaguar.

This performance continued till sunup, long after I had crashed on my bench. I got little sleep because the rooster started crowing well before dawn. (It did so every night, and I thought of many different ways I would enjoy cooking it.) As soon as I woke up, Luis took me outside for a purification ritual. He instructed me to wash my face and hands with the clove-scented fresca and had me rinse my mouth out with it, too. Then he waved some branches of stinging nettles around me as if to drive off any lingering bad energy. I felt refreshed and hungry. Luis slept some in the morning, then went about his daily chores, including chopping up more yagé for the weekend.

Luis has been using yagé for twenty-two years. He learned how by serving as apprentice to masters who came from Putumayo Territory. "The old people know much about the secret power of yagé," he says. "Now they are gone." But he is passing his knowledge on. As the weekend approached, a man named Victor showed up—an Ingano chief who lives half a day from Mayoyoque and has been Luis' apprentice for three years. Victor is a fine-looking man with parrot feathers in his ears. He explained to me that few people know how to use the yagé vision vine these days, and he wanted to be able to serve his people as a yagéro.

On Saturday, Luis cooked up more yagé, and he, Victor, Jorge, and a patient drank it at nightfall. I participated, too but only took a little. Victor and Luis sang and danced all night, periodically going out into the jungle to sing under the trees, then returning to the candle-lit house. Victor congratulated Luis on having made a really strong batch.

Luis gives yagé to anyone who wants it: to young and old men and women, sick and well. He says it cannot hurt anyone, and, though he gives it to pregnant women, young children and people with high fevers, no one suffers bad effects. Victor and he are both in good shape after taking enormous doses for years. Luis has seen hundreds and hundreds of people trip on yagé and knows all the ins and outs of the experience. He knows exactly how to minimize negative effects and encourage people to interpret their experiences in good ways. And many of the patients say they are helped. I talked with people in Mayoyoque who say that visits to Luis cured them of various ills.

Yagé is a strong drug, rough on the body physically when you take it but not harmful in any serious way. Used casually it might cause all sorts of bad trips. But treated with respect, made carefully and consumed in these elaborate rituals, it becomes a power for good in the hands of men like don Luis and his colleagues.

THE UNTOLD, REAL, TRUE, INSIDE STORY OF THE BEATLES' *SGT. PEPPER'S LONELY HEARTS CLUB BAND*

BARRY MILES

OCTOBER 1979

"Changing the lifestyle and the appearance of youth throughout the world didn't just happen—we set out to do it; we knew what we were doing."
—John Lennon, 1972

BETWEEN NOVEMBER 1966 AND March 1967 the Beatles recorded *Sergeant Pepper's Lonely Hearts Club Band* at the Abbey Road studios. This album, which sold one and a half million copies in its first two weeks of release in the United States, became an electronic bible for the emerging drug generation. Miles, then the editor of *International Times,* London's first underground newspaper, and currently the editor of London's magazine, went to the recording sessions at the invitation of Paul McCartney. In the following behind-the-scenes account he tells you what it was like to be there.

I remember it well. "The Return of the Son of Monster Magnet," the last track on the Mothers of Invention's *Freak Out* album, came to an end and Paul McCartney strolled across his huge living room to take the record off. In one corner a BBC color-TV monitor was mistimed to give a flickering abstract pattern; two René Magritte paintings glowed on the wall in the pale afternoon winter sun; and Martha, Paul's Old English sheepdog, lay content in front of a crackling log fire. I sat by the French windows enjoying a cup of tea. Paul returned and picked up the conversation where we'd left off. "This is going to be our *Freak Out*. Not like Zappa's. But when people hear this they'll really stop and think about what it's all about!"

"Fantastic, man!" I said, in that dull flat voice you sometimes get after smoking too much dope. Paul was talking about an album the Beatles had just started recording at Abbey Road. It was January 1967. The album was *Sergeant Pepper.*

In those days I saw a lot of Paul. The London scene was very small, and if you smoked pot in the mid '60s, you easily got to know every other head in town. When I first met him Paul was living in a large townhouse in Wimpole Street, the parental home of his girl friend, Jane Asher. I met him through Jane's brother, Peter, who was then still a member of Peter and Gordon and also lived at home and who, much later, went on to become the successful manager and producer of Linda Ronstadt and James Taylor.

Paul lived in a small attic room on the top floor of the Asher household, originally part of the servants' quarters, next door to Peter's room. Peter had an L-shaped room done out in modern style with lots of Norwegian wooden shelves, gold records and various trophies and awards from his career with Gordon Waller in the hit parade. A pair of Brenell tape recorders sat just inside the door. These belonged to Paul and were the machines on which he devised and recorded many of the Beatles' backwards tapes. "Brenells are the best, even if the knobs do fall off." He found that his own name came out as Ian Iachimoe when played backward on tape and suggested that we all write to him as that so he could distinguish letters from friends in amongst the sacks of fan mail. He published a short story under the same name.

Paul's room was next to the upstairs bathroom. It was a small plain room with a single window, a large brown wardrobe and a single bed, which occupied most of the floor space. A wall shelf held some interesting bric-a-brac: a couple of Jean Cocteau drawings from the *Opium* series, one in a cracked frame; a few first-edition books; a volume of Alfred Jarry; and some guitar picks. Under the bed where the chamber pot used to be were a pile of gold records and a presentation MBE. An electric bass was propped in the corner, and stenciled on the case in white letters: B E A T L E S. No room for more instruments. He kept some in Peter's room. No room even for records. The few that he had were kept outside on the landing in a rack on top of a chest of drawers next to the amateurly wired bell system that announced whom an incoming telephone call was for. I think there would be three rings for Peter, four for Paul. Paul had no phone of his own. In fact the very idea probably hadn't occurred to him. This was at a time when his accountant had already informed him that he was technically a millionaire. Not that he lacked money. Peter once went into Paul's room to borrow some socks, pulled open the sock drawer and was showered with dollar bills that Paul had forgotten about.

On the floor below lived Jane, a successful actress; but Victorian propriety meant that they couldn't sleep together in the parental home, so in 1966 Paul finally bought himself a house. Unlike the other Beatles, who had all bought huge mansions in the country, Paul decided to stay in the city and bought a beautiful free-standing Regency house next to Lords cricket ground. The house, which was built in about 1880, had a lamppost in the front drive and an orchard at the end of the garden. It was surrounded by a high wall and had a pair of gates covered in black expanded metal to prevent the ever-present fans from writing on them. You needed to know the bell code to get in. From the upstairs music room you could see the hands and heads of young girls who would hold onto the top of the wall for a few moments before dropping back exhausted. The house was within walking distance of Abbey Road, where *Sergeant Pepper* was being recorded.

From the very beginning everyone involved knew that this album was going to be special. It was going to work on all levels. Paul described it like this: "The idea was to do a complete thing that you could make what you liked of, just like a little magic presentation. We were going to have a little envelope in the center with the nutty things you can buy at Woolworth's, a surprise packet." Not just another Beatles album but something to look at, to do and to listen to—a complete experience. It also had another level: "There are only about a hundred people in the world who understand our music." (John Lennon, 1967).

In its time *Sergeant Pepper* was the most expensive album ever made. It took an unprecedented 400 hours of studio time and cost over £10,000 ($20,000), which nowadays would be cheap. The Beatles' first album was made in a day. The *Sergeant Pepper* sessions began in November 1966 and continued through March 1967. First came "Penny Lane" and "Strawberry

Fields Forever," numbers that gave a good idea of the new direction the Beatles were going, particularly "Strawberry Fields," with Paul's use of Mellotron, George on Indian temple harp, and with its use of cello, trumpet, and electronic drum track.

I recorded a conversation with Paul at his new house the day after "Strawberry Fields" was recorded. It was November 1966, and to the public and most of the fans the Beatles were still the Four Mop-tops. For this article I dug out the dusty old cassette and played it again. As I expected, ghosts hiding in old interiors came to life as Paul's Liverpudlian voice predicted the future:

"People, quite a few people, are prepared for the next sound. They're ready, they're waiting for the next scene in music, the next scene in sound. A lot of people now are ready to be led to the next move." He was fully aware of what they were doing.

As the conversation rambled on, he described his approach to music: "With everything, with any kind of thing, my aim seems to be to distort it. Distort it from what we know it as, even with music, with visual things. But the aim is to change it from what it *is* to see *what it could be.* To see the potential in it all.

"The point is to take a note and wreck the note and see in that note what else there is in it that a simple act like distorting it had caused. It's the same with film, to take a film and superimpose on top of it so you can't quite tell what it is anymore. It's all trying to create magic. It's all trying to make things happen that you don't know *why* they've happened. I'd like a lot more things to happen like they did when you were kids, when you didn't know how the conjuror did it and you were happy to just sit there and say, 'Well, it's magic!'

"Ordinary everyday thought is so messed up that you've got to allow for the possibility of there being a lot lot more than we know about. Therefore to take things that we already know about in one way: to bang one note on the piano, instead of trying to put millions of notes into it, just to take the one note of the piano and listen to it shows you what there is in one note. There's *so much* going on in one note, but you never listen to it! So many harmonics buzzing around, that if all that's happening in one note, and if in one frame of a picture all that's happening . . . the thing is, it could take a bit of looking into!" Paul had had a number of insights from his use of acid.

Generally speaking, most of the music on the album is by Paul and most of the words are by John, but there are plenty of exceptions. Not all the material was new. Paul originally wrote "When I'm 64" in 1962–3 during the Cavern days in Liverpool, but he revised it in honor of his father, who was 64 in 1967, and it was ideal for Sergeant Pepper since the album was supposed to have something on it for everyone.

Paul was also completely responsible for "She's Leaving Home." I arrived at the studio one night and ran into George in the corridor leading to Studio 2. He was dressed in a dragoon jacket, yellow crushed-velvet pants, and was carrying a smoldering bunch of incense sticks. When George talks to you he likes to get up real close, about eight inches from your face. "You should have been here yesterday, man," he said excitedly. "We recorded this beautiful song about a girl leaving home. It really says it all!" He gave me a stick of incense and left for the canteen.

The Beatles took many of their stories from the daily newspapers. "She's Leaving Home" came from a story in the Daily Mirror, the most popular newspaper in the United Kingdom. A girl left home and her father said, "We gave her everything, I don't know why she left home." As Paul said, "He didn't give her that much, not what she wanted when she left home." George Martin was almost moved to tears when he first heard it, and provided one of his most beautiful arrangements for it.

The "Sergeant Pepper" theme was worked on as a device to unify the album, which was originally intended to not have any spirals—each song was to segue right into the next—only EMI would not agree. The actual title was one of those random things songwriters come up with. Paul: "I was thinking of nice words like 'Sergeant Pepper' and 'Lonely Hearts Club' and they came together for no reason." The Lonely Hearts Club Band was the Beatles, who were themselves, with their North Country upbringings, a bit of a brass band as well as a rock 'n' roll band. "We went into it just like that. Just us doing a good show." As usual the influences on the music come from all over the place; for instance, the brass fanfares, applause, and laughter-off on the "Sergeant Pepper" reprise was an effect that Paul took, probably unconsciously, from Stockhausen's *Momente!* (he's on the album sleeve).

The huge scale and scope of the album was realized almost immediately when the Beatles embarked on "A Day in the Life" using a full orchestra. This was a John Lennon number. He was sitting at the piano with a copy of the *Daily Mail,* another popular tabloid newspaper, propped up in front of him and found a paragraph about 4,000 holes being discovered in Blackburn, Lancashire. John picked up on it: "There was still one word missing when we came to record. I knew the line had to go, 'Now they know how many holes it takes to fill the Albert Hall.' It was a nonsense verse really, but for some reason I couldn't think of the verb. What did the holes do to the Albert Hall? It was Terry Doran who said 'fill' the Albert Hall."

It's a rule on Beatles records that whoever wrote the verse sings it, unless it was written for Ringo. On "A Day in the Life" the bit sung by Paul was originally a different song entirely, but it just happened to fit. It was a simple little song of him remembering what it was like to run up the road to catch the bus to school, going upstairs to the upper deck and having a furtive cigarette before going to classes. It was written as a deliberate provocation, the only one on the album that could be taken two ways. It was one for their dope-smoking friends. Paul: "We decided, 'Bugger this, we're going to write a turn-on song!' "

George didn't attend all the sessions and at times felt that he was being ignored by Paul, but the Beatles always kept these disagreements very much to themselves. There were other times of course when George was in great form. I arrived one day and George, on seeing me, ran to his Stylist guitar, plugged into his Conqueror amp, yelled "Live at EMI!" and blasted one of the melodies he had written. Ringo joined in for a few bars from his sound box, but John continued to quietly tune his Gibson. The Beatles recorded with their microphones and amps set up as if playing for an imaginary audience.

They were very self-critical. Paul was always worried about the bass sound, and Martin was also concerned about how to get the bass notes onto record without them being lost. Martin's second biggest problem was Lennon's voice. John was convinced that he had a terrible voice and always wanted it changed electronically to sound better. Consequently Martin used a great many effects on the voices, some of which worked and a few of which didn't. Since these were the days before parametric equalization and the like, there were times when Lennon could be seen in the studio singing down a cardboard mailing tube to get a certain effect.

The actual making of the album was a fascinating process. As is usual with recording, there were large amounts of time when nothing was happening except that the engineers were fixing something or taking levels. The Beatles often used to work out the final form of songs in the studio itself, during which time no recording could take place.

There were never great crowds of people there to watch, but most sessions were attended by a few friends. Among those who came by were Mick Jagger, Keith Richards, Marianne Faithfull, Donovan, and Mike ("I'm a Believer") Nesmith. Slack periods were filled by smoking dope or drinking vile coffee or tea from paper cups from the canteen. The dope was smoked English style, mixed with tobacco, and more than once I was passed a laboratory test tube filled with white powder, usually speedballs, a mixture of coke and smack, though care was always taken not to expose George Martin to any of these things. Despite all this, there were times when Lennon would get pissed off at waiting around and grab the nearest live microphone and yell, "What's going on up there? Let's get on with it. You can't keep us hanging 'round for your fuckin' tea break. We're the fucking *Beatles!*" and George Martin would patiently try to explain what they were doing to the exasperated Lennon and at the same time mollify irate engineers.

One evening we arrived with Paul and sat out a full session from 7 P.M. until about 3 A.M. All that they recorded in that time was the two-second spiral leader that finishes the album and plays forever if you don't have an automatic pickup on your record player. At one point, all four Beatles were standing clustered around a mike, talking and singing anything that came into their heads, when Ringo said, "I think I'm going to fall over!" and as everyone watched in amazement he proceeded to do so. There was no problem, though, because before he hit the ground, Mal Evans, their trusty, burly assistant, was there to catch him and stand him on his feet again.

Ringo was always funny in a quiet way, but you had to be fast to catch him sometimes. One night there was a team from *Time* magazine taking photographs and interviewing for a feature. During recording, Ringo felt hungry and Mal prepared a meal for him, setting up a small table at the side of the huge studio. As Ringo tucked into a plate of baked beans on toast, the *Time* man approached, then stopped, horrified. "Good God, man, you can't eat that!"

"Why not?" asked Ringo. "Did you see someone put something in it?"

At the time of *Sergeant Pepper,* Lennon was at the height of his acid phase, taking literally hundreds of trips. He lived in a country mansion surrounded by five television sets, endless tape recorders, instruments, a huge altar cross, and a suit of armor called Sydney. He would buy a movie camera, paint it in psychedelic colors, the paint would run inside and jam up the works, and it would be thrown into the corner and a new one bought.

Of all the Beatles, John was the one who used his money to fulfill his every whim. At 2 A.M. in the studio he would turn to Mal Evans and say, "Apples, Mal," and sure enough, half an hour later, Mal would appear grinning, carrying a box of apples fresh from Covent Garden market. On another occasion he turned and said, "Socks, Mal." Fairly soon, Lennon was happily trying on dozens of pairs of brightly colored socks. This reached its peak years later at Apple Records when John and Yoko would make the most impossible demands of their loyal staff. John and Yoko would like to send an acorn to every world leader for peace. The trouble was, it was mid-winter. Where do you get acorns in the middle of winter? The whole staff of the press office was dispatched to the London parks to try to find where the squirrels had hidden their supplies and to dig them up. John and Yoko got their acorns.

John had his huge white Rolls Royce painted with bunches of flowers. He had bought an old gypsy caravan for his garden, and now he got a firm of caravan and barge designers to give the RR the once over. Rolls Royce lodged a formal complaint.

I saw John arrive at Abbey Road one evening dressed in a full-length Chinese brocade gown, carrying a handbag and wearing a large floppy hat tied with a white scarf that almost touched the ground. The fans loved it, but inside John was going through a very bad period. His relationship with Cynthia was breaking up, and his resolve to follow Tim Leary's suggestions in *The Psychedelic Experience* and destroy his ego was resulting in just that. Lennon never did things in half measures. He was subjecting his ego to a full frontal attack.

This made him somewhat unpredictable and sometimes unapproachable. I was having dinner at Paul and Jane's one evening and some of Jane's actor friends were also visiting. John was there, and the actors were more than a little nervous in the company of two Beatles. One of them, a young woman, needed an ashtray. Seeing none on the table, she asked Lennon if he knew where one was. Lennon sprang to his feet, ran to her side, crouched down, inclined his head to one side and pried open his nostril for her to stub out her cigarette. "Here, use this!" The poor girl froze in horror just as he'd expected her to do. Jane glared at John until he shrugged and stood up.

Since the sessions usually ran late into the night, it was always a problem finding somewhere to eat afterward. The Beatles usually finished up at one of London's "in" clubs. One of their favorites at that time was the Bag o' Nails. The Beatles never telephoned ahead for reservations because the managers always spread the word that they would be there and they were mobbed. They just arrived, like royalty, knowing everything would be all right. One night we arrived at the Bag o' Nails at 3 A.M., just as they were closing. The manager took one look at who was at his door and customers who were being cajoled into their coats ran joyfully back to their tables, music started up again, the kitchen was reopened, and we settled down to a nice meal of steak, chips and peas washed down with Scotch and Coke, the Beatles' favorite drink. Neal Aspinall—Nell as they always called him—carried a flashlight with him for these occasions in order to inspect the food in the dim light and make sure it was up to standard.

After the album was completed I arrived at Michael Cooper's photographic studio in Chelsea. The Beatles had already put on the Sergeant Pepper outfits designed for them by the American artist Jann Haworth, and she was fussing 'round them, getting the flowers pinned on John's epaulets and adjusting their medals. Her husband, pop artist Peter Blake, was still arranging the potted plants, constantly watering them in case the strong photographic lights made them wilt. Both Jann and Peter showed their work at Robert Fraser's Bond Street gallery, and Robert was there also, darting about rubbing his hands together in sheer delight and wearing a skintight purple-polka-dot suit from Hung on You. Huge, very strong joints were being passed about, and it took Michael so long to take his light readings that several people doubted whether the picture would ever get taken at all. But it did, and he shot off roll after roll of film since the sleeve required at least four different poses.

So what was the message that the Beatles gave to the world on June 1, 1967? Everyone read the album in a different way of course, but this is the way that Paul explained it to me at the time:

"We've been in the lucky position of having our childhood ambitions fulfilled. We've got the big house and big car and everything. So you stand on that plank then, having reached the end of space, and you look across the wall, and there's *more* space! And that's it! You get your car and house and your fame and your worldwide ego satisfaction, then you just look over the wall and there's a complete different scene there, that it *really* is. And which is *really* the scene. And looking back, obviously you can still see everybody in the world trying to do it. Trying to do what you've just done. And that's what they believe life's about! And it's right! Because that is what life's about at the moment I suppose, for them. But you know, I could tell a few people that I can see a few rungs further down the ladder, trying to do exactly what I've just done, I could tell a few of them: That's completely the wrong way to do it because you're not taking into account this scene on the other side of the wall. *This* is the bit you've also got to take into account and then *that* bit will be easier. It'll all be easier then!"

THE STATE OF ROCK

An Unsolicited Testimonial

JOEY RAMONE

JANUARY 1980

THE WHO IS THE perfect example of what rock 'n' roll stands for and was always meant to be. Whether it be the '60s, '70s, '80s, or '90s, the definition of rock 'n' roll is: Daring. Exciting. Bein'. Very visual—catchy and melodic tunes. Not half-hour, boring guitar solos or mindless songs about sex: She left me. Who the fuck cares!!! The kids of now are being deprived, cheated and brainwashed bad. It's not their fault, most of them just don't know better. Rock 'n' roll is dying 'cos the media are trying to kill it as they've always been trying since the days of Elvis and Gene Vincent. The media are spreading propaganda about how youth listening to this music are having their minds poisoned and are bein' turned into habitual sex-crazed, hard-core, trisexual, mindless, pill-popping, pot-smoking, dropout mass murderers, which we all know is bullshit, but it's always worked successfully to promote the clean-up-the-image campaign. Remember Pat Boone and Doris Day—the soft-décor public image that parents will approve of. Rock 'n' roll is for rebels and outcasts. Rock music was not meant for your parents' pleasure.

Anyone who is involved, it's 'cos they're dissatisfied with things and want change. They want to experiment. They're disgusted in general. But it's the same old story throughout the generations. Corporate radio is big business now, caring only about making money, not knowing or caring what music they're playing—neatly formulated. So the DJ (whose fault it is as well, 'cos if he cared he wouldn't be working at the station) doesn't have to think either. He just follows the color-coded chart: Play the red-dotted albums twenty times and hour; the blue, ten; the green, it, and so on. Or just follow the Top forty playlist and don't forget five commercials for every three songs played and everyone's happy.

In the '60s radio was incredible. It was the best. Radio was very adventuresome. They played everything, which opened up a lot of marketplaces for all kinds of music. Remember AM, the WMCA good Guys, WABC, Murray the K? The late '60s and early '60s were the best time for music.

Now everything is a copy of a copy of a copy because that's where the bucks are. Something bein' a major seller, they're out to re-create the success of the '60s, so record companies and radio stations are out to find and create another Led Zeppelin. Hearing a set of songs on the radio compiled of Led Zeppelin, Deep Purple, Toto, Foreigner and Van Halen, it is almost impossible to tell one from another, there bein' no difference between '68-era heavy metal and heavy metal now except, of course, that the quality of the songs—like Deep Purple's "Highway Star"—was better then. From Elton John to Billy Joel, who sounds as much like Elton John as Elton, everything financially successful has turned into '70s acceptability, like Kiss, Boston, Aerosmith, Ted Nugent. I gotta get off this topic or I'll go crazy. I mean, I'm happy Billy Joel made it, he deserved it, but his music, like Meat Loaf's or the Eagles', is for an older crowd—like ya mother or father. It should be played on the easy-listening stations. No way is that rock 'n' roll. And disco is mindless-at-heart music to dress up by and have all the big and little fashion designers make a buck off you (sap!!!). Take Quaaludes, sway by the palms . . . It's the most plastic, manufactured, sickening, disgusting, enraging, cheap shit I ever heard or had to compete against.

—An Unsolicited Testomonial
Joey Ramone
Lead singer of the Ramones.

POSITIVELY THE LAST UNDERGROUND INTERVIEW WITH ABBIE HOFFMAN . . . (MAYBE)

JERRY RUBIN

FEBRUARY 1980

STONED IS THE BEST way to appreciate Abbie Hoffman.

Once one of the most visible and persistent symbols of the '60s, the mythmaking co-founder of the Yippies (along with Jerry Rubin) has been a fugitive for the last six years, ever since his 1973 arrest in New York for conspiracy to sell cocaine.

Since then, the forty-three-year-old madcap political prankster has lived underground as another person, changing his features with plastic surgery and shedding identities as frequently as a snake does its skin. Unable as Abbie Hoffman to continue his marriage to his wife, Anita, he left her and his then two-year-old son, america, in February 1974, went underground and married someone else (Abbie doesn't believe in divorce). But vacating a persona is not so easy. At least twice during his travels Abbie has freaked out, including one time in Las Vegas where he ran through a casino yelling out his real name. Remarkably, he was never caught. But the overlapping personalities have left their mark. His sentences don't always proceed in logical order, the words are hieroglyphs of a bigger picture, precision alternates with metaphor, and there is uncertainty as to whom the personal pronoun I refers to. A puzzle for even the most astute psychology student.

Abbie, the son of a "legitimate" drug salesman from Worcester, Massachusetts, started out by studying humanistic psychology with Abraham Maslow at Brandeis University. But he was "born" in 1960, he says, when his massive and naive faith in the American myth ("truth, justice and the American way") was shaken by the intruding reality of war, racism, and generational revolt that characterized the '60s. After working in the civil-rights movement in the South in the early part of the decade, Abbie returned to New York and opened up Liberty House to sell poor people's products from Mississippi, then abruptly changed his lifestyle by becoming a digger (a political prehippie) on New York's Lower East Side. This was the start of a new American myth, and a new role for Abbie as a new American mythmaker.

Aided by television and its quick dissemination of image, the United States during the '60s underwent a violent metamorphosis of styles and values more rapidly than was ever possible before. It was Abbie Hoffman's genius to learn how to use the media, how to manipulate it to carry messages against the Vietnam War, for marijuana, for community consciousness. "The Sixties," as writer Marvin Garson once said, "were staged." Life and politics were transformed into theater for the television cameras. And Abbie Hoffman was one of its prime directors.

Hoffman wrote messianically of new lifestyles and values in his books Revolution for the *Hell of It, Woodstock Nation,* and *Steal This Book,* the latter a kind of kamikaze attack on corporate consumer society inspired by a digger pamphlet he authored earlier in his career called *Fuck the System,* by Free. But the culmination of these works, an autobiographical recapitulation of Abbie's life in the '60s, will be published in April [1980] by Fred Jordan Books, distributed by Grosset and Dunlap. Called *Soon to Be a Major Motion Picture* (the movie rights have been bought by Universal), it recounts the incredible rites of passage of the individual and the nation during that tumultuous decade.

Ordinarily, the issuance of a new book is not enough to make *High Times* jump to do an interview. In fact another interview was originally scheduled for this issue—until we received a phone call from the protean mythmaker himself. The message was clear: He was planning to come up soon, and this might be his last interview on the run.

For such a special occasion, we chose Jerry Rubin, Abbie's former partner in crime, to see if he could get Abbie, on a friend-to-friend basis, to open up as never before. Jerry as much as Abbie was responsible for the media absurdist politics of the Yippies, and his best-selling book *Do It!* was perhaps the most widely read example of the guerrilla theater of the time. In fact so intertwined were the activities of the dynamic duo that to the majority of the American public they often seemed to merge into a single entity known as Abbie and Jerry. The two of them have maintained a close friendship during Abbie's underground sojourn. Naturally we were curious about what kind of chemistry might transpire between them after long estrangement from public collaboration.

Another unknown was Abbie's feelings about a third figure of the '60s, Tom Hayden, who along with Jerry, Abbie, and four others became enshrined as a member of the Chicago 7. The 1969 trial was an attempt by the government to derail the counterculture by incarcerating its leaders on trumped-up conspiracy charges growing out of the demonstrations during the 1968 Democratic convention. It will go down in history as an example of the way political fights can be waged in the courts. Since that time, Hayden, whose Port Huron Statement led to the founding of SDS in 1962, has left radical politics, married movie actress Jane Fonda, and waged a nearly successful campaign for the Democratic senatorial nomination in his adopted state of California.

Getting Jerry reservations to go underground was not easy, but we did manage to send him there. While doing a college lecture he met Abbie at a hotel in Mississippi. This is what he reports: "Abbie is a tough interviewee. He likes to tell stories instead of giving direct answers. Later, when I confronted Abbie with this, he replied, 'Telling stories is an old Jewish form of defense.' I had wanted to slip past the defense, get at the man behind the myth."

Rubin: You've been a fugitive for six years now, ever since the State of New York charged you with conspiracy to sell cocaine. What are you facing?

Hoffman: Fifteen or twenty-five to life imprisonment, probably in some cage in Attica.

Rubin: Would you get extra time since you've escaped them so long?

Hoffman: Well, you get five for jumping bail; interstate flight—that's extra. If I get caught it's very, very bad, very hazardous. I could get killed. It's the fame factor. If you've been seen on television it's magnified into super power and magic by viewers, and the police translate this into violence.

They see you as ten feet tall. If they burst in here right now I'd have to immediately be calm and reassure them: "I know you're doing your job, guys. I'm doing mine. Don't worry, nothing is going to happen, just get out the handcuffs." I've played this scene so often in the past, you know. The danger is they misunderstand exactly who you are and can misuse their guns. I want to live as long as Abraham. I have a lot to do in life and don't want to go down at the hands of a shaky policeman or run down by drunken reality.

Rubin: But you occasionally seem so reckless to others. Not to me; I think you're basically deliberate.

Hoffman: Well, I enjoy the sensation of being swept along by my own reckless abandonment. That's my motto for the '80s. By definition of living an outlaw's life I must live every moment on the edge and to its fullest. But the planning is behind the scenes, in my mind's internal dialogue—where I'm constantly testing and rejecting—and in the years of discipline and determination required to be here now in this very spot being hunted while all around me is chaos and faulty communication.

Rubin: I see you as an outlaw. Is that your childlike romance coming out?

Hoffman: *Fugitive* is the government's word. Its derivative is Norman. *Outlaw* is Anglo-Saxon. Robin Hood was an outlaw. The people called him that, not the sheriff of Nottingham. This is extremely important. We in America, probably more so than any other place in time on earth, have such a problem being precise about our language. But language shapes our environment just as much as the opposite. You become what the media label you. It takes great power for anyone to resist media. It is the burning micro frying the brain. I see that all much more clearly now that I've lived in rural settings for so long. But to answer your question on childish romanticism, Herbert Marcuse, who was one of my great teachers, once told me we have all our creative thoughts by the time we're eighteen. Therefore, if we're interested in creating a new planet it's kind of stupid to scorn childishness. My kid america is already a wise old man, but you have to find and meet him on his terms. The same with animals and plants. City people don't have the patience for that.

Rubin: I still don't understand why you are not caught. You're so public. You appear in magazines, you contact people.

Hoffman: To use a Yippie four-letter dirty word it took a lot of work. It took a lot of work, it took a lot of discipline and maybe some luck. A lot of brains. I've learned to survive in a number of different kinds of jungles. I was lucky in that sense and in that I have the kind of friends that money can't buy, which unfortunately doesn't hold true for most of the other 300,000 fugitives, who are always on my mind.

Rubin: Maybe I'm going out of my role as an interviewer, but I think that you have an ability to get people to really love you. And that's the source of this support. Also you are a source of power to people. By being powerful yourself you're able to liberate people to their own potential. I think that's why you do have so many people who support you.

Hoffman: This is hard for me to take. I think I'm much more human than when you knew me back then. I'm humble because I cracked up on the run. The wife and I had to lick the gum off food stamps to survive and I had to separate from my kids and everybody I love. I had to deal with immense sadness, which I'm not exactly sure I ever had to deal with before. I had no choice but to do it or perish; to learn to love and survive or die. You probably experienced this when your parents died in your early twenties.

Rubin: But I was too young to mourn.

Hoffman: Too young to mourn? I don't know about that. I see some of those boat people's kids. "Boat kids." They look like they're mourning right off. Grief is grief. Loss is loss. Probably it's more drastic for the young, and that's why you've repressed the feeling.

Rubin: In the mid '70s you really made a personality transformation, living as a nonperson. You had to learn to live without the crutch of "Abbie Hoffman" actually. You have become a whole new person.

Hoffman: That's right. I'm at a party in Paris, this fashionable party, and I'm nobody. That's me. I'm a nobody. No fame, no money, no background. Part of the wallpaper. Right. And I'm trying to engage this pretty young woman in conversation. I usually avoid the '60s and things like this. But now I've got to have views. It's a verbal party. And the talk goes to this: "So, you're from America?" The U.S. and the '60s and what did you think of that? And I give a view of what I think of that. And this is a nobody talking to a woman. She says, "What do you think of the Chicago conspiracy trial?" And we talk a little bit about that and she says, "What do you think of Abbie Hoffman?" And I'm about ready to give a view and she says, "Excuse me, there's somebody I recognize," and she walks right out of the conversation because I'm a nobody. I'm not rich. I'm not famous. Incredible.

And what delighted me, what made me feel so good inside, was that I didn't take that too personally. I didn't feel threatened. I didn't have to announce myself. I didn't feel that my ego was being threatened. I just sat there and I said "Holy shit. Ain't people fucking interesting." I'd have to be the blindest schmuck ever to graduate Brandeis not to recognize that as "growth."

Rubin: I know people are more interested in me when they find out my name.

Hoffman: Yes. My past identity gave me access. My ceasing to be a nobody had to do with my community organizing during the last two years, when I became another person and assumed my underground identity. I was learning all these skills and living in a rural environment and I didn't even really have a last name. It's a small town. I was learning country things: carpentry, horse riding, about weather and wildlife, about listening to others, how to say excuse me and thank you. But something was missing: my reason for existence. Then along come the bureaucrats who want to destroy the valley and put in a nuclear power plant. Someone says to me,

"Your little peaceful scene that you built here, your home, is going to be destroyed." So I go and I study the plans of the engineers and bureaucrats and I say they're right. And I'm the only one in the valley that can beat them. I've won this battle a hundred times. I have no choice but to fight on every level. It's my home. I built it with these hands.

I care about democracy and the valley people isolated from power. What I learned in the '60s was how to penetrate the power structure from the street as a nobody. I call that a revolutionary. When lots of people do it it's a revolution. The '60s were *not* the second American revolution, but a civil war, brother against father, family against neighbor. In our valley everyone supports our committee. We are not to be confused with the antinuke marches. We are out to change America, and we, the '80s, are the true second American revolution. Believe you me, when you see *Soon to Be a Major Motion Picture* by the biggest movie company in Hollywood, you are going to see the people of every small town in America, my neighbors and my friends.

The people that are involved are farmers and hunters and small business owners and people like that, as well as your pot-smoking backpackers. In order not to get caught I had to be very cautious, very deliberate. I changed my accent, I had to learn the way everybody talks, their manners, the relationships of all these people. We won the battle, by the way, and have gone on to try to capture political control of our country, our state, and our nation.

Rubin: How did Three Mile Island affect you?

Hoffman: Well, what happened was it became fashionable to join the antinuke movement. Everyone got involved too quickly because a crisis had occurred and so people started noticing our work more. So Abbie had to withdraw from media land and rethink his whole thing. How many chances could I now take? How much should Abbie talk about the nukes? I've decided to broaden the discussion to the environment as a whole, to realize the war in Vietnam—all imperialism—is a war of ecology.

Rubin: But you didn't retreat. I saw you at the MUSE office one day.

Hoffman: I also wanted to help MUSE. I mean, the idea of musicians being involved in a cultural/political movement on that level—Jackson Browne, Graham Nash, Bonnie Raitt, John Hall and those terrific souls—is great. As are the feelings I have about David Fenton, Sam Lovejoy, Obie Benz, Harvey Wasserman, Holly Near. Hey, I wrote the goddamn book *Woodstock Nation*. This was a ten-year dream. I was at two of the concerts and the rally. For me this was a dream come true.

Rubin: Don't you have any doubts?

Hoffman: Yes, of course. I want to hear the Russians' point of view. I have great mistrust of Tom Hayden, "the candidate." I mistrust young whipper-snappers, wet behind the ears, who don't listen to people like Dave Bellinger, Dan Ellsberg, and who want to put one worker on the board of the big corporations. That's Uncle Tomism. I mistrust an audience that would go to see Bruce Springsteen (who I loved and who was the hero of the event) but wouldn't care if it was anti nukes or pro Nazis or pro banana babies. I question a movement dominated by spoiled rich kids who play at revolution and did not have to try and change America when it literally meant shedding your blood and going to prison for your beliefs—not being given Madison Square Garden and getting your cock sucked by the media moguls—back in the early '60s.

This, the '80s, is the real thing, and these young kids *better* be for real or America and the planet are lost. I agree with Ralph Nader: We don't need ten-year phaseout programs and compromises with the aerospace industry of California. We need to tear down the plants now! Nader is more honest than Tom and Jane at this point in time. He's making progress; he's the one I want to meet, not the Flying Fondas.

Rubin: Getting back to your alleged crime.

Hoffman: My what?

Rubin: Your coke bust.

Hoffman: I'm innocent. Completely innocent. *Crime* is one of the most complicated words to define. One person's crime is another person's means of survival. The prosecutor asked for $500,000 bail in my case as he adjusted his tie for the newspaper boys. He said, and I quote, "This is a crime more heinous than murder." That was six years ago. Now the prosecutor, that same guy, is a partner in a dope case with one of my lawyers; he goes into court and claims coke is harmless. He gets clients off. He's a good lawyer. So who's on first?

Rubin: Are you willing to go on trial?

Hoffman: Yes, I am. I'm willing to take a lie-detector test. The problem is the structure of the court system. You and I spent a lifetime in courts. We know it's got not very much to do with truth. Remember the time in our Chicago trial when the prosecutor read a few lines from my "handbook of revolution" *[Revolution for the Hell of It]*? Well, our attorney offered to let each juror have the entire book to read. No go. Remember how the former attorney general, Ramsey Clark, was kept off the witness stand? Remember the jury with a median age twenty years older than ours, remember the collusion, now on the public record, between the judge and the FBI? Before I went on trial the courts would have to convince me they, like I, are no longer living in the past. I'm in search of truth. The question I raise is, is our system of law in search of truth?

Rubin: How do you feel about coke?

Hoffman: Cocaine? Well, it's certainly not a narcotic as defined by every test other than legal. It's a beneficial stimulant if used correctly. Just ask the Peruvian Indians and all the executives. I've met coke dealers whose clients include many of our finest New York judges. The *New York Post* isn't quick to call those people "junkies" and demand the streets be swept clean. Cocaine, like any stimulant, has to be properly used, of course, or it can be dangerous. It can screw up the lining in the nose, and if overdone—Malcolm X had the best definition I've heard yet. He said it made you feel like Superman of the moment. I should include, as I say in the book, that making coke illegal was a political decision made by racist bigots many of whom were themselves either alcoholics or morphine addicts. I don't do it much because I can't afford it. Last night I saw the original version of *Modern Times*. Did you know there's a coke scene in that movie? In other versions I had seen it had been censored. I hate censorship. Like Cole Porter's publishers being forced to change "I get no kicks from cocaine" to "champagne." There are coke dealers that say I've done more for coke than anyone since Freud. There are smart lawyers that say I'm the one with courage enough to fight this through the courts to make coke legal.

Rubin: So why not surface?

Hoffman: Well, I really don't want to go down in history for that battle. I just don't want to misuse my energy working as a guinea pig for the court system. I know all battles are important, but right now I'm concerned about saving this beautiful land called America. They would have to make me an offer I really couldn't refuse.

Rubin: But what if you get caught?

Hoffman: Oh, a disaster. Aside from the accidental shooting I mentioned above, I'd ruin a good movie ending. No one likes to "get caught." How did you feel when your mother opened the bathroom door while you were masturbating? God, I'd probably pass out, my whole world would be shattered. Many of Abbie's friends find it difficult to believe, but I am only "acting" the role of Abbie. I am someone else. Let's call it my B identity.

Rubin: I think that's what is so fascinating about your six-year odyssey. The '70s were a time of changing identity—your ending of the book indicates that—and I want to compliment you on such a creative writing achievement. The ending implied you have metamorphosed into another person. You really *did* the '70s trip of self-awareness.

Hoffman: Yes, that's right. There were a series of changes and great confusion and agony, the crack-ups on the run I describe. I hope to do literary justice to the intensity of the experience. But R.D. Laing teaches that "breakdown" can also be "breakthrough." Each crack-up taught me important lessons about pacing one's energy, about humility, about being a better person. But I am a different person. *Really* different. I have an identity I refuse to give up no matter what happens, because I love who I am. It's not a metamorphosis in any Kafkaesque sense because Abbie was and is my hero, just as he is and will be for millions of others.

Rubin: Aren't you getting a little bigheaded here?

Hoffman: Well, I know the movie story. I understand movies, I learned about our country by watching movies. That's the significance of *Soon to Be a Major Motion Picture*. I'm an American hero. Hey, it's better than most jobs around. I'm lucky and I don't want to die, that's why I, me, this body, could never come back as Abbie. I just don't want to live last year's movie any more than Jean Stapleton wants to go on living as Edith Bunker, Archie's wife. I mean, would you want to go around being confused with a frizzy-headed doll wearing a flag shirt when you're eighty years old? The first thing I would do if I had to surface would be to legally change my name. That would be the quickest way to make a long story short. If they just quietly dropped the hunt and the charges, I'd make no fanfare, just keep right on doing what I'm doing.

Rubin: I've seen some of your other life. How much can you talk about?

Hoffman: Well, much of that will be in the next book, and the movie. I'm an environment activist, have been for over two years. I live in a beautiful valley. I dedicate the book, of course, to my wife and the valley people who taught me truth, justice, and the American way. I've been on radio, TV, spoken in barrooms, passed out leaflets, done office shit work, raised money. I work as hard as I did on the Chicago trials.

Rubin: I find it impossible you're not discovered.

Hoffman: Maybe I have been. My neighbors are very shrewd people. My model is the Clint Eastwood movie, *The Outlaw Josie Wales.* He's a fugitive renegade from the Civil War who's chased by a posse but eventually arrives and settles in a valley. His neighbors protect him when the posse shows up. There's no gun battle. They just point a different way: "He went thataway." For all I know that's happened already. There was a rumor, but right now I'm a valuable member, well respected and loved by many in my community. And the love is mutual. Angel, my wife, led me through the valley of the shadow of death up the mountain of hope and down into the heartland valley of life. She's my last wife, my running mate. We're very close and very in love.

Rubin: And Anita—I was moved to tears by the great love you show for Anita in the book and what a great pain separation from her and america, your newborn son, must have been. For a year I shared your grief.

Hoffman: Thank you. That's why no matter what happens to us down the road, we'll always be close friends. And as to Anita, she and I are lovers, but, well, like, I talk about all the fucking in the movement in the '60s. Let's just say now, I don't mix that sort of pleasure with business.

Rubin: Speaking of business, are you insulted if I call you a good businessman?

Hoffman: Not anymore. Fidel Castro and my father, Johnnie Hoffman, taught me that not only is there no contradiction between being a good businessman, a good man, and a good revolutionary, one *must* be all three, unless, of course, one is a woman.

Rubin: Abbie, let me tell you that when I go on the college trail these days I'm asked a lot of questions from a tiny minority. And there is the question that the reporters have: "Are you a relic of the '60s?" How would you answer that question?

Hoffman: I'm not sure I'd waste my time. Actually, I don't feel compelled to say I'm not a relic. Relics are very valuable anyway. I don't feel a need to explain myself. It's just a dumb question because why would a reporter be interviewing a has-been anyway?

I just want to show people what I can do because *what I can do, they can do*. I did it twice, and I'm just an average kid.

Rubin: How interested do you think people are in the '60s these days?

Hoffman: The '60s are an emotional attitude, which I'm sure is what we both understand it to be. An emotional stance. They are absolutely fascinating. Nostalgia for the decade is just starting. You can see it in Hollywood. This fall they are going to present a three- or four-hour reenactment of the Chicago conspiracy trial. Jeremy Kagin is the director, a perfect choice. There's the movie they're going to make from my book, there are several other 60s-type books, and I think that all of this is becoming of great interest to people because they're going to want to know about it. It's time. My kids want to know. My wife is curious what SDS means and she is my contemporary.

There were many '60s for many people. I learned that living underground, because you walk down the same streets on the Lower East Side or in Mississippi, or Berkeley or Chicago, and it's a you, the B personality, that did not experience the '60s as the A personality did. Everyone is such an egomaniac under capitalism. Think how we use the expression "Everybody's doing it" when we mean our circle of friends or Walter Cronkite's circle of friends. All that's going to change in the "We" decade.

Rubin: In the early '70s you couldn't get someone interested in the '60s for anything.

Hoffman: Well, the '60s for me never died on one level. And I said that on the tenth anniversary of the Chicago conspiracy trial case. Because we fought against an imperialist war and we won. We have to make this absolutely clear. That's what *Apocalypse Now* and all of those revisionist movies fail to make clear. The empire collapsed and good riddance to bad rubbish. There were two sides. There were the villains and there were heroes, as we saw it. And we, the antiwar forces in America and the Vietnamese, were some of the heroes and those bastards in the White House and the Pentagon were the villains and we won. The proof is that American troops are not fighting in Nicaragua, in Latin America, in Africa, in Iran. Until the troops go out again in force that way, I'll say the '60s still live. That's why my book is a true story: It's history. If some of the heroes don't write the history, the villains will. McNamara will get a peace prize. The villains' view of history will be the '50s going on '70s. It won't be '60s going on '80s. Do you see what I mean? To the villains the '60s will be only a momentary interruption in the building of the American Empire. We have a revolutionary duty to never let that happen, to follow through.

Rubin: You want to be a major interpreter of the '60s?

Hoffman: My book is to set the record straight. I wanted to start with what happened to me in 1960 and before. Not the '60s: 1968 to 1972. I wanted to show the transition of the building of a revolutionary and how my own consciousness was developing and how these events were happening to me. Here we were coming out of the '40s and '50s, you and I, with our great love for America. Great belief in all the myths. Total gullibility. Not even knowing the Rosenbergs had been executed. And then you see and experience what happens and you're just shocked constantly. It happened with HUAC [the House Un-American Activities Committee] end the execution of Caryl Chessman and it just kept going and you just didn't believe it. I didn't believe Kennedy was assassinated; I didn't believe we were put on trial in Chicago. I didn't believe we were being dragged before HUAC. I didn't believe we were being beaten up and not given a chance to protest. I didn't believe any of this stuff, because I believed in the American dream of democracy, and all that time those sons of bitches Nixon, J. Edgar Hoover, John Wayne, LBJ, *they* were spitting on the flag, not *us*. And now I can read government documents released under the Freedom of Information Act and now I believe it. We got Watergated before it was fashionable. You know what I mean. We didn't have Woodward and Bernstein and these other investigative journalists around. We were called paranoids by the press.

Rubin: But people said it's okay to Watergate us because we were calling for a revolution.

Hoffman: Calling for a revolution? Well, I grew up in Boston where *revolution* was not a dirty word. I wrote a long paper in college about the battles of Lexington and Concord. I can do an hour stand-up comedy routine about the battles. I know the whole history of the minutemen. I compared my youth to Samuel Adams's several times. I know they ran the first underground newspaper, the *Massachusetts Spy*. I know all that kind of history, and then to leave Boston and hear the word *revolution* was bad was weird for me. So that's why in the end of my book, when I write that when all today's "isms" are tomorrow's ancient history, there will still be reactionaries, there will still be revolutionaries. When ABC-TV during the '60s interviewed me on the Concord Bridge, the DAR and the Legion forced the Lexington City Council to try and sue ABC for illegal trespassing. As things now stand there's a town ordinance that you need a permit to film on the Concord Bridge. Ridiculous, because at this moment hundreds of people are doing it without a permit and no one seems to be screaming. Go tell me about the law!

Which side are you on? Because I think the word *revolution* implies growth. It implies change. It isn't as determined as evolution. It doesn't imply that Darwinian determinism. So I'm quite happy to say I'm a revolutionary, much better than to say you're born again. Well, I'm born . . .

Rubin: Now everybody knows you're very angry these days about Tom Hayden.

Hoffman: Disappointed.

Rubin: Why are you disappointed?

Hoffman: That's all in the book. But let's say it's political differences: Because. I see what he's doing as subversive and dangerous to the movement. He has a conflict of interest. He is "the candidate" and he is the "spokesman" for the antinuke movement right now. Now that's a movement that's growing and has to develop its own philosophy from the bottom up, and over here is "the candidate" wanting desperately to be elected at any price. Those two things come into conflict just as much as does being chairman of the board of General Motors and trying to be senator. You've got to resign one thing, you can't have the other. It's a conflict of interest. When he talks about strategy it has to be in tine with the needs of the aerospace industry in California. He has to separate the issue of nuclear weapons from nuclear energy plants. Because that connection is unrealistic to his right-wing component. He has to embrace Proposition 13. And try to align that with a whole welfare program that has to go on revitalizing the inner cities. That's something that can't be done without lying. What he's doing is sending out pollsters. He and Jane send out publicists, press agents, to spoon-feed the people. I'm not going to say feed the people what they want. They're going to feed the people what the people *think* or are told they want in order to get elected. And that's a long way removed from philosophy and statesmanship; it's a long way removed from truth. I fail to see any "new" politics here.

These are complex problems that have to be worked out by the people. Tom Hayden is not now and never was "of the people, by the people, and for the people." He was and is an elitist. He likes shuttle diplomacy, dealing with the top level of society in terms of changing things. He doesn't come from the bottom up and I don't think he gives a fuck about the sun. I could say a lot of good things about Tom if you feel it's necessary. He was a good organizer in Newark; the Port Huron Statement—but Tom turns too many people into objects to get what he wants. He betrays friendship. He places political ambition over personal friendship. Which I don't consider a new form of politics. And I'm not the only one. I'm not alone when I speak to you about Hayden. When I'm talking about Hayden I'm breaking a ten-year silence where I wasn't going to say anything bad about any of the people in Chicago.

Rubin: What's the story? What happened?

Hoffman: He told my wife Anita that I'm a common criminal. What does that mean? Of 450,000 people who were busted for dope, what does that mean? That they're all going to stay in jail. I knew he never liked the counterculture. I'm *common*. What does common mean? Common? What a jerk!

Rubin: Well, when did he call you a common criminal?

Hoffman: To Anita. She went to him for a job and he told her nobody in this town will hire you when your husband is a common criminal.

Rubin: On the telephone or in person or what?

Hoffman: Face to face he said it to her. She went to see him. He's insulated. It's hard for the wife of an old friend, a former cellmate, it's hard for a woman now working as a waitress in a Pizza Hut to reach "the candidate." If you asked him about this rejection, about why he didn't—of all the people in the Chicago trial—show up for the Bring Abbie Home Rally, he'd lie, say he forgot or no comment. That's how he handled the Jane Fonda–Joan Baez big debate on Vietnam, the boat people thing which was never really handled. He never signed the letter criticizing Vietnam. He said he lost the letter and wasn't dodging the issue. Liar. Politician. "The candidate." Fuck him. He'll be president, I'll be in the mountains fighting him. And then we'll have a real revolution going on. Just like in Latin America. Che Guevara's fighting his classmates. I'm not running for president. I'm just *running*. . . .

Rubin: So you wouldn't support Hayden for senator?

Hoffman: No. I wanted Shirley MacLaine last time and Tom blew it. Tom thought it was a good idea so the next morning he decided to run, and now he's his own candidate. I'm following his tour very carefully—every single speech. The latest good idea between Jane and Tom is that the first rule is to maintain a sense of humor.

Rubin: Where did they say this?

Hoffman: In Washington. In each stop they take back something from the past. It's incredible to watch the tour. They keep taking things back from the past.

Rubin: What do you mean?

Hoffman: They'll take back the Vietnamese when their kid's name changes from Troi to Troy. But here they are, back on the road again. Hayden and Fonda. The Honda. Honda baby. And what are we taking back? Jane is now taking back everything in Washington. Take a look at this article I've been saving, written by some ass-kissing groupie from the *Washington Post*. She's asked about Jane once saying that Huey Newton, the Black Panther leader, "is the only man that I've ever met that I could trust as a leader in this country." There are a few kidders in the back room waiting to see how she'll handle that one. The famous double take, the eyes roll. Take it back. "All I have to say about that is that I was naive and utterly wrong." Fonda sits down to a burst of applause. And each stop is like that. "Did you say?" "No. I'll take that back."

I want to go on record as saying that Huey Newton was a hero of the '60s and that in all my dealings with him he was a gentleman and a scholar. Of course I didn't go see him as a Hollywood starlet on the make. I went to see him about getting Tim Leary, an escaped convict into Algeria. . . . But I'm giving away too much of the book.

Tom really lied to me once. I didn't even tell this story in the book.

Rubin: Can you tell *High Times*?

Hoffman: Oh, the big climax in the trial when we've got to go for the judge's robes and all that. And we've got to disrupt him. We're not martyrs and we don't want to go to jail. Right. You remember that moment when Tom says Dave [Dellinger] should. You know, he's a pacifist and pacifists want to go to jail. Tom's always had that ability, which is very useful in politics, to make objects out of people. I pulled him aside in the ACLU in the toilet room after Dave was arrested, and Tom had indicated that we do nothing in the courtroom because he had some plans afoot. And I said,

"Tom, what are you going to do? You say you have this little group of people. Aren't you promising something?" And Tom said, "We're going to firebomb the *Chicago Tribune* at the end of the trial." So I said, "Can't you do it tonight?" And he says, "Yes." Well, nothing happened. You and I put on the world, he put on us. He put on me. He put on his friends. Well, we just put on the world. If we said 500 million people were coming to Chicago, that's considered a lie.

Rubin: At that moment in that bathroom was Tom Hayden planning that act? Was he maintaining a revolutionary pose to hook you in? Was it a total pose?

Hoffman: Well, total pose. But I'm not out to do him harm. This has not got to do with Tom, by the way. This is all constructive criticism. This is not revenge. This is not a war. I don't want to destroy Hayden. This has to do with constructive criticism, which is what I believe in, and truth.

I'm out to torpedo the image that he's projecting: "the candidate." I'm out to do "the candidate" *in* and try and help him become a statesman.

Rubin: So you're saying that Hayden was playing a role in the '60s as a revolutionary, and now he's playing the role of the candidate. And manipulating people. Why do you think Jane Fonda's giving Tom such cover, and what do you think of Jane?

Hoffman: I separate the two of them as individuals although they are moving together as, I guess . . .

Rubin: They're a collective . . .

Hoffman: You can *still* separate the two people. You must. You have to treat individuals as individuals on this level when we're talking, and I'm going to talk about the difference between them because it has to do with where you're coming from and where you're going with images. Jane Fonda. Hollywood. *Barbarella*. Movie actress. Moving toward brain. Thinking. Getting more sophisticated. And all that. That's a positive move. We have

Tom Hayden. Coalition activist organizer in the streets. Revolutionary. On trial. Destroy the system by any means necessary, moving toward a corporate position where he's willing to settle for one worker on the board of General Electric, put on a suit and tie, not legalize marijuana, and next you'll see him praying in church a lot. He'll not talk about the rights of the Palestinians for a long, long time because he's heard the Hollywood street gossip that he's anti-Semitic. You know, some people say that I didn't do Jerry Rubin justice.

Rubin: Me?

Hoffman: Yes. In the book: *Soon to Be a Major Motion Picture.*

Rubin: Who said that?

Hoffman: The book's editor.

Rubin: I thought it was okay. It wasn't a book about our relationship. It was a book about your adventures through the '60s, and I thought the things you said about me were with few exceptions pretty appropriate. Perhaps there were some unnecessary things.

Hoffman: Unnecessary. Uh-huh. Unnecessary. I was trying to get me and Rennie [Davis] together there. Wait. Unnecessary. Yes. There are some unnecessary things, but I heard you said to the editor, "Did he talk about how we fought?" And he said, "No, there's no fighting in there." You wanted me to be a little more . . .

Rubin: No, no, no, no. I say in my speeches that there was ego competition between us. It's just human. I mean, it's no judgment or anything. And maybe my insecurity was the source of my competition. If I had been a more secure person, there would have been no need for me to compete with anybody. Right?

Hoffman: I wasn't competing. I wasn't competing with you.

Rubin: Well, you're very competitive. You're incredibly competitive.

Hoffman: Maybe with Muhammad Ali. He said he was the greatest and I knew I was. Maybe we'll have to reduce this to sports.

Rubin: All right.

Hoffman: We have to see. We're in a game and we're competitive and you're the quarterback on this side and I'm the quarterback on this side and now the game is over and we'll go out and have a beer together and make jokes about *all* the spectators. That's the kind of competition that I can understand.

Rubin: Yeah, but the level . . .

Hoffman: I never practice the kind of competition that demands that I have to reduce you as a human in order for me to grow. I totally reject that sick shit. I'm not General Patton! Let's talk about a difference that I didn't put in the book that really fascinated me. What are different kinds of courage? Now, Jerry, you described yourself as a coward.

Rubin: Did I?

Hoffman: In *Growing (Up) at 37*? Yes. You're Jerry Rubin, this public guerrilla to be feared, and inside is a little boy who's afraid and. . . . Right?

Rubin: Oh, yeah. Right.

Hoffman: Right. You are describing this difference between the internal and the external. I studied psychology for all that kind of stuff with Abe Maslow. I played football and other rough sports. So in a certain sense, when things were sort of rough in the streets we rioted in together, I was sort of used to it. I didn't think you were, and you kept doing it over and over and I kept saying in my head, "Why is he doing this? This is so hard. He's working so hard *to overcome this fear.* This is incredibly courageous."

Rubin: Yeah, I see that now.

Hoffman: It's like what I wrote in the front of my book: just what you're supposed to do with fugitives. You're not supposed to point. We recognize you before you recognize us. We've got very good vision and the way you say hello is just smile and nod. You understood a little better than I actually. You taught me that because Bill Ayres and Bernadine Dohrn told me to thank you for not approaching them one day.

Rubin: Oh, I remember that yes, yes . . .

Hoffman: You know, someone said that once you reach thirty the friends you make are the friends for the rest of your life. What do you think about that?

Rubin: You mean the friends you have at thirty?

Hoffman: The friends that you make, say, in your early thirties. The first fifteen years are incubation. The next fifteen years are for study. Basically, power is fought between the people who are thirty to sixty. And this is the whole dynamic of history. And once you're over sixty, the grandparents, you can align with the people who are really younger. But the basic penchant of history is fought between thirty and sixty. And we saw that back in the '60s and the non-Yippies didn't. Have you ever studied demographics or looked at demographics as the reason for the '60s?

Rubin: Sure.

Hoffman: The baby boom and all that. We were the masses. We're still the most and by now we're over thirty.

Rubin: And so we're not pushing . . .

Hoffman: But we still are "the" culture. We still do determine it. If you look at the magazines, if you look at the fashions. If you look at what you call the '70s. What are the issues? How do couples relate, and myths, and childbearing, and men to women. Who's on top and who's on the bottom. You think seventeen-year-olds give a shit? Or grandparents? We were, as you remember, glorious about being action freaks. It was the apocalypse. It was war. We acted on impulse. We had to. There were some people quick on their feet. Some not so quick. We were certainly quicker than the generals in the Pentagon. If you read our books during that period they are cheering everybody on. Let's go team! Rah, rah! You know, it's not like "this is why we do things" and "this is how we didn't" and "this is because we were doing it!" We were doing it at the moment. Dwight Macdonald, my crotchety old friend, once said to me, "Whatever possessed you people in the '60s? The idea of acting on your ideas is so against the intellectual tradition. It just doesn't make any sense."

Yeah, I said, that's what it was. So now we have this period to think about what happened. We got a little bit over the surgery of the nostalgia of we're losing our youth, the Beatles broke up and I don't think they'll ever be united and I could care less. Jerry and Abbie don't see each other much, you know. Well, it's time to get through with depression and screw those old boring questions.

Rubin: But, along with what you say, there's importance to preserving the good of our history . . .

Hoffman: Of course. The decade thing that you understand real good— and there's someone before you that understands it much better. José Ortega y Gasset. He does the whole thing and the whole world in terms of generational revolt. He explains everything.

On top of all that I see the '60s as America's Renaissance period, *the Golden Age*. The greatest decade of the twentieth century and a significant decade for the entire world. We stopped the empire.

Rubin: How?

Hoffman: The other night I saw Clare Boothe Luce, America's dragon lady with bright wings. I lived through the great era of America—the '50s. Both my America and hers climaxed with the execution of the Rosenbergs in the '50s. America ruled the world, it had all the big bombs and it misused or didn't know exactly what to do with them. *No one force* is supposed to rule the world. That's why the Rosenbergs to me were great heroes, and I hope they tried to give secrets to the Russians (I would have), or whoever it was, and I hope there are some Rosenbergs over there in Russia doing their thing, because *no one force* is supposed to own the whole enchilada. So, it doesn't matter what it's called. The United States of Soviet, USSR, USA. I mean, it was fun when the Beatles mixed it all up. I think they came to this whole insight and of course that's one reason why this all happened. We had the Beatles and that was nice and fortunate. We had TV. We had the methods of communications. We had a certain kind of shifting in our perception that occurred in the '60s, and we had the climax and the fall of the American Empire. The quick rise and fall. It happened the moment the government threw the switch up in Sing-Sing: the quickest rise and fall in history.

Rubin: Why are there so many people in the '70s who say that there were no results of the '60s? The '60s didn't succeed and the world is either a bigger mess or nothing's happening. What do you think?

Hoffman: They're wrong. Just unhappy people. Back in the '60s I said I missed the '50s. It's that kind of a thing. You heard me talk about the '60s and it was all one big exhale. You can't exhale forever. Did you ever try to do that? One whole decade of a big exhale. You've got to inhale. Well, the '70s is an inhale. When I went into Mississippi in the early '60s it was psychotherapy, and some people said you're not supposed to use struggle and movements this way. Well, they were wrong. They were wrong because there is not that separation. The introspective period did occur in the early part of the '60s for me. The '60s lasted thirteen years. I guess we got up to 1973. It was so good we got three extra years. There were people asking me all about it. Maybe that's one reason why I got busted and took off. I got tired of people saying, "Are the '60s over?" It was 1973 already. It was 1974. They kept asking, "Are the '60s gone?" And meanwhile everybody was saying it was awful, yet wishing we were back in beads and saddles carrying Stop the War signs. What do they want it to keep coming back for?

Rubin: The questions about the '60s drove you underground?

Hoffman: For instance, going to trial again, dealing with the same role over and over. Asking the same questions, not growing, not learning anything. Oh, that was such a burden. Whew! I mean, *you* know. I don't have to tell you. You know. Sometimes I almost want to kiss those two narcs on the lips.

Rubin: So you went underground, in a sense, to escape being Abbie?

Hoffman: To escape being Media Abbie. The media came very close to destroying the real Abbie.

Rubin: Yeah, but you did it in an Abbie way. You kept a frame of reference of being a public outlaw. You actually continued the '60s into the '70s.

Hoffman: Well, it took me maybe a year of incubation, where I really had to learn lots and lots of other things to try and figure out exactly the kind of things that are a lot more important. And I might say this is a continuing process that doesn't end, this sort of thing that I'm describing. But I did not want to reject my past. That's why I'm against all conversions. I don't think it is really a healthy sort of a thing, the idea of rejecting your past. You must integrate your past into not only your present but your future.

Rubin: And you?

Hoffman: Well, I'm obviously going to have more influence. One decision that I've come to is that I'm going to try and concentrate on truth more and politics less. That's one thing. That's one sort of New Year's Revolution.

Rubin: What do you mean?

Hoffman: I think the process of politics as we know it in general involves lies. Lying is, of course, very intriguing to me. I'm all hung up in this because here I am on this truth kick and I am living a lie. I'm not Abbie Hoffman anymore. Although I love him very much, still have his good qualities, have eliminated some of his idiocies. And you know what?

Rubin: What?

Hoffman: I can beat him in tennis!

Rubin: If you were, say, twenty or twenty-one right now—a young radical man or woman—how would you express your political consciousness in the '80s?

Hoffman: Well, at the beginning of the '80s I would be asking a lot of questions—*a lot of questions*. I'd want to know a lot about what went on in the '60s. I'd want to know the stories that weren't told and the stories that were told. I'd question everything at the school: I'd want to know who discovered America, and I'd want to get twenty-six opinions on that. And I'd want to know answers to things like Is the CIA or the KGB lying about whether Julius and Ethel Rosenberg were spies? I'd want to know answers about who's lying and who's right about Three Mile Island. I'd want to know about why there are no blacks in high positions in the antinuclear movement. I'd want to know if it's enough to have an Uncle Tom approach to the problems of oil and distribution by putting one worker on the board of General Motors.

Since this is an election year, I'd want to know an awful lot about truth and an awful lot about who's *telling* the truth. And I would come to the conclusion that I'm going to study this election, because this is the most important event, both culturally and politically, that ever happened in the history of the United States. That the '80s are going to be far greater than the '60s, that the '80s are going to be the second American revolution, whereas the '60s were the second civil war. And I'd want to bring everybody together and say that *everybody's* right! And I'd want to deal with people who are not going to tell *any* lies, *ever*!

Rubin: Who are you going to support in the 1980 election?

Hoffman: My first choice for president of the United States of America is the person I consider the greatest American lawyer in the country, and that happens to be Fidel Castro.

My second choice is the person—the American closest to my roots, to my birth, to where I was born. The name has great significance to me because it played a crucial role in the beginning of the '60s, during which I certainly had a good time. And he's a Boston Red Sox fan, and he's running and he's going to need some guidance and help, because he's on the edge of life and he's got a lot to think about. And that's Ted Kennedy.

Rubin: Okay.

Hoffman: And my third choice—my third choice? That doesn't work out! We get all the men in the country, see, and we line them *all* up and we pick the guy with the biggest bleep! Every politician, every candidate, is a fucking liar. That's what it is—this country has to get out of lying! It has to get into telling the truth! If I was Ted Kennedy—and I tell you right now—I'm sitting here. When this magazine comes out, all right and I'm sitting here a year ahead—a year ahead—and I'm telling you: Teddy Kennedy is already president.

Rubin: Right.

Hoffman: We have to live in the future. Now what do I give? Me, "outlaw" in the hills. What advice, after I've learned all those how-to-survives when everybody was chasing me and bookmakers said I couldn't make it with my fucking big mouth and I've proved my point and I've learned my lesson? What do I say to Teddy? I say, "Teddy, hey, you know, you're gonna need a lot of help to stay alive." You know?

And why don't you go to see Fidel and find out why he eats his own lobster? Why don't you meet me in my home? Why don't you come over and meet me for lunch someday? Find out how I cook, I'll cook you a good meal, Ted. So, we'll talk on . . . I'll tell you about the time I ran a campaign against you, and we met in Worcester, and we'll bullshit and talk about tennis, and I'll come be in your tournament. I can beat anybody in your tournament in tennis. I'm great in any court; judicial, tennis, district, *Sports Illustrated*—it's all in there, see, and that's what the book is about. That's what my movie is about. Excuse me, you see, because I said my— that's not a good pronoun anymore. I don't like that pronoun. I like *we*.

Sometimes, when I feel that everything is in the right position, I think about having a nice party. *And* I plan to advertise it—full-page ads! In magazines. And I plan to fingerprint it. And I'd say "Mr. & Mrs. Blank would like to invite you to their home for dinner. You know the way, just don't bring any weapons." And if Fred Silverman comes, he's gonna have to bring a contract. And if Bob Dylan comes, he's gonna have to bring Rod McKuen, and he's gonna have to tell me why he keeps changing his name. I know why I keep changing my name.

Rubin: Do you think you'll be aboveground in the '80s?

Hoffman: That's a possibility. You're more concerned about above and below than me. 'Cause you don't know the B personality. B's friends don't worry about me at all, my sanity, my betraying them. They need B. I owe them my life and I made a pledge two years ago that the FBI and no other force was going to remove me from the valley and my work. Not even Hollywood, nor all Abbie's old friends. It's just a whole new ball game. So, to quote a great '60s philosopher, why don't we end the bullshit questions and just DO IT!

THE PERSECUTION AND ASSASSINATION OF THE PARAPSYCHOLOGISTS AS PERFORMED BY THE INMATES OF THE AMERICAN ASSOCIATION FOR THE ADVANCEMENT OF SCIENCE UNDER THE DIRECTION OF THE AMAZING RANDI!

ROBERT ANTON WILSON

AUGUST 1980

THE NOVELIST WAS WORKING on a huge, cyclopean, swords-and-sorcery epic set in eighteenth-century France, full of duels and seductions and revolutions and a cast that included such egregious gentry as Napoleon and the Marquis de Sade. It promised to be a rather juicy bit of work. Then *High Times* called and asked if he would cover the 1980 San Francisco meeting of the American Association for the Advancement of Science. The novelist was not at all sure he wanted to be dragged out of the novel while it was going well. But *High Times* hooked him, not just with $$$ but with the assignment to observe how the parapsychologists were handled, or manhandled, this time around.

You see, at the last AAAS meeting, in Houston in 1979, Dr. John Archibald Wheeler had damned and blasted the parapsychologists from here to hell and back. Dr. Wheeler is a real heavy; his contributors to quantum theory, gravitational geometry, and other arcane branches of physics are literally cosmic in import. He also has the distinction of being called the father of the hydrogen bomb, except in those circles that attribute paternity to Dr. Edward Teller. Wheeler has another distinction, for which the novelist loves him dearly. In a weak moment, or a whimsical moment, Wheeler put his name on a paper, with two other physicists named Everett and Graham, in which they proposed that everything that can happen, in effect, does happen; that there are millions of millions of millions of universes, each as fast in space and time as this one, in which slightly distorted Xerox copies of each of us are going through variations of the life scripts we are going through here.

Concretely, that seems to mean that in the universe next door, Dr. Wheeler never put his name on such a bizarre speculation; and in the universe two jumps away, he never became a physicist at all, but a ballet dancer perhaps; and s on and on through all possible permutations. If this theory makes you dizzy, take comfort in the thought that it only includes possible universes. The Everett-Wheeler-Graham model, or EWG for short, does not say that copies of you are wandering around in totally impossible universes. And yet in 1979 Dr. Wheeler, the man who loaned his prestigious name to this mind-boggling notion, denounced the parapsychologists for being weird. He had not just fulminated against the parapsychologists in Houston. He said they should be kicked the hell out of the American Association for the Advancement of Sciences for their heresies.

The novelist had no high regard for parapsychologists himself. (They seemed to lack imagination, poetry, and whimsy. He thought they should all expand their consciousnesses by studying modern physics.) But he was interested in heretics in general and how the scientific establishment treats them. His interest was particularly concrete because there was one part of his historical novel that was giving him trouble. His hero, Sigismundo Celine, had seen a meteorite fall. Celine had dragged the damned thing, which couldn't exist according to eighteenth-century science, to the Academy of Sciences in Paris, where he was roundly denounced and mocked for his troubles.

The problem was in re-creating the mental set of the scientists of 1780, those self-declared men of reason who were so sure of their own enlightenment. How did they convince themselves of their own rationality while refusing to look at the actual facts about meteorites? This novelist decided that checking out how the AAAS deals with unorthodoxy today would give him some insight into how the academy dealt with meteorites in 1780.

And so the novelist-turned-journalist arrived at the San Francisco Hilton the second day of the AAAS meeting to drink impressions from a panel called "Science and Pseudoscience." The journalist had a pretty good idea of what *pseudoscience* meant: People who had been reporting the current equivalent of meteorites were going to be dumped on. It was an axiom of his philosophy that *10,000* trained witnesses reporting something that doesn't fit current theories have less credibility than two drunken participants in an auto accident. You might call that a paranoid head set or a cynical point of view of how domesticated primates behave when they get together in groups to define the truth, but at least the journalist is up front about his own heresies.

The panel featured five speakers but only one viewpoint. If the pseudoscientists are those who think they have found meteorites, here was a debate on the issue by five men who knew damned well that there were no meteorites. The heretics were allowed into the audience, however, where they promptly clustered themselves up front, directly under the panelists, in what the journalist recognized as "the sinners bench." The configuration illustrated what Tim Leary calls the vertical polarity of the emotional-territorial circuit: Any primate group defines authority in terms of who is *higher* and who is *lower*. (That's why dictators like to talk from balconies, Leary says.) So the primates on the stage were the authorities here, and the heretics *down* on the sinners' bench had to look *up* at them all morning long.

The first speaker was Rolf Sinclair of the National Science Foundation. He said a lot of nice things about science, which was not surprising; if the first speaker had been the pope, one would have expected him to say a lot of nice things about religion. The journalist took only one note during his sermonette. It said: "Scientists intensively competitive." Memory (always less reliable than the trusty notebook) indicates that Sinclair thought it was good that scientists are competitive, but whether this was on Darwinian or Republican grounds is not clear. The journalist did get the impression that Sinclair was trying very hard to be decent to everybody, including the heretics on the sinners' bench.

The next speaker was livelier. This was Dr. Ray Hyman of the University of Oregon. He defined *pseudoscience* rather circularly as "pathological science," and then defined that as "the science of things that aren't so." The journalist began to feel that Lemuel Gulliver should have been reporting the discourse. "The first rule among these Learn'd Persons," Gulliver might write, "is that Heresy is False, and that Falsity is Untrue, and that, furthermore, the Untrue is Heretical." "But," Gulliver's host (who looks like a horse and talks like G.I. Gurdjieff) might press, "how do they determine what is Heretical and False and Untrue?" "They have an Infallible Method," Gulliver would reply, "which is this: They only Believe that which can be demonstrated to their Reason, and they are able to demonstrate to their Reason only those Propositions which they are willing to Believe."

At this point it was obvious that the journalist was goofing off and the novelist had seized the chance to take over the assignment. The journalist resumed control, and Dr. Hyman, not being a character in a satirical novel, then surprised both of us by arguing, rather somberly, that the pathology in "pathological science" was not just in the heretics but in the scientific establishment itself. What makes for pathology, Hyman said, beginning to sound like Gregory Bateson, is a jamming or warping in the communication process. The way to determine truth, Hyman went on vigorously, is to allow all viewpoints to be discussed.

This was such a radical notion, in these surroundings, that the sociobiologist expected Dr. Hyman to be ejected from the stage and sent to sit among the heretics on the sinners' bench. But Hyman made a nice recovery, rushing on to heap ridicule on the ideas of teleportation and "psychic force" (two of the most damnable of all heresies, according to the establishment). He was on the right side after all, and only the most Agnewesque establishmentarians would accuse him of being squishy-soft on heresy for believing in debate.

That psychic-force business is especially irritating to the establishment because, no matter how many times they condemn it as false, it keeps getting rediscovered, rehallucinated, by otherwise sober people. Dr. Stanley Krippner, former president of the Association for Humanistic Psychology and a leading candidate for king of the heretics, if such an anarchist group had a kind, lists more than nintey cases of the rehallucination of the psychic force in the history of science. For instance, Paracelsus discovered—or hallucinated—it as *munia* in the sixteenth century, and Luigi Galvani, the electrical pioneer, called it life force in 1790.

Indeed, the more the idea gets condemned, the more people seem to feel the force is with them. William McDougall called it the hormic energy in 1920; Henri Bergson, *élan vital*, also in 1920; Willhelm Reich, orgone, 1937; V.S. Grischenko, bioplasma, 1944; Margenau, quasi-electrostatic field, 1959; Charles Musés, noetic energy, 1972, and on and on. There sure is a lot of hallucination going on. Dopers *all* seem to have this hallucination; they call the force in question simply "the vibes," subdivided into "good vibes" and "bad vibes." Shows what Permanent Brain Damage will do.

And this brings up another thought to the historian, who pushes the journalist aside for a moment. Hyman, in speaking of the infestation of the establishment itself by "pathology," mentioned the attempt in the 1950s to suppress Velikovsky's book. Dr. Immanuel Velikovsky, if you don't remember, was the man who, among other things, claimed some of the miracles in the Bible actually happened, and were caused by a near collision of the earth and a comet. It is curious that Hyman should choose that example—an *attempt* to suppress books—when something far more pathological, from a civil libertarian point of view, occurred. For it was in 1957 that the feds seized all the books of Dr. Willhelm Reich from their publisher, Orgone Institute Press, and burned them in Rangely, Maine, where Reich had stood trial. The books represented thirty years of scientific research. The historian has yet to find *any* record *anywhere* that *any* member of the AAAS objected to this method of eliminating heresy. Thou shalt not discover or hallucinate psychic energy. Dig?

Dr. Hyman was even more sarcastic about teleportation than about psychic energy. Teleportation, the psychologist reflects, is what domesticated primates call it when something arrives somewhere and they can't figure out how it got there. For instance, if the Wright brothers had kept the airplane a secret, and I arrived in New York a few hours after you knew I had been in Los Angeles, that would be a teleportation, because you couldn't explain it. Teleportation is *possible* if and only if there are scientific principles we have not yet discovered. It is *probable* if and only if you accept the

evidence cited by various persons who aver that they have witnessed teleportations. The author is personally inclined to consider teleportation *possible,* because he doubts very much that primate brains have evolved to the
point, in 1980, where they know all the laws of the universe. Some things
probably can move around by methods we do not understand. On the
other hand, the author does not consider teleportation *probable,* because
the evidence cited for it by people who claim to have seen it is not quite
as good as the evidence, say, that there were two Oswalds in Dallas on
November 22, 1963, and considerably less good than the evidence that
objects in the earth's gravitational field fall at thirty-two feet per second per
second unless other forces are acting on them.

Dr. Hyman made it sound, as do many members of the AAAS, as if the
idea of teleportation is not only improbable but impossible. The only logical justification for that position would seem to be that they are personally convinced they know *all* the laws of the universe already. Blessed are
the meek, but they will never get to sit on an AAAS panel called Science
and Pseudoscience.

The best catalog of teleportations, or alleged teleportations, can be found
in the books of Charles Fort: *The Book of the Damned, New Lands, Lo!,* and
Wild Talents, if you are interested. Fort collected literally thousands of cases
of damned things appearing where they couldn't or shouldn't. Some of his
cases come from newspapers (not the most reliable sources of scientific
data) but a lot of them come from scientific journals. Fort himself didn't
know what to make of his data. Since he was willing to be offensive to theologians as well as to scientists, he said that if God were moving all these
things around, we should consider the possibility that God is a mental case.

The next speaker was an astronomer named E.C. Krupp from Griffith
Observatory. Krupp quickly set to the business at hand, which was smiting
Erich von Daniken. Krupp smote von Daniken's arithmetic (all wrong), his
scholarship (slipshod at best), and his integrity (questionable even to
those who try hardest to be charitable in judging our fellow humans). It
was very professional smiting, but the journalist had encountered it all
before in the occult journal *Gnostica,* which had smitten von Daniken by
cataloging the same errors in his works several years ago. It is hard to
think Krupp ever read *Gnostica,* however, since it is an "occult" journal

and always has words like *witchcraft* and *tantra* and *sex magick* on the cover. The journalist couldn't help wondering, though, if Krupp had read somebody who read *Gnostica*.

Of course, it is remarkably easy to smite von Daniken, whose books are a virtual encyclopedia of how *not* to prove an argument. His scholarship is careless at best and suspiciously opportunistic always. The trouble with smiting von Daniken is that his particular heresy—the idea that extraterrestrials may have visited this planet—has been espoused by many theorists whose writings are much more scholarly, careful, and scientifically honest than his. This list includes Robert K.G. Temple, an English astronomer who thinks people from Sirius visited here around 4,000 years ago; Jacques Bergier, a French physicist who believes we might have been visited many times; Duncan Lunan, a Scots astronomer who has suggested that there's been a probe from Epsilon Bootis in our solar system for several centuries, and many others. One can't escape the feeling that it is easier to smite von Daniken than any of these men, but that an attempt to smite *them* would yield more light and less heat.

Krupp then went on to what is known as the sociology of knowledge, in part a technique for invalidating the arguments of your opponent by showing that he, she or it has ulterior motives for subscribing to a particular doctrine. (The sociology of knowledge was invented by Karl Marx, but in capitalist countries sociologists like to pretend it was invented by Karl Mannheim, to avoid being called Marxists.) Krupp proposed that people who believe earth has been visited by outsiders believe so because this gives them psychological gratification.

That's the nice thing about the sociology of knowledge: You can use it to explain away anybody who has an idea you don't like. Even von Daniken, if he were in the audience and fast enough with a riposte, might suggest that Krupp is an isolationst (i.e., he believes we've never been visited) because that gives Krupp psychological gratification. Indeed, the sociobiologist thought of that himself. Domesticated primates are very territorial, and it fills them with anxiety and rage is outsiders seem to be impinging on their turf. Better we should argue about one another's motivations than actually look at the evidence that such outsiders might be peeping through the windows or oozing down the chimney, right?

By now it was clear that the panelists thus far were all liberals. The difference between liberals and conservatives is that conservatives want to hit heretics on the head with blunt instruments whereas liberals want to treat them for mental illness. The chief function of the panel, the psychologist thought, was to disseminate the liberal view that heretics are mentally ill. "Pathological science" is the science of the mentally ill.

The next speaker, a grim fellow with dark hair, dark mustache, and even dark eyebrows, looked like a physician on a soap opera telling the heroine she has only three months to live. He was Rodney Stark of the University of Washington and his subject was the geography of heresy. Most heretics, he claimed, live on the Pacific coast. No great surprise. We Californians even have a joke that California is like Granola because it consists of equal parts fruits, nuts, and flakes. But Stark was replete with surveys, charts, and data of all kinds that proved that the situation was not just Californian. It goes all the way up and down the coast, he said. Washington, Oregon, and even Alaska are infected. There are more cults here than anywhere else, he said. Most of the mail to *Fate* magazine (the journal of organized, or disorganized, heresy) comes from these states. There are more astrologers listed in the phone books of our major cities than in any of the cities east of the Rockies. Furthermore, membership in the conventional churches is lower out here than elsewhere in the country.

The journalist was reminded of Timothy Leary's argument, in his new book *Intelligence Agents,* that the mutant genes—which Leary also calls *futigue* genes, because he thinks they're searching for a new reality—have been moving steadily westward for the past 30,000 years and are now all piled up on top of one another on the Pacific coast, with no place left to go but outer space. Stark gave no indication of thinking all the weirdness on the coast is part of an evolutionary movement. He was content to note merely that there was a neurogeography of heresy and that the heresiarchs have all landed in the Wild West.

Then, the high point of the morning arrived in the form of The Amazing Randi, as he styles himself. Randi looks like Santa Claus and talks like the late Sen. Joseph R. McCarthy. Randi is not a liberal by any definition but a real, old-fashioned, honest-to-Cthulhu conservative, fire-breathing variety. He wants to hit the heretics on the head with a blunt instrument. The Amazing Randi is of the school of thought that holds heretics are a bunch of *sneaks, cheats,* and *liars.* This is the best rhetorical stance for a heresy hunter since it is rooted deeply in primate psychology. It is much easier to rile up a herd of primates by hollering "that gang over there are sneaks, cheats, and liars" than by the liberal path of saying "that gang has an honest difference of opinion with us." Every demagogue knows this, and Randi, an old showman, plays it to the hilt.

The journalist hadn't heard such oratory since Jim Garrison was in his heyday, finding new Kennedy assassins every second newsbreak. It was a smashing performance and the sociobiologist was convinced that most of the audience were breathing harder and starting to tense their muscles before it was half over. Primate mob psychology at its most primitive. But Randi was a bit unclear about who he was attacking. He kept referring to the heretics as "parapsychologists," but most of the people he denounced were not parapsychologists or any kind of psychologists. But parapsychologist has evidently become a generic term in Randi's mind. "Parapsychologist" means to Randi what "communist" meant to Joe McCarthy or "male chauvanist" to Gloria Steinem. It means he doesn't like your ideas.

Randi's chief targets were Drs. Harold Puthoff and Russell Targ, who are not parapsychologists but physicists. Randi's vendetta against Puthoff and Targ is so long, tangled and replete with charges and countercharges that it sounds like the plot of a spy novel. Among other things, he hates them for saying that Uri Geller can bend metal by *wishing* it bent. Puthoff and Targ deny they said this. Whenever the matter comes up, they quote their report on Geller in *Nature* magazine, in which they wrote: "Although metal bending by Geller has been observed in our laboratory, we have not been able to combine such observations with adequately controlled experiments to obtain data sufficient to support the paranormal hypothesis." That seems to mean that they saw him bend metal, but the conditions were such that they could not rule out the possibility of trickery.

Randi refuses to believe this, and continues to damn and blast them for saying Geller did it by *wishing* it. He has a good source for this; the source happens to be his own book, *The Magic of Uri Geller,* in which he says they said it was done by wishing. The debate between Randi and Puthoff and Targ is *all* on that level. There are two versions of *everything.* As Abbie

Hoffman once said, there seem to be a lot of different realities going around these days.

When Randi got through roasting Puthoff and Targ, he performed some magic for the audience; he was a professional magician before he became a professional heresy hunter. He got a volunteer from the audience and performed "psychic surgery" like the shamans in the Phillipines. He claimed that because this performance was a fake, all similar performances must be fakes. (There seemed to be an undistributed middle in Randi's syllogism. He must be using some new brand of non-Aristotelian and nondistributive logic, the psychologist decided.)

The psychologist had even more trouble with Randi's idea that "psychic surgery" and other shamanistic tricks are necessarily bad for their customers. Everybody knows about the placebo effect: Give a patient a powder and tell him it will make him better and quite often he *will* get better. In a tribal society that has heard of surgery but doesn't have any surgeons, "psychic surgery" could very well work as a *dramatized* placebo. Because Randi didn't quote any statistics on how people respond to psychic surgery (scientific method is strangely alien to him), one had only his bald assertion that it didn't work. In fact, we do know that all forms of faith healing, healing by suggestion, et cetera, work best with people who want to get well—who are, as it were, looking for an excuse to get well. For instance, *Medical Sciences Bulletin* (September 14, 1979) reported that these are the types who respond best to placebos. The types who want to stay sick ignore placebos along with all other therapies. It seems likely that the people who resort to psychic surgery are the former type; looking for an excuse to get well, and that those who would not respond to it wouldn't even *try* it.

When the psychologist turned himself back into the journalist, Randi was in the midst of his peroration. He repeated all over his denunciations of parapsychologists, building up steam as he went along. You could see he had the audience in the palm of his hand. If he had ended, "Let's get a rope and string the bastards up right now!" anything could have happened.

Most of the audience marched out, smiles of contentment adorning their faces. They had heard what they came to hear, and all was well in their little worlds.

And so (as Lemuel Gulliver might have reported), these Learned Men, having Inquir'd deeply into the Case for the Opposition, discover'd that the Opposition had no Case and were Devoid of Merit, which was what they Suspected all along, and they arriv'd at this Happy Conclusion by the most Economical and Nice of all Methods of Enquiry, which was that they did not Invite the Opposition to confuse Matters by participating in the Discussion.

At last the heretics were allowed to get up from the sinners' bench to make their five-minute rebuttals. Dr. Sinclair kept one eye on his wristwatch to make sure they didn't go over their limit. Dr. Russell Targ of the Stanford Research Institute spoke for fewer than five minutes. He said that everything Randi had said about his research was untrue, that the reports on the research were in print in *Nature* magazine and that anybody who wanted to form an impartial judgment should go and look up the reports. He sounded tired, as if he had said this so many times that he was getting bored hearing himself say it again. Randi jumped up and called Dr. Targ about seventeen kinds of liar, including damned liar and revolting liar and plain-and-fancy liar.

Dr. Harold Puthoff, also of the Stanford Research Institute, made pretty much the same speech as Dr. Targ, inviting people to read their reports instead of accepting Randi's version of their research. Randi jumped up and called Dr. Puthoff twenty-three kinds of rascal and scoundrel. Dr. Geoffrey Mishlove said that everything Randi had said about Ted Serios, the man who allegedly can put pictures on film by wishing them there, was inaccurate. You can imagine what Randi said about Dr. Mishlove.

Dr. Jack Sarfatti spoke for nearly the full five minutes. He said that the only reason for believing in the so-called paranormal was if it happened to you so often that it got to be normal. He said that it had happened to him that often. He also said that he as working on a new theory of quantum mechanics that might explain *why* these so-called paranormal events happen. Nobody at the AAAS wanted to hear a theory that suggested the paranormal was normal.

And so the novelist got a pretty good idea of how the French Academy of Sciences would have reacted to Sigismundo Celine's blasphemous meteorite in 1780. It would have appointed a panel of five men who didn't believe in meteorites to debate the issues impartially. One of them would suggest that prometeorite people should also be heard, but he wouldn't insist on it. Another would produce statistics showing that meteorites are most commonly reported in a part of France known to be full of kooks. A third would denounce the book on meteorites by a man who also believed in the tooth fairy. And a professional demagogue would round out the day by denouncing people who see meteorites as scoundrels, rascals liars, fools, and lousy no-good bastards in general.

The psychologist made one final note: "After this article appears in print, Randi will claim I'm a parapsychologist." The journalist found the whole experience entertaining but hardly edifying. The sociobiologist acquired a few notes for his projected nonfiction opus, "Dominance Rituals among Domesticated Primates."

The satirical novelist wandered over to a symposium on sociobiology held by a group called Science for the People. They all hated sociobiology as much as Randi hates parapsychology. They hated it because sociobiologists take Darwin seriously and really believe we are a primate species, with all the usual primate habits. They went on and on, denouncing sociobiology as degrading to humanity and sexist and reactionary. And all the time they were saying these things the journalist kept imagining he was watching another gang of primates working themselves up into a rage against a rival tribe. It was like watching the cast of *Planet of the Apes* argue about their own superiority and rationality. The journalist had to leave because he was afraid he would start to laugh in an uncontrollable way and, what with his press card saying *High Times*, they might think he was on some kind of weird drug.

RICHARD PRYOR

A Public Burning

MARK CHRISTENSEN

OCTOBER 1980

AT THE WHISKY IN Hollywood a couple of the local Antichrists are talking to a guy who says he's Johnny Carson's coke dealer. All the guy's really important circuits were probably burned out years ago, but he can still finesse a linear point. "If it don't lead to stupor or ejaculation," he reveals, "I ain't interested."

The event tonight is yet another wake for Jim Morrison and the drinks are on the house. Two pool table-sized television screens project twin images of the now-gone Jim writhing prone on a stage sometime in the late '60s or early '70s, microphone to mouth, howling. Cops take to the stage on screen. Doors fans are seen being cracked with long billy clubs. Cut to scenes of the National Democratic Convention in Chicago in 1968. More cops, more smacking. Cut to a closeup of J. Edgar Hoover. Cut back to the Doors, gothic maestro Morrison crooning, "This is the end, my only friend, the end . . ."

Welcome to uptown L.A., land of spandex and insanity. Where a snazzy hovel down the street in Bev Hills can cost you half a million and the best live entertainment is free: winos on roller skates, spike-heeled call girls from Mars wobbling delicately along Rodeo Drive, Ronald Reagan, you name it.

Here at the Whisky (née A Go Go), Cars mastermind Ric Ocasek stands three steps to the right of former Doors keyboard player, and now godhead of the punk group X, Ray Manzarek. New Weird and Old Weird respectively. The Whisky has brought 'em out of the woodwork tonight. At least two geriatric Doors fans are in togas, and Timothy Leary—or a Timothy

Leary hallucination—works the crowd. Posing for pictures and whatnot. Morrison continues to devolve in the two TV screens.

Fifteen or twenty miles away, America's greatest stand-up comic, the freshly flambéed Richard Pryor, is doing the same thing—'80s style. He has been charbroiled from the belly button up, is lying suspended on a protective mattress at the Sherman Oaks Burn Center in the San Fernando Valley, and has been given a one-in-three chance of living. A pioneer on the frontiers of feral zonkitude, Pryor fell hapless victim to an astounding freak accident: A glass of rum blew up in his face. Honest to God.

Now, sure, you've heard stories that he was using the wonderful cocaine derivative, freebase. And that he caught fire while cooking some up. Well, hey, don't you believe it. Puerto Rican did him in and that's a fact. Just ask his attorney. A hot ash from his cigarette was all it took and *bwaaamm-mooo!*

UCLA pharmacologist Ron Siegel estimates that here among the local rockers and TV folk an annual per body investment in cocaine of $250,000 is not uncommon. He would know. Siegel is one of the world's experts in the effects of brain-altering drugs. He has spent ten years investigating a whole slew of potions, everything from acid to belladonna. His work has included a study of everything from alcoholic lab rats to ketamine junkies and, in the wake of this, he has become convinced that sane people can handle a spectrum of drugs including pot, psychedelics, and cocaine without physical or mental detriment.

Still, a quarter of a million dollars a year for cocaine? That's about a garbage can full of the stuff per annum. Who would have a mind left after putting all that up his nose? Also, where would all the cash come from? That works out to about the cost of a new VW Rabbit a week.

"In the entertainment industry," Siegel says, "it all gets written off under 'food and cash.' Just business as usual. And these days, it doesn't go directly up everybody's noses. It goes to make freebase. Which is very pleasant stuff . . . and very dangerous."

Indeed. For the as yet uninformed, the wonder drug freebase is simply cocaine alkaloid. Coke sans hydrochloric acid; made by mixing ammonium or sodium carbonate. You mix equal parts carbonate with petroleum ether, add cocaine and shake. This elixir subsequently separates into two water-clear layers, the top one consisting of freebase and ether. You then suck the freebase/ether solution off with an eye dropper, squirt it into a petri dish, and wait for the ether to evaporate, leaving the white, talc-like powder in the dish's bottom. Voila! Freebase. Now the fun part. Because freebase will not burn, it must be superheated in order to be smoked. Unlike cocaine, freebase doesn't do its work when snorted, so . . .

Enter the blowtorch. Or at least the Bunsen burner like you used in Bsc. Chem. 107. Freebase is usually then inhaled through a glass hookah.

Siegel fires some up for demonstration purposes. We are in his office and the torch's long arrow of blue flame cooks the powder in its little screen cup. A thin tendril of smoke twists up into the air. Smoke worth about twenty-five bucks.

I inquire: Perchance a sample hit? For scientific purposes. Siegel shakes his head and passes me a copy of his now landmark report, *Freebasing: Hazards from Smoking Cocaine*. He estimates that freebase is a fad that swelled from nothing three years ago to about a million users currently in the USA alone. He details also an impressive smorgasbord of freebase liabilities: "Effects include dry lips, black sputum, mydriasis, rapid pulse, restlessness, insomnia, anorexia, tremors, paranoia, and psychosis." Sounds like the effects of the last job I held down, so what's the big deal?

"I'm surprised," he answers, "that the bodies haven't started popping up before *now*. We've had several freebase-related burn cases before this Pryor thing. People take hit after hit of base and then get so wasted, they lose track of the torch. A couple of them have had to be awakened *after* they've caught fire."

But that's just part of the freebase package. "The attraction to compulsive use is greater than heroin," Siegel says. "The initial rush is tremendous, but tolerance develops rapidly—users seek to replicate the original superhigh experience. Which they usually can't. But they chase it, using more and more base, and it really starts taking a toll on their systems."

Siegel estimates that it takes a minimum of three months to really lunch yourself on base, but once you've got the ball rolling, it's hell. Take the hallucinations, for instance. "Unlike LSD where you *observe* the hallucinations, with freebase the hallucinations become a direct part of your reality." He goes on to recite the already famous case of one of his patients (Siegel does extensive counseling) who became convinced that worms were crawling out of his body and brought Siegel bits of skin he'd tweezed from his arms. "The guy was totally convinced the worms were real," Siegel says. "All he wanted to know from me, in fact, was how they could have contaminated his cocaine supply to begin with."

But wait. There's more. "The freebase rush lasts only a couple minutes, but there's this huge compulsion to repeat it over and over at short intervals. Which really can string you out. It leads to subsequent use of a lot of downs. In fact, freebase fosters poly-drug use like no substance I've ever experienced. And if you make yourself too crazy on the stuff, well . . . in an emergency room situation, it's relatively easy to deal with somebody who's taken too much LSD—you can handle their fears by talking them down. But a guy who is really messed up on freebase may take seven to ten days just to detox."

What makes it so attractive then? "Well," Segel says, "its simple." He looks out the window of his Westwood office-apartment. A thin, youngish man with a high forehead, he wears jeans and a pressed khaki shirt. "The rush from freebase feels better than anything else we've ever encountered. We've had at least one case where a man got so excited over the stuff that he ejaculated through a flaccid penis. For a couple of minutes, you can feel better than anybody has ever felt before in his life."

The Sherman Oaks Burn Center has now been hosting an obligatory press circus for days and days. Guys with TV camera portapacks are thick as junkies on 42nd Street. They wander the portals of this little hospital, a trim structure that could double as a suburban police station or insurance office; *that* uninteresting.

There is, however—right this minute—some interesting activity hereabouts. A little woman, for example, is going bats. "This is it! I've had all I can take," she screams. "I don't want anybody talking to this writer! This is the last straw. I'm not talking to anybody from *High Times*. That's a drug magazine! They don't care anything about Richard Pryor—all they care about is drugs!"

She is Richard Pryor's P.R. lady. A little bird of a person. White. White skin. White dress. White eyes. It's been several days since Pryor's accident, and the night before, a TV announcer had intoned over the air, "Pryor is as sick as a human can be and still be alive."

We're standing in the lobby of the burn center. Pryor is asleep, still unconscious following surgery that included a flexible bronchoscopy, a myringotomy and the first-stage extensive debridement of his chest, shoulders, back, arms, neck, and face. Which means, in English, that surgeons have removed extensive secretions blocking his breathing passages, pierced his eardrums to facilitate treatment in the pressurized hyperbaric chamber and removed dead skin from all over the place.

Accounts still vary as to what actually had happened to the poor guy. *Time* reported that an "explosion" had taken place in Pryor's bedroom the night of June 2. Indeed. The cops found scorch marks on the walls and ceiling. But that was it. No coke, no freebase, no paraphernalia. No rum or Camel straights, either.

At any rate, this much is known—or at least agreed upon: After Pryor "exploded," his elderly aunt, Jenny, was alerted to the now-flaming comedian by Pryor's live-in watchman. She rushed into the bedroom and smothered the fire with a blanket. By then, probably already in shock and almost certainly in tremendous pain, Pryor rocketed out of his house on foot, running in order—as the *Los Angeles Times* put it—to "seek relief in sheer motion."

Outside, Richard, his shirt burned away and his chest and arms a bloody pizza, caused quite a stir. Traffic along the street in front of his house in suburban Northridge (where most of his neighbors were unaware a black person lived) congested as motorists slowed down and tried to talk to him. A passing squad car noticed the ruckus and stopped. Pryor kept walking, crying, "I can't stop. I can't stop! I'll die if I stop!"

Then he started jogging. One of the two cops radioed for an ambulance while the other leaped from the car and trotted alongside him, afraid to halt him physically for fear of causing further injury. A dithered Pryor had to be restrained when the ambulance arrived. Yelling and screaming, "Give me a second chance. I know I did wrong but I got some good in me," he fought the rescuer's attempts to place him in the ambulance.

Needless to say, physicians at the nearby burn center saw their patient as a challenge. Third-degree burns covered pretty much everything from the belt line up. Much of his epidermis was simply *gone*. Given a whirlpool bath and swathed mummy-style in antibiotic dressings, Pryor was sedated and put to bed for the night. And doctors were relieved when he lived to see the dawn.

Gary Shaye, a burn center spokesperson, reveals, "Richard is in pain, an extreme amount of pain; but pain, unfortunately, isn't the worst thing we have to deal with in medicine." A burn center staff person who asks not to be identified says, "Even if he makes it through the next few days or weeks, he's in such bad shape that he could go at any time. Burns like these really destroy the body's defense system. People seem to be getting well and then suddenly"—he snaps his fingers—"they die like magic."

This, of course, is but the latest of Pryors heavy scrapes with reality. A native of Peoria, Illinois, and a veteran of between three and six marriages—depending on where you get your information—the thirty-nine-year-old comic had had a rough go of it. To wit, the federal income tax. In 1974, he forgot to pay and was rewarded thereafter with a ten-day-all-expense-paid vacation in jail. Then, at dawn on New Years Day 1978, he got into a beef with his wife and a few of her friends following a party at his house, and, well, one thing led to another and Richard ended up ramming his Mercedes into a Buick occupied by the wife and the pals. Then, in his words, he "killed" the Buick. That is to say, he produced a gun and shot the car. About six times. The car died, Pryor paid another visit to the slammer and his wife moved out.

And, oh yeah, he did some other things, too. Like the time he got into acid and detonated his future in Vegas by saying, "What the fuck am I doing here?" before walking off the stage in the middle of a performance. Then, let's see; well, he broke actor George Memmoli's head with a chair, and then his heart also attacked him. Good old cardiac arrest. And now this.

"What I hear? God damn Ted Kennedy for calling him up. Funny thing, just around election time, too. God! *Damn*! That makes me mad. Blacks, we're an emotional people; now Ted Kennedy figures, 'I give Richard Pryor a call while he's so sick and look at all the votes I'll get.' Makes me sick." The man speaking is Prophet Jennings and he is pissed. A friend and consultant to Pryor off and on for years, Jennings is a painter, filmmaker, philosopher, ex-confidence man, and sportswriter. Right now we're holed up in his West Hollywood apartment. "I'm staying away from that hospital," he says. "Richard don't need me there. All'a hangers on be showin' up now scrapin' and bowin' and prayin' there. 'Cause they know. Richard die and it's gonna be the end of all the freebies."

Jennings's phone rings. It's Dizzy Gillespie, in town for the Playboy Jazz Festival at the Hollywood Bowl. They confer, the skinny and somewhat grizzled prophet pacing his living-room rug, receiver to his ear. The bull is shot and then Jennings hangs up and returns to the subject at hand. "Richard die, it's gonna be some loss. He's the only fellow I know in show business what can make great material just from livin'. That's right. He sit down with you and listen to you talk and then he takes what he hears and just changes it a little bit and all of a sudden, you never heard anything so funny. He picks up on everything. Reads newspapers, books, magazines, sees three, four movies sometimes in a day! Sees movies like a motha-fucka! A great man. Now I don't know anything about any of this drug stuff. That's none of my business. All I know is what a good man he is. I'll give you an example," he says, grimacing as if the memory is still painful. "This party he had one time on Memorial Day at his house. Invited every-body over to roller-skate at his house! Got two trucks fulla roller skates. One truck don't have all the right sizes so he sends for another! He took care of everybody. I've spent all my life studying great. Great athletes, busi-nessmen, musicians, politicians, pimps, artists, and whores—studied 'em all. And there is none greater than Richard Pryor."

John Moffitt, coproducer of ABC's late-night *Fridays*, concurs. "Pryor is a comic genius almost without equal. But he's one of those people who can't avoid extremes." Moffitt *knows*. He was directing the *Ed Sullivan Show* when Pryor made his first appearances. And Moffitt also produced Richard's disastrous NBC show a few years ago. "He always got to be very, very good or [he would] screw up completely.

"An example," Moffitt says as he leans back in his chair in an office whose furniture looks like it was cut directly from standing trees, "is when several years ago he made a deal with NBC to do a variety series. They made him a financial offer he couldn't refuse. Then he realized what he'd committed himself to. Richard writes 90 percent of his own material and he saw that he'd go crazy trying to do that on a weekly basis. He tried to squeeze out of the deal but NBC wanted four shows, minimum. By that time he hated the entire idea. He hated it so bad he cried. He thought TV would ruin his career. Then he got into some battles with the censors over material and the whole thing more or less fell apart. He'd come to shows so blasted that the audience would have to be sent home. One time I was over at his house and showed him a tape of one of his skits and he couldn't even remember having done it."

Morning, June 18. Pryor is mobile. He can walk to the john. To the therapy pool. Nevertheless, doctors at the burn center have announced that he has contracted pneumonia. And that the flesh around his chest is contracting like a "leather tourniquet." He is dying by increments and he is scared. His days are spent in a tiny room filled with body monitors, his only diversion a TV set. In the aftermath of his surgery, he is in even more pain, if that is possible. He spends most of each day reclining on a bed that resembles a foam egg crate. Sedation is minimal and he remains awake from dawn to dark.

Days pass. Pryor's condition does not change. Visitors are banned from his room. Physicians are checking him out at the rate of approximately one doc per organ. Prophet Jennings figures Jimmy Carter will be on the phone himself to Pryor any day now. Meanwhile, pharmacologist Ron Siegel reports that here in Hollywood, guys are so desperate for freebase "they're hawking their Rolexes right off their wrists" in order to grab money to score it.

Your narrator, meanwhile, is miles away, pitching lit Silva Thins, kitchen matches and flaming cigars into a bowl of rum, listening to Mr. Pryor's albums and talking to L.A. police lieutenant Dan Cooke on the telephone. Just for the record, Cooke, who was responsible for the original LAPD report on poor Richard, says that four patrol officers and numerous passersby heard Pryor state that he was freebasing up a storm just before he "exploded." Cooke also states that one of Pryor's physicians, Dr. Jack Grossman, first confirmed the freebase story and then, to put it politely, "changed his story" right after a visit from Pryor's attorney.

What has followed since is lots of Pryor exploitation. His role in publicity spots for the *Wholly Moses* film is suddenly brought to the fore in full force. Freebase is likewise exploited—if you can call it that. What happens is, everybody and his brother is going around wondering aloud, "Wow, where can I get me some of that stuff?" Most people don't even know what it *is*.

Minor mysteries are solved. Pryor evidently was running because, when he was in the army, that's what he was told to do in the event of major burns. Meanwhile, one neat rumor floats—that a man named *Bob* Pryor invented all this freebase paraphernalia and that he is Richard's cousin. A call to paraphernalia manufacturer Don Schar confirms that such a man exists but no one seems to know where he is.

Anyway, officially it's not an issue of freebase anymore at all. It's exploding rum. Shit, now Puerto Rico will probably go broke.

RICHARD PRYOR LIVE(S)

Richard Pryor spent no small amount of time in his monologues chatting about cocaine and death. A lot of this material doesn't translate well to print, depending as it does on his voice, timing, and delivery. Nevertheless, herewith, a Richard Pryor coke-and-death sampler:

- "I snorted cocaine for about fifteen years, my dumb ass. I musta snorted Peru. . . . I coulda bought Peru, all the shit I snorted . . . just give 'em the money up front and had me a piece of property. . . . I started out snortin' little pinches—so I wouldn't get hooked. . . . Can't get hooked on no coke. I got friends been snortin' coke fifteen years, they ain't hooked . . . [but] took me a long time to realize, this shit'll kill ya."

- "My mama did a voice that made me stop snortin' cocaine. . . . [I say] here mamma, I'm puttin it down the toilet . . . $1,600 worth a shit. . . . She found out how much it cost, she got mad: '*Ya dumb muthafucka!* You coulda sold some a that shit back to the man you got it from. I *told* you that stuff make you stupid.' "

- "Leon Spinks: There's a nigger that gets busted for a $1.50 worth of cocaine, a *dollar* and *fifty* cents worth of cocaine. . . . Have you ever *seen* $1.50 worth of cocaine? A-dollar-and-fifty-cents worth of cocaine melt before you open the paper . . . you gotta have a ballistics expert on the scene to examine

205

that kinda shit. . . . And I gotta theory . . . if you buy $1.50 worth of cocaine from any dealer in America, *he* gonna tell on your ass."

- "Death don't give a fuck where it goes . . . you can't fuck around with death, boy. Death gonna take you away and forget it. 'You thinking about dying [to himself, after his heart attack], aren't you? . . . Why didn't you think about that when you were eating the pork, drinkin' that whiskey and snortin' that cocaine?' . . . I woke up in the ambulance . . . lookin' up at all these white people . . . starin' down at me. I say 'Oh God,' I fucked up and ended up in the wrong heaven. . . . They [put me] in intensive care . . . they hook you up with all these wires and shit and you be lookin' like Frankenstein lying there with tubes and shit up your nose. . . . You get to see your life beep away [on the monitors] *do do do do.* If you hear *dooooooooooooooooooo,* cancel Christmas. . . . Life's a bitch ain't it? One day you're here, the next day you're gone."

FADED FLOWERS

The Day They Buried Jimi Hendrix

AL ARONOWITZ

NOVEMBER 1980

I HAD TO TALK Miles Davis into going to Jimi's funeral with me. What the hell, I told him, it was only a few days before he had to be out on the coast anyway and besides, the exposure would be good for him. There'd be a lot of press there. "I don't like funerals," he rasped. "I didn't even go to my mother's funeral." In the end he made the plane with his hairdresser, Vinnie, and Jacki, a girl he had picked up out of the crowd at LaGuardia Airport one day. "She had just come off a plane getting into the city," he explained, introducing her, "and I was catching a plane to fly out on a gig. I saw her on the other side of the lobby and I called her over and told her to get on the plane with me, and she did."

. . . *They buried Jimi Hendrix in the bright afternoon in a hilltop cemetery amid the sobs of people who hadn't really known him for years. It was a cloudless day. Several hundred kids watched from behind ropes. Seattle had never understood Jimi, and now it had to open its earth for him* . . .

Miles and Jimi hadn't known each other too long, but in the short time they did they had gotten pretty tight. Jimi was one of those kids who had grown up worshiping Miles as Miles kept getting younger. For as long as Jimi could remember, Miles had been a legend to him, and it was only when he felt secure enough as a legend himself that he came to sit at Miles's feet and ask Miles to record an album with him. Miles said shit, he'd be happy to do the album but he wanted $50,000 for it. For that much of his soul, he wanted that much money. Like when Sidney Poitier tried to hype Miles into doing the soundtrack for some movie, he told Miles not to worry about the money because the movie would make Miles famous. "Man," Miles answered, "I'm *already* famous!" Miles was a big influence on Jimi. Miles is a teacher, but he learned something from Jimi, too, learned about rhythms and something about phrasing and something about the rock 'n' roll lifestyle. It was Jimi who became the final inspiration to move Miles to renounce the classical forms of jazz—many of those forms created by Miles himself—and to start playing concerts in the rock halls. Miles knew how to stay as young as any kid. But what he wanted to find out was how come a kid like Jimi could make $50,000 in one night when Miles still couldn't make $10.

It had been nine years since Jimi left the vast green valleys that had sent him off in search of a home he could not find and now his flesh was back amid the airplane factories, the strip-mine quarries, the salmon canneries, the steel mills and the breweries that had tried to trap him . . .

Steve Paul was on the plane, Steve, the underground entrepreneur who used to run the Scene at 46th Street and Eighth Avenue, New York's most outrageous cellar rock club. Steve, host to the stars, had become a friend and confidant of Jimi's through the long, hangout nights at the club, where Jimi used to go to get so drunk and drugged he couldn't stand up anymore, and still he'd get onstage and jam 'til dawn. Steve was on the plane with guitar star Johnny Winter, the Albino Whisper, a tender, quiet, bashful sweetheart until he starts picking those Texas roadhouse blues. Steve and Johnny were married, in the music business sense. Steve was Johnny's manager, guiding him to the big time: Mr. Yokel and Mr. Brash. And then there was John Hammond, Jr., who had hired Jimi to play in his band in the Village way back when. It was while Jimi was playing with Johnny Hammond in the Caf au Go Go that Chas Chandler and Michael Jeffrey first laid eyes on the amazing spectacle of Jimi wasting a guitar. Chas was a big star then, one of the Animals. Mike was the Animals' manager. It was from Johnny Hammonds band that they lured Jimi away to England to become the world's next super-act.

. . . Jimi had become one of the greatest stars ever to make music, one of the sweetest poets ever to make the language dance. But back in Seattle all they could bury was the memory of a little black kid who used to play on his father's two-stringed ukulele.

On the plane it was like a party. It *was* a party. We were all Jimi's invited guests, flying first class according to his wishes as expressed by Mike Jeffrey, Jimi's manager, in collaboration with Mike Goldstein, Jimi's press agent. We seat-hopped all the way to Seattle, with the two Johnnys, getting off on getting to know about each other and me tap dancing between Steve and Miles, the Black Prince, who was holding court at the table past the airliner's galley. I guess the real reason I talked Miles into coming was for his company. When we got to Seattle, Steve, the two Johnnys and I went to the Hilton Inn at the airport, where Jimi was paying for our rooms. Miles grabbed a limo to the Washington Plaza, the brand new glass, steel and granite showpiece in the center of town, where he checked Vinnie, Jacki, and himself into a luxury suite. He said he'd pay for his own rooms.

. . . At the Dunlap Baptist Church on broad Rainier Avenue in south Seattle, Mrs. Freddie Mae Gautier, a woman Jimi knew well enough to call Mom, presided at the services and read from Jimi's liner notes on the Buddy Miles album, Expressway to Your Skull: "The express had made the bend, he is coming on down the tracks, shaking steady, shaking funk, shaking feeling, shaking life . . . the conductor says as they climb aboard, small we are going to the electric church, the express took them away and they lived and heard happily and funkily ever after and—uh—excuse me but I think I hear my train coming. . . . "

At the motel, our party from the New York plane was amalgamated into a bigger party. There had been other planes from L.A. and London and even Barry Fay, Jimi's promoter in Denver, had jetted in for the mourning. All of Jimi's sidemen were there, all the roadies and managers who had ridden his express, all the little people along the way, like myself, who had given Jimi whatever breaks they could—the flagmen of his career. Even

Nancy, Mike Jeffrey's ex-old lady, who loved to draw. Jimi hadn't passed her by either. In the end, he wrote her letters. His first album after he died had her drawing of him on the cover. . . .

. . . In the pews were rock stars Johnny Winter, John Hammond, Jr., and Mitch Mitchell and Noel Redding, both of whom had played with Jimi in the Jimi Hendrix Experience. Drummer Buddy Miles, who also had played with Jimi, collapsed at the coffin when it was opened for the invited guests to pay their last respects. Inside the coffin, Jimi looked waxen and unreal . . .

Jimi wouldn't have loved the party so much as the idea of it, hosting a bacchanalia on his own grave. I mean there was plenty of feasting, drinking, smoking, rapping, snorting and picking, with most of the musicians sitting in with the local rock group in the nightclub downstairs. But none of the girls took off any clothes in public and even the craziest of the English contingent kept their manners zipped up. Steve Paul and I had a good time daydreaming about Miles and Johnny Winter touring together. Otherwise, we were less than the pirates we would have been if Jimi were there—Jimi, the eternal swashbuckling buccaneer, with his plumed hats and ferocious presence, and I sometimes could even imagine a sword hanging from his wide leather belt. Not that the party was lame—but what was missing was Jimi. The biggest excitement came out of a rumor spread by press agent Goldstein to the effect that Paul McCartney was going to show up, due any second. The rumor turned out to be so effectively planted that the next day one of the wire-service reporters sent a story out to the world saying that Beatle Paul did indeed attend the funeral.

. . . Outside the church there was a crowd of 200, including reporters, photographers, and TV crews. A half dozen police cars were parked across the street. A dozen police motorcycles were waiting around the corner. Twenty-four limousines lined the curb . . .

In Jimi's absence, Mike Jeffrey played host. This consisted mainly of sitting in a booth in the coffee shop so people who recognized his power could come over and pay their respects. Of course, aside from his power there was very little to recognize in Mike. He certainly didn't stand out in a crowd and unless he was trying to hustle you, you'd have trouble detecting any personal dynamism from his direction. People who talk about him say geniality did not come easy to Mike except for profit. But I found Mike easy. His problem was that he suffered from an occupational hazard among music business managers known as eclipse. When you're managing a star, the bigger he grows, the bigger the shadow he casts over you. The Mike I knew constantly seemed surprised by his success, except in the safety of his own small circle of hand-picked friends. Mike learned early that when you're a star, nothing you say is wrong. Mike, on the other hand, would rather say nothing than say something wrong. If this made him a cold fish, it also made him a better shark. Being invisible helped Mike become a hit manager. But what he wanted most was to be recognized. At the Hilton coffee shop, everybody took a turn coming over to his booth. The party was for Jimi but it was Mike's party. Still suffering from eclipse, he presided over the festivities without ever getting in the way of them. Even beaming, he dimmed his light with the cloak he was most comfortable in: anonymity. To turn Jimi's funeral into a circus was to Mike's advantage because he had a legend to maintain for profit. Jimi still had an album or two in the can and maybe a movie. Jimi was dead but he was still product. I never doubted Mike knew what he was doing. For him the party at the Hilton may have been his finest moment. A year or so later he went down in an airliner that fell into the sea off the coast of Spain. . . .

. . . *Alongside the coffin were a dozen floral sprays, including one six-foot white and lavender guitar made up with velvet strings. The family had chosen Dunlap Baptist Church because Jimi's nine-year-old stepsister, Janie, was a parishioner there. Janie, in fact, was the only member of Jimi's family who went to church . . .*

In the morning I took a cab into the center of the city to meet Miles in his suite at the Washington Plaza. Miles always travels first class. He had sent Vinnie on ahead to the Hendrix house in south Seattle to fix up the family's hairdos for the funeral. Miles will give you his last buck, too, if he cares for you. We sat and had breakfast and then Miles dawdled as he dressed. He was almost ready by the time the chauffeur got back from taking Vinnie to the Hendrix house. On the ride there we talked about how Seattle runs at a pace twenty years behind New York; it felt like we were back in the '50s, maybe even the '40s. It was a comfortable town, but you could see where it could get boring. At Jimi's father's house, a small, gray, one-family home in a mixed residential district, I couldn't keep track of all the members of the family I was introduced to. Jimi's father looked just like Jimi. And Devon was there, dressed in black with a black veil over her face. "Are you playing the merry widow already?" Miles asked her.

. . . James Marshall Hendrix was born in Seattle on November 27, 1942, to James Allen and Lucille Jetter Hendrix. Mrs. Gautier read from the church podium: "His mother preceded him in death. . . . Jimi, as he later became known to all his fans, felt that his hometown did not afford him the outlet to express himself with his musical ability . . ."

Devon was the closest thing Jimi had to an old lady. He left her a widow's pension in his will. She was one of the most beautiful and sensuous of the groupies and one of the most successful, too. I first met her in the '60s, I forget with whom, but whenever a rock star came to New York, the chances were you'd find Devon in his hotel room. They used to recommend her to one another. Her sex was overwhelming. Somebody once told me she was a teacher and I used to wonder of what. In all the times Devon and I talked to each other, we really never got to know what we were all about. We would just gossip. It got to be amazing how her relationship with Jimi survived. She could never totally belong to anybody, just as Jimi couldn't, but somehow they came to depend on each other. I saw her a few times after Jimi died. She was hard not to love. I was writing a column for the *New York Post* in those days and she kept asking me, "When are you going to write a column about me?" And I kept saying to her, "When are you going to do something?" I think it was in March of 1972 that she took an OD and died.

. . . On the podium Mrs. Gautier read from a poem sent anonymously by a student at Garfield High School, where Jimi had been kicked out for sassing a teacher who had become annoyed because he was holding hands with a white girl. "So long, our Jimi," Mrs. Gautier recited. "You answered the questions we never dared to ask, painted them in colorful circles and threw them at the world . . . they never touched the ground but soared up to the clouds . . ."

After Jimi's funeral, I went to Monterey for the pop festival and then spent some time with Miles in San Francisco, where he was working a club. I was backstage at Winterland with the Grateful Dead and the Jefferson Airplane when word came that Janis had been discovered dead in her motel room in L.A. I didn't know what it all meant then and I still don't know, but even as I write this there's a moth beating itself to death on the electric bulb of my lamp. And in a little plastic cup on my desk near my typewriter there are two dried-out flowers, faded blue, from Jimi Hendrix's graveside.

August 1980 $2.50

HIGHTIMES

Will success spoil Cheech & Chong? Of course. See page 32.

High Times #60, August 1980

A ROTTEN INTERVIEW WITH JOHNNY LYDON

Slashing Through the Public Image

ANN LOUISE BARDACH

NOVEMBER 1980

JOHNNY LYDON ALMOST SINGLE-handedly defined the "punk" in punk rock. Not the textbook version coined by Marsh and Bangs in Creem over a decade ago to describe a certain late-'60s recording sound that has once again become fashionable, but the nightmare visions of brain-damaged apocalypse kids bent on demolishing everything and everyone in their path. He was the vile and repulsive Johnny Rotten, lead vocalist of England's most cursed and celebrated Sex Pistols. Rotten was too good a name for the astounding character he created in this guise, as he built one of the most sensational images in rock history. His antistardom, right dawn to the green teeth he cherished as a symbol of his foulness, became his calling card as he cursed out every rock band, TV commentator, record-company employee and virtually every reporter he ever met.

The Sex Pistols disintegrated in one awesome, vulgar swoop after their brief, aborted 1978 U.S. tour when bassist Sid Vicious died of an overdose. Rotten reverted to his given name, John Lydon, and formed Public Image Ltd. His character hasn't changed much in exchanges with the press, as witnessed by his recent battle with Tom Snyder on the *Tomorrow* show. It took Ann Bardach, whose coverage of the Vicious murder case gave her an international reputation, to get Lydon talking. The results are pretty interesting . . .

High Times: Can you describe the transition you went through, from being the ultimate media-contrived hype product, to being an artist, performer—a musician who calls the shots himself.

Lydon: I'm not an artist or musician. And I definitely don't perform.

High Times: We go from the ultrahype of the Sex Pistols to—

Lydon: Well, I got nauseous. I had enough of that. Just a farce.

High Times: Are you unhappy with Virgin Records?

Lydon: Yes. I'm totally unhappy with all record companies. They're bullshit. They're liars—third-rate frauds. They've no fucking sense of anything, no perception. They don't want to take risks. Which is why their crummy industry is falling to pieces. I mean, they're frequently moaning about album sales dropping. Why shouldn't they be. They're just selling the same old dirge forever and a day. In the last fifteen years music has changed practically not at all. How many retreads of Chuck Berry are still going on? All those long-haired, platform-booted, flared-jeaned, fucking imbeciles. That still goes on. And that's fucking old as the hills. God! Grandad Rock!

High Times: I was going to ask you about that—how you felt about all the renaissance of music from the '50s and '60s.

Lydon: It's vile! I don't need history. I can go to a museum for that, thank you very much. And they did it so much better the first time around anyway. They made their mistakes. And there's people desperately trying to do the same thing.

High Times: How do you like the revivals of two-tone groups, girl groups, and all the '50s music? Do you see it as inspired reinterpretation, or just regurgitation?

Lydon: Just farcical imitation. Well, I mean, we all know there's going to be a psychedelic revival, *[laughs]* right? It's so obvious, it just has to happen.

High Times: Are you looking forward to that?

Lydon: No! It is going to be the worst Woodstock, part two. Woodshack.

High Times: But you don't see reggae, which you like, as being part of the '50s revivalist music movement.

Lydon: I don't mind reggae, I don't mind a bit of jazz, I don't mind classical, I don't mind cocktail music or cabaret. I don't mind rock in its place. I don't mind anything. It's fun. Just so long as they don't pretend it's the be-all, end-all of the universe. Which is the way it seems to be.

High Times: The Clash?

Lydon: The clap.

High Times: The clap is the Clash?

Lydon: Same thing. They're both a disease.

High Times: You told a story once in a piece in the *New Musical Express,* where Joe Strummer comes over to your flat in London and shows you a book in which Bernie Rhodes [the Clash's first manager] had underlined passages for him.

Lydon: Yeah, Bernie used to give them Marxist theories and stuff like that. Books on it. And he'd underline certain lines and sentences. Then they'd write about it.

High Times: Did you get to see any of the titles of these books?

Lydon: Oh, I don't really know about that dreariness. He [Strummer] was a wank for even considering it. "Here Joe write a song about this, I've underlined it for you." Such trash. What can you do?

High Times: Why do you think Strummer was interested in Bernie Rhodes' Marxist theories?

Lydon: I don't think he was. I don't think he knew what he was getting involved in. If you look at the Clash and its various succession of

217

managers, you'd notice that they've adopted the styles given to them by those managers. They are very easily influenced people. They don't seem to have direction of their own. I don't like that.

High Times: You don't see any value in their songs?

Lydon: No. None at all. Completely ineffectual. Waste of time. Politics was always a definite thing to avoid.

High Times: Are most of your friends musicians?

Lydon: No. None of them. No one in the band is a musician. We all hate that term.

High Times: Excuse me. What are you?

Lydon: I'm not sure. Something close to factory workers. Machinists. Skilled operators.

High Times: Do you work for a living?

Lydon: Uh huh. Who doesn't? Mind you, I'd love not to work for a living.

High Times: You wouldn't want to be or live like Mick Jagger?

Lydon: Oh, *god,* no! It's not doing him much good, is it?

High Times: Yet you're very pragmatic.

Lydon: What's that?

High Times: Sensible.

Lydon: Yes. I'm definitely not an intellectual. I keep getting asked, am I an intellectual or am I a poet. And all that dreariness. All those labels just reek of boredom. Bookworming. Ooooh! Ugh!

High Times: In other words, you think of an intellectual as being a poser, like Joe Strummer leafing through Bernie Rhodes's crib notes on dialectic materialism.

Lydon: Dia- what?

High Times: Marxist theory.

Lydon: All right, you backed me into a corner. I give up. *[Laughs.]*

High Times: What college did you go to?

Lydon: Kingsway, CFE. The College of Formal Education.

High Times: And shortly thereafter, you ran into Bernie Rhodes?

Lydon: Wobble!

High Times: Oh you met [Jah] Wobble [Public Image's bassist] at college, that's right. And then one day you're in the Sex Store and Bernie Rhodes comes in and sees you miming to records.

Lydon: No. I was insulting Malcolm McLaren when Bernie was there.

High Times: McLaren turns around and says, "You too can be a star!"?

Lydon: Malcolm never spoke to me.

High Times: What did Bernie say?

Lydon: "You're unpleasant enough to be in a band."

High Times: What did you say?

Lydon: I just did it. To me it was just a huge joke. I really didn't give a shit, and it struck me as being mighty humorous that someone could want *me* as a singer.

High Times: Never occurred to you to be in a rock band?

Lydon: Never. You see, I've always hated rock music and that was my chance to really wreck it.

High Times: You hated rock music. Then what kind of music did you listen to?

Lydon: Anything but. Anything but that long-haired dreariness.

High Times: Name a few. I'm trying to remember what was before long-haired dreariness. Short-haired dreariness?

Lydon: Brylcreem dreariness!

High Times: So you stopped listening after Buddy Holly?

Lydon: I never listened to even that. I hated it. Besides, I was too young for that.

High Times: You never listened to the Beatles, the Rolling Stones, or the Who?

Lydon: Oh, no. I couldn't bear them.

High Times: When you were fourteen years old, you never listened to them?

Lydon: I did not like them. No. It's so detached. They were in a dream world. Just didn't want to know about them.

High Times: You said in an interview that you would like to change the music industry and "this time [you] would do it right," as opposed to the Sex Pistols. You said "it would take years." When you said "change the music industry," how?

Lydon: Well it was a bit of a rash statement, I admit. That I could change the entire industry in one fell swoop. But I'm making a bash at it. I could *only* fail.

High Times: How would you do it? You still need Warner Brothers here, which is one of the largest multinationals.

Lydon: They are seen here merely to distribute our records, nothing else.

High Times: They're lackeys then, for the Public Image?

Lydon: Yes. And they don't like us treating them like this. But that's just too bad.

High Times: Did you ever hear that Warner Brothers is the mob?

Lydon: Uh huh. I've been told that. They must be curious then, how we got the gall to say "shove it."

High Times: Public Image taking on the biggest mob in the music world?

Lydon: Horrible fun. And all we can do is lose, right? That is if the worst comes. Oh, we won't lose. I've no intention of losing. I never back a dead horse. I look a bit like a horse as well, don't I? *[Sings:]* "I'm getting near the winning post, get out the way."

High Times: So, you were always listening to American black music?

Lydon: Yeah. Tamber what from the early skin days. We were skin heads when all the hippies in the universities were going to see the Who. It meant nothing to us.

High Times: When Malcolm McLaren said, "You too can be a rock and roll star," you said "why not"?

Lydon: It was never put like that. I had no faith in the Pistols that amounted to anything other than a damp fart. The prospect looked pretty grim. Oh, it was something to do, and then it got so huge. I saw the humor in it for a while, and then it crawled up inside my ass. I felt embarrassed about being alive. We just fell apart when we got to America. Too much of everything.

High Times: Do you think Malcolm McLaren was ever honest, at any point?

Lydon: No, and he had very little to do with the Pistols as well. That was what was the farce of it. He was always a remote, distant figure.

High Times: But he made a lot of money.

Lydon: Uh huh. He wasn't too remote about that. He sent me the tax bills too. That was real good of him. And when the Pistols broke up, they left me stranded in fucking L.A. Sorry—San Francisco. No ticket, no plane ticket and twenty dollars and no hotel. So there I was in a hotel lobby with a suitcase [laughs] like a fool. Destitute, as usual. Fucking poncing money off journalists.

High Times: You came back to New York though?

Lydon: Yeah, I had to.

High Times: Have you talked to Malcolm McLaren since then?

Lydon: *[Snickers.]* Words wouldn't be passed between us, I'll tell you that. Quick-firing metal projectiles would be aimed at his direction. He doesn't deserve to live. I feel very righteous about that one.

High Times: After the Pistols broke up, and Sid had this murder rap—

Lydon: Uh huh. It was so dismal.

High Times: Malcolm was in town [New York]—

Lydon: Yeah, see how Malcolm helped him. He got one hell of a failure of a lawyer [F. Lee Bailey]. I never got through. Well, Sid wanted to talk to me. But his old dear never put me through.

High Times: His who?

Lydon: His mother. She's a bitch.

High Times: Wasn't she arrested?

Lydon: In jail?

High Times: I heard she got busted for smuggling dope back.

Lydon: Yeah, she did. I don't know what's happened about it.

High Times: I heard she got busted again a few months ago.

Lydon: Probably, that's highly likely with her. Right irresponsible human being. I remember she bought him a pack of needles once for his birthday. With substance in white packets. Never liked to be quoted on that one.

High Times: What birthday was that?

Lydon: This was years ago.

High Times: When you were still in the band or when you were in school?

Lydon: Before then. You see, he'd cleaned himself up.

High Times: My understanding is that Malcolm was trying to manage a murder.

Lydon: That's how I understood it. Yeah, that's how it appeared to me.

High Times: Malcolm was very cooperative with all the American reporters, who knew nothing.

Lydon: Our Malcolm loves dealing with people who don't know nothing. That way he can shine.

High Times: Where do you think Sid went wrong? At what point did he go from being the kid you knew in school, a fairly nice bloke, to a total disaster?

Lydon: He believed in his own publicity. He fell for it, hook, line, and sinker. He was called Vicious because he was such a wanker. Really, he couldn't fight his way out of a crisp bag. He'd lose all the time.

High Times: Then why did you ask him to join the band and fire Glen Matlock?

Lydon: Because Matlock was into the Beatles. *[Laughs.]* He had nice melodies. Sid was into no melody whatsoever, which struck me as a damn good right conclusion. I mean, so what if he couldn't play when he joined—Wobble couldn't play when we [Public Image Ltd.] started. He learned as he went along. That's what we all do.

High Times: Yeah, that's what you did. You began the Sex Pistols as a joke and you learned to sing. Then you started to love it.

Lydon: I perfected the joke and it backfired, I must admit. Slightly like scrambled egg on face. Sunny side up.

High Times: You say Sid went wrong when he started believing his own publicity, as opposed to doing a lot of junk.

Lydon: Maybe that was the reason. He just lacked humor, took it all too serious. I don't think it deserves a lot of sentences.

High Times: Even posthumously?

Lydon: Well, heaven! Pretty wanky way to go.

High Times: By a drug overdose?

Lydon: Yeah. So dreary and typical, isn't it?

High Times: Was he using junk before he joined the Pistols?

Lydon: No. Speed then.

High Times: Which you approve of?

Lydon: I don't approve of nothing.

High Times: I mean favor.

Lydon: No, I wouldn't advise anyone to take any kind of chemical.

High Times: Who do you think brought him into the realm of junk, Nancy Spungen?

Lydon: Yes. There was that horrible movement from New York to London, and they brought their dirty culture with them.

High Times: And that was the beginning of the end for Sid?

Lydon: He was impressed by the decadence of it all. God! So dreary. Too many Lou Reed albums I blame it on.

High Times: Do you think there are drugs that are useful?

Lydon: No. They just put off what you've got to face sooner or later: blandness.

High Times: Do you know that book written by Julie Burchill and Tony Parson, *The Boy Looked at Johnny*, that has your photo on its cover?

Lydon: Uh huh.

High Times: Burchill and Parsons advocate speed. About it being a useful drug. There's an entire chapter on the benefits of amphetamines.

Lydon: Well, that's just stupidity.

High Times: They credit some of your genius to your intake of amphetamine.

Lydon: *[Laughs.]* That's a typical journalistic approach. I mean, that's all they are, toss-bag journalists, desperately trying to get in on something.

High Times: They came up with a very interesting unknown scientific "fact" that amphetamine raises the IQ.

Lydon: I doubt if that's true.

High Times: Did they ever discuss this with you?

Lydon: Tony Parsons I've met briefly, for about two minutes. He was shaking like a leaf. Snorting lines. He just looked like a pathetic character to me. He didn't strike me as having a high IQ.

High Times: So you don't see any utilitarian value in using drugs?

Lydon: Each to his own. It's just as simple as that I would never advise anyone to do anything.

High Times: You say you can't see anything remotely political like the Clash.

Lydon: No. What I really mean is naive political. I mean, they're spouting these theories and not knowing what the fuck they're talking about. And *that* I find offensive.

High Times: Because they don't have the academic muscle to personally read it and figure it out themselves.

Lydon: They don't even read all of it. It's just what they're shown. They're very narrow-minded. Go into it totally or not at all. I can't bear people not knowing things totally. Just spouting out ignorant, half-assed statements that don't mean fuck-all. I mean, you've got to understand what you're talking about.

High Times: But say in your case you sang "Anarchy in the U.K."

Lydon: That's not political.

High Times: Yes it is.

Lydon: How? Anarchy is a mind game for the middle class. It doesn't mean anything.

High Times: It was very threatening to the Labor government at the time.

Lydon: I never thought so.

High Times: Threatening enough to get you bruised.

Lydon: No. That was "God Save the Queen." That's what got me bruised.

High Times: For all intents and purposes, it *was* political in that it frightened the authorities to action. It brought the whole police department down on you.

Lydon: So what. They're still coming down on me. I just got raided recently.

High Times: Where?

Lydon: Oh, they've been around quite a lot, the police. They kicked the house to pieces. And then they go off and wait for another month. In the last couple of months I've been raided on suspicion of bomb making, of hiding runaway juveniles and, last week, for drugs. They've raided me for drugs and found *nothing*. Not even *one* marijuana seed, and it made me very happy. They done me instead for a gas canister. I have to put the case forward until I get back to England or else I wouldn't have got my visa.

High Times: So essentially you had to plead guilty. Which you would not have done if you didn't need a visa.

Lydon: So this might be my last time in the U.S. of A.

High Times: As a kid, what were the charges against you?

Lydon: Oh, silly things. Minor burglaries, jaywalking. Out on the streets late at night.

High Times: Does it make you feel paranoid?

Lydon: No. It's just a way of life. It's always been there and it just gets worse.

High Times: It strikes me that you take things very calm, one at a time.

Lydon: You have to, God! I couldn't be one of those people who sit down and think, "God, if I go out I'll arrested." That would be terrible. Wow.

High Times: Do you have any prophecies for the world for the next ten years?

Lydon: We're damn lucky if there will be a next ten years.

High Times: What do you see yourself doing in the next ten years should the holocaust not happen?

Lydon: Being very embarrassed.

High Times: How old are you now?

Lydon: I'm twenty-four.

High Times: You'll be thirty-four.

Lydon: Oh. I'll have to move over for the next big mouth. It won't be me ranting and raving then, will it? I'll too old then and past it.

High Times: Have you seen any of the Pistol movies, like *The Great Rock 'n' Roll Swindle?*

Lydon: I've seen the *Swindle,* yeah.

High Times: How about that?

Lydon: What about it? Really, it's not worth spending money on. It's very dreary. It's just Malcolm's ego, isn't it.

High Times: Were you ever enthusiastic about making that movie?

Lydon: Never. I had nothing to do with that film.

High Times: How about *D.O.A.?*

Lydon: What's that?

High Times: A movie about the Sex Pistols.

Lydon: No. I don't know about that.

High Times: You say you read newspapers and magazines, which ones?

Lydon: All magazines. I like *Omni*.

High Times: What else do you like?

Lydon: Well, any kind of glossy magazine.

High Times: Do you read *Rolling Stone*?

Lydon: No. That's so boring. Oh God! What in earth do they got in mind with that rag? *That's* showing its age.

High Times: Do you think people will rely upon drugs and sex more as we approach impending nuclear war?

Lydon: When I get my seven-minute warning, I'm going to go pretty over the top, I think. Do it all in one glorious swoop. Everything all at once. I have the supply ready here, put that way.

High Times: What's your favorite day or night?

Lydon: Monday morning. I watch others go to work.

High Times: Do you think you'll always want to live in England?

Lydon: Yeah.

High Times: Does your family live in London?

Lydon: I've got family in England, Ireland, and Canada.

High Times: Are you close with your family?

Lydon: Umhum. There's three others. All boys. They are all younger.

High Times: Oh, you're the first one?

Lydon: [Whispers.] Yes. I was the experiment. Then they decided to have some more.

High Times: Do you want to have children at some time?

Lydon: No, definitely not.

High Times: Why not?

Lydon: One of me is quite enough.

High Times: Can you envision yourself as an old man?

Lydon: No. I can't conceive myself being old.

High Times: No old age and no progeny.

Lydon: What?

High Times: Children.

Lydon: No. Well, I'm happy. I wouldn't wish it on anyone else. I couldn't cope with kids. It would drive me nuts. I'm totally irresponsible. Me as daddy. I'd be rotten.

High Times: I don't believe that.

Lydon: I'd like to get married to Dolly Parton, though. Maybe I'd consider it then. "Dolly Rotten?" God! What a glorious name.

High Times: Were you religious?

Lydon: No.

High Times: But you were raised Catholic?

Lydon: Yeah, that's enough to make you not religious.

High Times: But you know what they say about Catholic boys: always an altar boy.

Lydon: I never thought of that. I was almost an altar boy when I was young. But the priest who wanted me died. Definitely an act of God.

High Times: How did you feel about getting scooped up by the National Front a few years ago?

Lydon: Scooped up! They hate me. They always did. Right from the start. Yes, right from the very beginning. The National front, just after *Anarchy* was recorded, had their magazine, *Spearhead,* with its front page a picture of a gorilla and underneath written "Johnny Rotten—the White Nigger." That's their opinion of me and they can go shove themselves.

High Times: Did you ever receive any phone threats from them?

Lydon: Oh yeah, lots. But if people mean to do you harm, they don't let you know about it first.

High Times: How do you stay sane?

Lydon: I drink permanently.

High Times: Is that the only way?

Lydon: It lets me stay asleep a lot. What's wrong with being asleep on and off? I suppose there's not too much to get up for, is there?

High Times: Do you get a lot of groupies?

Lydon: No. No one wants to know us. If we do get any, they're fat and ugly. We get a lot of loonies: lunatics and dangerous people. Like one who commits suicide in your presence.

High Times: Has anyone ever done that?

Lydon: Tried to.

High Times: What did you do?

Lydon: Push them out the front door. "Don't do it here. Away!"

High Times: One last question: Do you have any advice for our world leaders?

Lydon: Drop dead! Move over!

ME AND BIG JOE

Michael Bloomfield

December 1980

IT WAS THE EARLY '60s at a Chicago nightclub called The Blind Pig that I first met Joe Lee Williams. He was a short and stout and heavy-chested man, and he was old even then. He wore cowboy boots and cowboy hat and pleated pants pulled way up high, almost to his armpits. Just visible above the pants was a clean white shirt, and a tiny blue bow tie decorated his bullish neck. He played a nine-string Silvertone guitar and to keep others from copying his style he'd put it up in a very strange tuning. I was familiar with all stringed instruments and eventually worked that guitar every way possible, but I never learned to play it and to this day don't know the tuning he used.

Big Joe, as he was often called, had been a well-known artist in the '30s and '40s and wrote one of the real standards in the blues field, "Baby Please Don't Go," a song cut by, among many others, Mose Allison and Muddy Waters. At the time I met Joe Lee I was trying to meet as many blues artists as were alive in America, because music was the field I most wanted to pursue and blues was the music I most wanted to learn. So between sets that night I talked with Joe, or at least I tried to—he lacked teeth and had a thick pineywoods accent and at first I found him nearly indecipherable. I had to ask him to repeat himself over and over, but he didn't seem to mind and after a while I caught on somewhat to his speech. He told me Crawford, Mississippi, was his birthplace, and that since the early '30s he'd done nothing but hobo around the country with his guitar. Now, most bluesmen I'd met had two jobs—they'd play and sing nighttimes, but during the day they kept up a straight gig of one kind or another. But Joe never did that—he traveled and he played, and that was it.

Joe and I got along very well that night, and as he packed his guitar away after his last set he invited me to visit him sometime. He was living in the basement of a record store on Chicago's Near North Side and I dropped in to see him often. The shop, which specialized in blues and jazz, was run by a very odd guy named Kaercher, and Joe, down in his basement, had a rather strange relationship with him. Physically, Kaercher was a cross between Steve Allen and Peter Sellers, with none of their good features and all of their worst; sexually he was ambiguous, and politically he was bizarre. Along with the store he owned a record company, and though I was never sure he knew a good record from a bad one, he was straight with the musicians he recorded and had a real reverence for their art and skill. But Joe and he would have many fights, sometimes due to Kaercher's obtuse nature and at other times to Joe's drinking. Joe would get a few beers or a little hard liquor in him (Peppermint Schnapps and Gordon's Gin were his choices) and you wouldn't be dealing with a normal man—he couldn't talk coherently and nothing made sense to him. Behind larger amounts of alcohol he could get physically violent. But as nasty as he could get when he was drunk, that's how compassionate and big-hearted he could be when he was sober.

As I got to know Joe better we became more and more friendly and he began to assume a sort of paternal sort of role in the lives of me and my wife, Susan. His manner around her was touching. He was a real Southern gentleman—very gallant and sweet. Soon he began to carry me to see old friends of his. I'd say, "Listen, Joe, d'you know where Tampa Red's living?" And Joe'd reply, "Sure I know where Tampa's at—I'll take you on by right now." And we'd go. Tampa Red was a singer whose career had begun in the '20s and who'd become very popular in the '30s and '40s. I knew his records well. He'd had a big hit called "Tight Like That," and had recorded with the man who is now the king of all gospel publishing, Thomas G. Dorsey. But Tampa, by the time I met him, was just a frail, wizened little man whose hands shook uncontrollably. He had an expensive old Gibson in a case beneath his bed, but all he could do was show it to us—his hands wouldn't let him play.

Another singer Joe took me to go see was Kokomo Arnold, who had also recorded in the '30s and '40s. His big hit was "Kokomo Blues," a song about that bright city, that seven-light city, that sweet old Kokomo. He told me I was the first one to ask about his music since the early '50s, when some people from a jazz magazine in Belgium had come to see him with Charlie Musselwhite. Kokomo'd had to have much of his insides cut out, and he was just a shadow of the man I'd seen with Joe.

Joe also carried me to see Tommy McClennon, who recorded for RCA Victor in the '40s. We visited him in Cook County Hospital, where he was dying of TB. He was just a skeleton, but his eyes were like hot coals burning at you. And his music was like that, too—it had a savage, burning sound. He was a fierce man.

Then there was Jazz Gillum, who was just about the craziest man I'd ever met. Joe took me to see him on a very uncomfortable summer day, with both the temperature and humidity up in the '90s—the kind of day when doing nothing makes you sweat and dirt forms under your fingernails for no reason at all. We drove out to the West Side and stopped in front of a little house, just a shanty, really. When we entered the place I thought I'd gone to Hell—as hot as it was outside, it was insufferably worse within. All the windows were shut down tight, and standing beside a woodstove, clad in a huge brown overcoat, Gillum stoked a raging fire. He was sweating profusely and was extremely paranoid. He'd written the very successful "Key to the Highway," and had never gotten the publishing money for it, and he was afraid I'd come to steal his other tunes. And we didn't stay long enough to change his mind.

Eventually I sat in so many bars and met so many singers that the South and West sides of Chicago ceased to be new territory for me. Joe, from his travels, knew blues singers from all over the country and when he suggested that we make some field trips I was quick to agree. The first jaunt we took was to Milwaukee so I could sit in with Sonny Boy Williamson. Now, this Sonny Boy thing can be confusing. The original Sonny Boy's name was John Lee Williamson. He was a big star for Bluebird Records and recorded many songs that Joe liked to sing, such as "Decoration Day," "I Can Hear My Black Name Ringing," and "Katie Mae." The second Sonny Boy Williamson's name was Rice Miller. He was a much older man than the original Sonny Boy and had been recording even longer, but he didn't become famous until after the original Sonny Boy died—stabbed by a woman in his Chicago doorway.

It was this second Sonny Boy, Rice Miller, that we went to Milwaukee to see. We found him in a funky lounge in the black section of town. He was an old man—God only knows how old he was. He had a baleful stare and a sour mouth, and he'd check you out with cold, squinty eyes that said you didn't matter. He sat at a table among the customers with his harmonicas and mike and old hotel towel, and to start the song he'd spit blood into the towel and then blow a little harp. He wouldn't tell the band what song or key or anything, and they'd just stagger in behind him. He didn't care if they were there or not—he'd just tap his feet and play along by himself. I wasn't real crazy about approaching him to play, but I did, and he asked me if I knew, "Help Me," which was a hit at that time. I said, "Yeah, I believe it's like 'Green Onions,' " and he said, "That's right, go ahead and play." So I sat in with him and the people seemed to like us.

Big Joe was at a table with some older, heavy-set black women, and he was getting drunk with them. After Sonny Boy's last set he came up to me and said, "Michael, there's some real fine leg sitting here." Now, besides being of advanced years, these women had a combined weight of several tons and didn't fit my idea of good leg at all. But as an inducement to stick around and maybe go home with one or two of these women, Joe said, "These ladies have their womanhoods way up high on their bellies." Considering their weight, I could see how that might be true, but I told him, "Joe, I don't believe this is something I want to get into—I think we'd best head back to Chicago." Joe got pretty irascible at that, but didn't really wig out, and we made it on home okay.

"Drive me down by Gary," Joe said one day, "and I'll carry you to see Lightnin' Hopkins—him an' me is old, old friends." So Joe and I and Charlie Musselwhite and Roy Ruby, who for a time played bass with Barry Goldberg and Steve Miller, climbed into Roy's car and headed east to Indiana. Actually, we had to go out beyond Gary, into the countryside, where eventually we came to a barbeque pit, or roadhouse. This kind of place was also known as a barrelhouse or chockhouse, and seems to have pretty much disappeared from the North, and maybe the South, too. The roadhouse was run by an older black couple and consisted of a barbeque pit in front and a large bare room in back. This back room was heated only by body heat—when there were enough people in the room, the place got warm. And that night it was hot.

Joe had gotten himself a center seat and was buying drinks and ordering people around when the opening act, J.B. Lenoir and His Big Band, came on. J.B. was a short man in a zebra-striped coat that hung down low behind him. He had straight hair, but it wasn't up in a high process, it was slicked down flat against his head. He looked a little like a seal. The band he had backing him featured three horn players of such advanced stages of age and inebriation that they had to lean against one another to avoid collapse. J.B. played guitar and sang through a microphone on a rack around his neck. He had a fine, almost feminine voice and was a fine singer. He danced through the crowd as he played and sang, and Joe sat nodding his approval—he liked J.B. quite a bit.

Then old Lightning came on, and he was as sly and slick and devilish as a man could be. He had a real high black conk on his head and wore black, wrap-around shades. He had only a drummer behind him, and when the blue lights hit that conk—man, that was all she wrote. Lightnin' ran his numbers and everything was cool.

When the set ended Joe went over to Lightning to say hello, but before he could get a word out Lightning said, "What are you doing here? I'm the star of this show, you know." "I know you're the star," Joe replied, "and we don't mean no trouble. I carried these white boys down here to see you, and I just wanted to pay my respects." So Lightning mellowed and bought Joe a drink, but that was a mistake, because Joe didn't need it. Sure enough, Joe got rummed out and quarreled with Lightning, and we got turned out of the place. When we got to the car, Charlie hustled into the back seat and pretended to fall asleep. I rode shotgun and feigned sleep, too. Roy was driving and Joe was between us, trying to direct Roy where to carry him. Joe was hard enough to understand sober, but drunk you had no chance at all—it was just syllabic noise.

What Joe had a penchant for doing when he was drunk was to look up distant relatives of his, sisters-in-law or whatever, and see if their husbands were working a nightshift so he could screw their women. So he had us driving through all the ghetto areas of Gary, Hammond, and East Chicago, ranting and roaring at Roy, who was unable to understand a word of what he was saying—he might as well have been speaking Tagalog. And Roy would look over and say, "Michael! I know you're not asleep—you've got to tell me how to get home!" And when I wouldn't respond he'd turn to Charlie and say, "Charlie, goddamn it, wake up—you've got to show us how to get out of here!" But Charlie'd just lie low, too. Joe's eyes were tiny, squincy red slits, and we weren't about to go up against that moaning, cursing, grousing, heaving indecipherable angriness. If Joe wasn't ready to return to Chicago, that was it—we weren't going. And we didn't—not that night anyway. But as dawn finally broke over the smokestacks and railyards and cracking towers of northern Indiana, Joe directed Roy home.

Around the Fourth of July, Joe took it into his head to visit some people of his down in St. Louis. The owner of the record store, Kaercher, thought it was a good idea. "Yeah, Joe," he said, "you go down there and be a talent scout. Take a tape recorder along and say you represent my company. Record some people, see what kind of deal we can make and bring back some tapes." Joe needed a ride, as usual, and asked if I wanted to go along. Well, I'd begun to have doubts and trepidations about taking these field trips with Joe, because once outside Chicago my friends and I were pretty much at his mercy, and you could get into some strange situations with the guy. But St. Louis was new territory for me, and I knew there were supposed to be some famous old blues men living down there, so I said okay. I called up another pal of mine, George Mitchell, and asked him to join us. George was a college student, originally from Atlanta, and had once worked at the record store. He wore those Kingston Trio-type button-down shirts and had a real neat Ivy League haircut. He really dug blues, and while in his teens had gotten to know many people in the South. He got along well with older black people, and especially well with Big Joe, so I thought he'd be an ideal guy to have along.

The drive to St. Louis was real nice. Wonderful, in fact. Joe talked to George and me about things from thirth years ago as though they'd happened that morning. He reminisced about Robert Johnson and Willie McTell and Blind Boy Fuller, he told how Sunnyland Slim had helped Muddy Waters get a record contract and explained how Big Bill had gotten rich. Being with Joe was being with a history of the blues—you could see him as a man and you could see him as a legend. He couldn't read a word of English and he couldn't write a word, but he had America memorized. He was a wise man in so many ways—from forty years of hiking roads and riding rails he was wise to every highway and byway and roadbed in the country, and wise to every city and country and township they led to. Joe was part of a rare and vanished breed—he was a wanderer and a hobo and a blues singer, and he was an awesome man.

It was nightfall when we got to St. Louis. It was a Fourth of July weekend and it was hot—lord, it was hot. I couldn't imagine what the days would be like. The first place we stopped was the home of Joe's sister, or sister-in-law, or step-sister, or something. When we walked in, there were little kids sleeping on every available surface, so we all sat down in the kitchen and Joe said to his relative, "Now you know I play the guitar, and this boy Michael do too, so we'll play some while we visit." He brought out his guitar and, with it, a bottle of schnapps. I took George aside and said, "Man, we better not let this guy start drinking. It's a long weekend, and if he starts now his brains'll fly right out the window—we'll have a lunatic on our hands the whole time!" But Joe was set on drinking, and when he said, "Michael, why don't you have a little taste?" I went ahead and put some down. I figured if Joe was going to get drunk and go crazy I was going to get drunk and go crazy right along with him. So I drank as much gin and schnapps and beer and wine as I could get in me that night, and I sat with Joe and played the blues. And man, I got sick. For the first time in my life I got king-hill, shit-faced, tore-up drunk. I puked all over the house. I puked in the kitchen, I puked in the hall, I puked on the sofa and I puked on the wall. I was just rolling in puke—I was sick, sick, sick.

I woke up the next morning to find Joe standing over me. He had stayed up all night drinking and he was more than drunk—he was on a bender.

His nostrils were flared and his eyes were red and runny. A barbeque fork was in his hand and on it was a pig nose, and hot grease from the nose was dripping on my chest. He opened his mouth and his schnapps breath hit me in a wave. "Snoots, snoots," he shouted, "I promised you fine barbeque, and snoots is what we got!" My head was throbbing and my stomach still queasy, and when I looked up and saw this horribly fat and greasy pig nose an inch from my face, I lurched out of bed and threw up again. Joe began to curse me. "Man, you done puked all the damn night and into the mornin' an' now you pukin' up again! Can't you hold that stomach down?!" And I slunk out the house with George, who wasn't on top of the world himself, to try and find something to settle my stomach. Joe stood roaring at us as we left. "Where do you think you is, you think you home in Chicago now? You *ain't* home in Chicago now, an' those niggers out there'll kill ya!" But my head and stomach were already killing me, so I took my chances on the street. And it was the funkiest street I'd ever seen. I thought I'd seen funk when I'd gone out to Jazz Gillum's in Chicago, with the sealed house and blazing fire—but this section of St. Louis we were in made Gillum's shanty look like a penthouse on Lakeshore Drive. But we found a drugstore with no problem and got some aspirin and bicarbonate and Coca-Cola, and they seemed to help a little, but they sure didn't help a lot.

When George and I got back to the house, Joe was on the porch with his relatives and their friends, strumming his guitar. And he was crazy. Every woman who came by he clawed at, and every man who passed by he argued with. If there was a woman in the street he'd shout, "Say sweet mama, come on over sweet mama, an' set down your daddy's knee!" And she'd look around and see a seventy-year old, three hundred-pound man yelling at her, and she'd get a funny look on her face and keep on walking, maybe a little faster than before. Finally, I said, "Joe, I thought we came down here to do some scouting and find us some singers. Let's do it!" But Joe just said, "Now don't you rush me—it's the Fourth of July, and I want to spend some time with my people."

But his people got put out by his rowdy behavior, and an older woman, a church woman, finally threw him away. "You can't act this way around here," she said, "Just where do you think you is? You nothing but a damn crazy animal what ought to be in a cage! Now why don't you up an' leave an' let us right folks be?!"

We piled in the car and drove aimlessly about the city under that scorching July sun. A thermometer on a downtown bank building read 107, but I believe the inside of the car was twice that, and the fumes from Joe's breath were so thick I thought George's cigarette might blow us up. My head was still pulsing and my stomach pitching again, and finally, I said, "Joe, let's stop somewhere—the heat and this car are getting me." So Joe directed us across the Mississippi River to a nightclub in East St. Louis. It was still daytime, and no one was performing, but the bar was pouring and there were a few guys sitting at the tables playing cards. Joe drank beer and George and I watched those fellows play games with names like "Coon Cat," "Tonk," and "Pitty Pat." And balefully, malevolently, they watched us watch them. "Joe," I said, "I think these guys would like to see us die— maybe we should go someplace else, while we can." So we got in the car again, and I suggested to Joe that we find a tourist area called Gaslight Square, where I'd heard a fine player named Old Mr. Graham hung out. But Joe started ranting again.

"Don't you be tellin' me where to go—who here carryin' who?"

"Well," I said, "It's my car and George has been doing the driving—"

"I don't care who been driving—this is my city an' I'm doin' the carryin', an' we gonna be with my people in my part of town!"

And he got madder and madder and reached into his pocket and brought out a little penlight with a blade no more than an inch long. I started to laugh—it looked like a toy. But he suddenly reached over and popped it right into the palm of my hand. I leaped out of the car, howling. "Now you did it, you fat old sonofabitch! You cut me—I'm bleeding! I'm going to the police and have your ass in jail!" But I don't believe Joe heard me—he'd passed out. He just lay there in a mess, sweating and snoring. "George," I said, "let's find the county hospital—I've got to get fixed up."

At the hospital, they put some butterfly stitches in my palm and wrapped me up. I left the emergency room and walked across a steaming asphalt parking lot toward the car, and from forty feet away I could smell drunken, sweaty, seventy-year-old blues singer. I got in and Joe seemed to regain his senses, what ones he had left. I showed him my bandaged hand, and he claimed not to remember a thing. He behaved as though nothing had happened. "Listen, you boys," he said, "now we goin' to find the best blues singer of them all—the finest that I ever knew, yes sir!"

He directed George to a place that didn't even have front steps—they'd all just rotted away. We walked around behind the building to try the rear stairs, and in the backyard was a monstrous collection of refuse—every kind of filth imaginable was back there. There were old, moldering mattresses, shredded and stained with springs sticking out, there were pieces of cars that had rusted and reddened from years of exposure, and I don't think the garbage from the tenants had ever been collected—I believe they'd been throwing it in the backyard ever since the apartment was built, and from the looks of the building that had been a long time ago.

We started up the rickety stairs to the second floor. George struggled with Kaercher's big tape recorder while I lugged Joe's ancient amplifier, which, to judge from its weight, must have been sheathed in lead. I was soaked with sweat, my head was pounding and my cut hand was throbbing, my stomach was sour and the stench of eons-old garbage tore at my nostrils, and as we approached that second-floor landing I didn't care, I really did not care at all, just how great a blues singer was up there waiting for us.

A middle-aged brown woman in a loose house dress and bare feet let us in the apartment, which was stifling. We dropped our gear in the kitchen and followed her to the front room, and the first thing I saw in there seated on a couch, was a twelve- or thirteen-year old girl who weighed at least four hundred pounds. She was dressed in flour sacking, and you could tell by the shape of her head and the look of her face that she was an idiot. I don't mean a person with no common sense, I mean a complete retard. She was mumbling and drooling, and her face was smeared with grease. On a table in front of her were some rib bones and a jar of mayonnaise that looked like zinc ointment left in the sun too long. She'd take a bone and dip it in the mayonnaise, then run it back and forth through a gap in her front teeth to get the meat off.

As sick as I felt, and as bad as my hand hurt, this was it. I mean, things had been funky before, but daddy, this was freak city.

"Joe," I said, "let's not stay here. I'm not feeling well at all—I think we'd better go."

"Shut up!" he yelled. "I don't want to hear nothin' about it. I'm the talent scout here, I'm the boss, an' you people are workin' for me! Now get in there and set up our machine."

So George brought the tape recorder in from the kitchen, and as he was threading a new tape through it a bedroom door opened, and in hobbled this legendary blues singer that Joe had been touting. He appeared to have been sleeping, or passed out, and he looked as though he'd been lying in there with all his weight on his face. Joe introduced him only as Jimmy. He was old and toothless and looked only slightly less demented than the girl in the flour-sacking. From under the couch he dragged out a scratched and stained violin with only two strings on it. "Now you're really gonna hear somethin'," said Joe, pulling out a new bottle of schnapps. I asked for it. I had heard that more drink would sometimes cure a hangover, and besides, I thought if I could get enough down me I might go numb, and at that point, feeling numb seemed like just the place to be. I took a big swig of schnapps and gagged. Joe snatched the bottle away and commanded George to turn the recorder on.

Jimmy picked up his bow and began sawing off strange tonalities in no particular key and mumbling incomprehensible lyrics. My stomach started rolling again and I was sure I was going to be sick. I asked the woman of the house where the toilet was, and she led me to a door at the end of a hallway. I opened the door and found not a toilet, but a closet. There was nothing in the closet but a few sheets of newspaper and a hole—a hole about eighteen inches in diameter, in the floor. I turned to the woman and tried to stammer out a question, but she just waved at the hole. "Don't worry none," she said, "no one livin' down 'neath us now. Ain't been no one there for months." She walked away and I got down on my hands and knees and got sick with no trouble at all. But I faced away from the hole. There was just no way I could look down that thing.

When my business in the closet was finished I returned to the living room and took George aside. "George," I said, "this is about enough. We gotta go back to Chicago, *now.*" "Yeah," he agreed, "this is a pretty sorry scene—let's hit it." So I told Joe to pack up. His eyes popped.

"You wait a minute! Just who here carryin' who?!"

"Joe, I don't care who's carrying who—George and I are going back."

"You don't like my people!"

"I like your people fine, Joe, but it's just not my scene—I'm sorry."

"Yeah, you is sorry, all right. Well get on back to Chicago! Go on an' go wherever you wants—I'm stayin' here!"

I looked at George. He was fidgeting with the car keys. Joe pulled on his schnapps and glowered at us over the top of the bottle.

"Joe, look," I asked, "do you want us to drop you somewhere before you leave?" He thought a moment.

"Yeah," he finally said, "you carry me over to East St. Louis, where my cousin live."

So George and I crossed over to an old iron bridge into Illinois and Joe directed us to the outskirts of town, where we drove down a narrow dirt road full of potholes. We stopped in front of a ramshackle frame house set well back off the road and Joe, carrying an old battered suitcase, got out. George pulled Joe's amp from the back seat while I handed him his guitar, and the three of us stood there in the road, Joe looking sullen. "Well, see you back in Chicago," I said, somewhat apologetically. "Take care, Joe," said George. Joe just grunted something and George and I got back in the car and drove away.

A hundred yards or so down the road, I turned around and looked back. Joe was still there in the road, fumbling with his suitcase and equipment. He was an image from the lyrics of a blues song, or from the cover of a record jacket—Joe and his suitcase and guitar, looking down a hot, dusty road, alone. "George," I said. "We can't just go off like this—it's like we're abandoning him or something. We gotta turn around." And we did. Because, for better or for worse, he was a man of stature. There was a great pride in this man, a great strength in this man. And there was poetry. He was a poet of the highways, and in the words of his songs he could sing to you his life. And to hear him talk about Robert Johnson or Son House or Charlie Patton, to hear life distilled from fifty years of thumbing rides and riding rails and playing joints—to hear of levees and work gangs and tent shows, of madness and whores, pimps and rounders, of gamblers and roustabouts and bootleggers, of circuit-preachers and medicine-show men—well, it was something. Because to know this man was to know the story of black America, and maybe to know the story of black America is to know America itself.

Joe didn't look at us as we pulled up beside him in the road.

"Come on, Joe," I said, "come on back to Chicago with us."

"No, I want to stay some while longer. You boys go on back to your peoples—you don't belong here."

And he was right. I had thought I could be part of his culture and live out on the street with him, but I couldn't. I was a stranger in a strange land, and it was nobody's fault but my own. So George and I wheeled around and drove away again, and this time when I looked back, Joe was gone.

Back in Chicago, I avoided the record store for a couple of weeks. For one thing, I was afraid Joe might be hostile toward me, maybe even physically if he'd been drinking. But the real trouble was that I could only talk Joe's life—when it came down to living it, I couldn't do it, and Joe knew it. And I didn't want to confront that aspect of myself and I didn't want to confront his knowledge of that aspect.

But staying away got to be worse than any confrontation, so finally one day I went into the store and headed for the basement. Joe was sitting down there in old serge trousers and an electric-green shirt with spangles all down the front. The spangles looked like the little things you see on sugar cookies at Christmas time. He had a bottle of beer in one hand and his guitar strung across his lap, and on the floor beside him was a six-pack. As I approached him a strange look came over his face. It was a hard look to describe—it was shy, but at the same time, it was sly, too. "Joe," I said, my voice a little tentative, "how are you?" Still with that odd expression on his face he looked up at me. "Well, Michael," he said, "we really had ourselves a time in that St. Louis, didn't we?" Then he reached in the six-pack for a beer and held it out to me. I took it and pulled an old hardback chair over and sat down, facing him. He picked up his guitar and struck off some chords and notes, and for a while I watched his fingers make those nine strings ring. I opened the beer and took a pull. "Yeah, Joe," I said, "we sure did have a time. We really did indeed."

MY ACID TRIP WITH GROUCHO

See the Sacred Word and Win $100

PAUL KRASSNER

FEBRUARY 1981

IF YOU TAKE THE name of a certain former vice-president, Spiro Agnew, and scramble the letters around, you can rearrange it to spell out Grow A Penis. Such appropriateness can give your boundaries of coincidence permanent stretch marks. After all, when Sen. Charles Goodell came out against the war in Vietnam, it was Agnew who called him "the Christine Jorgensen of the Republican Party"—thus equating military might with the mere presence of a cock.

Years ago, when Mike Wallace interviewed me for *60 Minutes,* and asked about the difference between the underground press and the mainstream media, I told him about the above anagram and said, "The difference is that I could print that in the *Realist,* but it'll be edited out of this program."

My prediction was accurate, so naturally I took an immediate vow never to appear on any TV show again unstoned. Which in turn explains why eating magic mushrooms was practically a prerequisite for my being interviewed by Tom Snyder.

Now, Andy Friendly had only been doing his job when he was reading the Sex and Dope issue of *High Times* in September 1978. As a producer for the *Tomorrow* show, he was always on the lookout for potential guests, and there was a particularly bizarre interview with me in that issue, so he called up to invite me on the show.

There were a few follow-up phone conversations to explore areas that the televised interview might cover. The subject of drug use came up, and I said, "Well, maybe we could talk about my old psychedelic macho. I've taken LSD in all kinds of unusual situations: when I testified at the Chicago Conspiracy Trial; on the Johnny Carson show—Orson Bean was guest host—I was sort of a guide for Groucho Marx once; while I was researching the Manson case I took acid with a few women in the family, including Squeaky Fromme and Sandra Good. It was a kind of participatory journalism. . . ."

The interview was scheduled for November 30.

"That's my birthday," said Abbie Hoffman, still on the lam at the time. "Would you wish me a happy birthday on the show?"

The *Tomorrow* show flew me from San Francisco to Los Angeles, and a chauffeured limousine delivered me to a fancy hotel, where I proceeded to partake of those magic mushrooms. My mood was intensely sensual. What I really wanted was an exquisite massage. I called an old friend who is a professional masseuse.

Since she was also an old lover, it was not totally surprising that we began fucking on the bed before she even set up her table. She finally broke the sweet silence of our postcoital afterglow with this whisper: "But I'll have to charge you for the massage."

November 1978 was the month of that unspeakable Jonestown massacre and, a week later, the political assassination of San Francisco mayor George Moscone and gay supervisor Harvey Milk by ex-cop Dan White. The mushrooms were really coming on strong when Tom Snyder—who has an FM mind in an AM body and was apparently doing his impression of *Saturday Night Live's* Dan Aykroyd doing *him*—asked me, in effect, to *justify* San Francisco as the locale of such sequential horror.

"Nyah, nyah," I began, "my city's more violent than yours. . . ."

When he asked me about the trip with Groucho, I replied, "Well, there's a whole *context*"—but due to the demands of televised pacing, we barely got into it before Snyder wanted to know about my six months as publisher of *Hustler* and what it was I said to the Hare Krishna pushers at the airport. Just before the show ended, though, I managed to remember to wish Abbie Hoffman a happy birthday.

Recently a *High Times* editor recalled seeing that interview on TV and invited me to write the story, which finally completes this media cycle.

THE TIMOTHY LEARY CONNECTION

Think of this as a piece of combat history. To fully understand the context in which this battle for the will has been taking place, you need only retrace the chronological profile of G. Gordon Liddy—from his role as a Pough-keepsie district attorney who raided the Millbrook mansion where LSD was an experimental sacrament to his function as a CIA operative who offered to assassinate Jack Anderson on behalf of the Nixon administration.

Had Liddy been given the go-ahead, columnist Anderson wouldn't have been around to embarrass the Carter administration into not invading Iran, and we might be in the middle of World War III at this very moment.

In 1963 in my capacity as editor and Zen bastard of the *Realist,* I had assigned Robert Anton Wilson to investigate the game being played at Millbrook. In my capacity as stand-up comic and drug virgin, I had been poking fun at all the highs I'd never tried.

Wilson came back and presented me with our cover story, "Timothy Leary and His Psychological H-Bomb." After it was published, Leary called to invite me for a weekend at Milbrook. Working with him were Ralph Metzner and Richard Alpert. Somehow, despite all the accoutrements of Eastern religion, the scene was quite American. Even this top level of the psychedelic hierarchy consisted of a Catholic, a Protestant, and a Jew.

Yet they were performing a cosmic task, this trio of Ph.D. dropouts, helping to spread the expansion of consciousness in the middle of a sado-masochistic empire whose perpetuation depended upon the mass contraction of consciousness.

Originally, the CIA had intended to use LSD as one more means of manipulating the population. That scenario backfired. A generation who trusted their friends more than their government deprogrammed themselves from the society that had shaped them, and then reprogrammed themselves into an infinite variety of incarnations.

The think tanks had not formulated a contingency plan for this counter-culture that was refusing to be brainwashed into becoming consumer and military zombies. This—*mutation*—would certainly have to be discredited.

LSD influenced music, painting, spirituality, and the stock market. Tim Leary let me listen in on a call from a Wall Street broker thanking him for turning him onto acid because it had given him the courage to sell short.

Leary had a certain sense of pride about famous folks he and his associates had introduced to the magic potion. Cary Grant had become a father at age seventy-four, thanks to LSD, and likewise, Herman Kahn of the Hudson Institute now talked about "spasms" of information.

Years later, I gave Kahn a superficial tour of the Lower East Side. We stopped in a bookstore. Among this thinker of the unthinkable's purchases was *LSD and Problem Solving* by Peter Stafford.

Meanwhile, I had become a gung-ho acidhead, a public propagandist. I wrote a lot about LSD. Sometimes I would take a tab right onstage at the beginning of a performance, verbally sharing my journey with the audience, hoping I could get a few laughs while simultaneously maintaining my juggling act without dropping any chromosomes and damaging them.

THE CHARLES MANSON CONNECTION

There's a new-wave band whose name itself—Sharon Tate's Baby—is a tribute to time warps everywhere. For it is now nearly a dozen years since Charles Manson, a victim-executioner sired by the prison system, dispatched his perverted commune to mutilate and kill a group of people in the privacy of their home. Among the slain was Sharon Tate, a pregnant actress.

Her husband, Roman Polanski, director of *Rosemary's Baby,* was out of the country at the time. Now he is out of the country again, this time to avoid prosecution for consorting with a voluptuous thirteen-year-old.

Young idealists on their way to the Woodstock Festival that weekend in the summer of '69 kept passing newsstands with headlines of the gory multiple murder. Not all the details emerged. Others dead:

- Jay Sebring, hairdresser, dealer of marijuana and cocaine—earlier that evening, a member of a coke ring had appeared at the house—his body would later be found stuffed in a car trunk in New York;
- Voytek Frokowski, who with Sebring was preparing to became U.S. distributors of MDA;
- Abigail Folger, coffee heiress, girlfriend of Frokowski, and campaigner for Tom Bradley, L.A.'s first black mayor—she

was a far cry from the conservative image of Mrs. Olson in her father's TV commercials.

Manson was an eclectic. He borrowed techniques from Transactional Analysis and Scientology alike. There was even a Scientology E-Meter (lie detector) on the blind man's ranch where Charlie kept his harem. He used sex and music and isolation and ritual and fakery—whatever worked. He was a pimp and a hypnotist. He dispensed LSD tablets as though they were timed-release Dog Yummies.

I interviewed Preston Guillory, who had been a deputy with the Los Angeles Sheriff's Department when they eventually busted the Manson ranch. He stated that before the murders, they had been told to leave Charlie alone—despite complaints about his violations of parole (including, ironically, statutory rape)—because "something big was coming down."

"Why were you given such an order?"

"I don't know," Guillory replied "We didn't question our superiors."

"Did you at least *speculate* as to the reason?"

"Oh, we just figured they were gonna kill Black Panthers."

Thus did the racism of the sheriffs render them collaborators of Charles Manson, who had wanted to start a race war. He instructed his followers to leave clues making it appear that black militants were responsible for the killings. When the family was arrested, however, it merely served to give hippies a bad name.

Before Willie Nelson made the look respectable again, there was John Liney Frasier, a long-haired, headbanded freak in the Santa Cruz mountains who was involved in an awesome mass murder a year after Charles Manson. He later became a prison mate of Manson, mentioning in a letter that "me and Charlie are still trying to figure out how long our leashes were and who's been pissin' on them. . . ."

And so it came to pass that Charles Manson was stuck in solitary confinement at Folsom Prison when a new inmate was placed in the adjoining cell. It was Tim Leary fresh from being hounded around the world. He was eventually captured with Joanna Harcourt-Smith, who later admitted working for the Drug Enforcement Agency.

"They took you off the streets," Manson informed Leary, "so that I could continue with your work."

Charlie couldn't understand how Leary had given so many people acid without trying to "control" them. Still, I remember a certain vested interest Leary had in having been a catalyst for their transformation. He enjoyed whatever influence he had wielded in the change of attitude toward LSD that Henry Luce had brought to *Time* and *Life*.

But, Leary once remarked, "I consider Otto Preminger one of our failures."

THE OTTO PREMINGER CONNECTION

The FBI has been getting a bad press lately. They were being accused of hounding Jean Seberg to suicide. Documents proved they had spread a story that she was pregnant by a leader of the Black Panther Party. Then, in order to *defend* itself, the FBI released their tape of a tapped phone conversation wherein Jean Seberg tells a surprised Panther how *pleased* he should be that she's carrying his baby.

It is enough to make the left and right lobes of your brain start humping each other. What will the next layer of reality be? Will yet another document reveal that the Black Panther was actually an undercover agent?

But the FBI was not the first to toy with Jean Seberg's destiny. She was originally chosen from among thousands of contestants by Otto Preminger for the starring role in his film, *Joan of Arc*. While she was being burned at the stake, her garments actually did catch on fire. Jean Seberg screamed with such a passion for survival at that moment, it seemed to preclude the possibility of ever taking her own life.

And Otto Preminger, bless his professional heart, knew that this was one scene he had on the first take.

I've met Preminger on two occasions. The first was in 1960. I was conducting a panel on censorship for *Playboy*. Preminger had defied Hollywood's official seal of approval by not censoring *The Moon Is Blue*. In retrospect, it hardly looks courageous, but Preminger refused to take out the word "virgin."

Anyway, at the end of our interview, he asked, "Ven you tronscripe dis, vill you fix op my Henglish?"

"Oh, sure," I replied quickly. "Of course."

He glared at me and shouted, "Vy? Vot's drong viz my Henglish?"

The second time I saw Preminger was a decade later. We were both guests on the Merv Griffin show (Orson Bean was guest host again). I had taken mescaline for the occasion. Another guest was comedian Jackie Vernon. Responding to the length of my hair, he said, "Why don't you take a bath?"

Nobody had ever asked me that on network television before. Later, Monday morning quarterbacking, George Carlin would have an Aikido-like suggestion—"You should've said, 'Why, thank you, Jackie, I hadn't considered that.' "—but at that instant I was caught off balance and just kept silent. So did the audience. The tension was broken by Otto Preminger.

"Dot iss duh seekness ov our society, dis stereotypical ottitood."

Now the audience applauded. And then we went to a commercial. There is a definite rhythm a director brings to a TV talk show. . . .

Between those two occasions, Otto Preminger made a movie called *Skidoo*. It was proacid propaganda thinly disguised as a comedy adventure.

And the part of God was played by Groucho Marx.

Recently Tim Leary cheerfully admitted to me: "I was fooled by Otto Preminger. He was much hipper than I was."

THE LENNY BRUCE CONNECTION

Steve Allen became the first subscriber to the *Realist* in 1958. He sent in several gift subscriptions, including one for Lenny Bruce, who was busy fighting the press label "sick comic." Lenny and I developed a close friendship. In 1962, *Playboy* assigned me as editor of his autobiography, *How to Talk Dirty and Influence People,* which they were serializing.

Traveling around with Lenny Bruce was an incredible delight. It was a theatrical education to watch him sculpt his offstage perceptions into onstage routines. But, as his environment became more and more the courtroom, so did the contradictions of the law become more and more the canvas for his craft.

Although Lenny was a tremendous influence on me as a performer, I was not at all into drugs at the time. Once I asked him about the apparent inconsistency between his free-form lifestyle and his having to stop everything in order to shoot up. He replied, "Well, you stop to *eat,* don't you?"

He described heroin—"It's like kissing God." And who could fault him for that?

In the winter of 1964, stoned on a combination of DMT and LSD, Lenny fell backward through the window of his San Francisco hotel room. At the precise moment that he was suspended in midair, he uttered: "Man shall rise above the rule!" Then he surrendered to the law of gravity and plummeted to the sidewalk below. Both legs had to be put in casts, and for a while he became the Hermit of Hollywood Hills.

Around that time, Jerry Hopkins—who had opened the first head shop in L.A., and later became the biographer of Elvis Presley and Jim Morrison—was producing the Steve Allen show. He arranged for me to do a one-night stand at the Steve Allen Theater. Lenny Bruce was in the audience, and so was Groucho Marx.

At one point in the show, I was talking about the importance of having empathy for other people's perversions. During a question-and-answer session that followed, Lenny stood up on his crutches and asked what I had meant by that.

"Well, once I was sitting in the subway—it was rush hour and really crowded—and an elderly lady's buttocks kept rubbing against my shoulder, and I began to get aroused . . ."

"You're *sick!*" Lenny yelled.

"Thank you, Mr. President," I responded, ending the show right there.

Later, I met Groucho Marx for the first time.

"That was very smart, the way you finished," he said. "Besides, I was getting fidgety in my seat."

THE RAM DASS CONNECTION

By the mid '60s I had become such a dope fiend that I kept my entire stash in a bank-vault deposit box. Once a week I would don my *Cosa Nostra* sweatshirt ("We aim to please!") and get my supply of LSD—to give away, sell, swallow, whatever.

It was, for you brand-name fans, Owsley White Lightning—300 micrograms of separate reality. I bought my acid from Dick Alpert to finance his trip to India, where his guru renamed him Baba Ram Dass. "Come fuck the universe with me," his postcard beckoned, but I already had an American guru—Mortimer Snerd, ventriloquist Edgar Bergen's dummy. One time Bergen asked his main dummy, Charlie McCarthy "What are you doing?" Charlie answered, "Nothing." And then Mortimer Snerd said in his goofy buck-tooth country bumpkin style, "Well, how d'ya know when yer *finished?*"

Anyway, Ram Dass kept seeking illumination and having his feet kissed by strangers, while I stayed home and got a call from Groucho Marx.

He was going to be in an Otto Preminger film called *Skidoo,* and it was pretty much advocating LSD, and he had never tried it but was not only curious but also felt a responsibility to his audience not to steer them wrong, so could I get him some pure stuff and would I care to accompany him on the trip?

I did not play hard to get.

The acid with which Ram Dass—in his final moments as Dick Alpert—failed to get his guru higher was the same acid that I had the honor of taking with Groucho Marx. As I left the bank vault that week, I was breathing slowly and deeply so that I would not laugh my ass off in the lobby.

THE GROUCHO MARX CONNECTION

We ingested those little white tabs one afternoon at the home of an actress in Beverly Hills.

Groucho was interested in the social background of the drug. There were two items that particularly tickled his fancy.

One was about the day acid was outlawed. Hippies were standing around the streets, waiting for the exact appointed minute to strike so they could all publicly swallow their LSD the exact second it became illegal.

The other was how the tour bus would pass through Haight-Ashbury and passengers would try to take snapshots of the local alien creatures, who in turn would hold mirrors up to the bus windows so that the tourists would see themselves focusing their cameras.

I told Groucho about the first thing I ever sold to the old Steve Allen show. It was a sketch called "Unsung Heroes of Television." Among the heroes was the individual whose sole job it was to listen intently the whole half hour for somebody to say the secret word on *You Bet Your Life* and then to drop that decoy duck when the word was said.

He told me about one of his favorite contestants—"a gentleman with white hair, on in years but a chipper fellow. I inquired as to what he did to retain his sunny disposition. 'Well, I'll tell you, Groucho,' he says, 'every morning I get up and I *make a choice* to be happy that day.' "

We had long periods of silence, and of listening to music. I was accustomed to playing rock 'n' roll while tripping, but the record collection here was all classical and Broadway show albums. After we heard the Bach "Cantata No. 7," Groucho said, "I may be Jewish, but I was seeing the most beautiful visions of Gothic cathedrals. Do you think Bach *knew* he was doing that?"

Later, we were listening to the score of a musical comedy *Fanny*. There was one song called "Welcome Home," where the lyrics go something like, "Welcome home, says the clock," and the chair says, "Welcome home," and so do various other pieces of furniture. Groucho started acting out each line, as if he were actually *being* greeted by the clock, the chair and so forth. He was like a child, charmed by his own ability to respond to the music that way.

There was a point when our conversation somehow got into a negative space. Groucho was equally bitter about institutions such as marriage ("like quicksand") and individuals such as Lyndon Johnson ("that potatohead"). Eventually I asked, "What gives you hope?"

Groucho thought for a moment. Then he said just one word out loud: "People."

After a while, he started chuckling to himself. I hesitated to interrupt his revelry. Finally he spoke: "I'm really getting quite a kick out of this notion of playing God like a dirty old man in *Skidoo*. You wanna know why? Do you realize that irreverence and reverence are the some *thing*?"

"Always?"

"If they're not, then it's a misuse of your power to make people laugh." And right after he said that, his eyes began to tear.

When he came back from peeing, he said, "Everybody is waiting for miracles to happen. The human *body* is a goddam *miracle*."

He mentioned, "I had a little crush on Marilyn Monroe when we were making *Love Happy*. I remember I got a hard-on just *talking* to her on the set."

During a little snack: "I never thought eating a fig would be the biggest thrill of my life."

He held and smelled a cigar for a long time but never smoked it.

"Everybody has their own Laurel and Hardy" he mused. "A miniature Laurel and Hardy one on each shoulder. Your little Oliver Hardy bawls you out—he says, 'Well, this is a *fine mess* you've gotten us into.' And your little Stan Laurel gets all weepy—'Oh, Ollie, I couldn't help it, I'm sorry I did the best I *could*. . . .' "

Five years later, my book, *How a Satirical Editor Became a Yippie Conspirator in Ten Easy Years*, was published by Putnam's. Editor William Targ sent an advance copy to Groucho, and he sent back a postcard that was as eerie as it was complimentary: "Thanks for the book. I am sending this card to you, because I don't know where Mr. Krassner lives. Or even if he is alive. At any rate, it's a hilarious book and I predict in time he will wind up as the only live Lenny Bruce."

The year after that, I was heavy into my Manson investigation. During the acid trip with three of his family members—Squeaky Fromme, Sandra Good, and Brenda McCann—I got an even more awesome compliment.

Sandy Good had once seen me perform at The Committee in San Francisco. Now she was saying to me, "When people used to ask me what Charlie was like, I would compare him to Lenny Bruce and Paul Krassner."

My heart thumped rather strangely.

Sandy had been a civil-rights activist. But Charlie Manson stepped on her eyeglasses, threw away her birth control pills, remolded her personality, and transformed her value system. So now she was parroting Charlie's racism and asking me to tell John Lennon that he should get rid of Yoko Ono and "marry his own kind."

I've never met Charlie Manson, although I've corresponded with him. But I have heard a tape of his rap, and he definitely used humor as a tool for evil.

For the first time I understood in my guts what Groucho Marx had meant about misusing the power to make people laugh.

THE JERRY RUBIN CONNECTION

After our acid trip, I had only a couple of contacts with Groucho.

The first concerned a rumor that he had said, "I think the only hope this country has is Nixon's assassination." I wanted to verify whether he had actually said that.

"I deny everything," he joked, then admitting he had indeed said it over a luncheon interview with a now-defunct magazine, *Flash*.

"Uh, sorry Mr. Marx, you're under arrest for threatening the life of the president. I can't tell you how much I enjoyed *A Night at the Opera*. Here, now, if you'll just slip into these plastic handcuffs. . . ."

I wrote to the San Francisco office of the U.S. Department of Justice, asking about the status of the case against Groucho, particularly in view of the indictment of Black Panther David Hilliard for using similar rhetoric. Here's the reply I received:

> Dear Mr. Krassner:
>
> Responding to your inquiry, the United States Supreme Court has held that Title 18 U.S.C., Section 87 prohibits only "true" threats. It is one thing to say "I (or we) will kill Richard Nixon" when you are the leader of an organization which advocates killing people and overthrowing the government; it is quite another to utter the words which are attributed to Mr. Marx, an alleged comedian. It was the opinion of both myself and the United States Attorney in Los Angeles (where Marx's words were alleged to have been uttered) that the latter utterance did not constitute a "true" threat.
>
> Very truly yours,
> /s/ James L. Browning, Jr.
> United States Attorney

The second occasion was at the Los Angeles Book Fair in 1976, where Groucho was scheduled to speak, along with Tim Leary and Jerry Rubin.

Leary was dressed all in white except for a black string tie. He was now advocating suburban space colonies.

"Migration," he proclaimed, "is the number one tool of the DNA code."

There was speculation that this might really be a metaphor about the way we ought to behave on earth. Utopian planning for life on a celestial way station is bound to serve as a model for people changing themselves, their institutions and systems on our own planet, whether or not we actually start sending out satellites covered with Astroturf.

Leary took a slight swipe at Rubin, mentioning an ex-radical who said "Kill your parents" and had now written a book on how to contact your deceased parents through astral travel. Rubin had issued a press release requesting the media not to refer to him as a former Yippie leader. Somewhere there must have been a headline: FORMER YIPPIE LEADER ASKS NOT TO BE CALLED FORMER YIPPIE LEADER.

A few years previously, Jerry Rubin had helped organize a press conference to denounce Tim Leary as a snitch, although Leary insisted that he never got anybody in trouble. Now, Rubin was scheduled to appear at the Book Fair on the same evening as Leary but he rearranged it for the next evening in order to avoid a public confrontation—or, worse yet, a public embrace—in front of all those eagerly popping flashbulbs.

Nevertheless, Jerry Rubin served as a unifier at the Book Fair.

It had been announced that Groucho Marx would not speak from the stage in the Ambassador Hotel ballroom, but rather on a one-to-one basis with folks whose books he would be autographing. This turned into a mob scene. So Jerry found Groucho's companion, Erin Fleming, and suggested that if they walked back around a certain way it would bring them directly onto the stage. She followed his advice.

Groucho looked frail and unsmiling, but he was alert and irreverent as the audience fired questions at him.

Was he working on a film now?

"No, I'm answering silly questions."

What was his favorite film?

"*Duck Soup.*"

Nixon?

"He should be in jail."

Is humor an important issue in the presidential campaign?

"Get your finger out of your mouth."

What does he dream about?

"Not about you."

What inspired him to write?

"A fountain pen; a piece of paper."

I couldn't stand it any longer. I called out, "Groucho, what gives you hope?"

This time he said, "The world."

There was hardly any standing room left in the auditorium, but one man sat on the floor rather than take the seat occupied by a rubber Groucho Marx doll.

WAR ON DRUGS

The Strange Story of Lyndon LaRouche,
Sinister Mastermind of the Anti-Drug Coalition

CHIP BERLET

MAY 1981

IT SOUNDS LIKE A script from a grade-B movie, or a nightmare experienced by an overly paranoid dealer: a national "war on drugs" launched by a bizarre political cult group with ties to the organized right-wing and intelligence agencies.

It's real, however, and it's called the National Anti-Drug Coalition. The coalition has chapters in some thirty cities, and worked feverishly in last year's elections to unseat legislators who favored decriminalization of marijuana and on behalf of politicians who support tougher penalties for drug users. Marijuana is not the only target of the coalition; they are also "dedicated to forming a national machine capable of ridding the nation of the menace of psychotropic substances."

Representatives of the coalition have been appearing nationwide at local public schools with lectures on the dangers of marijuana use and have been guests on radio talk shows, where the message reaches a wider audience. They publish a glossy-covered sixty-four-page monthly called *War on Drugs*, which recently summarized the group's goals and accomplishments:

"We have stemmed the tide of 'drug decriminalization' in state legislatures. We have succeeded in having some states recriminalize marijuana where decrim bills were passed. We seek tough laws, and tough enforcement. We want mandatory antidrug education programs in schools; a free hand for parents and administrators to stop pushing in the schools—without ACLU or others' interference in the guise of protecting pushers' "civil rights"; we will keep the entire public informed of all legislation, and where local, state and federal candidates stand on the issue. . . ."

Mighty strong stuff, but not surprising considering the source, because the National Anti-Drug Coalition is not a grass-roots organization of confused and concerned parents, but a highly sophisticated fundraising and recruitment scam for a political cult group led by Lyndon LaRouche, Jr. You might have seen LaRouche on television forecasting nuclear war or imminent economic collapse. He ran in the Democratic presidential primaries and pulled 170,000 votes in 14 contests—a move that qualified him for over $400,000 in tax dollars through Federal Election Commission matching funds.

LaRouche is no fly-by-night crackpot operating on a shoestring budget; he is a well-financed crackpot with some 600 cult members and another 1,500 supporters who are willing to spend long hours organizing for the political goals of their leader. Right now, Lyndon LaRouche wants a war on drugs—so to understand the National Anti-Drug Coalition requires an understanding of LaRouche and his minions.

Most of the key organizers of the National Anti-Drug Coalition are members or supporters of LaRouche's various front groups, which include the U.S. Labor Party, the national Caucus of Labor Committees, the Fusion Energy Foundation, the Humanist Academy, the New Democratic Policy Committee, and the New Solidarity Service. LaRouche has masterminded at least a dozen other such groups in the past ten years, and like the National Anti-Drug Coalition, they generally operate out of the same offices and share the same phone numbers of LaRouche's various fronts in the cities where he operates.

Lyndon LaRouche spent the late 1950s and early 1960s as a management consultant developing a unique view of world economy. He organized a small circle of followers out of the militant SDS chapter at Columbia University in the late '60s. LaRouche's "labor caucus" in SDS was expelled over political disagreements, so LaRouche established the National Caucus of Labor Committees.

LaRouche and his followers began as a small inward-directed organization pounding esoteric economic views. In 1972, however, things began to change. LaRouche returned from a trip to Germany after his wife had left him for a younger member of the Labor Committee living in England. Shortly thereafter, LaRouche became convinced of a secret conspiracy of evil people directed by British agents controlled world politics—and was out to assassinate him.

Labor Committee members who challenged LaRouche's rather arcane view of reality were called CIA agents or psychologically hung up on what LaRouche called "mother's fear."

NCLC members who were suspected agents were simply isolated in a room and harassed until they admitted they had been brainwashed. Chris White, the English NCLC member LaRouche's former wife had taken up with, was called before LaRouche in December 1973 for a "deprogramming" session. White was kept awake until he "admitted" he had been programmed by both the KGB and CIA to help set LaRouche up for assassination.

In January 1974, LaRouche publicly announced he had successfully untangled the brainwashing of Chris White. LaRouche claimed White had been "brainwashed by the CIA to simulate a brainwashed KGB agent" through a process he called "psycho-sexual brainwashing." In the course of the rambling, virtually incoherent speech, LaRouche described part of the alleged brainwashing technique:

How do you brainwash somebody? Well, first of all, you generally pull a psychological profile or develop one in a preliminary period. You find every vulnerability of that person from a psychological standpoint. Now the next thing you do is you build them up for fear in males and females of homosexuality, aim them for an anal identification with anal sex, their mouth is identified with fellatio. Their mouth is identified only with the penis—that kind of sex, and with women. Womanhood is the fellatio of the male mouth in a man who has been brainwashed by the KGB; that is sucking penises.

LaRouche went on to claim that the programming played upon guilt fears about masturbation and homosexuality, and forced the person being programmed to engage in degrading acts. According to LaRouche, the programmers would show the victim a picture of a man performing intercourse with a sheep. "Wouldn't you like to do that? How about this dog?" The key to the technique was summed up by LaRouche thusly:

"What brainwashes is the victim's knowledge that he is degrading himself in order to avoid pain. It's not the pain that brainwashes, it's forcing the victim to run away from the pain by taking the bait of degrading himself. This persistent patter of self-degradation, self-humiliation, is what essentially accomplishes the brainwashing."

The preceding explanation of brainwashing is pretty raunchy, but former NCLC members claim it forms the basis for the technique used by LaRouche to maintain strict obedience and loyalty from his followers. It is what turned LaRouche's inner organization into a cult. LaRouche's charges of a KGB/CIA brainwashing operation against him were a fantasy, but he believed the only way he could prevent further assassination plots was to subject followers he distrusted to a "deprogramming" session in which he "discovered" the psychosexual brainwashing. It was no surprise he was able to discover such brainwashing, since during the course of his "deprogramming" sessions he was conducting it himself.

NEO-FREUDIAN RASPUTIN

LaRouche began to use his twisted Freudian psychoanalytic techniques to intimidate members during weekly meetings. One early research report on the LaRouche cult, titled "NCLC—Brownshirts of the Seventies," concluded that "the 'self-consciousness' sessions that LaRouche introduced were ostensibly to train the 'leadership' to withstand psychological terror and destroy opposition within the leadership—and eventually within the whole organization."

Former NCLC members say they experienced strong fears of becoming impotent as a result of the psychological conditioning. In one memo, LaRouche overtly linked the political with the sexual: "I am going to make you organizers—by taking your bedrooms away from you. . . . What I shall do is to expose you to the cruel fact of your sexual impotence, male and female. . . . I shall show you that your pathetic impotence is a mere aspect

265

of your political work such that you will know that you cannot cure one without solving the other."

According to former NCLC members, many LaRouche followers were subjected to sessions where LaRouche or his handpicked aides would strip down a person's psychological defenses to the point where they would be sobbing hysterically and begging to stay in the Labor Committee. A former member told the *New York Times,* "I've seen them destroy people. They made me blow my guts in front off the whole group and then they used it against me. My mother came to see me and they ripped her up, screaming that she was a lesbian and had castrated my father."

As part of the psychological manipulation within the group, LaRouche announced "Operation Mop-Up"—a series of physical attacks during 1973–75 on meetings held by other political organizations on the left. NCLC members with brass knuckles, sticks, and chains would invade a meeting and beat people up, sending some to the hospital. "We shall be cruelly ruthless in carrying out those duties which are necessary to build the kind of mass force required" to seize power from other groups, said LaRouche.

"Our hearts were not in it," recalls one former NCLC member who asked to remain anonymous. "We were all intellectuals, only LaRouche was up for [the attacks]. We knew it was an aberration but it was all or nothing. The attacks were supposed to harden the membership. Most of us now find the whole thing was crazy." The former member, whom we will call Mark, says the nature of the organization changed rapidly during the period of Operation Mop-Up. "LaRouche was an incredibly good speaker, he still is. . . . He's brilliant, but he has gone absolutely bonkers."

Mark was doing graduate work in the social sciences when he was recruited into the NCLC. Now, after leaving the cult, he recalls with disbelief what he did for LaRouche. One night during Operation Mop-Up he found himself with a group of NCLC members on a night mission to attack a political meeting:

> We were wearing hockey helmets covered with sky hats to try to disguise them. We had on knee pads, and were carrying sticks, trying to hide them under our coats. Imagine, it was the middle of the summer, and here we were marching through Harlem dressed like

that. I remember seeing the blacks on the stoops looking at us in amazement, and thinking, 'My Good, we are going to be made into mincemeat.' But instead, for blocks ahead, people were going inside and locking their doors.

A locked meeting-hall door stymied that mission, but the experience helped ensure Mark's loyalty and obedience to the NCLC and LaRouche.

After solidifying unquestionable support within the NCLC, "LaRouche began to move away from the issues," says Mark. What had started as an intellectual study group had turned into a militant cadre of conspiratorial fanatics. LaRouche evolved a paranoid worldview in which Nelson Rockefeller was behind a conspiracy to assassinate LaRouche and spread famine and disease across the globe in order to seize power for the British oligarchy. "People who disagreed were called brainwashed and put in isolation," recalls Mark. The proof of their brainwashing was that they opposed LaRouche's policies, and only LaRouche possessed the intellect and perception needed to "deprogram" the dissidents.

Soon, "there were no economic policies left," Mark says, "only conspiracies; everyone hated everyone else. You couldn't talk to your wife because she was trained to rat on you. We were all pushed to do such crazy things. . . . we were totally exhausted. . . . it was very much like a Moonie operation." Mark says it was this atmosphere of fear that prevented objections when LaRouche moved to the right.

To bring his strange message of evil cabals and unseen plotters to the American public, LaRouche formed an electoral arm—the U.S. Labor Party, which ran candidates for public offices in 1973. The USLP articulated a theory of imminent nuclear war with Rockefeller's finger on the button. Since Rockefeller was the main enemy, LaRouche began to contact other anti-Rocky forces, who tended to represent the most extreme elements of the organized right-wing such as the paramilitary Minutemen and the Washington-based Liberty Lobby. The campaign against Rockefeller launched by the USLP dominated the group's work for several years, especially after he was named vice-president.

One former USLP member, Gregory F. Rose, revealed in a *National Review* article that the anti-Rockefeller campaign focused the group's interest "in extremist right-wing organizations." Rose produced one memo telling USLP cadre: "Operations reports from our organizers in the field indicate growing sympathy for our 'Impeach Rocky' campaign among right-wing circles. We must move to take advantage of the situation."

A RIGHTWARD LURCH

The memo suggested right-wing groups could be tapped as a source of contacts, recruits, and money, and then when the Rockefeller conspiracy was broken, it would be "comparatively easy" to eliminate the cooperative right-wing groups. In late 1977 NCLC chief of staff Costas Axios told a reporter, "We must establish an industrial capitalist republic and rid this country of the Rockefeller anti-industrial anti-technology, monetarist dictatorship of today." After accomplishing this, Axios said, it would be a simple matter to "win over the people's minds."

By the fall of 1977 LaRouche was talking about a "humanist capitalist alliance" and openly recruiting right-wing support. He also detected another in the endless series of assassination attempts on his life, and hired a former Office of Strategic Services spy with close ties to the CIA to serve as his security adviser. Mitchell Werbell not only advises LaRouche on security, but also trains LaRouche cultists in what are called antiterrorist techniques. Former members call them hit squads, and point out that Werbell operates an arms-manufacturing company and has garnered the nickname "Wizard of Whispering Death."

With the untimely death of Nelson Rockefeller, LaRouche was forced to concoct a new archenemy. He came up with a series of real and imagined organizations that were part of a global conspiracy. LaRouche declared that the Anti-Defamation League of B'nai B'rith, a Jewish human-rights lobby and educational group, was the control network for the conspiracy in the United States.

This charge against the Anti-Defamation League surfaced shortly after the ultra-right-wing Liberty Lobby criticized the USLP for leaving the Jewish organization out of a booklet detailing the global conspiracy. Liberty Lobby complained that the USLP publication, *Carter and the Party International Terrorism*, had neglected to include any of the "major Zionist groups such as the notorious Anti-Defamation League" in the list of conspirators in the terrorism apparatus.

U.S. Labor Party researchers went to work and prepared a series of articles in their publication, *Executive Intelligence Review*, a ten dollar-per-issue weekly aimed at corporate executives, which outlined the conspiracy they called Dope, Inc. Behind the conspiracy of drug trafficking "discovered" by the USLP were a group of individuals who generally shared one common denominator—they were Jewish. The articles appeared in late 1978, and almost immediately USLP supporters founded the Michigan Anti-Drug Coalition.

By early 1979 the USLP had published their research in a four-hundred-page book titled *Dope, Inc.: Britain's Opium War against the U.S.*, in which they charge that U.S. heroin peddling is controlled by British and American Jews. Dennis King, a LaRouche watcher in New York, points to other anti-Semitic charges that began to appear after the Liberty Lobby complaint. "LaRouche and his followers began to publish articles claiming that the murder of six million Jews in World War II never happened, that B'nai B'rith is a nest of treason against America, that the Jews in ancient times plotted mass murder against the Christians, and that Zionism controls the drug traffic in America."

The anti-Semitic nature of the USLP and its charges concerning the heroin drug trade were downplayed when the USLP newspaper, *New Solidarity* issued a call for a "National Anti-Drug Coalition" on July 10, 1979. For months the newspaper had been running a series of articles drawn from *Dope, Inc.*

From published reports of *Dope, Inc.* co-author David Goldman's tour, it was clear that the USLP was considering a major campaign around the antidrug issue. The fundamentals of the campaign were outlined in typical LaRoucheian rhetoric in a May 4, 1979, article in *New Solidarity*:

The explosive nature of the antidrug battle nationally has been highlighted by the situation in northern Indiana, where Goldman adressed [an antidrug] group. In the city of Highland, following months of U.S. Labor Party antidrug organizing and the door-to-door mass sales of *Dope, Inc.*, a successful crackdown on drug use in the schools was launched by local officials. Dozens of drug-abusing students were caught and subjected to strict reprimands and exposure by school authorities and parents.

269

The growing momentum of the antidrug movement clearly alarmed the phony "liberal" establishment. Working on behalf of their drug-pushing British masters, the American Civil Liberties Union (ACLU) has threatened court actions to disrupt the drug clean-up. The ACLU, a front for Zionist-British crime interests and a recent defender of the Nazis, is charging that students' "rights" are being violated when they are caught carrying dope in the schools!

Furious at the ACLU's defense of drug use by young people, Highland citizens marched, over 200 strong, along with a U.S. Labor Party contingent, calling for a strong antidrug fight and carrying signs identifying the ACLU as the "Anti-American Creepy Liberals United.

When the U.S. Labor Party perceived it had stumbled across a goldmine issue, it went into high gear. The call for the National Anti-Drug Coalition in the July 10 issue of *New Solidarity* was accompanied by an endorsers list of over 120 community leaders, legislators, union leaders and clerics. The founding convention of the group was set for September 29, 1979, in Detroit's Cobo Hall.

As a warm-up for the September meeting, the U.S. Labor Party scheduled a series of state and city meetings of antidrug forces, including an annual awards banquet for the Illinois Anti-Drug Coalition, a neat rabbit-out-of-the-hat piece of organizing since the Illinois coalition had only recently been invented by USLP cadre. At first several prominent political, civic, and religious leaders were lined up to appear at the Illinois awards banquet, but as word of the LaRouche connection spread—he was the featured guest speaker—people began to back off.

Typical of USLP paranoia, its cadre fired off a message on the group's international telex network:

Chicago event targeted by Kennedy . . .
LaRouche campaign is determining U.S. politics.
The Illinois Anti-Drug Coalition event scheduled for this Sunday in Chicago is coming under heavy attack by the Kennedy-controlled drug-running networks in the state. The event has become a battleground around which speakers are being targeted by various

Kennedy networks including the congressional Black Caucus, the University of Chicago, and Mayor Byrne. This is the line-up: Bennet Stewart (U.S. Rep), has been forced to withdraw by members of the Black Caucus, the same group of lackeys proposing "Auschwitz-syle" camps for the black unemployed.

According to well-placed sources, this deployment against LaRouche and the Anti-Drug Coalition is unprecedented in the history of political events in the city. With the kind of destabilization scenario now going on in Washington, the enemy is afraid of the potential we have to capture the American population.

It's this kind of paranoia that makes the LaRouche cult so dangerous and unpredictable. Unlike other cults, their conspiracy theories change from week to week, but they approach their tasks with a zeal that is characteristic of all cult groups. Despite the unstable nature of the group, it can be coldly calculating when it comes to organizing support. A secret internal USLP memo obtained from the group's Chicago office outlines the real goals of the Illinois Anti-Drug Coalition: "In general our strong point is our inroads into the World Community of Al-Islam in the West (WCIW) and our work with the police department and related organizations." The WCIW is a Black Muslim religious organization the USLP was trying to recruit at the time. The memo went on, "The strategy for the WCIW is to open the base" to the Illinois Anti-Drug Coalition and allow WCIW's religious leader, Wallace Dean Muhammad, "the breathing room he needs to nationally come out in the open for the Coalitions and for LaRouche at a later date. Our primary concern now is to engage the WCIW membership and significant leaders in the World Community at whatever level they want to work with us."

The memo continues, saying, "The police work is moving along extremely well," and describes a conversation with the head of Chicago's Narcotics Division. The memo reveals two thrusts of the Anti-Drug Coalition—organizing blacks into the LaRouche support network and solidifying ties with police agencies through the drug angle.

The USLP has long supplied "intelligence" on its enemies to local and federal law-enforcement agencies. For instance, in 1977, USLP security "experts" met with representatives of the New Hampshire State Police and handed over a report claiming that antinuclear activists protesting the Seabrook nuclear power plant were part of an international terrorist conspiracy. The USLP also publishes *Investigative Leads,* a newsletter sold to public and private security agents.

The organizing of the black community through the Anti-Drug Coalition has been successful in many cities across the country, and a majority of those attending the Illinois Anti-Drug Coalition awards banquet were black parents with their children.

HARDLINE TACTICS

The highlight of the Illinois banquet was a slide show by Philadelphia autopsy technician Edward Christian that featured mangled bodies of narcotics users who had "all started out on marijuana."

The slide show was also shown at the founding convention of the National Anti-Drug Coalition in September of 1979. The official report of the meeting started with pride: "After the presentation, a number of people, including children in the audience, fainted. 'We must make our children faint,' said Juan Torres, Michigan Anti-Drug Coalition chairman, 'to burn in their minds the destruction drugs mean.' " Such neanderthal sentiments were right at home with the convention speech of Dr. Gabriel Nahas, whose marijuana research studies are so ludicrous and biased that serious researchers have dismissed them for years.

In the audience were a number of state and local elected officials who have become key contacts for the campaign to stop the decriminalization of marijuana. They included Georgia state senator Culver Kidd, who told the seven hundred assembled delegates: "We need laws that make it so that anyone caught with one hundred pounds of marijuana faces ten years in prison with no parole."

Coming out of the conference were a series of resolutions on education, legislation, and organizing, and a network of antidrug activists who have begun organizing lobbying efforts in state capitals against decriminalization. There are also significant efforts to introduce the National Anti-Drug Coalition's "educational" materials into public- and private-school curricula. Dr. Christian and his gruesome slide show have toured the country, appearing at schools and town meetings drawing audiences of up to eight hundred.

In June of 1980 the National Anti-Drug Coalition launched its slick magazine, *War on Drugs*, which has grown at a tremendous rate. According to an internal USLP financial telex, last year, after only a few issues, USLP cadre were selling up to 1,300 copies of the two-dollar magazine *every day*. Memberships in the National Anti-Drug Coalition and sales of the book *Dope, Inc.* also continue to grow. The sale of materials produced by the National Anti-Drug Coalition is quite lucrative but represents only a small part of the income-generating empire of LaRouche. On a good weekend day, the LaRouche cult raises over $30,000 primarily in publication sales, although their weekly income usually averages between $50,000 and $60,000.

The National Anti-Drug Coalition is just one component of the political movement being assembled by LaRouche. His other highly successful front group, which also funnels in money and recruits, is the Fusion Energy Foundation, a pronuclear group that specializes in fund-raising at major airports. Recently, LaRouche decided to drop the names U.S. Labor Party and National Caucus of Labor Committees from his public repertoire and has been conducting most of his organizing through various front groups, especially the National Anti-Drug Coalition.

Many of the same psychologically manipulated cultists who have been with LaRouche for years continue to carry out his master plan through the various front groups. And that plan is fascism. The word *fascism* is tossed around rather carelessly by some people, but a number of writers and researchers point out LaRouche's economic and political goals fit the classic fascist pattern of seeking rapid industrial growth through a highly centralized government that enforces cooperation of all sectors of society. LaRouche believes that only he has the ability to ensure the necessary cooperation in social, political, cultural, and economic arenas; he dismisses technology as "the rule of irrationalist episodic majorities."

As with most fascist ideologies, the LaRouche cultists want to police our morals—and their standards are very stringent. The National Anti-Drug Coalition is already grooming its contacts for their role as the moral mind police in LaRouche's drive for fascist power. Issues of *War on Drugs* now include articles on how sex education is "brainwashing by perversion," and that rock 'n' roll is a plot to destroy the minds of America's youth. Jazz is labeled a racist and inferior musical form. LSD is reputed to be part of "the expansion of British intelligence's fifty-year campaign in the United States to create cult formations among the general population through the use of drugs and Dionysian rituals." The mind control envisioned by the moral gendarmes behind the Anti-Drug Coalition extends to removing rock, disco, jazz, and blues from public-school curricula, and from public television.

"Jazz, disco, rock, and blues have been inseparably linked to the use and dissemination of mairjuana, heroin, and other mind- and body-destroying drugs throughout this century. This is as true of blues and jazz as it is of rock and disco," states an article in *War on Drugs*. "The pornographic content of today's rock and disco echoes the role of jazz and blues in the 'Roaring Twenties' as the music of organized crime and prostitution."

By tying together drugs, rock 'n' roll, and sex education, the LaRouche forces have been successful in organizing among the same fundamentalist and "new right" forces that helped give us Ronald Reagan as president, but they have also been extremely successful in organizing in the black and Latino community. This year the coalition is targeting state legislatures with antiparaphernalia bills and calls for stiffer penalties for marijuana use and sale. They are highly organized and motivated. They are directed by a zealous cult of political fanatics with a neofascist political philosophy. They have a multimillion-dollar publications network to finance their activities. They should be taken very, very seriously.

High Times #115, March 1985

THE TAXMAN

Fiction

BRUCE JAY FRIEDMAN

MAY 1981

LOCKED IN COMBAT WITH the government over back taxes, Ullman won some points, lost a few, but could not get the revenue service to accept his plush East Side apartment as a "working office."

"What do they think I use it for?" Ullman asked his accountant.

"They don't know," said Tisch. "They just sense it isn't for work."

"Then let them come up and see it," said Ullman. "I've got nothing to hide."

"I wouldn't do that," said the cautious Tisch. "I'd settle."

"No way," said Ullman. "I'm entitled to have whatever kind of office I like. Send 'em up."

In truth, Ullman worked a little in the apartment and played a lot. But what business was that of the government's? For all they knew, he slaved away in the place from dawn till midnight and never had any fun there. The plush decor? He needed it to put him in the mood for hard work. Howard Hughes probably had twenty such places, all over the globe, each of them a clean tax deduction. Why not one for Ullman?

On the day before the agent arrived, Ullman ran around and tried to give the place more of an office-type look. He wheeled the bar into a closet, put away his erotic statuary, and scattered paperclips, rubber bands and file cards on the end tables. Here and there he set up tired piles of manuscripts.

The agent's name was Gowran, a fellow who kept his teeth gnashed together as though he were in severe abdominal pain.

"Would you like a drink?" Ullman asked him. "I don't know the protocol."

"Not just now," said Gowran, running his finger along the edge of a handsomely designed leather couch. "So this is the so-called office."

"Not so-called," said Ullman. "Just the office."

"Some place" said Gowran. "Must have cost you a bundle to furnish it."

"Not really," said Ullman. "You use tricks. Decorator short-cuts that make a little go a long way. Look, let's not fool around. This is my office. I work here. I happen to like nice surroundings. What's the government saying? That I have to work in a drab little place?"

"The government is saying take it easy," said Gowran, easing himself into a white futuristic armchair and practically disappearing in the cushions. "What about the bedroom? You work back there, too?" Ullman had hoped he wouldn't get around to that. He had devoted most of his money and effort to that room, paneling all four walls with mirrors, and the ceiling as well. He had bought the thickest rug made and put in a heavily gadgeted bed—in the great man-about-town tradition. Just his luck, the revenue agent had taken a peek at the set-up on the way into the living room. "I take naps back there," said Ullman. "Half a dozen a day. That's my style of working. Work a little, take a nap, then work some more. You want me to stop that and not take any naps, is that it?"

"Let me see your calendar," said Gowran. Ullman could not tell if he was winning or losing with this fellow, who kept his teeth gnashed together but otherwise had a neutral expression. He was prepared to go along with Gowran until the fellow stepped out of line, at which point he would ask that his case be turned over to higher-ups. Tisch had told him he could do that. But it was difficult to tell if Gowran was stepping out of line. He probably wasn't. So Ullman handed over his daily record book. He had worked on it for two weeks to make it look completely legitimate.

"You certainly take a lot of cabs," said Gowran, flipping through the diary. "No, the government isn't saying you should walk. The government is merely making an observation."

"The government is cute," said Ullman. Gowran snickered, a gray civil-service exhalation of breath, and then plowed on. "Who's this guy Berger?" he asked, still studying the diary. "You've had him to lunch six times and I'm still in January. You both must be very hungry guys."

Actually, this was a break for Ullman. Most of the Berger lunches were legitimate, and in addition, he had called Berger, a public-relations man, and put him on alert that the government might be in touch. And to please back him up all the way. He was in great shape on Berger, not so good on Hellwig, Danziger, and Ferris, all of whom were down for fake lunches and might not come through if Gowran checked them out. "Why don't you call Phil Berger and ask him if we talked business all those times or not," said Ullman. "Here, I'll give you his number."

"That's all right," said Gowran, making a few notations in his record book and then putting it away. "Let's take a break. I know about these calendars. Everybody bullshits their way through them. You probably just got finished padding yours the second I got here. How about that drink you mentioned before?" Gowran loosened his collar, kicked out his legs and made himself comfortable. Ullman winced at the thought of this fellow with his two-bit civil-service suit getting comfortable on his fine furniture, but he rushed to mix a drink all the same. If it ever got down to a pitched battle, he could say that Gowran drank on the job.

"You go to a lot of restaurants," said Gowran. "Try a place called Andy's. Terrific parmigiana and you get unlimited pasta and fruit for the same price. You get out of there, you feel just like you're gonna bust."

Ullman could just about imagine what kind of place Andy's was. With its all-you-can-eat policy on pasta and fruit. He almost threw up at the thought of it, but he made believe he was jotting down the name and address for future reference.

"I don't care how many restaurants you know," he said, joining Gowran in a drink. "You can always use another one."

"Must be nice work you do," said Gowran. "Going to all those lunches and then sitting around in a place like this to do your work. With this view."

"I really do work up here," said Ullman, still defensive. "I just happen to like nice surroundings. I've worked in flophouses and now I figure I deserve this."

"Hey," said Gowran, waggling a finger. "We're taking a break, right?"

"Right," said Ullman, relaxing slightly.

"You must meet a lot of nice people," said Gowran, "a lot of good-looking chicks."

"That's right," said Ullman. "They do sort of drift into the theater if they're good-looking."

"What do you *do*," said Gowran, "you get these thoughts and then you sort of write them down on paper?"

"Something like that," said Ullman.

"That's nice work," said Gowran. "Hey," he said, looking at his watch and springing to his feet. "I'm supposed to meet my new girl. Can I use your phone?"

"Sure," said Ullman. "If it would make it more convenient, she can pick you up here." The drink had evidently made him feel a bit more convivial than he realized.

"That'd be terrific," said Gowran. "She'd love to see a place like this."

Gowran gave the girl the address over the phone, Ullman wondering how he could speak through those gnashed and battered teeth. He called the girl "little one," and Ullman figured this was internal-revenue style. Romantic internal-revenue style. He could just about imagine the girl.

Actually, she wasn't that bad. For one thing she probably should have been called "big one." She was a heavy-set girl, probably German, with languid, somewhat dazed eyes and an attractively slow-rolling style of movement. From the moment she showed up, she slowed everything in the room down. It took a few beats for Ullman to realize how attractive she was and when he did he was a little annoyed. For one thing, it had to change his view of Gowran. He had put the fellow into some kind of cramped and pretty second-rate internal-revenue slot. If that was his proper category, what was he doing with Ingrid? Also, it made Ullman look bad. He worked in the theater. He was supposed to be the one with Ingrids.

"The thing about this girl," said Gowran, who suddenly looked a bit dashing, "is that she'll do anything."

"Nothing bothers me," said Ingrid.

"Do something crazy," said Gowran, with a heavy-handed wink at Ullman.

Slowly, lazily, the girl stood on her hands, using Ullman's expensive bookshelves to balance herself. Her skirt poured over her head, Ullman dazzled by the erotically chunky spectacle. "It means nothing to me," said Ingrid, lightly regaining her feet after just the right amount of time, and with a single movement getting her blond hair to fall back over her shoulders. The doorbell rang and Ullman braced himself. More Ingrids! It was the dry cleaner, after Ullman's dirty suits. Ullman had them ready in a bundle and tossed it to the fellow. As the cleaner sorted it out, Gowran said, "Let's have some fun," and motioned to Ingrid. She took off her blouse, undid her bra, and thrust a heavy breast against the startled dry cleaner's face. "Say," he said, "what kind of party is this?" Ingrid allowed him to enjoy it a moment and then dismissed him with a light kiss on the forehead. "She something?" said Gowran, with a chuckle. "Whatever you like," said Ingrid, with an almost bored snap of her fingers, "I do it."

"Yet I feel sorry for the kid," said Gowran, when the puzzled dry cleaner had left. "They're going to send her back to Germany." He spoke almost as though Ingrid were not in the room.

"You said you'd get me girls," said Ingrid, removing her bra entirely now, as though it were an annoyance.

"I'm working on it," said Gowran.

"I like it with girls."

"Listen," said Gowran, "how's the grass situation up here?" The question put Ullman right on the spot. He had some, but what if he produced a few joints and Gowran slipped the cuffs on him, booking him not only on tax evasion but also on a drug rap. Maybe that's what Ingrid's presence was all about. On a simpler level—if he brought out grass it would be clear-cut evidence that the apartment was more than just an office. Still, a certain inevitability began to surround the evening. He went and got some. From the second Ingrid had walked in, he had felt a little stoned anyway. Gowran seized his joint and began to suck on it elaborately in the style of the suburban experimenter; more predictably, Ingrid declined, saying, "I don't need this. It is a waste of time. Come. What do you want to do?" She took a seat between them on the couch, cradling both Ullman's and the tax collector's head against her giant bosom and saying, "Poor babies." Ullman wasn't sure if it was the grass or a certain drugged aroma that came from the girl's flesh, but there was a jump in time, some minutes or perhaps a large part of an hour that fell out of the evening, like a skipped piece of film, and the next thing he knew the three were standing on his Swedish rug, arms around each other, none of them wearing clothes. *A little music,* " the tax collector whispered to Ullman. Gowran's voice, in a whisper, had none of the reedy internal-revenue style to it. It was surprisingly continental. As Ullman made the adjustments on his stereo set, he became aware of a sharply attractive fragrance which he took to be Ingrid's Germanic cologne. Then, too, there was the possibility that it might be Gowran's aftershave, a subtle concoction which Ullman would never have dreamed was favored by federal tax agents. Selecting an album somewhere between hard rock and the big-band sound of the '40s, Ullman turned and for a panicky moment saw that the couple was gone. But then he tracked them into the bedroom and found them on his heart-shaped bed, a hundred versions of them reflected in his craftily arranged wall-and-ceiling mirrors.

Ullman slipped in beside the couple, who had begun, tentatively without him, and soon caught their rhythm, he and the tax collector wandering across the girl's heavy-duned body, Ingrid, not bored, but somewhere beyond them, as though she were a huge piece of experiential statuary stretching herself voluptuously in the sunlight. The unspoken rules were that Ullman and the taxman were to make love to her, but that both were to occupy separate zones and never to make contact with one another. Until one moment, deep in the night, when Ullman heard the revenue man whisper "over this way" and it seemed natural to alter the rules somewhat and finally, to abandon them altogether. And then, in an even deeper chamber of the night, the girl was gone and Ullman could recall no effort on either his or Gowran's part to keep her there.

In the morning, Ullman awoke with an awareness that he had not slept very long. At the same time, he felt none of the staleness that generally went with lack of sleep. A moment later, Gowran, fully dressed except for the thin civil-service necktie, stood above him with an opened can of condensed milk, wanting to know if it was fresh enough to use with his coffee. "I think it's okay," said Ullman. He brushed his teeth then, put in his contact lenses and showered, deliberately keeping his thoughts vague in the stream of hot water and preferring not to confront just yet the central new fact of his existence: that no matter how he sliced it, he had spent the night in a tax collector's arms. After changing the sheets and making the bed, he dressed, making sure that everything he wore was spotlessly new and clean—and then he appeared in the breakfast alcove.

"Get some sleep?" asked Gowran, sipping his coffee and riffling through Ullman's daily record book, making a note or two.

"Not bad," said Ullman. "What happened to your girlfriend?"

"Nice kid, huh?" said Gowran. "She had an appointment. You want to start now or get some breakfast first? I've got some questions about April 1968. Your figures don't add up."

"All right, hold it right there," said Ullman, pouring some juice and then slamming down the container. "I don't think you quite realize what's happened. You know, I just don't do this. This is a very big thing to me, I've never done this in my life. I won't kid you. I've had the thought a few times and maybe I even knew that some day I'd get around to it and give it a try. But I've never actually done it before. Never even come near it. This is a very strong new thing for me. I haven't even begun to assess the effect of it yet. I may not even be able to function normally when it hits me. My whole personality could be out the window. For Christ's sakes, I haven't done anything like this since Roger Lacey in Bunk Nine at Camp Deerfleet and that was nothing compared to last night. That was just a harmless little cupcake. For all I know this may turn out to be the single most shattering thing I've ever done in my thirties. I may get a goddamned nervous breakdown over last night and you want to casually jump in and review calendar notes for April '68."

"That's right," said Gowran, munching on a toasted English muffin and turning the pages of Ullman's diary until he came to the page he wanted. "Now who's this fellow Benziger and what do you fellows find to talk about three times a week at expensive French restaurants?"

"Bitch," said Ullman and was shocked by the unmistakably female hiss that accompanied the outburst.

BEDTIME FOR GONZO
Down and Out at the Reagan Inauguration

MIKE WILMINGTON

JUNE 1981

TWO HUNDRED DOLLARS' WORTH of expense money—shot to hell! Two days of my life—shot to hell! Two days in Washington, D.C., watching Ronald Wilson Reagan become the 40th president of the United States, and I have nothing to show for it! I've gone nowhere, seen nothing. And the few notes I did jot down are lost somewhere in a D.C. lady's apartment. The IBM Selectric typewriter is humming at me in the afternoon gloom—mocking me! Laughing at me! And the paper—its staring at me. White, creamy, blank. *Impotent little jerk, it sneers. Pathetic, worthless motormouth . . . Where are they now: your jests, your fancies, your lightfooted gambols?*

Washington had been reeling in the throes of a horrendous cold snap for weeks, but on the day of Ronald Reagan's inauguration (Tuesday, January 20, 1981) the sun, in a burst of whimsy sliced open the threatening clouds with all the perverse energy of Richard Nixon dumping his files into the paper shredder. Radiant sunbeams bathed the streets of Georgetown in a golden shower. A sense of hope filled those suddenly honeyed streets— hope and faith (if not charity). Nature itself was pouring down, bending its beneficent rays upon Ronald Wilson Reagan, the man they had laughed at, ridiculed, dismissed as a third-rate actor and howling bigot with no brains and Grecian Formula waves, but who now was ready to ride down Pennsylvania Avenue in triumph.

Not bad, not bad. A little purple, maybe have to cut it later. But at least it's something. Reagan, the sun, Washington, ah . . . what comes next? Explanations? Scene setting? Christ, what a bummer!

Let me set the stage. I was there when this revolutionary transition took place. I was there clutching my press credentials and my letter from *High Times* editorial director Ratso Sloman (demanding, politely, that I be extended every courtesy)—there as the *official* representative of that magazine read with enthusiasm and devotion by God knows how many loyal, patriotic, hard-working Americans.

You see, I know my editor. I know the fierce reverence in which he holds the doctor of gonzo, Hunter S. Thompson, who inhabits his personal pantheon, along with Dylan, Andy Bathgate, Joni Mitchell and some sleazeball called Kinky. Eight years ago we covered the Republican convention in Miami together for the University of Wisconsin *Daily Cardinal* and Ratso babbled nonstop about Thompson and his *Rolling Stone* campaign coverage; he was dissuaded at the last minute from titling our piece "Fear and Loathing in Miami."

So I offered myself—sneakily—as a legitimate (but much cheaper) substitute.

"Great!" shouted the editor, irrepressible, ebullient. "Great! Gonzo! Perfect! I'll set it all up this afternoon!" Sloman whipped up his phone, began stabbing at the dial. "Listen, we'll send you down there with an artist—Ralph Steadman, if we can get him. I'll pull out every credential you could ask for. You'll get into everything! I'll have you in the Goddamn presidential box! It'll be you, Nancy Reagan, and her New York butt-boy— what's his name—Jerome Zipkin! By God, by the end of the inauguration I'll have you in Nancy's pants! Go to it! Gonzo me, baby! Gonzo me!"

And the pollution-shrouded Manhattan sun set upon a wildly enthused Sloman, touch-dialing his way into the Halls of the Mighty . . .

But three months later things had taken a turn for the worse. I knew by then that Ratso had struck out. I knew that the cartoonist and I had no credentials. I knew we had no cooperation. We hadn't even established a level of civilized discourse with the Reagan mob. The magazine's request for credentials had been turned down, by a mysterious, unreachable figure named Dixie Dodd, the Inaugural Press Queen.

For the next four days I tried, with increasing frustration, to reach Dixie. No dice. Dixie was skulking somewhere behind a battalion of glib, rude flak catchers who gave terse responses and then hung up. This wasn't necessarily because they were pissed at *High Times*. They had no idea who I was. They were just naturally and congenitally, it seemed, rude and unmannerly assholes. Perhaps, I began to suspect, there *was* no Dixie Dodd. Perhaps she was a fairy tale, or a comic strip.

Dawn broke on the day before Inauguration '80, crisp and bright and right on schedule. Quickly I set up a command post in my temporary accommodations: one telephone on a crumb-strewn dining-room tablecloth. My first, second and third calls are all to Dixie Dodd—which makes about thirty-two all told during the past four days—no luck. But I do locate my major journalistic contact: an ace investigative reporter. He answers my queries with an insider's weariness, as if—God help us—we'd all been over this dull, plowed ground a hundred times before; it had yielded up every last, desiccated root you could expect.

"The inauguration?" he asks. "You're covering the inauguration? What in hell for? That's got to be the dumbest, most depressing assignment I can think of. How did they stick you with that?"

"I asked for it."

"Why?"

"Well, ah, you see, I figured this is an important moment, a crisis. A turning point in American history. After all, no political change of this magnitude has occurred since 1932. Or maybe 1952."

"True, true!"

"So I figured somebody ought to be there. To keep an eye on things. Ridicule them. Do a sort of Hunter Thompson–style piece."

"Hunter Thompson, huh?"

"Yes. It really doesn't matter if it's dull. The point is to get close to these people and expose them."

"Well, good luck. My feeling is that if you *do* get close to them, you'll probably expire from boredom. This is a *dull* crowd. This is a *dull* event. I doubt if anyone in Washington even really gives a fuck. You have no idea of the stupidity, emptiness, and banality these Reagan people represent. They're in a fucking class by themselves."

"Well, what are they doing? Somebody must be doing something spicy."

"Nothing. Nothing. I tell you, you're *dreaming* if you think you can get anything exciting out of this. Besides, I don't think they're going to *let* you get anywhere near them. I think your perspective on this gig is going to be something like the field nigger out in the cottonfield, watching the white folks at the Cotillion Ball through the French windows. Listen, these people have a motto, a creed. It's becoming obvious to everyone: Fuck the press."

"Fuck the press?"

"Right. Fuck the press. And fuck the poor. These people and their vision of grandeur come from a world view and a cultural perspective about an inch high. I don't envy you at all. This is one of the worst fucking assignments you could possibly come up with."

I begin nudging the ace investigative reporter with questions about the Teamsters, Jacky Presser, "Weasel" Fratianno, and the Reagan transition team—which he fields disinterestedly.

"Listen," he finally parries. "The guy you want to talk to is this friend of mine in the Justice Department. He says the whole campaign is a criminal enterprise."

"He says what?"

"You heard me. And he *knows*. He's been investigating the Teamster-Mafia connection for years. Talk to him. He's got more information than you'll know what to do with."

My adrenaline started running again. I had visions of a hot, epochal, transcontinental scoop.

REAGAN REVEALED AS BAGMAN FOR THE MOB.

HOLDS OFF POLICE IN DESPERATE SHOOTOUT.

"Come and get me, coppers, come and get me," snarled "Dutch" Reagan, as he plastered himself against the Oval Office wall to avoid another hail of bullets from the D.C. SWAT team outside. He pressed a drenched handkerchief to his nose to ward off the effects of the acrid tear gas—the gas that was drifting everywhere through the blackened, gutted shell that had once been the "White" House. Outside, a deadly tattoo of occasional rifle fire crackled. It sounded just like popcorn, just like the popcorn his grandma used to make in the steamy, hot, comfortable kitchen back in Tampico, Illinois! No more tomorrows. Dutch had pulled his last copy, and he was about to kiss tomorrow goodbye.

"Give up, Dutch!" roared a voice from a bullhorn out on the line. Outside, the White House lawn was choked with police cars and barricades. Searchlights knifed through the evening gloom, cutting holes in the veil of tear gas. Helicopters wheeled overhead, making an ominous hum.

"No dice, coppers!" he roared.

Suddenly, all the lights in the outer hallway went dead.

"Dutch! Dutch!"

It was a high-pitched, frenzied voice, coming from somewhere at the rear of the room. Dutch swiveled, warily, his heater in his mitt.

"Who is it?" he yelled back. "I'm warning you, mister, I've got a roscoe in my hand and a bullet with your name on it."

"Don't shoot, Dutch! Don't shoot!" came the frantic whisper. "It's me, Frankie!"

Through the boiling clouds of tear gas, flashes of light sweeping the windows, Dutch saw a familiar, squat little form scurrying toward him. He gasped.

"Frankie!" he cried, "Frankie! Is it you? They told me you was singing, Frankie. I thought you'd either turned stoolie, or, or . . . or they'd iced you."

"Nah, Dutch. Nah, not me. They tried to grill me but I gave 'em the slip. It ain't me that's singin'. It's that ratfink Tricky Dick. He's blown the whistle on everybody."

Dutch nodded as outside he could hear the helicopters making closer and closer passes, filling the inky night with their sinister hum. Tricky Dick! The worthless, lying bastard. He might have known. Well, it was all over now. Suddenly the entire room was illuminated by a vast flood of light, and Dutch could see—perhaps for the last time—the Woodrow Wilson chair, the bust of George Washington, the Abraham Lincoln table, all turned over and piled near the doors as a barricade against the bulls.

The bullhorn began blaring with a renewed intensity: "Dutch Reagan, this is your last chance! Come on out with your hands up!"

And, another voice, quavery and old, but with the fondly remembered touch of Irish syrup in it . . .

"Dutch, boy, it's me, Father Pat. I'm out here to guarantee your safety, Dutch. For God's sake, boy, give up. I've told the authorities you fell in with bad companions. Nancy's out here, Dutch. She's been waitin' for you. She loves you. Give up, Dutch, and throw yourself on the mercy of the Lord. He's a good ol' sod, Dutch, and he wont let you down!"

Frankie was whispering in his ear: "It's a lie, Dutch. A lie! I know what they're planning. Father O'Brien's juiced to the gills. They're going to cut you to ribbons as soon as you set foot outside. It's Bush and Tricky Dick—they're behind all this."

"Well, Frankie," said Dutch, as the light blazed around them and portraits of Chester Arthur and John Quincy Adams beamed down oily benevolence. "Then I guess this is the end. Are you with me?"

Frankie clutched Dutch's shoulder and then was the trace of a tear on his aging tough-kid features. "Always, Dutch, to the end."

"All the way?"

"All the way, Dutch."

A grin broke out on Dutch's boyish face as the racket of the helicopter came closer and closer. "We had high hopes, didn't we Frankie?"

Frankie nodded, and now the tear was unashamed. "It was a very good year."

"Dutch! In three minutes, we're coming in!"

"Okay, Frankie," Dutch whispered. "Let's give them something to remember us by . . ."

It's 2:00, I'm at Union Station. I'm there to pick up the cartoonist, who's buzzing in on the Amtrak from New York with our expense money. For all I know, I've blown this one, too.

Ah, *there* the guy is. Thank God for small favors. Jeff ambles over with a distinctly low pressure, amiable expression, skinny, hippie-style beard and hair, in a nondescript brown outfit. No mistaking. This is the guy. I'm feeling bitter, feisty.

"Listen," I say to Jeff, trying to muster up a little machismo. "These bastards can't get away with this. They're going to regret not giving us credentials. What we do is this: We besiege them. We storm them. We *demand* credentials. We turn *that* into the story. And, of course, the lousy good-for-nothing pricks won't give us any. But that's the beautiful part of it, because then we get to describe them. You, with your satiric pencils, me with my mastery of wit and invective. We'll immortalize these cretins. They'll cringe whenever they hear the word *high* from now on."

"Right," says Jeff, amiably. "Sounds good."

"Are you with me?"

"All the way."

But our expedition hits another snag. Sloman has conceived an ingenious plan for the story. Total sleaze. A note from the underground. He wants us to check into some scumgutter of a hotel, overrun with winos and junkies, the paint peeling off the walls, and maybe a "lounge" with fading red plastic stools and Patti Page songs on the jukebox. The lower depths.

So we set out down Avenue K in search of sleaze. Jeff vaguely remembers a sixth-rate hotel called the Ambassador. We walk past housing project after housing project, trash blowing past us, through vast open fields of grayish dirt. Plenty of sleaze but no Ambassador Hotel. Jeff gets us booked into something called the Presidential. By then, unbeknownst to either of us, our last chance to harass the now mythical Dixie Dodd has vanished. The Inauguration Press Committee has closed up shop at 4:00 and is no longer in existence.

The Presidential is no junkie hangout, but it seems to be well located, only a subway stop from the White House. An ideal command post. The name of the hotel, actually, is not the Presidential, but the Presidenti l, since one of the neon letters has gone winking off into oblivion. It is filled up not with winos and junkies but with foreign dignitaries, a high proportion of them speaking Russian and a few other Slavic languages.

Also, the Presidential's dining facilities consist of a small cubicle resembling a boiler room, where an Indian gentleman is dispensing Saran-wrapped fruit pies, Mars bars and bologna sandwiches. Bone-weary we head out to catch some dinner before the start of Frank Sinatra's inaugural gala. A fresh surprise awaits us. Up and down Avenue K we go. Down and up. Every place we hit is either closed or looks formidably expensive. Downtown Washington is close to a ghost town. We find one hamburger joint. But the bouncer—a blond, glowering hulk in a polyester suit—informs us we're in violation of the dress code. "To get in here, you have to look like me," he growls.

As we wander off, I begin fuming and ranting. It's not enough that we can't get into the inaugural balls—we can't even get into the goddamn hamburger joints! We shuffle on, find a pizza place with no dress code and, after splitting a small sausage-and-pepper pie, arrive back at our room in time for the gala.

Capitol Center is crammed to the gills with the Republican faithful. I doubt more than a handful of the working press was able to squeeze in at all. There's a sadistic edge to the evening, a sense of accumulated nastiness. Deprecatory jokes about Jimmy Carter or George McGovern are greeted with howls of hilarity; the audience, stuffed into their evening gowns and tuxes and no doubt basted to a fine golden shimmer with booze and rich cuisine, give off an almost tangibly malicious gleam. The people there have been shined to such a high polish that they could practically send semaphore signals to each other from across the auditorium.

On television, every five-minute snippet of "entertainment" is surrounded by three or four commercials (for oil companies, American Express, toiletries, cars and booze). Johnny Carson sneering about McGovern, and a quick cut to the Alaskan pipeline, Donny and Marie flailing around with a perversion of Chuck Berry retitled "Ronnie B. Goode," a cut to the president beaming and cackling, and then another cut to deodorants and toilet cleaners. Grim-faced Marines escorting everyone up the stage. A tight shot of a Budweiser beer can, and reaction shots of the crowd, holding their bellies in and grinning in slack-jawed triumph.

My mind begins to reel. Is this really happening? Is that really Ben Vereen out there, shuffling and scratching and rolling his eyes like Little Black Sambo? (Charley Pride goes Vereen one better when he grins bashfully toward the presidential box and thanks "Miz Nancy" for inviting him.) Is that Ethel Merman belting out "Everything's coming up roses and jelly beans"? And—most numbing of all—is that really Jimmy Stewart, drawling and stuttering out a tribute to his new commander in chief? Brigadier General Stewart is there as the official escort to Gen. Omar Bradley, who is pushed onstage in a wheelchair, looking like a withered old zombie stoned on morphine who'd just been disconnected from his respirator and stolen from the hospital by pranksters. "Ya . . . ya just do-don't know," stutter-drawls Jimmy, "ha-'how happy it makes me to call you Mr. President." And—as he and the practically comatose General Bradley salute—bouncing Ronnie, like a windup doll, pops to and snaps off a brisk, Norman Rockwell-*Boy's Life*-cub-scout salute.

The closing act is Sinatra, however—an act that shouldn't go wrong. Unfortunately it does. Clutching the mike, he stares at Nancy Reagan and warbles, without a trace of shame, a new version of one of his old hits, "Nancy with the Laughing Face" now retitled "Nancy with the *Reagan* Face." The first lady responds by blowing him a schoolgirl kiss.

Finally Reagan bounds onstage, beaming from ear to ear. "Well," he begins, mimicking Rich Little's mimicry of him. (Jeez, what a regular guy!) He then launches into a condescending prose-poem by Irvin S. Cobb describing actors and performers as adorable little children who bring sunshine into the world and should be allowed to pass through the gates of heaven. (Reagan, stiff as ever, mispronounces Cobb's name as "Irwin S. Cobb.")

After two hours of this degraded spectacle, we escape to the Counter-Inaugural Ball in a state almost as comatose as General Bradley's.

Next morning I wake up on the other end of town. The house is deserted. The radiance of the day before has passed, and the first day of Ronald Reagan's presidency has a chilly, white clarity.

The Washington subway mirrors my barren mood. It is a science-fiction subway: It looks like a set for Kubrick or Lucas—a huge, wformblike tunnel, softly lit, through which the train itself seems to pad along on cushions of foam, and where the constant darkness on the platforms carries a whisper of sterile elegance and dangerous Utopias. The D.C. subway would be a good setting for a chase between the Dream Police and the Last Free Man in the year 2084. It shoots me along like an aluminum crossbow, and within minutes I am back at the Presidential, where, naturally, I have missed connections with Jeff. I spend an anxious two hours prowling the corridors with the constant guttural jabber of the Russians stabbing at my paranoia.

Finally desperate, I head out alone on the subway toward the White House and Reagan's inauguration—the sorry spectacle that has precipitated all this unthinkable misery and idiocy. But I have waited too long. The subway is packed. Full to the brim and running over. Not, however, like a Manhattan subway at rush hour. What I am observing now is a ghastly ghoulish spectacle, a surreal madhouse, a plush, foam-footed nightmare.

All along the platforms of this sinister, elegant subway in which all the conductors might be cousins of Hal, the computer, there is a howling, crazed, shoving, stampeding throng. But not the usual subway crowd, the mixture of working class and professionals elbowing each other for a seat home. The D.C. police have cordoned off all the streets, emptied them of taxis, cars and buses, emptied them of everything, in fact, but VIP cars and vans, the top-chop participants—and all these wildly enthused Republicans, these capering realtors and insurance agents and YAFers are forced to travel to the White House by subway. The same mink coats and ermines and evening gowns and morning suits and Harris tweeds that adorned the festivities last night are once again in evidence, but they are pinching, biting, scrambling, jostling, lunging all over each other in their frenzy to be seated. It is a grotesque spectacle. In the middle of the car where I end up, shoved forward by the sweating, beminked wave, there is all kinds of room, but no one moves to fill it. These are either subway neophytes or bone-lazy dullards. They all pile up near the exits, jammed together like gropers—and at every station they press back and forth like a bloodthirsty mob, determined to keep the Bastille from falling. People in Bill Blass creations and tuxedos are kneeing each other in the groin, swearing. At every stop, the doors are held open for what seems hours, as the black conductor pleads with his passengers to behave with some modicum of sanity and civilization—but the caterwauling mob only greets him with cries, jabs, and more knees to the groin. It is like a barroom brawl in the middle of Bloomingdale's. I am next to a merry giggling, obviously upper-crust Italian-American family that keeps yelling across the car and warning each other to watch for pickpockets. Unlike the grim marauders who keep waging the battle of the subway doors, committing unspeakable atrocities on each other, they are treating all this as a game, a madcap soirée. At the White House stop the frenzied mob is disgorged like toothpaste mashed from a tube.

Three huge escalators angle up toward the chilly sunshine, and they are crowded, crammed with the desperate mob—still jostling, falling all over each other in their wild, insatiable desire to see Ronald Reagan become their next president. They have abandoned all reason and restraint. They are practically slavering with glee. Two of the escalators are moving upward;

292

the other is still, a solid mass of people biting and elbowing each other on each one. I take my place on the central escalator and the mob closes around me like lemmings. All around there seems to be a fervid, rabid hum, a groundswell, an insistent beat: "Reagan, Reagan, Reagan—hypnotic, chanted like a voodoo incantation against the outer darkness. Suddenly— wild screams! A catastrophe. The right-hand escalator, for no apparent reason, has gone berserk and is carrying its full cargo of passengers back down to the depths where they are falling off and rolling all over each other like oranges. Shrieks! Howls! Then bursts of crazed laughter as the chosen ones, the ones who will make it through the gates of paradise, mock their falling brethren. "Start spreading the news" carols the family ahead of me. I stagger off the escalator like Dante emerging from the seventh circle.

"Mr. President! Mr. President! It's the crowds. We can't control them any longer. They've gone insane with joy!"

"Great, Dixie, great. That's what we need: enthusiasm! By gosh, I can remember the crowds at the Big Ten football games, back when I was a boy. The warmth! The spirit! That's what this country needs *to get back on the track again!*"

"*But Mr. President . . .*"

"*Don't call me Mr. President, Dixie. Remember what I told you. No formality. It's just plain Ron.*"

"*Yes, Mr. President . . . I mean Ron. You don't understand. I mean these people have gone* really *insane! They're rioting in the street. They're tearing down the Capitol, uprooting trees! We have reports of howling mobs literally ripping each other to bits and devouring each other. Sir, Ron, we can't handle it any longer. What in God's name can we do?*"

I let the eddies and currents of the crowd carry me to the west White House lawn where President Ron will face the Pacific as Warren Burger administers the oath of office. By now the frenzy has abated. Clots of people are pressed against each other in the mud, peering over barricades. The president, the vice-president, the Supreme Court justices, the wives, everyone is a distant blur over the fences. Reagan takes the oath—but the speakers are malfunctioning. "About time" screams an obese gentleman in a Stetson, a cigar clamped between his teeth, a transistor-radio plug in his ear. He applauds and looks around wildly. Reagan's speech begins, crackles, blurs, and then dims out completely. The speakers have broken down, and you can only hear bits and scraps over the various transistor radios. I catch a smidgen of Reagan bawling maudlinly, his voice cracking, over the diary of some World War I casualty. He seems to be beside himself. "Thattaboy!" screams the man in the Stetson.

"God!" I think to myself. "This is probably the worst coverage of a major media event in modern journalistic history! I can't even see or hear what's going on. For all I know, Reagan is reciting 20 Mule Team Borax commercials up there."

"Thattaboy! Give it to 'em!" screams the fat man in the Stetson, blood-lust in his eyes.

"My friends and fellow Americans, as I stand up here, staring out upon this broad and proud land, with its waving wheat fields, its giant oaks, its industry its verdant fields and blue skies, I think to myself—I think—by crackie, what is it I think? Heh, heh! Seems to have slipped my mind completely! Whatever it was, it was a good 'un. Yessirreebob, when old Ronnie Reagan comes up with an idea, he doesn't shit around. But, meanwhile, I thought I'd tell you a little joke, about the Polack nun and the dwarf with the vibrator . . ."

Plunged into what seems a permanent funk, I let the ermined crowd, still chuckling and cackling, whirl me back through the subways. No more jostling. No more gnawing at each other. A deadly glee seems to have set-tled over everyone. At the Presidential, I hook back up with Tiedrich, and we wander back up the streets to get a vantage point for the inaugural parade. The crowds seem to have turned surly. When we reach a rise in a little park, people are tearing up bricks and piling them on top of each other to get a better view. We stand next to a pimpled, uniformed character whose name tag reads "Presidential Chauffeur, Manson" and who eyes us suspiciously. We stand. We stand some more. Jesus freaks prowl through the park, screaming at everybody to repent. A bum is swaying precariously on his little pile of bricks. A helicopter keeps passing overhead. More people are scaling the brick walls of nearby buildings and clinging to the windowsills. We wait. The hours stretch into days, weeks! An evil gray pall has descended—over the entire world.

Finally, after what seems to have been a delay of several centuries, it appears. The presidential motorcade. Slow. Stately. An open convertible, and on each side of it, a troupe of grim-faced Secret Service men—all suitably attired for the hamburger joint—plodding along in grim unison. Perched on top of the convertible is what looks to me from this distance, like an inflatable rubber Ronald Reagan doll, smiling and waving and turning around. I can practically see the revolving key in its back. The crowd cheers, waves hundreds of little American flags. The bum teeters on his pile of bricks, catches his balance. He belches. Then the president has passed. And behind him, Bush, another little American flag in his hands, waving it and flailing his arms, a truly demented expression on his face. What seems to be the sound of a dozen or more military bands wafts in from the distance, along with the clop-clop of hundreds of horses, all of them, apparently, dropping huge turds on the streets as they pass. (This has become a matter of some concern, especially to the marching bands who have to wade through the stuff.) We amble on back to the hotel. The bum is still swaying back and forth. Bush is still waving his little flag. Along with hundreds of other people, we try to cut through a vacant lot and wind up clambering along huge, tottering piles of jagged cement, while over on one side two people dressed as M-11 missiles are dancing a jig. Someone passes us an incomprehensible Marxist pamphlet full of misspellings, which advises us to disregard everything that is being written and broadcast, including the pamphlet itself. We finish a meal at a fast-food vegetarian restaurant and swing back in time to see the end of the parade: an equestrian squad of bearded mountaineers in coonskin caps, carrying rifles, and, behind them, the Mormon Tabernacle Choir on a float, lip-synching "God Bless America." Then the parade passes by and the crowd closes in from both sides. The streets are being drenched to clean away the horseshit, and the park is in a shambles.

Nighttime in Washington, D.C. The first evening of the New Age. Fireworks explode over the Washington Monument in chains of coruscating color, streams of fire, accompanied by the kind of crackling and banging Napoleon must have heard at Waterloo. Another counterinaugural. Night, blessed night, descends on Washington, D.C., hides it, surrounds it.

The next morning I am on the Amtrak back to New York City. Back to the city of slashers and Jesus-freak assassins and puke-soaked subways and the *New York Post*. Back to relative sanity and coherence. Like leaving Hitler's Eagle's Nest for the comforts of Auschwitz. Munching on a cheeseburger, I notice an incredibly fat gentleman in a checkered suit across the aisle. He has rubicund cheeks and a Salvador Dali mustache, and he's fondling a little plastic model of Godzilla. I also notice that he's scribbling away in a notebook and poring over three days' worth of copies of the *Washington Post*. I catch his eye and smile. He grunts back. "Reporter?" I ask.

"Yup," he responds, and stuffs what seems to be a sardine-and-lettuce sandwich on pumpernickel into his mouth, washing it down with a can of 7Up. "Inaugural, huh?"

"Yup."

"So was I." I extend my hand. "I'm Mike Wilmington."

The fat man wipes his palm on his tie—it has a phosphorescent picture of Rita Hayworth spread across it—drops his little Godzilla, and extends his hand. "Glad to meet you. Hunter Thompson."

I stare at him in disbelief. "Hunter Thompson?"

"Yup."

"*The* Hunter Thompson?"

"Yup. Here—want some of my Kit-Kat bar?"

"But, but . . . I've seen *pictures* of Hunter Thompson. You don't look anything like him."

The fat man stares at me a second, takes another swig of 7Up, and blows his nose into his sleeve. He shakes his head. "Oh, *that* guy. That's just some terminal drug patient from Lexington we hired as a model. Don't believe everything you see on book jackets."

I watch "Thompson" for a second or two. "You mean, *you* write all that stuff? You wrote *Fear and Loathing in Las Vegas?*"

The fat man, looking bored, begins to thumb through a copy of *Rona Barrett's Hollywood Gossip.* "Sure, sure."

"You were covering the inauguration?"

"Yeah, but not as Thompson. I was using my other pseudonym: David Halberstam." I stare at him, utterly speechless. His little plastic Godzilla perched on a heap of chicken bones stares back. Under his breath, the fat man hums a few bars of "Yes, We Have No Bananas."

"Well," I say, finally, "bummer of a convention, wasn't it?"

Thompson begins picking his teeth with a little mint-flavored tooth-pick. "Wouldn't know. I never went *near* Washington. I've been covering the whole thing from a motel in Davenport, Iowa. I just dropped down there to validate all my expense vouchers." He looks over at me and, above the phosphorescent lewd twinkle of Rita Hayworth, gives me a baleful glance. "Didn't like it, huh?"

I shake my head, numb. Outside, Wilmington, Delaware, rushes by in a blur.

"Well, kid," says Thompson, picking up his copy of *Rona Barrett's Hollywood Gossip,* "you got a lot to learn."

MY SCROTUM FLEW TOURIST

A Personal Odyssey

KINKY FRIEDMAN

SEPTEMBER 1981

FORMING A COUNTRY-WESTERN band and calling it the Texas Jewboys was either a very smart or a very stupid thing to do. I was a Peace Corps volunteer in Borneo. I was stranded in the jungle for a year and a half once and the idea just crossed my desk.

I was living in a Kayan longhouse upriver from the town of Long Lama in Sarawak. The Kayans had been headhunters as recently as World War II and they still kept souvenir skulls in hanging baskets on the porch. The skulls in baskets were to the Kayans what green hanging plants are to many nonsmoking vegetarian roller skaters today.

Most Americans are too civilized to hang skulls from baskets, having been headhunters, of course, only as recently as Vietnam.

I remember we were returning from a fishing expedition one night, paddling up-river by torchlight. We were chewing betel nut and drinking tuak, a brutal, gnarly, viciously hallucinogenic wine carefully culled from the vineyards of Lord Jim.

The Kayans don't give a flying Canadian whether they catch any fish or not. They claim to be "visiting the fish." This quaint and primitively poetic little notion, unfortunately for them, does not culturally compute.

Yet I came to share their timeless, tribal outlook. I visited the fish. I watched the river flow. I got so high that I started to get lonely. It was a strange, gentle feeling, like warming your hands in a Neanderthal campfire. Not cosmic. Not mystical. But not the kind of thing you'd really want to share with the Charlie Daniels Band.

I never saw God in the jungles of Borneo, but it was during this time, on a dark, primeval night, that I did see a nine-hundred-foot Jack Ruby.

I still vividly remember what Jack said to me. He said, "Kinky, this is Jack. I, like yourself, am a bastard child of twin cultures. You know, I just never could forgive Dallas for . . . what they did to Kennedy. Didn't like what they did to the Redskins either . . . Kinkster, baby it's up to you now, sweetheart . . ."

In the monsoon months ahead I became almost obsessed with Jack's messianic words. Again and again I saw him in my dreams, jumping out of the shadows. I felt his warm, comforting, sleazy presence rushing through my veins in the middle of the dank jungle night like the screaming of an endless subway circus train. I saw American dreams going up like little puffs of smoke from the infamous Texas Cookbook Suppository Building in Dallas. I was proud to share Jack Ruby's heritage. Proud to be a Texan like Jack. Proud to be a Jew like Jack. I felt almost elated that he had shot Lee Harvey Oswald. It seemed fitting and proper that one of my countrymen had taken the law into his own hands and actually assassinated the assassin. "Jesus" I remember thinking at the time, "Ol' Jack must have really had some pawnshop balls!"

Years later, of course, I was a little surprised and a bit disheartened when they finally exhumed Lee Harvey Oswald's grave and found Ernest Tubb.

Jack Ruby's spirit was already abroad in that land. I had determined to form a country-music band as soon as I returned to the States, and I had sworn to myself that it would be known as Kinky Friedman and the Texas Jewboys. The torch had been passed.

A Peace Corps psychiatrist was flown in by helicopter to give me a checkup from the neck up. By this time I was pretty much cookin' on another planet. (The only other visitors I'd had in almost twenty-four months had been my parents, Dr. and Mrs. S. Thomas Friedman from Austin, Texas, who had taken a Borneo taxi, incredibly enough, all the way to the last outpost on the river. I was, naturally, thrilled to see them. I was also rather amazed to see that the driver of the taxi was Harry Chapin.)

The Peace Corps psychiatrist listened to a few of my songs and determined that I was definitely out where the buses don't run. Finally much to my chagrin, the Peace Corps director ordered that I be returned immediately to my own culture. Little did he dream that what was the Peace Corps' loss was soon to become country music's loss.

I left Borneo with nothing but my guitar and my wheelbarrow. I had run into a bit of elephantiasis in the jungle and I had to carry my scrotum in a wheelbarrow.

The very next day I was winging my way back to the States. The Peace Corps was gracious enough to buy me a first-class ticket. My scrotum flew tourist.

I got to New York just as Robert Young began filming the first of his Sanka coffee commercials for television. These, I felt, were a step down from "Father Knows Best" but certainly a step up from "Marcus Welby, M.D." Robert Young was, fortunately, a rather distant friend of the family. I had always admired him, and now I thought I'd drop by the studios and have a few words with the wise old bird.

When Robert saw me he was shocked and disturbed at how pale and thin I was. I weighed about twenty-nine pounds and was in a rather deep state of culture shock at the time. I told him I liked Borneo but that my Peace Corps director had recommended that I be returned to my own culture because I was getting very nervous in the service. Robert Young recommended that I and a rather irritable young Negro airline stewardess who was also on the set switch to Sanka brand.

Three weeks later, Robert said, "Well, Kinky; *now* how's our returned Peace Corps volunteer feeling?" By then, I weighed about 28 pounds and was in a severe case of culture shock.

"I'm feeling great, Robert," I said. "That goddamn Sanka brand really did the trick! In fact, I'm leaving for Texas today. You might check on that stewardess, though, if you get a chance."

The young Negro stewardess was hanging from a shower rod right there in the studio. Robert Young walked right up to her and put his hand on her shoulder. As I walked out he smiled and I heard three short, rather hollow laughs: "Ha-ha-ha." "Maybe that's the way Robert Young always laughed," I remember thinking. But it gave me kind of a strange, gentle feeling. Kind of like warming my hands in a Neanderthal campfire.

I went back to the ranch in Kerrville, Texas, to round up the band and rehearse and hit the road to country music's hall of fame (or shame, depending on how you looked at it). The songs I had written while in Borneo, including "Ride 'em Jewboy," "We Reserve the Right to Refuse Service to You" and "They Ain't Makin' Jews Like Jesus Anymore," had a little something to offend almost everyone. I knew if I could just reach one person out there that I'd be a success. But little did I dream that I would go on to become probably the best nationally known Jewish entertainer from Texas. That is, of course, unless you want to count Tom Landry.

In those early days I could sing, burp, tell jokes, smoke a cigar, and play two instruments—the guitar and the Jewish cornet (sometimes referred to as the nose). But not unlike the great Hank Williams, I had serious problems with my personal life. It was not a pleasant sight for many audiences or fellow band members to see me wheeling my scrotum off the stage after the show into the waiting U-haul trailer. But the band played on.

We had rehearsed for six days back at the ranch, and on the seventh day we had a sound check. The band contained many former greats and many future greats and no bass players from Los Angeles.

When the Jewboys were hot they could really send your penis to Venus. But some people and some places were not quite ready for our music. So we barrel-assed across the country—a dusty station wagon pulling a U-Haul trailer down those lost highways. From Kerrville to Nashville, from Austin to Boston, from Luckenbach to Los Angeles. Schizophrenic Sons of the Pioneers—providing bad taste in perfect harmony—setting out to prove that the world wasn't really square.

At first, we got run out of town so often that once we didn't get to go home, take a shower and get changed for three months. But that didn't bother us. Even our harshest critics had to admit: "Their music may occasionally suck bog water, but this band consistently smells bad." Actually, we kind of dug it. We figured we probably just smelled like real outlaws, like hardworking Negroes, like people smell who live in Europe.

Probably the whole thing started with Bob Dylan back in Greenwich Village where he never bathed, shaved, or brushed his teeth for years at a time. The only time he ever brushed his hair was before he went to bed. I once asked Bob why he did it. He said, "You know, Kink, I gotta make a good impression on my pillow."

Pretty soon Bob had the whole country looking and smelling like Sirhan Sirhan. "Talent's one part inspiration and nine parts perspiration," Bob wrote in one of his songs. "Now, Annette Funicello, won't you lay across my big brass bed?"

One might say that Bob's total disregard for personal hygiene, either dental or mental, ended the golden age of blond-haired Aryan dominance and brought about a new kinky-headed, more funky, fairly tedious era. It marked the end for Tab Hunter, Sandra Dee, and Fabian, but it would herald a new beginning for Isaac Hayes, Ira Hayes, Woody Hayes, and Gabby Hayes. And purple haze, for that matter.

We played one of our very first gigs in Luckenbach, Texas—a small German ghost town where they still tied their shoes with little Nazis. This was before Willie or Waylon had ever heard of Luckenbach. It wasn't on the maps or the charts. The jukebox contained mostly old German drinking songs and warped Wagnerian polkas. The only two popular titles I recognized were "You Light Up My Wife" and the great all-time standard, "Send in the Kleins."

I was a bit nervous until I looked out over the krauts. They were big and friendly and goose-stepping in time to the music. Soon they stopped polishing their Lugers altogether, clicked their heels, and broke into a moderately Teutonic variant of the bunny hop.

The days ahead were filled with excitement for me and the Texas Jewboys. We were attacked by wild Indians onstage in San Francisco for wearing those funny little dime-store Indian war bonnets and singing a funny little Indian song, "We Are the Red Men Tall and Quaint." We were attacked by dykes on bikes in Buffalo for singing "Get Your Biscuits in the Oven and Your Buns in the Bed." One called me a "male show business pig." We needed a police escort to get out of town. Negroes chased us in Denver. Rednecks ran us out of Nacogdoches, Texas, on two different occasions. Mild-mannered, pointy-headed, liberal Jews called us a *shanda* in New York and born-again nerds in the Richie Furay Band tried

to shut us down in Atlanta when I sang "Men's Room, L.A.," a religious
ballad:

I saw a picture yesterday
In a men's room near L.A.
Lying on the floor beside the throne
Had I not recognized the cross
I might have failed to know the boss
I thought "Lord you look neglected and alone."

I picked it up with loving care
I wondered who had placed it there
Then I saw there was no paper on the roll
I said "Lord what would you do
If you were me and I were you
Take a chance, save your pants or your soul?"

And a voice said "Kinky, this is Jesus
I ain't square I got these pictures everywhere
From Florida on out to Frisco Bay
So boy, if you're hung up on the pot
Feel free to use my favorite shot."
I saw a picture yesterday
In a men's room near L.A.*

Finally, I had to send the Texas Jewboys off on sabbatical for a while.
"When the time is right," I vowed to myself, "I'll bring them all back and
give them each two or three hundred dollars." I hope someday still to
make that dream a reality, though I'm not too sure about the two or three
hundred dollars.

The point was people were beginning to hear my songs. The point was
also, rather unfortunately right on top of my head. People were beginning
to accept me for what I was—a highly ambulatory, somewhat unpleasant
American with a terminal case of Lone Star Beer and a tertiary case of

syphilis that I had apparently run into somewhere in the jungles of Borneo. In his unbridled eagerness to give me and my scrotum the hook, the Peace Corps doctor had overlooked the latter.

Meanwhile, I kept traveling the American countryside playing my songs, telling my jokes, and consciously infecting toilet seats practically everywhere I went. This included (in what was to prove an unfortunate career move), Kenny Rogers' brand new forty-foot jade toilet seat.

I still vividly remember emerging from Rogers's extremely ornate dumper into his sequined living room. The Southern California sun was ricocheting ferociously from the chandelier to the swimming pool to the tennis courts and back again into my right iris.

"You ol' storyteller, you," I said humorously. "I can understand the chandelier, the swimming pool, the tennis courts . . . but Kenny," I asked, shaking my head incredulously, "why in the world would you need a forty-foot jade toilet seat?"

"Well, Kink, you know," he said rather wistfully, "we never had one when I was growin' up."

But "the times they were a'changin'," as Willie Nelson sang in one of his songs. Negroes were coming out of woodpiles, Christians were coming out of their mobile homes, women were coming out of the kitchen, and homosexuals and Jews were coming out of the closet.

I was coming out of a men's room in Denver, Colorado. It was one of the last stops on Bob Dylan's Rolling Thunder Revue, and back then I was as happy as the shah of Iran. I had just taken a rather large and highly gratifying nixon . . . I had walked miles and miles of bathroom tiles . . . I was thinking of many things. Weird phrases peppered my cerebellum. "Save Soviet Jews— Win Valuable Prizes." . . . "Here I sit/Straining my pooper/Tryin' to give birth/To a Texas state trooper." I flashed on other times, other dimes, other walls, other stalls, other balls, other halls, other words, other turds, other nerds . . . young couples shopping for flavored toilet soaps in Georgetown, D.C. . . . myself teaching Frisbee to the natives of Borneo . . . some of the

* *Words and music by Buck Fowler Kinky Music, Inc BMI*

natives stealing the Frisbees . . . using them to make their lips big . . . setting back my Frisbee program. I saw the best minds of my generation destroyed by Holiday Inn sanitary wrappers shimmering in the night . . . truckstops . . . rubber machines before the Trojan War . . . airports and runways and young couples buying ludicrous, Freudian-flavored thought associations.

When I came to, a steaming cup of Sanka brand coffee was on a tray at my side and Robert Young was smiling down at me. An orderly was wheeling a wheelbarrow with a white sheet over it out into the hallway. "What happened?" I asked. "Where am I?"

"Take it easy now, Kinkster," said Robert Young. "You've had a bad accident and you're in the Cedars of Tedium Hospital. Apparently you were run over by a bookmobile as you were coming out of a men's room in Denver, Colorado. To save your life we had to give you a transfusion using the blood of a person of the Negro persuasion."

"That's moderately unpleasant," I said.

"Well, there's a good side of things, too," said Robert Young. "Your welfare checks should start coming in a few weeks, and your penis just grew twelve inches. Ha-ha-ha."

SAY CHEESE

Frank Zappa

November 1981

IT HAS BEEN SUGGESTED that the GNP is perhaps not the best indicator of how well we are doing as a society since it tells us nothing about the *Quality of Our Lives* . . . but, *is this something worth dwelling upon as we grovel our way along in the general direction of the 21st century?* When future historians write about us, if they base their conclusions on whatever material goods survive from Present-Day America, we will undoubtedly stand alone among nations and be known forevermore as "THOSE WHO CHOSE CHEESE."

As you will recalls, folks, nobody ever has as much going for them in the beginning as we did. Let's face it . . . we were fantastic. Today, unfortunately, we are merely *WEIRD*. This is a shocking thing to say since no Red-Blooded American likes to think of him- or herself as being *WEIRD* but when there are other options and a whole nation CHOOSES CHEESE, that is *WEIRD*.

Our mental health has been in a semi-wretched condition for quite some time now. One of the reasons for this distress, aside from CHOOSING CHEESE as a way of life, is the fact that we have (against some incredibly stiff competition) emerged victorious as the biggest bunch of liars on the face of the planet. No society has managed to invest more time and energy in the perpetuation of the fiction that it is *moral, sane, and wholesome* than our current crop of *Modern Americans*.

This same delusion is the Mysterious Force behind our national desire to avoid behaving in any way that might be construed as INTELLIGENT. *Modern Americans* behave as if intelligence were some sort of hideous deformity. To cosmeticize it, many otherwise normal citizens attempt a peculiar type of self-inflicted homemade mental nose job (designed to lower the recipient's sociointellectual profile to the point where the ability to communicate on the most Mongolian level provides the necessary *certification* to become ONE OF THE GUYS). Let's face it . . . nobody wants to hang out with somebody who is smarter than they are. This is not fun.

Americans have always valued the idea of FUN. We have a National Craving for FUN. We don't get very much of it anymore, so we do two things: first, we rummage around for *anything* that *might* be FUN, then (since it really wasn't FUN stuff in the first place) we *pretend* to enjoy it (*whatever it was*). The net result: STRESSED CHEESE.

But where does all this CHEESE really come from? It wouldn't be fair to blame it all on TV, although some credit must be given to whoever it is at each of the networks that GIVES US WHAT WE WANT. (*You don't ask, you don't get.*) Folks, we now have got it . . . lots of it . . . and, in our Infinite American Wisdom, we have constructed elaborate systems to insure that future generations will have an even more abundant supply of that fragrant substance upon which we presently thrive.

If we can't blame it on the TV, then where *does* it come from? Obviously, we are weird if we have to ask such a question. Surely we must realize by now (except for the fact that we lie to ourselves so much that we get confused sometimes) that as *Contemporary Americans* we have an almost magical ability to turn anything we touch into a festering mound of self-destructing poot.

How can we do this with such incredible precision? Well, one good way is to form a *Committee*. *Committees* composed of all kinds of desperate American Types have been known to convert the combined unfulfilled emotional needs and repressed biological urges of their memberships into complex masses of cheeselike organisms at the rap of a gavel. *Committee Cheese* is usually sliced very thin, then bound into volumes for eventual dispersal in courts of law, legislative chambers, and public facilities where you are invited to *eat all you want*.

If that doesn't fill you up, there's the exciting *Union Cheese*, the most readily available cheese type offered. The thing that's so exciting about *Union Cheese*, from a gourmet's point of view, is the classic simplicity of the mathematical formula from which it is derived. In fact, it is difficult to avoid a state of Total Ecstasy if one contemplates the proposition that *no import quota yet devised has proven equal to the task of neutralizing the lethal emissions generated by the ripening process of this piquant native confection.* Should we not be overtaken by some unspeakable emotion when we consider the fact that . . . the *smaller* the amount of care taken in the preparation of each *Union Cheese Artifact,* the *more triumphant the blast* as the vapors steam forth from every nook and cranny of whatever it was that the stalwart craftsperson got paid nineteen dollars per hour to slap together.

Still hungry? *Union Cheese* might be the most readily available, but no type of cheese in America today has achieved the popular acceptance of *Accountant Cheese.* If it is true that YOU ARE WHAT YOU EAT, then surely our national willingness to eat *this stuff* tells us more about ourselves than we probably wish to know. Obviously we have found *The Cheese to Believe In.* Why not? It is manufactured by people who *count money,* endorsed as *nutritionally sound* by Civic Leaders, and delivered by The Media *door to door.*

The Quality of Our Lives (if we think of this matter in terms of *"How much* of what we *individually* consider to be *Beautiful* are we *able to experience* every day?"*) seems an irrelevant matter, now that all decisions regarding the creation and distribution of *Works of Art* must first pass *under the limbo bar* (a.k.a. "The Bottom Line"), along with things like *Taste* and *The Public Interest,* all tied like a tin can to the wagging tail of the second *Prime Rate Poodle.* The aforementioned *festering poot* is coming your way at a theater or drive-in near you. It wakes you up every morning as it droozles out of your digital clock radio. An ARTS COUNCIL somewhere is getting a special batch ready with little tuxedos on it so you can think it's *precious.*

Yes, Virginia . . . there is a FREE LUNCH. We are eating it now. Can I get you a napkin?

SEX & DRUGS & TOM FORÇADE

My Eight Years With High Times *(And Then Some)*

DEAN LATIMER

JUNE 1982

"WHO DISTURBS MY REST?" It was obviously my yearlong office mate, Bob Lemmo, but I made my voice baleful as possible anyway. It was barely eleven in the morning, a beautiful June morning in 1979. Even *Lemmo* ought be discouraged from ringing my phone at any such damn-fool wholesome hour.

"It's Gabrielle!" It could have been Godzilla, from the tone of his voice. "She just came up with a bunch of goons and took the place over. Lawyers, too! There's Silver Streak Cadillacs from one end of the block to the other. You gotta get over here and see this, Latimer. It's Gabrielle!"

"Awwww, *fuck!*" The phlegm flew straight across my top-floor hooker-hotel room, and said "whop" against the plaster. "At eleven o'clock in the Goddamn *morning* she's got to pull this? I'll get my britches on and be straight over."

"It's out of sight the way that drug works." Tom Forçade could use cheering up, early November '78. It was not so much that you felt an obligation to try to alleviate this wretched human being's pain; you just got all cheery and positive in self-defense, sort of, when he was around, to try to shield yourself from his positively *radioactive* misery. "It's the *flashback* mechanics, Tom. Nothing else exactly like it in pharmacology. Lookee here."

I flipped open Carl Sagan's *Dragons of Eden* to the paper-clipped page and laid the detailed cross section of the human brain open before

Forçade's face, as you would move a dinner tray before a paraplegic. "It goes into your head sort of ass backwards, see? It collects in your spinal fluid, because it's got this special affinity for body acid, and spinal fluid's the most acidic part of your body. Then it creeps up into your medulla, this big bulge here. That's sort of your clam brain, the basic reflex-response part: heartbeat, knee-jerk, tactile sensation, real basic functions. So you're totally anesthetized when the PCP creeps up in there out of your spine, see? Then it tamps down your limbic system—hypothalamus, amygdala, hippocampus, see up here? That's what Sagan calls your lizard brain; it's involved with emotion, basic fear, rage, lust, ambivalence. PCP doesn't exactly shut it down, but switches off the connections between your limbic system and the orbital frontal neocortex. That's your 'me' part of the brain, right up front here, the observing, learning, self-aware structures. Which is why dustheads love PCP: It tamps down activity in the clam brain and the lizard brain, and absolutely disengages the whole animal part from the abstract 'me' part. So you feel like you're a disembodied entity floating in outer space, and your body's sort of in the *next room* over, arms and legs a hundred miles long. That's how come they rave about this out-of-body horseshit. Totally spurious, but try to tell *them* that. They're dustheads. That guy Lilly, the doc who talks to dolphins? He's big into taking Ketamine in sense-dep tanks, they're making a big pop-horror movie out of it. Ketamine's *exactly* like PCP, only it—"

Forçade was stirred to momentary interest. "You can draw a straight line through the me brain, the lizard brain and the clam brain. . . ."

While Forçade's body was still in the respirator up in St. Vincent's, one evening about three weeks later, the waiting room downstairs was entirely populated by young women. Only his wife, Gabrielle, was admitted up into those ghastly precincts where battlefield surgery is performed. But just about every *other* woman Tom had ever met in his life had been absolutely head-over-heels in love with him, and they were all, seemingly, gathered in the St. Vincent's waiting room, radiating a cloud of collective misery so intense it rivaled any of Forçade's profoundest depressive phases. So I only stood around long enough to determine that he had shot himself in the head that afternoon with his pearl-handled .22 pistol, and I retreated to McGowan's, the gloomy intimate little tavern catty-corner across 11th and Greenwich Street.

McGowan's was and is a terrific spot for picking up St. Vincent's nurses when they come off shift, but this night I had a different quarry. "Can you do me a favor, Lynda?" I asked the waitress who laid out my veal parmigiana and baked potato. "Have the barmaid keep an eye out for any St. Vincent's surgeon who comes in looking real shook up, okay? Any doc who looks really at wit's end, pale and shaky, and orders doubles quick, okay?"

Lynda, a freelance *Soho News* scribe herself, was intrigued. "What is it, a murder? A rock star overdosed? What?"

"I can't talk about it. I'm eating."

The doctor was shook up, but he wasn't pale. He was African, probably Nigerian. The barmaid tipped me to him right around 10 o'clock. I gave him time for a couple quick doubles, and then gently intruded into his brood.

"Have you been working on a suicide attempt, .22 pistol?"

In his mahogany face, the bloodshot in his eye-whites told a terrible story. "He's dead. We stopped everything. It was no good."

"What was the trajectory of the bullet?"

"Perfect." He forefingered a spot on his forehead, then turned in profile to trace a straight line that passed just across his earlobe. "It was like surgery. He could have done no better with a .22 bullet. If he had used a .38, it would have completely stopped action in—you know, the medulla oblongata? There would have been no need to try the respirator, nothing for it to work with." He went back to his straight double bourbon.

"Jesus."

"You are a friend? Or a journalist."

"Both. I knew the guy for years. Since we were kids."

"He *was* a kid," the doc said disgustedly. "He was thirty-two, a child. Why this now?"

"I don't know. Thanks, Doctor. I'm sorry I bothered you like this, but I knew the guy a long time."

It was a long time okay, but I didn't know him *that* well, and never once, before he was dead, had I ever thought of Thomas King Forçade as a "kid."

Still, we were exactly the same age, and I know *I* was a kid back in '68, when this Forçade guy commenced weird-vibing around the East Village. That's what we called the Lower East Side then, while it was slowly evolving from a *shtetl* of refugee European Jews and their former Ukrainian concentration-camp personnel into the *barrio* of third-generation Puerto Ricans and the latest refugee influx of island people it is today. For a while there, at the beginning of this process, a batch of low-rent artists and writers and performers and dancers moved into this immemorial and unredeemable *slum,* and started up a hippie newspaper called the *East Village Other.* The local realtors were so infatuated with this new euphemism for the horrid old Lower East Side that they call it the East Village to this day, and use that to soak the poor people there for every possible anna in the rupee with it.

Now, this Forçade person could hardly be called, even by the most charitable construction of these terms, an artist, a writer, a performer or a dancer. People who liked him have done so in print since November '78, but only by dipping *very* deeply into metaphor. We at the *East Village Other* immediately typed this Forçade as one magnificent fake-out and ripoff artist, potentially right up there with Abbie Hoffman and Jerry Rubin. I still hold by that characterization, but I give it a transcendently tragic twist now.

It was a loony morris dance. Jerry did Marc Antony, Abbie did Falstaff and Forçade did Iago, all very proficiently; and thus Yippies were generated in the earth, and pester it to this day. Jerry and Abbie everyone knows plenty about—everyone over thirty, anyway (gotcha!)—but you had to be just exceedingly *infra dig* to have knowledge of Thomas King Forçade, the *eminence gris* of the flower-people-gone-political. The most public thing Forçade ever did was to pitch a custard pie into the face of a congressman at a Washington obscenity hearing. Why exactly he did this I'll never figure out, since that particular congressman was *fiercely* committed to absolute strict construction of the First Amendment. Maybe Tom was in the grip of a seasonal Maoism recurrence—it came over him regularly, like malaria—and figured he could Heighten the Contradictions by pie-killing a free-press proponent. Or maybe it was just the only public figure within a likely custard trajectory of Tom's location on the spot. In assessing Forçade's behavior, one always dangles out into loose ends like this.

Anyway, like I say, I really hardly knew this sinister individual over the decade we co-conspired rather tightly together. I mean, *look* at the picture of this guy pieing that congressman.

Would *you* want to cozy up to any such sinister, black-becloaked, slouch-hatted, Fu Manchued caricature of Lee Van Cleef out of a late–'60s spaghetti Western?

Well sure, no way around it, there are a lot of people in the world who romantically gravitate to sinister romantic figures like that. I'm just not that way, myself. People like Forçade scare me to fucking *death*, so no matter how often soever the trade of garret journalism brings me within their orbit, I stay an asteroid, never a satellite. Keep the bastards at *arm's* length.

Forçade knew that, so early on he periodically doffed the cloak and slouch in my *EVO* office, perched himself yogi-legged in his deerskin boots atop my gorgeous American-flag desk, rolled up the reefer, and Got Down with me. Getting Down with Forçade basically involved getting so comfortable with the guy—a real *person,* y'know, like, underneath all that Fu Manchu spaghetti-Western horseshit, really man—that you wound up spilling your whole autobiography, philosophy of life, plans for the future, and so on. (Of course, you never learned from him that *he* was just an air-force brat in typical ambivalent rebellion against a much-bemedaled and entirely dead father.) Forçade was nearly as good at this Getting Down riff as the fatherly FBI agent who, in '68, tried to seduce me into *snitching* on the Yippies after what appeared to be a chance encounter and Get-Down in a West Village coffeehouse. Filthy mind-fuck artists. Keep 'em at arm and *leg's* length.

Tom, y'see, was recruiting likely propaganda hacks for his various Yippie adventures, and when it comes to flashy dopenik propaganda hacks, I have *always* been the best and cheapest on the market. (Think about it a minute; there is no immodesty at all in such a confession.) He and the Yippies developed so many dynamite ideas—running a live seven-hundred-pound Landrace boar, named simply Pig, for president in every Democratic primary in the '68 election, like wow man—my *EVO* column briefly became one of their most colorful media mouthpieces. After the bloody Gehenna they structured in Chicago that summer, though, I soured considerably on the motherfuckers.

No, that's mildly misleading, that epithet. The Motherfuckers, styled as such themselves, were the East Villagers who started blowing themselves up with dynamite after Chicago, and committing various other such psychopathic stunts to this day, like murdering policemen; or publishing their psychopathic autobiographies the minute the statutes of limitations lapse. Forçade, like me, was specifically diagnosed by the Motherfuckers as part of the Problem, not the Solution, and lived in daily apprehension for some time of their righteous revolutionary retribution; so we had that experience in common too.

Forçade first became my boss, briefly, in late '69. By that time he'd taken over what's now called the Alternative Press Syndicate: an informal transnational arrangement, back then, of several hundred pinko-faggo-dopenik papers like *EVO*. Forçade formalized and streamlined it. All the three-hundred-some publishers involved formally signed an agreement that any APS journal could reprint any art or text from any *other* APS journal without fear of copyright violation. Since this was how we all worked anyway, we were just as happy to have it casually formalized on these swatches of legal paper.

Then Forçade, chairman and sole proprietor of the APS, landed a fat contract with the New American Library to produce, bimonthly, a "paperback magazine" of counterculture art and literature. And thus he mysteriously showed up at my personal East Village railroad flat late one night with a big brown portfolio of documents: "Turn this into an article by next Thursday, and you get $350. But don't tell *anybody* about it, Latimer. It's important." A swirl of the cape, and he was gone in the night.

Now, $350 all at once, for me, was a sum so vast I'd have to *bank* it, lest the junkies discover it whilst shortcutting through my pad from the airshaft to the street, as they regularly did. So I wasn't about to ask any questions, just write that wonderful article by Thursday.

The portfolio contained mainly letters from political prisoners and their radical attorneys: Black Panthers, counterculture mouthpieces doing heavy time in the Midwest for petty pot possession, the usual LBJ-Nixon crackdown casualties. But there were some among them who had fucking *bombed* places, a revolutionary gesture I consider detestable; even if you're scrupulously careful not to blow up any human beings or yourself (an ethical risk no one short of a Special Services vet is qualified to take), the only effect of bombing is to scare the living shit out of the selfsame proletariat you're supposedly trying to mobilize with such romantic revolutionary gestures. "Look them crazy muthafughas blew up an AT&T office on Park Avenue yessiday. I see them chumps on *Amsterdam* with they muthafughin *nitro*-glycerine, I gone come up side they white hippie heads with a muthafughin .38, bro." So when I wrote up their cases, I went outside of Forçade's portfolio and entered the substantiated indictment dirt along with the radical hearts and flowers.

Forçade always *hated* that, I was to learn to my pain later on, any time his hack went outside the propaganda portfolios he assembled for us. But in this case, when I delivered my ms. to the APS office, he slipped a prewritten NAL-account check to me without even glancing at the title. "Don't tell a soul about this 'til the book comes out, Dean. It's important."

Not for some *good* while after the book came out did anyone explain this hugger-mugger to me. An extremely pissed off feminist writer finally brought it to my attention, after plumbing it from top to bottom. Besides a half dozen or so original pieces from myself and other garrett scriveners along Forçade's personal Grub Street, all the text and art in that paperback magazine were *reprints* from APS papers. Damned if old Captain Bad Vibes hadn't took and put the *New American Library* into his own personal APS, with unlimited reprint rights from three-hundred-odd counterculture journals. I will not quote the sums relayed to me from this wet-hen women's libber, but word (totally unsubstantiated, mind you) was that Forçade and his art director on that paperback magazine were divvying up a *seven-figure sum* between themselves each time it came out.

No wonder he was so blessed urgent I shouldn't tell my friends—all writers and artists of the East Village—that he was *paying* for my propaganda, while ripping them off cold. They probably would have broken my legs before going after his, once the word got out.

The paperback magazine itself did fine on the racks, I understand, but the NAL shut it down after just a half dozen issues, just about the time word of this seven-figure ripoff commenced unsubstantiating around. Technically, I suppose, the *East Village Other* could have reprinted the whole copyrighted NAL fiction line if we'd cared to just then; and though radical chic was all the craze that season, it's unlikely the NAL stock-holders were *that* crazy about it.

This, to my knowledge, is where the financial nut for *High Times* came from. There are plenty of glamorous, esoteric stories about Tom person-ally airlifting the first ten tons of Santa Marta gold out of La Guajira in 1973 to simultaneously launch *High Times* and knock Mexican skankweed off the national market—but I take all that razzmatazz with a hefty snort of uncut sodium chloride, personally. The notion of Tom Forçade, with his barely premorbid paranoia quotient, surviving even a couple hours on the same premises with any *really* felonious tonnage of weed simply does not compute for me. The guy was, to be blunt but accu-rate, Not Kool.

[*Editor's note from 1981: For an alternative view on Tom's involvement in the dope trade, see (sidebar by) Bob Lemmo, Dean's old officemate. (An) inter-view with "R," our dope connoisseur, also provides another glimpse into Forçade's unique, multifaceted personality. Perhaps Tom felt that Latimer was too paranoid to survive even a couple of minutes on the same premises with himself and any faintly felonious tonnage of weed.*]

Consider this very atypical episode in very early '72. Flush with *National Lampoon* mazuma, I had ambitiously landed a *two*-room apart-ment near University Place, a very sweet little flat with a fireplace and all, in a neighborhood which you can only designate as white. What landlord, you ask, would lease such a swell joint to any longhaired freelance pop-journal scrivener, be he ever so flush with gelt this particular season?

No way, Jose. I was *subletting* the pad from one Gabrielle Schang, an exceedingly white young piece of West Side Landed Gentry who had scored the place herself, and shared it till recently with her best prep-school friend from Rye, a sometimes *inamorata* of mine. Six months or so before this I had, God forgive me, introduced these two fresh-out-of-prep-school young rich bints around among the East Village artsy-litsy-dopsy-

Yipsy scene. Forçade, amongst many others, took an instant supernova *shine* to this Gabrielle, and the glow was never to fade a single kilowatt as long as the poor obsessive jackass was alive.

This is how bad it was for him. Gabrielle and her chum, see, had abruptly resolved to just abandon New York for the West Coast, drop overnight whatever complicated arrangements, romantic and otherwise, they were into, and start a whole new heartbreaking binge around the Bay Area. So they gave their nice place to avuncular old laid-back Deano—more a cuddler than a stud, all my life—and skied away quick as you could say "MasterCharge."

They didn't even take their *clothes*, just their teddy bears and prep-school albums and other sentimental adolescent trivia. So it was that when Forçade came barging in a week later, there I was in a place with *her* B. Altman's clothes in the closet, *her* authentic Spanish guitar on the bed, and even *her* snazzy leather fleece-lined Korean War flight jacket on my back (I'd been getting ready to go out).

I mean, he *barged* in. He blammed on the door like a fucking *cop,* and when I slipped the bolt he charged right past like a narc into a cocaine cut house. "Where is she?"

"Gabrielle? She's out West, Tom. She and Kathy both just up and—"

"Where is she, Latimer?" Dear God, he was rooting through the place *exactly* like a narc, looting the closets, lifting up the bed, looking *into* her beautiful expensive Spanish guitar . . .

"She's in California, Tom. California. You go to fucking New Jersey and bear west-southwest for about two thousand miles. . . . "

He grabbed me. By both fleece-lined lapels of *her* jacket, straight out of a late-night Ronald Reagan movie. At least he didn't shake me, though he was shaking amain himself. "I want you to tell her," he said with infinitely *honest* grief and reproach in his voice. "I just want you to tell Gabrielle that when she needed *me, I* was always there."

"Whatever you say, man." And he was gone. No swirl this time.

Although I never bothered to relay this anguished romantic tidbit to the lady (before now), I daresay that in the fullness of time she set his poor mind at ease on this *j'accuse* issue, me in her place with her clothes and all. Though Gabrielle may, for anything I know to the contrary, have discussed Bolivian politics with every *other* counterculture scrivener who got his byline in places like the *National Lampoon* around that time, there has never been the faintest hemidemisemiquaver of psychobiological flux 'twixt the two of us. We've been pals, sure; but I don't glow all over skinny little Wasp blondies for some reason, and I know she prefers men who take baths and have a reasonable assortment of visible teeth in their mouths.

So sure, if she may never have been quite so nuts for Forçade as he for her—that speaks *well* for Gabrielle, man. He was nuts out of his flaming *gourd,* as this very atypical episode demonstrates.

If you had a few tons of Santa Marta gold to dispose of, would you have *any* time for a natural-born wig like this Forçade, anywhere along the pipe? This is how I'm fairly confident that, contrary to popular post-mortem *roman de la rose,* my boss and old buddy Thomas King Forçade was never a heavyweight dealer in any substance more controlled than bullshit.

As Tom clearly put it to more people than me alone, the first 1974 issue of *High Times* was supposed to be a joke, a lark, a one-shot spitball into the eye of Spiro Agnew's Silent Majority. (Remember *that* Majority, ye over-thirties?) It was to be *Playboy's* sexual materialism lampooned in terms of dope materialism. Pornographic studies of red Leb slabs shot through Vaseline-smeared lenses, dead serious consumer pieces on state-of-the-art smuggling craft and high-tech head gear, and the white lady in the center-fold—well hell, we *all* knew what White Lady meant up north of 125th Street, Jack.

But those white folks out there in Darkest America, they didn't know hardly *any* of this dope stuff then. It would be fun to teach them about it, Forçade put it to all us scriveners along his personal Grub Street. We take the filthiest muck on the planet—the dope trade—and just glossy it up to *hell* and gone with super pro printing and page design, and rub Mr. and Mrs. Silent Majority's nose in it. And who knows? Once they get a couple snorts, they might turn out to *like* it . . .

That was typical of Forçade. He couldn't just dangle the money in front of your face, he had to feed you some byzantine bullshit "motivating" hype to go with it. Otherwise it wasn't *Professional* with a capital *P*, like in all those books he was studying on Professional business management, Professional corporate economics, and Professional staff management.

But I didn't know all that, I just swallowed the hype and the money. The first *High Times* office, in a basement on West 11th in the *Real* Village (just down the block from St. Vincent's, in fact), had a satisfying counterculture ambience of potsmoke and rubber cement, with the art director's light table adjoining the single freelance desk. There was once electric typewriter, some ancient Kraut model with an umlaut where the ampersand should be. You could sometimes spy a teenager crashing in the office cubby that had a rug on the floor. *EVO* was two years dead now, and I would've liked the place from nostalgia alone, if the vibes in there hadn't been so *almighty* Professional.

Forçade actually set my 18-year-old sweetheart up as his secretary, a job I suffered her to keep for exactly eight working days. The poor little freckleface would come home every night absolutely *strung out* on anxiety and fatigue, exactly the same as some damned account executive commuting home to Rye after a nine-to-five in some Madison Avenue malebolge.

"He does these awful *tricks* on people," she'd shudder. "He's got this one editor, Bob Singer, and he's always secretly *pitting* him against this other editor, Ed Dwyer. Neither of them's *really* out to get the other one's job, but Forçade makes each of them *think* the other one's out to get him. They're *friends,* but at work he's got them at each other's *throats.* And the art director, that sweet little guy from Kansas City? Forçade just stands over his shoulder for like 20 minutes at a time, watching every slice he makes with his razor blade, saying nothing. Just stands there, saying nothing, and goes away. Finally, the guy finishes the flat, takes it into Forçade's office, and closes the door. Ten minutes later he'll come out with one piece of torn-up flat in each hand, looking like he wants to *cry,* but he's too *scared* too."

Now, I've read about what happens to women whose husbands work nine-to-five in corporate hellholes like this. Since I was just then very much addicted to copious and enthusiastic pussy from this particular freckleface sweetie, I called Forçade in the middle of her second week and told him thanks but no thanks: "Fire her, Tom."

"But Dean, she's exactly what I need right now. A clean slate. Tabula rasa. I can teach her the ropes from the bottom up, and as the corporation develops, she'll become the best executive secretary this side of Ogilvy & Mather."

"Fire her, Tom. Today. Give us a break, huh?"

She was so happy to be cut loose from that terrible place, neither of us left the house for the rest of the week.

In fact, I could *not* have gone back into the *High Times* office for at least a couple of years after that. Darkest America turned out to have such a spectacularly prurient fascination with *dope,* as it somehow happened, Forçade's corporation quickly expanded to much cushier premises on West Broadway. HIGH TIMES vets still speak of the West Broadway place and all the great nitrous parties they threw whenever Tom was away. But I never once set foot in the West Broadway office; I don't know where it was or what it looked like. [Editor's note from 1981: *The Sordid Affairs editor is not whistling Dixie here. The office he refers to was on* Broadway, *not West Broadway. We are thankful that he occasionally manages to locate our present premises.*] I gave my manuscripts personally to Bob Singer, and talked business with him, exclusively at the Bells of Hell, our mutual Real Village liquoring trough.

Thus I am no proper historian of *High Times* in its heyday. Loved the magazine, loathed the people there. Forçade sort of bird-dogged poor Gabrielle into formally marrying him over this period, I understood through industrial gossip. His classic manic-depressive syndrome was getting completely out of hand as he got along. Par for the course in such cases, when they go along untreated like that, he would be industrious, charismatic, brilliant for maybe three months, until he'd worked himself into a state of total exhaustion and anxiety-fatigue, signaling an imminent hormone turnover into what the docs call "serotonergic depression." The turnover was commonly signaled by the day Tom would stride, all becloaked and slouch-hatted, into the office with a couple meatball body-guards, personally rip every phone in sight out of the wall, fire every third person who happened to be on the premises (employees, freelancers, his own lawyers, Xerox repairmen, visiting rock stars and wire-service journalists all got fired by Forçade from time to time), and stalk out. No one would see him for another two-three months, whilst he privately endured who knows what John Donne agonies of serotonergic depression and exaltation. Then gradually he'd *remanifest* on the premises, charismatic and personable, playing his hideous Professional mind-fuck games again . . .

So I much preferred hanging out at *Screw* magazine's office, even, where Goldstein actually kept closed-circuit TV cameras trained on his staff, feeding into a bank of spy monitors in his executive suite. Goldstein's a champion mind-fuck artist too, but at least he's not in visible *pain* all the time.

But the *High Times* parties were terrific; or so I'm told, and there appeared to be a terrific camaraderie among much of the staff when I finally came aboard full-time in early '78. I suppose firing and rehiring your employees, once or twice apiece each year, *is* listed in one of those Professional books as a capital way to actually promote fierce corporate loyalty over the long term.

Never mind exactly *how* I capitulated to a full-time staff job here. The fact is, with inflation running the way it is, you can't even be a starving Grub Street scrivener anymore. No way. If any of my previous remarks here have tempted the Youth of America to try a fling at poor-but-honest garret journalism, I take it all back. Better you should go on drugs: They'll finish you off less painfully and with more dignity. Wait till the Reaganauts turn this economy around, Youth, before you go try to make a living from an unfettered pen.

Suffice to say, Forçade installed me and Bob Lemmo as co-news editors, in our pleasant little office cubby looking out on East 27th Street, the very week the paraquat panic broke, in April of '78.

Yeah, that was a most *auspicious* month to come aboard HIGH TIMES. You had to *instantly* start boning up into a paraprofessional's conversance with toxicology and pharmacology. Straightaway you learned the ins and outs of media dope scares, and how to take the edge off them: mainly, which media people to call *right* away, to explain it all to them in words of one syllable, so that at least they don't automatically take the word of every headline-seeking county coroner from Poughkeepsie to Biloxi that he's got an adolescent on ice who just croaked from this season's brand-new scare drug. There would've been an *epidemic* of teenage nitrous oxide deaths in the media around early 1980, if *High Times'* Sordid Affairs Editor hadn't been on the case; as it was, that's one national dope scare that zipped past without properly frightening a soul.

I am often asked where the title Sordid Affairs Editor came from, and what it means. All right, I will proceed now to tell you, I will tell you all.

It was just a few months after the lovely July morning Gabrielle came up with her lawyers and their meatballs to grace our corporation. That day was the first time I'd seen her in maybe five years, and pretty though she may be in her skinny, Waspy way, I'd been doing my level damnedest best since then to keep her out of my eyeshot. Luckily we had two floors then, and her office was upstairs.

Look here. You have a ninety-four-pound woman who comes in one day and says she's your publisher. Okay, you've worked for Al Goldstein and Tom Forçade, what could be worse? This lady, day one, before you even got your britches on, had canned the treasurer and circulation director and staked out their offices with her meatballs. That's understandable—they could take the money and scoot if they decided, on first impression, that this blondie might be a little—ah—*balmy*—to be publishing a national magazine. Gabrielle does have this problem with first impressions; guys tend either to go wholly galley-west over her extraordinary good looks, or take her for a *royal* space case. Either way, they are only falling victim to their idiot masculine prejudices, and are certain to suffer for it sorrowfully in the fullness of time.

Day *two*, though. The ninety-four-pound publisher hauls the editors all up to her new office for an editorial conference. She is going to change the look and tone of this magazine from the bottom up, from the logo to the staples. She's going to do all sorts of magnificent new, wonderful new things— no *end* to the unprecedented miracles this ninety-four-pound Jann Wenner's gonna perform—but mainly she's gonna *change* it. Total metamorphosis. *Flux* the fucker.

She is determined, you gradually come to suspect inside yourself, as she goes on, to take their rather nifty-looking and brisk-selling Professional package that was put together by her late husband, and tear out, cast down, tread under, obliterate, and spread salt over everything in it that *reminds* her of the guy. Your suspicions definitely do not lighten after this colloquy with your new ninety-four-pound publisher:

"Dean, I hear you and Bob write this part on the newsprint paper in back here, the Planet section. What's that about?"

"It's nondrug news from around the world. International stuff the regular American media never cover. We rewrite it out of international journals like *Africa, El Tiempo,* and *London Sunday*—"

"But why can't it go up here in front, in *this* newsprint-paper section?"

"That's Highwitness News. It's all dope news, one-hundred percent dope news. The Planet's all nondope news."

"But the *paper* looks so . . . I mean, why do we have to have *two* newsprint sections, anyway?"

"I beg your pardon?"

"Look, I know you guys work hard on this, and you're proud of it. I'm not criticizing you, I just want to know why we have to have *two* newsprint sections."

"Uh . . . Gabrielle, um . . . that's the way it *comes,* you know? You have one newsprint section, you *have* to have two."

"I know! I know exactly how to solve this. We just take the Planet section and move it up front with the Highwitness News section. Run them back to back on newsprint in the front of the book. That way the whole back of the book is glossy, and everybody's happy. Right? Everybody agree?"

And of course nobody says anything, they're all looking at *you,* helplessly. "Ah-*hum,* Gabrielle. Look . . . hold the magazine up, spread out, in your fingers. See how it's stapled? Look real close at the binding. Now see how all those newsprint pages are *really* single, 17-by-22-inch sheets of paper, stapled in the middle so they *look* like lots of 8 1/2-by-11s? With glossy sections fore and aft, sort of?"

"Yeah. But I don't see—"

"If you wanted to run the whole newsprint section in *one block* you'd have to run it in the centerfold. And then we'd lose our snazzy, pretty, glossy dope centerfold every month."

Long pause, deep concentrated frown. "Well, I'll take it up with the guys out at the plant. Maybe they can rig something up. Now, as to the table of contents, from now on I want to . . ."

Months had passed since that colloquy. We were calling her the Ayatollah Schang now, what few of us remained. Gabrielle had called in some top-notch efficiency experts, who had asked all of us to describe for them, in our own written words, our jobs. Recognizing in this a prelude to whole-sale butchery, I had composed a heroic one-page scorcher saying essentially blow it out your rich white asses, you stooges. I'm damned if I'll make it any easier for you to fire me and my friends. But I did it so elo-quently and *precisely*, see, you'd have to be plain *crazy* to fire an editor who can write like that, and will work for a take-home that's lower than some of the secretaries. Not so almighty heroic after all, y'see.

Months had passed, then. The Ayatollah had machine-gunned two out of three personnel in every department (today we would call her "Mother Stockman," I'm positive). I had just helped my old chum Jeff Goldberg pack up his half ton of documents for *Flowers in the Blood* and haul them off to a taxi, humming "Dead March from Saul" very loudly and nastily under her new treasurer's nose. So when my phone rang that day, and her little voice came leaping over the wires, I automatically checked to see if the coast was clear between my office IBM Selectric and the fire-escape door.

"Dean," says she, "I'm putting together a whole new *masthead* for our whole *new* staff. I'm moving you right up under Managing Editor. What *title* do you want?"

Oh, for Christ sake. A *stroke* from the Goddamned *Ayatollah!* "I dunno," sez I, manfully fighting down my gorge. "Lemme think on it a bit."

"I've got just the title. You'll love it. *Guess*."

"Gee, I got no idea. Really."

"*Gonzo Editor!* What do you think of that?"

"*Ktchu!*" The gorge hit the back of my nose, pure hydrochloric bile. "Aw, golly, Gabrielle, Hunter would really kick my ass for that."

"Do you think so? Do you know Hunter?"

"Just from bars. The Lion's Head, the Bells of Hell, the Roadhouse, you know. Writer taverns." *Stone* lie. I've never met the guy in my life, nor read more than the first thirty pages of his first wretched *Fear and Loathing* book, either. *Doonesbury* is where I know Hunter Thompson from. "He'd kick my ass, man. I mean, he'd get me 86ed out of all the places I can *drink* in."

"Well, I like it a lot. Can you think of anything better just offhand? I have to messenger it out right now."

"Sure." Well hell, I *introduced* her to the poor guy didn't I? "Sordid Affairs Editor."

"Assorted Affairs Editor?" she asked doubtfully.

"No, no. Sordid. S-O-R-D-I-D. Sordid Affa—"

"*Sordid Affairs Editor!* That's *fantastic!*"

And that's where the title comes from, God's witness, scout's honor. Born in a blurt of bile, in sheer inspired self-defense.

I work good, and I work cheap.

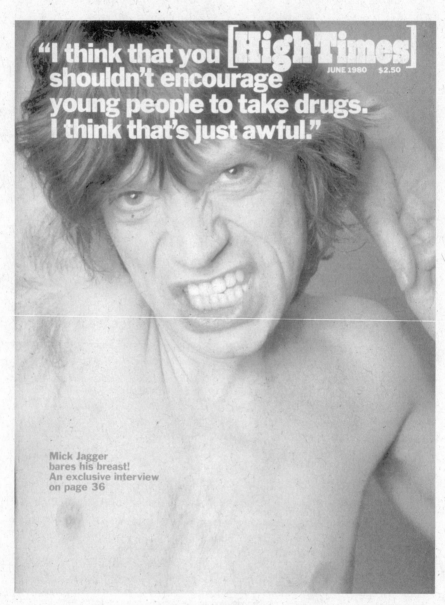

High Times #58, June 1980

WHY THE MISS AMERICA
PAGEANT SHOULD BE ABOLISHED

JOSH ALAN FRIEDMAN

JANUARY 1983

AT THE GREYHOUND GATE to Atlantic City, three ticket-holding blind persons were swiftly refused entry by the bus driver. The seats were oversold; the door pumped shut and off he drove. One of them began to cry because she had been separated from a blind companion already on the bus. The two others were shaken up, their dreams of attending Miss America pretty much shattered. A dozen last-minute beauty-pageant freaks stood cursing on the Greyhound ticket line at Port Authority New York, in a desperate attempt to make the show. It was the final night of the 1982 Miss America Pageant.

I was able to make a 5:30 New Jersey Transit bus, hoping to land an interview with the First Runner-Up on the morning after. Who cared about Miss America? The First Runner-Up was a hotter subject; she'd be neglected, bitter, dying for an interview, suffering from the pain of the greatest *almost* in her life. She wouldn't get her face on Kellogg's Corn Flakes or see herself in Nestle ads. But what were the functions of First Runner-Up? Was she sort of the vice-president, ready to jump in should Miss America get impeached or assassinated? Furthermore, I'd get to blurt out great questions, like, "Do you believe in premarital sex?"

During the three-hour journey, we passed through eight toll booths, which many folks can't afford on the way back. At the outskirts of Atlantic City was a mile-long stretch of makeshift parking lot, filled to capacity on the climactic night of the seven-day pageant. From the bus depot, I made a beeline to the stadium-sized Convention Center, adjacent to the Playboy Hotel. Only four contestants were put up at the Playboy, the least of any hotel. The other 46 girls were divvied up by the remaining eight casinos, who boasted their pictures in the lobbies.

Swarming over the boardwalk was a Halloween-like procession of Miss America freaks—clean-cut families with little girls decked out in Jr. Miss America gowns and crowns, sending little boys into breathless double takes—for a minute, by golly, you might mistake one for a real contestant.

I made it to the Press Hospitality Center in the nick of time. Here was a spread of ham and cheese sandwiches, sodas, TV monitors, and eight courtesy typewriters. A few hundred members of the straightest press I'd ever seen warmly greeted each other at this blessed event. They would spread the good news into every town and hamlet in the USA. Priority One Badges were given only to "wire service personnel," reps of "area newspapers meeting deadlines," official Miss America Pageant photogs, NBC News. These folks were given runway seats, and first privileges for interviews and pictures. I don't recall what publications Priority Two encompassed, but they invented a brand new Priority Three for *High Times*. I picked up my press badge, with my name badly misspelled, and was directed to two wrong locations before being seated light-years from the stage in these subbleachers. An old, drunken photographer shared my location, hiccuping in a stupor. Above me was a thirty-foot-high monitor screen, the transparent backside of which I could see through if I craned my neck. From this I observed the pageant.

But no matter. Miss America was a good thing, not a negative thing, the most glamorous high-school graduation ceremony around. Hundreds of girls won fat scholarships through the bush leagues of the Miss America system, learned poise, dignity, the spirit of competition. These fifty angels had won local and state pageants, they were the pride and joy of their communities, an inspiration to millions of little lassies who dreamed of someday winning the coveted crown. The Miss America Pageant could also be a springboard to talk-show hostdom, the most sought-after goal among contestants. These were Positive Girls, my favorite kind.

The show opened with a slapdash medley of pop songs that contained so many metaphorical references to prostitution, I gagged on my soda. "I'm a Working Girl," they sang, leading into a chorus of "*Les* girls," and some out-of-context lines from "I Am Woman." Next, they introduced ten semifinalists in evening gowns to the tune of "Send in the Clowns." Gary Collins was host—a second-rate sub for the out-to-pasture Bert Parks. His wife, Mary Ann Mobley, was among the parade of former Miss Americas who walked the runway before the show. Miss America 1933 got the largest applause on the 50th anniversary of her title, and there were many missing and/or dead Miss Americas who couldn't make it.

Among the distinguished panel of seven judges were Foster Brooks, professional "drunk," Rod McKuen, who recently saw fit to publicize himself as a victim of homosexual child-rape, and Wink Martindale, host of some atrocity called "Tic-Tac-Dough." Now, here were fifty gals who had spent years training for this, the Olympics of beauty contests, and it all rode on the judgment of Foster, Rod, and Wink. Or perhaps they *were* befitting judges for these slick, well-packaged, professional beauty contestants, carefully groomed by their town fathers to give two-sided answers and smile on cue, as they sought TV careers. But something about Wink irked the shit out of me.

The most bizarre "talent" of the evening was displayed by Miss Arizona. Although the program described it as "Free Form Gymnastics," it was nothing short of contortion. She whipped her legs back over her spine into some grotesque spiderlike posture and crawled around the stage. Apparently, her sponsors felt this hideous contortion would cinch the crown, but who the hell needed a tarantula-woman for Miss America?

When the new Miss America took her celebrated walk down the runway, a brigade of eighteen New Jersey state troopers followed closely behind the TV camera, in case one of those Priority One press people made a lunatic lunge for the Miss.

The drunken photog awoke. "I'm gonna see what's-iz-name, Brooks Foster," he bragged, tripping past me. "And then I'll say hello to my good pal, Wink."

The big press conference for the Newly Crowned was held in the carnival tent Press Center. With her splendid-girl Court of Honor and a police escort, Miss America, having had an ample half-hour to wipe away the tears, and probably change panties, posed for ten minutes of pix (photogs only) in a sealed-off tent. Then, with cameras still whirring, she was escorted to the podium for questioning. Miss California she was, and just a tad slurry-looking compared to last year's Elizabeth Ward, who was as wholesome as bleached Wonder Bread. Debra Sue Maffett, blond, twenty-five, former drum majorette, all-round Positive Girl, first defended her nose job as a "medical operation for a deviated septum"; all of her family had required nose jobs to correct this breathing problem. Debra Sue dated several men ("No one seriously"), and was a member of the National Man Watcher's Association, which led her to hand out Well Worth Watching cards to men at random.

It was later revealed that this winner, Miss California, had failed in three attempts to be crowned Miss Texas. After the third try at Texas, she had "extensive cosmetic surgery" before entering the California Pageant, according to the muckraking director of the Miss Texas Pageant. "Her nose, her chin, and I'm not sure what else."

Besides the twenty-grand pageant prize, Debra Sue would bring in over $100,000 during her Miss A. reign from public appearances and ads. "I'm still just Debbie and I'll still be just Debbie when it's over," said the sweet thing. "I'd like to have a talk show, be a wife and mother, there's so much I want to do—"

After the Saturday-night broadcast, at midnight, the pageant officially relinquished its supervision over all contestants, save for the new Miss America. The forty-nine losers were on their own, and most would skip town first thing in the morning. I had to act fast, and spent the following hour seeking the whereabouts of First Runner-Up Desiree Denise Daniels, Miss Tennessee. She was on the sixth floor at the Tropicana. Only four messages awaited her at the front desk when I added mine—request for interview with *High Times* mag at her convenience on Sunday. I hit the blackjack tables till 4 A.M., checking the front desk every half-hour, but Miss Tennessee hadn't answered her red message light. There was no answer each time the desk clerk phoned.

At 4 A.M. I discovered that every hotel on the boardwalk was booked solid. But I hadn't counted on the flophouses being sold out, which they were during Miss America week. The next chapter of my Miss America nightmare unfolded with an endless series of NO VACANCY signs, all the way to the back streets of the Monopoly board. Fleabag motel clerks found it laughable when I asked if they knew of any vacancies. I took to the streets, a loser at the casinos.

At 8 A.M., Room 217 at the Bull Shippers Plaza Motor Inn on Pennsylvania Avenue became available. I grabbed it. There was even a telephone, on which to make frantic backup calls for other contestant interviews. A black hooker tried to bust into my room, but no dice, honey, I was here for the First Runner-Up. A dozen calls later, I broke through the incredible protective layers of hostesses and hometown security nets that surrounded Miss Tennessee. These girls were harder to reach than Bo Derek. Everything had to be cleared through some men in Room 4425 at Caesar's—her "state traveling companions." A fifteen-minute interlude could be arranged if I showed up at Caesar's front desk by 11 A.M. Lying on a firm mattress at the Bull Shippers Inn, I nauseously refined my twenty Runner-Up questions.

Needless to say, some good old boys from Tennessee—tough-looking ones in their forties—showed up by noon. They explained something about "gals and schedules"; the women were still packing at the Tropicana, they apologized, and they'd have to catch a plane, so no interviews. I made a few more calls to sponsors of other contestants, but couldn't even pin down Miss Alaska. The prettiest contestant of them all, Miss Georgia, was reportedly packing her last bags right there at Caesar's, but her people also gave me the runaround. Out in the streets, Miss America contestants and their entourages were leaving in unstoppable droves. But I had been a bad little reporter, who came with no connections, and unfortunately, couldn't even land whoever came in fiftieth. I guess I would have even settled for Wink fuckin' Martindale, after all.

TITO BANDINI (IF INDEED THAT WAS HIS NAME)

Fiction

TERRY SOUTHERN

MAY 1983

ONE RECENT RAINY P.M. in the none too distant, I found myself quaffing a monstroid sundowner at ultrasmart Elaine's Restaurant, where the good, the true, and the incredibly nifty are apt to hang. It was at the height of the perennial New York August dope-drought, and the conversation—having run its usual labyrinthine gamut of who-is-sucking-who, where, when, and everything but why, the talk turned to that very subject, Big D. dope, or more precisely, the remarkable lack of anything other than the old New Jersey Graveyard, Miami Make-Believe, Canadian Catnip, or whatever other unspeakable yak-dung was being force-fed to your average Big A. hemphead.

"It's a question of *harvest*," some quasi-knowledgeable asshole piped up. "This time next month, it'll be coming *out your ears*—red, green, gold, brown, black—man, it will be Rainbow-ville-oh-roonie!"

"I'll bet you do horoscopes, too," said thin blond Laura, sitting next to me, and quite icily she said it, not being one, it was quite apparent, to set much store in palmistry or grain futures, at the same time leaning forward to put out her cigarette, doing this in such a totally beautiful way that her white and barely buttoned silken blouse gaped exactly right, from the POV of yrs trly, to present the no-bra distention of a perfect pink nipple from a perfect pert breast, freeze-frame, pink nip touching white silk, holding the silk away from the breast to form an exquisitely structured miniature. And what a bod! Willowy but voluptuous—*quel fab combo!* I took a prolonged hit of my tequila sunrise, carefully tonguing aside a rosebud-shaped nipple-size piece of half-melted ice, savoring its contour, devoutly, my mind seething with imagery and reflection: nip-distention in mid-afternoon? Was she excited? Was she wet? Did she *know* it was distended? Pulsating? Thrusting forward hungrily? Girls' nipples invariably distend when they have orgasm. Had *I*, through a chance word, a gesture, a glance—somehow made her come? We barely knew each other. Hey, awright! Way to go!

"Thees is all the true bullshit," said Jean-Pierre, rather abruptly, or so it seemed at the time. Jean-Pierre was a French (wouldn't you know it) connoisseur of—and to hear him tell it—one of the world's great experts on every aspect of sense-derangement, and especially that afforded by top-drawer wog-hemp. He spoke with a rather heavy accent, so that whenever he said "bullshit," which, for one snob reason or another, he often did, it sounded like "bowl-sheet." Also, and this is amusingly ironic I think, his favorite drink was a "bull-shot," which, when he ordered it, always came out an absolutely perfect "bullshit." "Give me a bullshit," he would say. He was fairly mixed up in a good many additional ways, too—chemically, physically, mentally—but that is another story, for another time. Sufficient for the mo to say he was fairly hip in certain regards.

"Now is the time," he went on, in his imperious and pain-in-ass manner, "for all good dealers to be *en vacance*—East Hampton, Martha's Vineyard, Provincetown, south of France, Cap d'Antibes, Venice, Capri, Costa Brava, Corfu—" he sighed, exhausted from his trip. "And that," he summed up, "is the true state *du drogue* at this point in time."

He was probably right. He was a correspondent for *Paris-Match* and, not that there's any connection, but he was very often right about little things like that—odd facts, dope, sex, what have you. Anyway, a little later he said to me, more or less privately, "Hey, listen man, I just thought of a guy—" And he starts rummaging about in his wallet and then comes out with a business card. "Now dig this," he said, laying it on the table:

TITO BANDINI
Import-Export
1040 Park Ave. 743-2914
By appointment

"Dy-nee-mite stuff," he added with great assurance.

333

I studied the card with a slight bemusement. "Import-export. Well, he's, uh, certainly up front about it, isn't he?"

"Up front, yes, he is very much up-front cat."

Jean-Pierre was inclined to be perhaps a bit overly enthusiastic about hippy-dippy dope talk, and so occasionally went the old malaprop route. "I am quite sure," he continued, downing the dregs of his "bullshit," "that he is still at present in the city, because of the, how do you say, 'dog show'—and he will have a good head-stash of primo-primo!"

I didn't respond immediately—not that I wished to avoid appearing as your basic drooling Pavlovian dope-nut, but because I wasn't entirely sure what the hell he was talking about—with that obscure "dog show" reference. *Dog show?* Was it a new slang expression for a snuff flick? For being on the *set* during a snuff flick? For fab preteenie ball-and-suck? For watching a strychnine hotshot? For some kind of disgustingly weird coprophilia *extraordinaire?* I didn't get it. But it did occur to me, I must admit, that a modest score for heavy green (brown or gold) might well be the most direct means of scoring Laura's fabulous pink nipple, indeed her entire perfect knocker, into my salivating chops—with boss gentleness and aplomb, natch.

"You think so, do you?" I said thoughtfully. "Because of the, uh, *dog show?*"

"I think he will tighten our wig something very *bad,* man," he said, grinning like a death's head and tapping the card briskly on the table. "Shall I make the, you know, appointment?" And he gave a slight nod in Laura's direction and a knowing wink which was practically conspiratorial.

The door of the posh pad at ten-four-oh Park was opened by a girl of nineteen or thereabouts, face of an angel, body of a saint (Bernadette came to mind), wearing a see-through blouse and devil red short-shorts. The hurt and confusion I had felt earlier, when Laura had declined to accompany us, began to fade.

"Hi there," she said with a lip-glistening, teeth-glittering Close-Up smile, like she might have been doing a parody on a *Cosmo* mag deepthroat-type heroine, slightly laid back, natch—Wendy her name, yumminess *extraordinaire* her game.

The pad itself was boss luxe—obviously dope-inspired—heavily electronic, with free-form divans, floating bookcases, a bank of TV monitors, all silently aglow, three with cable imagery and one with your heavy Thirteen. More centrally located was a monster Advent, so that if and when one particular channel was favored, a flick of the proverbial console switch would put it right up front, in living color and large as life. But the images were, as I say, without sound for the moment, and instead we were being treated to a soft and soothing electronic purr from a nonapparent 360-degree source, and the air was awaft with what could have (certainly *should* have) only been the fabled *frankincense*. All in all, quite a comfy scene. My companion, Jean-Pierre—an outrageously smug and supercilious asshole if the truth be known (though not wholly devoid of a certain *je ne sais quoi* type charm, at least in the eyes of various Miss Cutie Pie Dumbbells, if one were to place full credence in their constant "oohing" and "aahing," which yrs trly most assuredly did not)—was now in the midst of an elaborate frenchie snow-job intro, in which he did have the good grace, I must admit, to describe me as an *"écrivain très serieux,"* but immediately went on to insinuate *he* might like to use her on the cover of a forthcoming issue of his frenchie mag, which, as it turned out (ha-ha) she had never heard of.

It was about then that Bandini came in. I'm not sure what I'd expected—the name (a bit swarthy), the place (fairly exotic)—in any case, I was surprised to see a super-clean-cut All American Michael Parks-Bronson bike-type; a few years younger and he could have been on the back of the Wheaties box saying, "Gosh, Mom . . ." And yet, seen in certain half-lights, deep in those deep blue eyes, was the tiger-trace. The moment we were introduced he made some cabalistic sign or indication which caused fab Wen to lay out a fairly infinite number of long lines of Peruvian flake on the glittery black onyx coffee table before us. Then she indicated a small jade vase of thin ivory tubes, like straws at the old neighborhood soda fountain, and we each selected one and had a good toot, or several. It was king coke, no doubt about it, crushed so as not to burn holes in the old snoz, but rocky enough to flash on.

"Et bien, Tito," said Jean-Pierre, just wanting to make conversation I suppose, "where are all your beautiful *dogs?"*

"The dogs?" He smiled. "Oh, well, the dogs are at the beauty parlor, being groomed. There's a big show on Thursday, you know, at the Garden. The dogs will stay there, at the grooming place, until show time."

"Ah, yes," said Jean-Pierre, by now completely whacked out. "I was telling my friend here about it, about your . . . how do you say, *interest* in dogs."

Tito looked at me and smiled. "Your friend, I take it, is not with the . . . Treasury Department?"

"Comment?" said Jean-Pierre, whose sense of humor was of a rather special, perhaps limited, nature; but he was also resilient. "No," he said, obviously irate at this show of distrust, "but he *is* the illegitimate, and highly favored, son of Henry J. Anslinger."

Tito just smiled, blew a line, and had a toke of some heavy dark (Colombian, I later learned) which the adorable Wendy was proffering. Then the phone rang and he excused himself.

Jean-Pierre, by now in a state of calm and collected, but extreme, wipeout, cleared his throat. "In the import-export," he said, with a knowing nod in Tito's direction, "he has met plenty heavy dudes."

"Oh?" I, too, now found some difficulty in speaking without preparation. "Uh, just what do you mean by that?" He looked at me, more hurt it seemed than annoyed at his failure to communicate. "Heavy dude, man, you know—" he pointed his thumb and forefinger at me like a gun, "bang-bang, you're dead. Ha-ha."

I threw up my hands as if it had gotten me full in the face, two barrels of three-inch twelve-gauge Magnums packed with worn dimes, edges honed to razor sharpness (they say that's the worst, really messes you up).

Jean-Pierre was not amused. "Well, I do not mean you, *naturellement,*" he said peevishly, mostly annoyed I think because it had gotten a good laugh from the fab Wen. (And you know what they say—"Make 'em laugh, and you're halfway to clit city.")

"He does not do the *reportage,*" Jean-Pierre said, when Tito returned, "he does the purely *creative*—the *roman,* and the *conte.*"

Our host shrugged. "A cover blown is a cover blown," he said, "even if it's in a *sonnet.*" Then he looked over to me, only the hint of a question in his blue killer-eyes.

"I would say that is definitely right," I carefully said.

He laughed and hit his remote, throwing the big beautiful six o'clock news up on the monstro screen. "I dig Walt Crankeit," he said, "the cat knocks me out."

"Ah, *bon*," said Jean-Pierre, checking his watch, *"les nouvelles!* In my profession, I am obliged to watch each evening," but, of course, could not resist adding, "I personally, however, prefer the CBS." And, so saying, he leaned forward in the chair, preparing to give the program 100 percent of his serious professional scrutiny, but doing so with such out-of-skull eagerness that he pitched forward headlong onto the carpet, only catching himself at the last minute with outstretched arms against the floor.

I could scarcely suppress a chuckle at this combination of zeal and dumbbell-ness, while Jean-Pierre, momentarily on all fours, looked around in blinking surprise at the host. "Hey, man," he said, "that is *some heavy shit* you got there."

Tito nodded. "Glad to have you aboard." He indicated the black-top table. "Hit another line of that flake—it'll tighten your wig."

As for yours truly, I had eased in behind the flake and the hemp, and was now lolling back quite comfortably in the big chair, ready to take an interest in whatever John and Dave might have to say about the human condition at this point in time. Then I was rather astonished when the fab Wendy was solicitously leaning over me, air-stewardess style (also braless, incidentally, but nips, mercifully, in repose) with a tray of drinks, including what was unmistakably a tequila sunrise—tall and shimmering magically, like a Robert Penn photograph. A welcome sight, granted, yet I knew I hadn't requested it, so it was somewhat eerie.

"Is that," I asked, referring to the drink, "what it would appear to be?"

"Everything here," and she smiled delightfully, "is exactly what it would appear to be."

"Then you are gifted," I said, taking the tinkling drink and raising it toward her toast-wise, adding with what I trusted was a meaningful look, "in more ways than one."

She laughed, moving on. "No, I'm not *psychic*—I read the piece you wrote about traveling with the Rolling Stones, and about the tequila sunrises that everyone was drinking. So I just took a chance."

And then I was pleasantly surprised to learn that Tito had also read the piece and liked it, or at least said he did. In any case, the recollection of it seemed to put him more at ease.

"Well, I'll tell you," he said, "that dog thing Jean-Pierre mentioned, that was a sort of one-shot operation."

And I could feel him settling into his "raconteur" mood—a quality, I have noticed, that is curiously prevalent among dealers, both in and out of jail. He smiled. "What you might call a 'six-dog night.'" He looked at Wendy. "Put on some sounds, baby, something soothing," and he switched off Big Wally C. in mid-prophecy, as though the greater truth might come from a much nearer source, and he began his tale.

"Well, I'd been scoring coke from this dude in Bogotá, off and on for a couple of years, more or less *sociably,* you know, maybe five or ten grand at a time, but never any real *weight.* Then one day he gets in touch with me by phone—which was unusual to begin with—and makes this terrific proposition, ten keys of *one hundred percent pure pharmaceutical rock* for a hundred thou—this was about *one-quarter* the usual price and could have been turned over, like uncut and immediately, for eight-fifty, or maybe even a cool million. Well, right away, I figured it for a setup of some kind—that the dude, call him Gomez, had gotten into a bad heat situation. You know how it is: *Orders from the D.A., gotta bust in early May*— that old number. Anyway, that's what seemed to be coming down. Gomez owed somebody in Narcville a favor. On the other hand, I thought maybe it's *legit,* maybe *I'm* being paranoid, because, you see, he had a very logical explanation for the whole deal—the weight, the price, the urgency— it seems that a freighter, going from Hamburg to Rio, got wiped in a storm off Cape Verde, total breakup, all hands lost—except for the first mate and the ship's doctor, who managed to make it out of there, in a lifeboat—a lifeboat containing not merely your basic three-days ration of food and water for seven, life jackets, signal flares and so on, but *forty-four pounds of pharmaceutical coke* as well, which the good doctor, in his infinite wisdom and an ultraflash of last-minute cool-headedness, had remembered from a retro-glimpse of the ship's manifesto and was quick to salvage.

"And only the doctor, as it turned out, survived the difficult voyage in the longboat, finally putting ashore at Sierra Leone, on the coast of West

Africa, to be picked up six days later by a Norwegian freighter bound for Venezuela—whence, following a day or two of the big-hello, news conference, guest-shot on the local Mike Douglas show and so on, split for Rio— and the rest, of course—" he paused to indulge himself with a self-indulgent chuckle—"is U.S. of A. dope-history."

I was suddenly glad that I'd brought along my fab Sony TC-55, a remarkable unit for your bottom-line unobtrusive eavesdropping— wouldn't spook a gazelle, and, with a supercasual flourish, I placed the unit on the table between us. "Just want to get all the facts, ma'am," I said, adding with a winner smile, "Naturally the names will be changed to protect the innocent . . ."

"Dig it," said Tito with a nod of acquiescence, and he laid on the following, transcribed more or less verbatim:

"Like I say, I made the whole thing as a setup going in, but at the same time, at those prices, it came on as a kind of interesting *challenge*. I looked at it from every angle—up, down, sideways, and maybe one or two others. I figured the actual buy would come down okay, because it was obviously a border bust they were after—probably some dumb U.S. of A.–inspired Melvin Purvis–type operation . . . C.I.A.–time, trying to stem the unauthorized flow of blah-blah-blah—'unauthorized' meaning *they* weren't in. Of course the first thing I did was check with the Maritime Registry to see if there really was a ship named so-and-so sunk off the coast of Madagascar, et cetera, and that all checked out. Not that it affected my attitude toward it being a setup. But anyway, as I say, I figured the buy itself would be cool—after that, it would be a question of creating a super Pavlovian rat-maze of false-drop possibilities, so that when they couldn't locate it right away at Customs, they'd be prepared to conclude I'd switched it. I had already determined the transport of choice, because, one day when I was looking over the shipping news—arrivals and departures—I noticed, in the same section of the paper, the announcement of an important Colombian international dog show in, of all places, Bogotá. Well, as it so happened, I had a couple of Wiemeraners—*big* mothers, a hundred and fifty pounds, boss credentials, ancestors were sort of Rin-Tin-Tins of the kraut hunting-dog world. I wired Gomez, said something like: 'Showing at Bogotá International, May 2 to 5, Wiemeraner section. Hope to see you there. T.' "

339

He paused to do a line of flake, and take a hit of dark, proffered by the fab and ever-at-hand Wen, from a rose-water-filled hookah. And I was beginning to think of her as a sort of Flo Nightingale in hot-pants.

When I raised my head to receive the niplike end of the hookah tube, my eyes went beyond (by chance only!) the flawless girl, and into an alcove, where Jean-Pierre and a new and unknown nifty were moving in languorous quarter time to "Jumpin' Jack Flash." Despite any or all dalliance on my part, however, the miraculous TC-55 was not idle, catching every nuance and oblique insinuation put forward by a certain Mr. Tito Bandini (aka not quite the same, natch), and he resumed: "So I had two dogs and I bought two more. Then I called an acquaintance, a dog-fancier, who also owned a couple of the same, and asked if he would like to show his two at my expense. Naturally he was delighted. Now I had six dogs to show at the Bogotá International . . ." he paused, had a quick toot and toke, before adding, ". . . *and* six shipping crates.

"They were all standard specifications for air-freight dog shipment— four by three by three-and-a-half feet—floor, ceiling and the two ends of one-inch pine boards, aluminum bars: net weight, without beast, fifty-one pounds.

"On one cage I switched from one-inch pine to one-eighth-inch *oak,* using two each, so there was a three-quarter-inch space between them. You see, one-eighth-inch oak will support the same weight as one full inch of yellow pine, and on the sides I used a sixteenth, so that gave us a stash space of one-quarter-inch by four by three by blah-blah-blah in the floor and ceiling—I wanted the extra strength in the ceiling, too, in case they stacked the crates, or maybe even got them upside down, the maniacs. And then, of course, we had a three-quarter-inch space by three by three on the two sides that didn't have bars—giving us a grand total of *ninety-six cubic inches of stash.* And finally I used hollow bars on that cage—not for stash, that would be too obvious, but for keeping the weight down. I also thought if they started tearing that cage apart and hit on those hollow bars—*empty*—well, they would just have to figure *that* cage was clean for sure. I mean, where the hell would you stash a stash if not in the *hollow bars* of a cage, right? So, this cage, identical to the others, was twenty-one pounds lighter. The dogs averaged a hundred forty-eight, with the lightest one being a hundred thirty-seven and the heaviest a hundred fifty-nine. On the trip over I put the heaviest dog in the stash-cage, so it brought the weight up to normal—the idea being that on the return the lightest dog would be in the stash-cage, along with the forty-four pounds of flake, bringing *it* up to a normal weight. So there would be no noticeable weight discrepancy in the cages, either coming or going. Dig?"

"Yes," I said, allowing myself another glimpse into the farther room, where now Wendy and the new and nameless nifty were moving in languorous, sensual entwinement, while Jean-Pierre sat looking on, his face a mask of stoned bemusement. "Yes, I understand. But tell me something, while I can still think of it—what happened to the first mate in the lifeboat? You said only the *captain* survived—"

My host smiled. "My, my, you *do* have an inquiring mind," and still smiling he leaned forward, did two parallels, a nostril each. Then he nodded an indication that I should join him, and I felt obliged to do so.

"Well, actually," I said, totally whacked, "it isn't *me,* it's the *machine,*" and I stared momentarily at the TC-55. "It would want to know." I really meant it, and he understood.

"Yes," he agreed, "otherwise there would be, how do you say, a *gap* in the tape."

"Right, right, that's it exactly." Our rapport was staggering.

"Well, it was quite simple," he resumed. "The mate was washed ashore a few months later, a hundred miles or so south of the Cape, dead of course, and with about two inches of a six-inch distress flare protruding from the back of his skull."

I could not resist toying with the image in my mind's eye. I tried to recall the construction of a distress flare—something like a mortar shell, with flanging tail stabilizers—a miniature space rocket, protruding from the back of the mate's head. "Far out," I muttered.

Tito, however, did not appear to share my taste for the visually odd. He nodded toward the languorously swaying beauties in the adjacent room. "That's Kim," he said, and added with a cryptic smile, "She's sort of Wendy's . . . 'cousin,' you might say. They made the run with me, yes? Okay, *en route!* Well, everything was cool at JFK. And why not? The dog-cargo check-in was totally separate from the passenger check-in. Wendy and Kim handled it—Gal Friday–style, but heavy, like early Joan Craw-ford, you dig, and maybe Ida Lupino, very correct and career-girl-like, tai-lored-suit time, tortoise-rim glasses, everything cool and groovy, almost *formal* you might say." He paused, smiled as though at some odd flash-recall, did one quick line (left snoz, if memory serves), picked up a pair of rose-colored shades from the table, observed of them, breathed on them, rubbed of them, lifted of them, peered through them and, finally satisfied, very carefully put them on—he, too, it seemed, was whacked right out of his gourd. "Yes," he continued, still smiling, glancing briefly at the girls, "quite formal—who would have guessed they gave the best head east of L.A.? *Boss*-head . . . *king*-head . . . *queen-head. I don't know, man, but I really* dig head at thirty-three thousand feet . . . it's all in the mind, of course, but pop an amie in each snoz just as you come, at thirty-three thou, wow, it's something else."

I was quick (or so it seemed) to nod agreement. "Dig it," I managed, "but like you say, 'all in the mind'—I mean, the pressurized cabin and so on, it couldn't really be any different—"

"Right. Head-in-the-head, you might say—"

We shared the almost soundless chuckle of the hopelessly zonked.

"Well, back to biz," he said, suddenly brisk, having a quick toot. "I'll tell you about Bogotá. Far out. Coke there—street coke—is so cheap that *everyone* is on, all the time; they use it like the Victorians used *snuff* . . . truck drivers, bellhops, elevator operators, everybody has runny noses, sneezing, blinking, red-eyed. Of course, the stuff is cut up till it's pure garbage, but they snort huge amounts, like it's flour or something. It makes for an interesting scene, gives the city a curious pace—business deals included."

"Well, anyway," he went on, "we arrived about two in the afternoon, without incident—aside from the super-head I mentioned—and checked in Bogotá Hilton, natch—adjoining suites, one of them, presumably, for the girls, and one for me. They're fairly *straight* in Bogotá regarding excess weirdness of a sexual nature. Not that there isn't an enormous amount of balling and sucking going on at all times—in fact, I think that's the whole basis of the 'siesta'—but a *ménage à trois* might have raised a brow or two. Now, on the way to the elevator, I spotted what's-his-name, Gomez, sitting near the front desk. Neither of us crack. He gets up, gets into the elevator with us. I say 'Sixth floor, please,' he says 'Seven,' and we know the buy is set—that was the drill: whatever floor we drew, he would say the one above if the deal was on, the one below if there was a hitch. Then he asked the operator, 'Is the hotel bar open at *four* o'clock?' 'Oh, yes, sir,' he said, 'the bar opens at blah-blah-blah.' So that meant the first meet would be at four. The reason for doing it like that, talking aloud in an elevator, is to avoid *phone* conversations—you gotta figure every phone is tapped, right?"

He seemed to expect an affirmation of this fairly paranoid notion, so I gave it to him, in the form of a sympathetic nod and a couple of quick toots.

"Well," he went on, "Wendy handles the dogs, you see, and Kim is the maven."

"The maven?"

"That's right, she's probably the best flake maven in the world. It's almost like a sixth sense—she can taste the purity of coke, within *half a point*. I always run it through my chemistry set, but she's never been wrong. She's also got a way of doing it with litmus paper and a catalyst mixture—big trade-secret—but, you know, a talent like that is invaluable, because sometimes it can get a little awkward, carrying around a big sophisticated dope-analysis kit, and then trying to ditch it."

"Yes, I can well imagine," I replied, recalling the elaborate junk-testing apparatus in *The French Connection*.

"It's a gift," he said solemnly, "a genuine gift."

"Not like giving great head."

He smiled in appreciation of my understanding.

"Right. Any girl—well, *almost* any girl—with full sensuous lips and regular teeth, can learn, or be taught to give great head—an acquired skill, you might say—but this, dope-tasting infallibility, is truly a god-given talent."

"Like perfect pitch," I suggested.

"Yes," he agreed, "but far more rare—closer to *genius*, like being a child prodigy, a Mozart."

I began to think of Kim in a new, even more attractive, light. A coke maven! *To fuck a coke maven!* Hey, we're talking *Nirvana City!*

"Must be a moral there somewhere," I ventured.

Tito Bandini (if, indeed, that was his name) shrugged lightly.

"Well, for openers," he said, and leaned forward for a quick double, "it proves that a smart girl can use at least *some* of her bodily orifices for things other than playing 'Hide the Jelly Roll.' " And he laid his boss charm and winner smile on me, and proffered a veritable mound of it—as seen from very close now, all shimmering and sparkling like a diamond-crusted snowbank, pure and inviolate forever . . . or at least until I could put the old snoz to it. Ho-ho!

RICHARD BELZER

An Interview

GEORGE BARKIN AND LARRY "RATSO" SLOMAN

JULY 1984

IT AIN'T EASY BEING a stand-up comic. Just you and a stool and a mike, frozen in the spotlight, onstage before (hopefully) an audience full of people who spent good money to get in the damn door and now are getting hustled for even better money for watered-down drinks and, as likely as not, are probably paying more cash for the babysitter back home.

And you gotta make them laugh. You gotta glom on some situation that they all face, whether it's the nuclear bomb or their mothers-in-law, and give it that special little side-zinger so they see it in a way they never saw it before and it touches them, either with a reassuring pat on the back or a sardonic elbow to the ribs, and the resultant emotional catharsis comes out as laughter. It ain't easy.

Of course, the easy way to connect is to paint yourself as some sort of schmuck—the guy who don't get no respect, the henpecked nerd who pleads you to take his wife, the hopelessly neurotic bumbler, the jerk. It's easy for people to laugh at people.

It's harder to elicit laughter when the basic comedic mode is attack—which is the way Richard Belzer operates, and operates brilliantly. All the obligatory comparisons to Lenny have been made by the critics. And in this case, there may actually be something to what they're saying. He's got the same kind of passionate engagement with society that gets clothed in an almost arrogant, cynical coolness. He can talk social issues like a goddamn university professor, spouting Hegelian dialectic one moment, then vomit up a cesspool of Brooklyn street-corner scatology the next.

Of course, his name is not so obscure now as it was, say, a year ago. Though he's been doing his stand-up for almost fourteen years, he's beginning to channel his talent into other areas. Like the *Thicke of the Night* show, where Belzer was the street-smart antidote to the Velveeta Canadian. Then there were the film bits, the cameos in *Author, Author* and *Night Shift* and *Scarface*.

And now Belzer is poised on the brink of upping his recognition quotient on his HBO/Cinemax show, *Caught in the Act*. But what kind of woman is Richard Belzer?*

Well, they call him the comic to the stars. He was the Hollywood/New York hip film and music community's pet comedian, the dangerous, on-the-edge underground legend who either had too much integrity or was too self-destructive to even surface out of the after-hours scene.

Of course, the latter was the interpretation of the cigar-chewing moguls who book the college circuits and the talk shows and the studio projects. For them, Belzer's danger might backfire and freeze their Amex gold-card accounts.

But in 1981 *Rolling Stone* magazine did a feature on Belzer, and in a confession mode, fueled by about fifteen sakes, he laid out his whole sordid past. His abused childhood, the suicide of his father, his heroin habit, his broken marriages—the whole sadness that seemed to have permeated his life. Then came the sympathy backlash to the article.

George Carlin insisted he come on the *Tonight Show* the evening he guest-hosted. Ron Howard got him for a few bit parts in his movies. And slowly but surely, the agents realized that this guy Belzer wouldn't shit on their rugs if they took a meeting with him.

Today, he's punching forty in the face and he's traded his coke-dealer leather jackets for nice, sleek Georgia Armani suits (courtesy of the Thicke show wardrobe department, he hastens to add). And it's almost as if he's happy now, and it's certain that he's more mature, and it's wonderful that he's every bit as funny.

High Times: How did you get hooked up with Alan Thicke, and what in the name of Groucho Marx are you doing on such a patently lame show?

---

* *[Editor's note: This refers to a line from Belzer's routine]*

Richard Belzer: Those are two good questions. And to answer your first question, Alan used to have a show in Canada: *The Alan Thicke Show*. It was an afternoon talk show, which I did about three years ago. And after the show taped, he invited me to his suite and I hung out with him, and for some weird reason, I was funny that night. I don't know, maybe it was a drug or something. But I made him laugh for seven hours in a row—he was falling off his couch. I was on, and I worked it and he never forgot it, so when he got this show, he called me and wanted me to be on it.

And the way this show was described to me before it went on the air was, we're gonna have Alan Thicke as the host, we'll have five or six repertory people. We're gonna be like *Saturday Night Live* and *SCTV* and the *Tonight Show*, and you can be yourself and ba ba bee, and I said, "Fucking great," you know? And we felt like we were the new kid on the block. We're taking on Carson, we're gonna be hip, we're gonna be big, and we started to do two ninety-minute shows a day for three days in a row, which is physically impossible, but we did them.

And the show just fell apart. It became utter chaos. It's like an intelligence test: The more intelligent and hipper people are, the more they hate Alan. And people have all these long diatribes about him—

High Times: Well, the entertainers he's gathered around him are, with the exception of yourself, aggressively un-talented. Then there's his stable of media circus freaks—a gossip columnist from the *National Enquirer,* a professional right-wing talk-show asshole and assorted dippy Hollywood soap-opera actresses. And people can't understand how someone like Richard Belzer, who prided himself on his "artistic integrity," could sell out to such an actively vulgar and stupid show.

Belzer: When I first did the show, I honestly felt that we were gonna get great ratings and be totally different. Because on paper it sounded great. But the center of the show is a disaster, and that's Fred Silverman's fault, because Alan Thicke does not have charisma. And you cannot blame a person if they're not charismatic.

High Times: Whose idea was it to add the gossip columnist and the professional right-wing talk-show asshole?

Belzer: See, when you have a sinking ship, you'll try anything. It's like bunker mentality. It's Hitler in the bunker and what do we do now? So first they had tits out on the show. Then they had faggot columnists. So who's the show for? There's a faggot and there's a chick, and then they had rock 'n' roll. I mean, who's gonna watch this fucking show? A schizophrenic on Thorazine, who one minute can be gay and then like tits and then like rock 'n' roll? It's like, they try to please everyone, they please no one.

High Times: Weren't there a lot of routines you had to do where you said to yourself, "Why am I doing this?"

Belzer: I rewrote some of the sketch material that I didn't like. Yeah, there were a few times where I was embarrassed. Not as much as you would think, from the way the show looks, because after a point they got afraid of me and I would take a script and I would go into the producer and say, "Babe, do you want me to do this in front of two million people? You read this line."

High Times: It seems we can't get you to bad-mouth Alan Thicke. Who do you want to bad-mouth? How about Lorne Michaels?

Belzer: Again? Well, to tell you the truth, I was genuinely thinking of calling my show "The *Real* New Show," but was voted down. I'd even let *him* on *my* show. You can quote me on that. I don't mind that at all. After all, he had me on "Saturday Night."

High Times: Well, he seems to have defined comedy for a whole generation.

Belzer: And then undefined it.

High Times: And then beat it into the ground. All those "Saturday Night" people making a lot of money, doing a lot of great things, killing themselves and becoming instant legends. How do you view that whole phenomenon?

Belzer: That's a hard question. Well, the irony to me is that now I'm being hired to do the very thing that terrified everyone for the last ten years. You know, HBO Cinemax said, "We want you to be Richard Belzer." No one had ever asked me to do that before. They hired me to do all the things that lost me all the work that I've lost. Not lost, but didn't even get asked for.

High Times: But what do you see as the difference between what you do and the "Saturday Night" crowd?

Belzer: See, at the risk of being immodest, or whatever, my theories and feelings about comedy, terms like "don't compromise" come into my mind. And not milking the joke to death. And not doing an obvious joke and steering away from easy laughs. So I'd rather maintain my integrity than go on and do a really bad, embarrassing, stupid, sexist, drug-laden, fucking sketch unless I wrote it.

It's true, a lot of my friends did become millionaires, some are dead, and I used to say, "Everyone but me." That was my catch phrase. "Everyone made it but me." But now it's my turn, even though it's on a much smaller scale, and will build longer . . . I'm not sure I know how to answer the question really.

High Times: Look at someone like Steve Martin or Chevy Chase—Eddie Murphy, I guess, is the latest example—comedians whose popularity far exceeds the talent they have. How do you keep from falling victim to that— from getting puffed up to the point where you're a walking bag of hot air?

Belzer: Exactly. That's the thing I'm terrified of and will never happen to me, and if it does I hope you guys get me in a corner and kick the shit out of me. I saw this happen a lot at Catch when I emceed over the years:

Example, Bill Cosby comes onstage. So the audience already knows it's Bill Cosby because he's Bill Cosby. And he takes the mike stand and says, "I'm gonna put this over here." Big laugh.

Now, if a guy was auditioning on Monday night and you didn't know him, and he said, "I'm gonna put the mike over here," the audience is gonna go, "Yeah, and?" So the most dangerous thing in the world for a comedian is to have the instant recognizability that you are funny and then do anything you want and people will laugh at it because it's supposed to be funny because you're doing it.

Don Rickles is one of the primary examples of that. Where, you know, in 1965 it was hip to do what he was doing, but now he comes off as a racist, misogynist, fucking jerk lounge-comic scumbag. And he'll do a hockey-puck line and the audience will laugh like they're Pavlovian Russian wolfhounds. I'm very cognizant of that.

High Times: Who would you rather end up like?

Belzer: End up? I'd like to start out first, then I'll end up. I'd like to end up like Jack Benny.

High Times: This is like an essay question. Who would you rather end up like? Someone like Lenny Bruce or Chevy Chase?

Belzer: Neither. Right in between.

High Times: Like who?

Belzer: Richard Pryor, who transcended the live performances, got into film, who can still go back and forth and do both and maintain his integrity and make a lot of money and not sell out. And it cost him every fucking inch of it.

You know, I'll tell you something about all of those "Saturday Night" people. They begrudgingly did a network television show—a few of them, anyway. There was a lot of friction and conflict about this drug-oriented, youth culture being in a network format. I'm sure you guys are well aware of the history and the whole thing, but one of the things that psychologically fucked up John, I know for a fact, and Chevy, also—is that they did sell out. They did in fact sell out, and took huge sums of money and did things that they would have made fun of and had scorned and had been against their whole careers. And I know that John, in particular, was very troubled, although he didn't articulate it the way I am articulating it now—he was very disturbed about the movies *Neighbors* and *Continental Divide,* because John was a fucking, Second City genius, rebel, antiestablishment—he was everything that we thought he was when we first saw him on *Saturday Night Live,* that first year. And more. Because that was network television. I mean, have you ever seen him live anywhere? The guy was amazing. Harpo on acid. But then he's getting a million dollars to make a terrible picture, and then another terrible picture. And then another terrible picture. And then finally he's going to write his own screenplay and that gets rejected. So the rebel in him succumbs. The reason he was doing so many drugs was because he wasn't happy.

He wasn't happy because he wasn't the John Belushi that he set out to be. Chevy has done a 180 degree. He is now like a Republican candidate on Phil Donahue, with a suit, talking like he's running for office. Now he'll talk about his "naughty" days on *Saturday Night Live,* like, "Yes, I used to do those things." Everyone got jealous of Chevy because he stole the show the first year and it became the *Chevy Chase Show.* And then he left and got a major picture deal. But Chevy had some well-publicized drug problems that I feel were related to the fact that he was making a million dollars to dub Benji's voice. I was over at his house one day and I said, "How the fuck can you do this?" We were medicated, and after a while you say anything, right? I said, "How the fuck can you like dub a dog's voice in a Benji movie?" And he said, "For a million dollars and points." And I said, "Oh."

High Times: Wouldn't you have done that?

Belzer: I knew that was your next question. I'll tell you something. I don't know. I don't know.

High Times: Two million dollars.

Belzer: I don't know. I don't know.

High Times: You know who came out really great from *Saturday Night Live?* Bill Murray.

Belzer: He's a little bit smarter about his career than these other people. I mean, even though Chevy makes millions of dollars, he's a fucking pawn of the studios. And now he's trying to play the role of statesman. He's no longer hip and antiestablishment. Now he is the establishment.

High Times: Can you blame him?

Belzer: I can because I didn't fucking sell out.

High Times: Well, not yet, anyway.

Belzer: What?

High Times: Who knows what the future may bring?

Belzer: That's a good point. But I think the reason that I'm so vehement in securing my integrity is that if I've gone this far, getting my own show on Cinemax, so by the time something happens in a few years that might be so tempting—like a huge sum of money to do some bad picture that I know is bad—I'll turn it down.

High Times: Let's talk about drugs and performing. Does the vulnerability of being a comedian make drugs indispensable?

Belzer: I'll tell you something. I used to go onstage every night. I'd be fucked out of my mind on drugs that you guys can't pronounce. Okay? I've done everything. And things have done me. I've gone onstage using every type of drug and I've embarrassed myself; I've been great; I've been okay; I've given every level of performance on drugs.

And then I stopped using drugs. Not totally, but to go onstage with. I was on the road, it was a very cathartic experience for me. I was on the road with Warren Zevon, touring, opening up for him in these clubs all over. And every night before we went on, you know, it was like "Get out the shovel."

He introduced me to Stolichnaya, by the way. So, we'd be drinking Stoli from the bottle and doing coke like, you know, Jimi Hendrix's nephews, and before I went on I had to have that, you know [*snorting*], and I just felt I had to do it. And one night we were late. The bus was late and for whatever reason, I had to go on straight. God forbid I should go on straight.

And I had this moment: I said, "Wait a minute. I'm funny. I'm not high. Okay."

So I went on and I fucking killed. And it just taught me a little lesson. Because since I first started doing stand up, I always had to have a couple of drinks, I always had to do something before I went on.

First it was just drinking. Then it got to be pot. Then it got to be coke. Then there were nights I was onstage on mescaline. There were nights onstage I was on heroin. There were nights onstage on every fucking drug known to man.

High Times: 'Ludes. Let's not forget Quaaludes.

Belzer: And Quaaludes.

High Times: How can you tell a joke on heroin?

Belzer: Slowly. Very slowly.

High Times: Which drug made you the funniest?

Belzer: Hands down.

High Times: The big C?

Belzer: Yeah. Of course. It's called "the comedian's drug."

Comedian "X," a rich, famous comic, came up to me in the basement of a club—there are many famous "dressing-room" stories—and he said, "Rich,"—I hate when people call me Rich, but I let him do it—"Rich, you know, you're gonna make a lot of money in this business, and you're going to be a very big star."

I'm saying to myself, "What the fuck is this?" We just did coke, and I'm going up the stairs, I gotta go on, and, you know, what is this?

"You're going to be a very big star, you're going to be very rich." He said, "When you got the money, it's so easy to get . . ."

In other words, he's telling me that he has a coke problem, that I shouldn't have one because I make $35 a night and he's got $400,000 in the bank. "Fuck you. Don't warn me. Get off it yourself. I can't afford to have the habit you have." He's like giving me a thing: "You know, when you make a lot of money, you can get a lot of coke."

I said, "God, I wish I had the money," you know? "That's one habit I'd love to break." If I had so much money, I could buy as much coke as I wanted. [*Jewish accent*] What a catastrophe that would be. My word. Oh, my God, I got big cans full of coke. What am I gonna do? Maybe I should smoke some of it. Maybe I should give some away. Maybe I should cut it with something else. Who knows what?

High Times: What comics influenced you?

Belzer: I was always a student of comedy, as a kid . . . Lord Buckley, Lenny, Jackie Mason. I loved Jackie Leonard when I was a kid. Jerry Lewis . . .

But I think the greatest, the single greatest influence on me, if I had to pick one, would be Groucho. Because for twelve years, once a week, I watched him every night on "You Bet Your Life." And I know that some part of him is in me. I'm not doing Groucho, but he's very much a part of me. And so is Jack Benny, but it doesn't show as much.

High Times: Apart from Richard Pryor, who do you really admire among your colleagues?

Belzer: Albert Brooks. George Carlin.

High Times: What do you think of Eddie Murphy?

Belzer: What do I think of Eddie Murphy? I think that Eddie Murphy is a consummate talent. I think that he's grossly misguided. I think that with all the money that he's making, which I don't begrudge him because the nature of our business is so illogical—I'm not gonna be bitter because some schwartze has five minutes, grabs his dick and gets fifteen million dollars. Far be it for me to be bitter. But they should take some of that money and . . .

High Times: . . . and give it to you . . .

Belzer: . . . and get some good writers. The kid is great. There's no question about it. He was fantastic in *48 Hours*. He's real good on the floor, but his material is repetitive.

High Times: Well, they all compare him to Pryor.

Belzer: That's absurd.

High Times: Why is it absurd?

Belzer: Because he's black and he grabs his dick. But he's not a genius. But *I'm* not bitter that I'm 39 and I'm hiding from my Arab landlord.

High Times: There's an amazing comic renaissance now. Why? Do you agree with the socioeconomic theory of comedy: that in bad times people want to laugh?

Belzer: There are more comics now than ever before in history. When I first started there were maybe three clubs. Now there's hundreds of clubs. There's Zanies, and Chuckles and Laugh Up Your Ass and Bagels and Tongues and Jews and Jokes and every fucking street corner in every fucking town has fourteen comedy clubs in it.

See, it used to be every kid got a guitar and got in front of a mirror and wanted to be Elvis. Now every kid wants to be Eddie Murphy, they want to be Richard Pryor, they want to be Steve Martin, which I think is great.

They say people want to laugh in hard times and I think there must be some correlation on that level.

But there's something else at work besides that that I can't quite define. I don't know why there are more comedians than ever before. I know I like it, but I think that it may be some collective unconscious reflex that people are terrified of a nuclear holocaust and of not having any money and living in uncertain times, so they reflexively turn to comedy at some deep level.

I do believe that. That's too Jungian for your magazine.

High Times: We have a very Jung audience.

Belzer: But I genuinely believe that there may be something to that, that there's this thing going on on a national psychic level.

High Times: Well, I guess if you have a comedian in the White House.

Belzer: That's right, [*does Reagan*] "Well, I never thought of myself as a comedian, but I did know one joke, but I forgot it. I know it was a good one, too." That's a good point: there's a comedian in the White House. I think we have to get political this year, gentlemen. Anyone but Reagan. I'm willing to back either Mondale or . . .

High Times: Why don't you describe the Richard Belzer persona?

Belzer: Oh, it's been done so much better than I could. Uh, how do I describe it?

High Times: Well, what kind of woman is Richard Belzer?

Belzer: It's an eclectic character. I don't know. My director, Bruce Gowers, calls me the black Italian Jew because I can lapse in and out of all these different attitudes.

High Times: A seething pile of ethnicity.

Belzer: Yeah. I don't know, really. I could get embarrassed if I have to start saying how great I am. I mean, we all know I'm great; that's why we're here. [*lapses into Jackie Mason*] He's from the street, all of a sudden he's from a university, then next, he's a heroin addict dis day, he's a newspaper reporter dat day, one second he's a poet, next minute he's a pimp. Who does this guy think he is? He's a fuckin' limousine driver; he can fix the car, he can be in the back of the limousine. He could be driving it, he could be fixing it, he has all this, one side to another. So I don't know. Jackie Mason. He's as funny as anyone in the world.

Richard Pryor, Albert Brooks and Jackie Mason to me are the three funniest men on earth.

High Times: Jackie Mason may be a hero to you, because he gave Ed Sullivan the finger on national TV, and as a result was blacklisted from the business.

Belzer: Yeah. I guess on some level he was. I didn't think of it that way. But he hurt himself. We've both recovered from disasters. I did things where I was told I was through in the business.

High Times: Well, like what? I mean, how did you get this rep? I mean, you must have done something.

Belzer: I was doing a special in 1978 called "Chevy and Friends," for HBO. And Chevy wanted me to be on it and to cohost with him and introduce new comedians and ba ba bee, ba ba ba. So I was hanging out with Chevy a lot. And it was just towards the end of the Zevon tour. The famous 1978 Zevon tour that's now a legend. Where he took out a .45 and shot a cockroach in his bathtub. Another story.

High Times: Those rock stars.

Belzer: Um. Zany, aren't they? "Go ahead, make my day." Um, so I was at Chevy's house. I was supposed to open for Warren Zevon at the Universal

Amphitheater. One show; it was a big job for me then. I think it was $1,000 for one show, in those days that was a lot of money for me. Today it's a lot of money for me.

Um, and I was at Chevy's house, doing that white stuff that you put on mirrors—

High Times: Windex.

Belzer: And we're doing tons of it, and it was getting right around the time I was supposed to show up at Universal Amphitheater. And I just waited a little bit too long. I got a ride there. I pulled into the back. And I hear, inside the amphitheater, "Richard Belzer will not be here tonight. He called, he's sick," you know, something. You know, oh, no.

So I run back to Warren Zevon's dressing room and he's fixing his tie and I say, "Warren, I'm here and they just said I was sick." You know, he never got mad at me. He *was* mad at me, but he couldn't show it. He just shrugged.

So, after that incident, my agent at the time said, "I have gotten calls from the whole West Coast office of William Morris, promoters all around the country. You'll never work again. No one will ever book you again. How could you not show up and not have a good reason? What were you doing? Coke with Chevy Chase?"

I said, "No, no, no." You know, I made up some lame excuse for something about not knowing the way or something. But that, to this day, that's a famous story in certain circles. I found out years later why certain agents wouldn't take a call from me. As time goes on, I hear what people have thought of me over the years and some of it amazes me. I mean, how people are so terrified of me.

I mean, to this day, it's just a thing that I have to use to my advantage, I guess.

High Times: But terrified?

Belzer: Because they see me onstage and they think, "Well, this guy, he gets me alone in a room or in my office, he's gonna fucking bury me. He's gonna say, 'Fuck you' and 'Suck my cock' and 'How's your wife's cunt?' and 'I see the roots on your wife's hair' and 'I heard you fucked the maid' and 'I heard your son's on heroin' and 'You're a fucking douche bag and you have tax shelters that aren't legal and you're fucking your secretary and fuck you.' "

And that guy's gonna make a deal with me?

High Times: In the *Rolling Stone* article you talked about going through almost a cathartic period with your comedy and the black side of your soul, you know, living a Lenny Bruce scene. You've obviously transcended that and gone past that. Is Richard Belzer happy?

Belzer: Yeah, I'm much more serene and serious.

I think my time has come and I'm ready for it, I'm not gonna put a bullet in my head or stick a needle in my arm now, whereas I might have five or six years ago. Not a bullet, I would have gone out with drugs no matter how crazy I was.

High Times: Does the serenity scare you—I mean in the same sense it seems to have scared Pryor?

Belzer: It's not the kind of serenity where I would be complacent and just go stand up onstage and take the applause because I am who I am. I mean, I'm not a big star, obviously. People in the business know who I am and I do have a cult following that is kind of going overground now because of the Thicke show and because of the HBO special, and my career has been an accumulative series of events rather than this meteoric rise.

The thing I feel really good about is that I am now in a position to put my art where my mouth is and I've always felt that I've had an obligation to be not just a comedian but to be a journalist and to be a poet and to report things and educate people, and I know that sounds professorial for a comedian to talk like this and I hate when anyone does, but I genuinely believe that I do have something to say and that I can affect people's lives, even if it's just through laughter.

I feel very proud of the way that I handled disagreements with the Thicke people—I didn't go berserk and say, "Fuck them, fuck them, fuck them," which I would've a few years ago. But I can't relate to network people with their arbitrary artless bullshit, parroting what they think the audience is gonna like. One thing I've learned in this business, nobody knows anything. And anybody who says or claims they think they know—anything—they're full of shit.

Nobody knows anything because the worst elements in the world have worked and become big hits, and the greatest elements in the world have failed and everything in between. So if I have an idea, why isn't it as good as anybody else's idea? I mean, I'm not stupid. On the Thicke show I had great writers around me; I had intelligent, supportive producers, I had a great director, and if I believed in an idea, it was just as valid as some schmuck's. Who knows how he got it—what are his fucking qualifications, was he on the stage for ten years, no. He was drinking martinis in the boardroom. I've earned the right to say, "I don't want to do this this way." I'm not totally incorrigible, and I do relent on certain things; it's a very diplomatic thing and I've learned to do it . . . to survive. For the greater good of my work—I mean I want to add that in all seriousness.

High Times: Well, were you—essentially what the *Rolling Stone* article pegged you—a self-destructive genius, afraid of success—

Belzer: No, that's too psychoanalytical for me. I don't know if that's true. See, I refused to read for certain sitcoms; I was offered certain things and I didn't want to do them and they said, "Oh, he's afraid." Not because I was afraid, but because I don't want to be the dumb fucking neighbor who has five gestures and one inflection that he does for twenty-six weeks for eight years. I don't want to be the guy who comes in and goes—and gets the recognition applause and does the goofy joke and leaves. I mean, fuck you. I'm not Lennie and Squiggy, okay.

It's strange—it always used to be, "Richie, Richie, clean it up." Now they're paying me to be dirty. So HBO now says, "We want Belzer to be dirty, political and intelligent . . ." That's a direct quote.

High Times: What a crazy world—

Belzer: And years ago I was like plutonium rods.

High Times: So now they want you to be dirty. What's the dirtiest joke you ever told? Or the sickest?

Belzer: Here's one Chevy told me: A theatrical agent is in his office. A guy comes in, says, "I have an act." The agent says, "Okay, what does the act do?" The guy says, "Well, it's a family act. It's me and my family. First, my son comes out. He pulls down his pants and shits on the stage. Then my wife comes out and she rubs her face in it. Then my little daughter comes out and takes all her Tampax from all her periods and sticks them in the shit. Then I jerk off. Then I take my whole family and we rub our faces in the shit and the come and the blood, then I shit in my son's face while my daughter puts a dildo on and fucks him in the ass, while she's eating her mother. Then my wife shits on my face and then I kiss my daughter on the mouth while my son's fucking my wife in the ass. Then my father comes out—he's a very old man—he comes out and is just barely able to throw up. We mix all the stuff together with that and we start eating it. Then my mother's mother comes out and my father puts a dildo on and fucks her in the ass while she's throwing up, because of the smell of all the shit that's already on the stage. Then we all take off all our clothes and roll around in all this shit and start throwing up because of the smell, how disgusting it is, and then we start fucking and sucking each other and then I fuck my wife in the ass while she's blowing my son while his sister is fucking her in the ass with a dildo while my grandfather and grandmother are going sixty-nine." So the agent says, "Oh yeah? What do you call the act?" And the guy says, "The Aristocrats."

IT HAPPENED IN THE HAIGHT

COOKIE MUELLER

MAY 1986

THE FOLLOWING STORY TAKES place in Haight-Ashbury in 1967. It is a sample day from the period based on my personal experiences. The facts are exactly as I remember them. Nothing is exaggerated.

The golden age of the Haight did not last long. Late in 1968, a new element appeared in the neighborhood. Unlike the high-minded peace-lovers who founded the community, the new arrivals were sub-intelligent, violent, sleazo types who carried guns, stole drugs, and raped girls. Heroin appeared on street corners where there previously used to be free LSD. The street got ugly.

The few hippies who remained decided to form a vigilante squad—their own police force actually—but this didn't work too well. Eventually the slime took over and the place got really low-down. One of my friends put it this way:

"Remember when you walked down Haight Street and everybody was smiling and bright? There was actually a light around these people, a bright aura. When the sleazos moved in, the first thing I noticed was the darkness around them, their gloomy auras. The neighborhood got dirty. There was garbage and broken whiskey bottles all over the place. One couldn't go barefoot anymore. One couldn't even live there anymore. It wasn't safe."

At first glance one might not be able to tell the difference between the new sleazos and the hippies. Both groups had long hair. Both were of all races. But the new group was so unlike the former. There was something in the eyes, something in the faces, something rough, uncivilized, brutish, bitter. They looked the way a German Shepherd does after being kicked for many years . . . all scarred up and potentially lethal. Charlie Manson is a perfect example of the type I'm trying to describe.

Anyway, it all died in 1968. Even the tourist buses stopped coming. I've heard the Haight is nice again . . . different, of course, but nice. Even so, the spirit of that era can never be duplicated. It was a very special time in history. There was a sense of communal movement, a feeling of oneness with everyone. I'm glad I was part of it.

HAIGHT-ASHBURY, SAN FRANCISCO, CALIFORNIA, 1967; NEAR EASTER

An earthquake woke me and rolled me off the mattress onto the floor. It was nothing too unusual considering the San Andreas fault. All the buildings along Page Street were crooked from past tremors. This one was 4.6 on the Richter scale and struck at the uncivilized hour of 10 A.M.

It was too early to get up, but I decided I couldn't sleep any longer in the same bed with this person who I liked just fine yesterday when we liberated two T-bone steaks from the Safeway Supermarket—which we cooked and ate, much to the disgust of the vegetarians I lived with. After the steaks we drank a gallon of cheap Napa Sonoma red wine and dropped Owsley purple barrels. But now he was sweating too much in bed, staining the one sheet I owned with all that wasted power from his pores. It meant he couldn't hold his liquor or his drugs, which irritated me so much I had to escape.

I went to the bathroom quietly so I wouldn't wake the eleven people I lived with. My roommates were spread out among five bedrooms, one of which was a glassed-in porch off a kitchen that overlooked a dismal cement courtyard with another building where Janis Joplin lived. On some mornings I could see Janis rattling her pots and pans in her kitchen and sometimes we talked across the concrete abyss like housewives.

After I put on my eye-makeup (a throwback to the time when I teased and bleached my hair—no one else wore eye-makeup in the Haight . . . an occasional dayflower or third eye on the forehead perhaps, but definitely no eye-makeup), I went out on Haight Street looking for something novel. The first thing I saw was a school bus painted black with the words HOLYWOOD PRODUCTIONS (one "L" was missing in Hollywood) scrawled in gold by what appeared to be a retarded person. A tall, hambonish-looking guy was sitting on the bus stairs. He had nicotine stains on his index finger. I asked him for a cigarette. "No cigarettes," he said, "but why don't you come in and smoke a joint with us?"

I followed him in and sat down among paisley throw pillows, bare mattresses, and hanging sand candles. The interior was painted sky blue with splashes of red. Five or six girls were lounging around inside. They looked my age, but seemed younger. Maybe it was their dull eyes, maybe it was their girly prattle, but they seemed like dumb, happy ducks quacking at each other and I immediately felt superior to them. There was something missing here, faulty brain synapses, low wattage cerebral electrolights, maybe.

One of the girls asked, "Would you like to join us? We're traveling up and down the coast in this bus." Everyone thought it was a good idea if I joined them. I thought it was rather sudden, but these kids were just weaned from Wonderbread and Cheese Doodles into free love and peace. They were disgustingly enthusiastic.

I tried to picture myself traveling "up and down the coast" with them but my blood turned cold. "I don't think so," I said. "I have a flat here with eleven other people and I'm sort of set up, you know? What's the situation on this bus? I mean, how many of you are there?"

"There's eight right now. Six girls and two guys. You should really wait for Charlie to come back from the store before you decide. He's the one to talk to. He's really far out and spiritual. He's in there buying oranges for us." She pointed to the Korean fruit store. I decided not to wait, so I thanked them for the joint and left looking for a diversion from this bunch. (It wasn't until years later while reading "The Family" that I remembered that bus. It was described in the book exactly as I remember it. Those girls were Susan Atkins, Squeaky Fromm, Mary Brunner, etc. I missed Charlie by five minutes.)

Next I noticed a group of women gathered on the sidewalk. I thought this was odd since it was long before the days when women felt it was their duty to exclude men in their conversations. As I got closer, I realized the blonde in the center of the group was extolling the virtues of Jimi Hendrix, after having fucked him the night before. It all seemed pretty silly to me since I'd fucked him the night before she had.

I moved on to Golden Gate Park. As usual, the sky over Hippie Hill was dark with Frisbees, kites, and sea gulls. Hundreds of hippies' dogs were barking and walking on the people lying on the grass. The air was thick with the smell of marijuana, patchoulie oil, jasmine incense, and Eucalyptus trees. The music was deafening. Black guys were playing congos; white guys were playing flutes, harmonicas, and guitars. It was as crowded as Coney Island on the Fourth of July. Hippie Hill was like this every day of the week.

I ran into some friends and sat around drinking wine. Around noon I stopped back at 1826 Page Street. An acid capping party was in progress. It was the sort of party that only happened where an acid dealer lived. The object of the party was to put acid powder into gelatin capsules, but since the acid assimilated through the skin, everyone got pretty high. Consequently, the party usually went on in shifts and when someone got too stoned to continue, another person would take their place. So when Kirk, one of my roommates, dropped out, I slipped into his place in front of a large mound of white powder. After filling around three hundred capsules, I decided I was quite high enough. Someone took my place and I went back out on the street.

I walked down Page Street, which runs parallel to Haight. The sidewalk was lined with dealers and hippies. The acid was beginning to take effect, so I dropped into a Catholic church to cool down. The doors were open, probably because it was close to Easter. The church was empty except for an old lady sitting in a pew who didn't notice me. The altar was tastefully decorated in purple and gold. The atmosphere was peaceful.

Since I wasn't raised Catholic, the confessional fascinated me. I looked into every booth. There were booths on both sides of the priest's box, but the priest's box looked the best. It had a velvet armchair and gold and purple raiments hung over the backrest. The booth was bathed in blue light. It looked so comforting on acid . . . a great spot to sit for a while, I thought, so white and holy. I wasn't a Catholic so it wasn't a sacred spot to me. I didn't know one wasn't allowed inside. I was tripping my brains out and I think even if I had been a Catholic, it wouldn't have mattered. I went in, sat down, and decided to stay until I stopped peaking on the acid.

A minute later, the door opened. A man entered and quickly closed the door. We were cramped in the narrow, tiny space. He had glasses and short hair, which immediately led me to mistrust him. (In those days, the longer the hair, the more versed one was in the scene.) He was shaking like a Chihuahua in a snow storm. I thought he must be a custodian and expected him to discreetly ask me to leave. Instead, he fell on his knees. His glasses fogged up. He began sweating. He wasn't an employee, just a pervert and no greater fantasy could have been his fortune than to discover a stoned, hippie chick in his confessional box.

The acid rendered me pure and guileless, so I didn't recognize a sexual deviant. I just didn't think about sex on LSD. I felt more like a flaccid fungus, inhuman and unphysical.

"Let me eat you," he said in a barely audible voice. "Please let me eat you."

Even on acid, when the strange is accepted, I thought it rather odd and unbecoming for a supposedly religious man to be saying such things. Perhaps it was an hallucination. Where did this guy materialize from? He wasn't in the church when I came in. I said something like, "No, my son, but you're forgiven. Please leave me now to my prayers and solace." But he wouldn't leave. He grabbed my shoulders and tried to hold me down. By sheer adrenaline force, I managed to push him off, jump over him, and run out the door, past the pews and back into the eye-damaging sunlight of the street.

A flatbed truck came lumbering toward me, carrying amplifiers, guitars, drums, a group of hippies, and The Grateful Dead. I must have looked shaken for they stopped, extended a hand, and pulled me onboard. Suddenly, we were on our way to San Quentin to give a free concert for the prisoners. Not much happened out there, but the prisoners liked it.

By the time I reached home, everyone was shooting heroin to come down from the acid capping party. I helped myself to some and lay down for a bit.

A friend named Patrick, who I hadn't seen for a while, woke me up and urged me to visit his new guru, Anton LaVey, America's foremost demonologist and devil worshipper. It sounded interesting, so I went.

First, however, we had to stop at Patrick's sister's house to borrow her car. She was having what appeared to be a sit-down dinner for a bunch of

Indians. However, it turned out it wasn't a dinner at all, but an authentic peyote ceremony. Her husband, a full-blood Sioux chief, was presiding while four other Indians munched on peyote buttons. We ate some and they asked us to return the next day so we could all drink each other's urine and get high all over again. I thanked him and promised to return, but I kept thinking how inappropriate it was—all these Sioux Indians sitting in Patrick's sister's high-rise, pre-fab apartment performing an ancient ritual that should have been done on the plains and under the stars. It was a sad sight, those red men in polyester outfits sitting on plastic chairs. What would their ancestors have thought?

When we got back to LaVey's house, which was painted black, all of it, down to the drainpipes and Victorian woodwork, Patrick asked me to sit in the livingroom and wait for him to return. It's not easy to frighten me, it never has been, but this place was definitely spine-chilling. LaVey entered wearing velvet robes. He seemed surprisingly cordial and human. He brought some sort of liquid for me to drink. Patrick returned carrying a bag. LaVey nodded to Patrick and left.

"We're going to have some fun now, Cookie," he said. "We're going to Mount Tamapious to evoke one of Beelzebub's footman. Whataya say?"

It was fine with me. I was pretty sure LaVey was a fraud supported by naïve fools like Patrick . . . although . . . at the same time I couldn't dismiss the creepy feeling I got inside the house.

As we crossed the Golden Gate Bridge, Patrick told me he had personally performed a black ceremony that resulted in the *San Francisco Chronicle* newspaper strike. I decided Patrick was nuts.

The summit of Mount Tamapious was entirely too dark. There was hardly a moon that night and the trees, rocks, even my own feet beneath me were frighteningly distorted. Maybe the knowledge this spot had been a sacred Indian burial ground had something to do with my sudden fears.

Patrick opened his bag and produced a blood-stone talisman, a jar of blood, a black-handled knife, a bag of herbs, the hooves of a goat, and a black book. He scratched two nine-foot circles and a pair of pentacles in the dirt. After seeing this, I began suspecting Patrick might be dangerous. I knew enough from books about the black arts to know when someone was serious.

It got so dark that the edge of the mountain disappeared and the earth beneath my feet was no longer visible. Patrick told me to stand in the middle of the circle. He said I would be okay since this was the protected spot. I thought, if this was the protected spot, then why wasn't Patrick standing there with me? But I stepped inside the circle anyway and Patrick began reading from his black book. Just as I was beginning to relax, sure this was all ridiculous, I heard something with little feet running toward us from distance, screeching with a voice that was half human, half bird. It was definitely not imaginary. For what seemed like a light-year, I tried to categorize the sound . . . but fear overtook reason. I felt my body go ashen as the thing got closer. The little hairs on my body rose and waved like a wheatfield in the wind. For the first time, I knew the feeling of one's hair standing on end. I looked at Patrick, who was obviously not in command of the situation. He looked like someone being disemboweled.

If this was a test of courage, I lost. If this was a ritual for human sacrifice with me as the victim, I won because I didn't wait around to find out. I couldn't stand it. No one with a shred of sanity would have been able to stand there.

So I left Patrick to his evil deed, left him in the dust the way a roadrunner would. I ran faster than I ever had in my life, probably crossed paths with the footman himself, jumped into the car, took the keys from under the floor mat, and tore down the side of the mountain, tires squealing around the narrow precarious curves, gunning it full blast to the Golden Gate Bridge. When I finally saw the bridge lights (fear had altered my vision), the superstructure was melting and the houses on the other side were disintegrating. I wanted to scream to the passersby but they looked shockingly inhuman. The road rose and fell like storm swells in the sea. I was sure someone or something was in the back seat behind me.

When I got home, I leapt out of the car and ran inside so scared that everyone was horrified (most of them were on STP and THC). They calmed me down and soon we were back in Patrick's sister's car and on our way to Winterland to see Jim Morrison and distribute the Blue Cheer acid that had gone through the laundry by accident, since that's where Susan had stashed it the day before. Mark hadn't known it was there and washed the whole load (about four hundred dollars' worth of the stuff) with the detergent Cheer. Now the whole batch of acid was Blue Cheer and Cheer combined. We planned to give it away free, providing, of course, people didn't mind the accompanying side effects of the detergent.

Jim Morrison was good, as usual, and so was the acid. We even handed a lump of the goo to him on stage and he happily ate it. After the concert, we left to smoke opium at home, leaving Kathy and Eve to go backstage to fuck Morrison. While smoking the opium and listening to KMPX (the best radio station at the time), we heard an unfamiliar song. I was elected, since we didn't have a phone, to go out into the three o'clock morning and call KMPX to get the title of the song.

While I was in the phone booth, a black man with short hair (again) walked up and stood behind me. I thought perhaps he was waiting to use the phone, but no, when I finished, I found he was waiting for me.

"How do you like Stokely Carmichael?" he asked.

"I don't care one way or the other about him, really," I said, unsure of the relevance of the question.

"Would you like to meet him?" he asked.

"Not really, not right now. It's a little late, don't you think?" I answered.

But he drew a gun from an Iceberg Slim book. I looked around feebly for help. There was none.

"Come with me and we'll meet him," he said.

We never did.

Actually, it would have been nicer to meet him because it turned out this was rape. It wasn't even done well and he was stupid to boot, just like the young girls on the Manson bus. But he did give me a musical jewelry box from his trunk and I ingeniously cajoled him to drive me back to my neighborhood by telling him I had wall-to-wall carpeting, air-conditioning, a huge color TV set, and heroin waiting for him. When we got into the neighborhood, I saw a few big hippies walking by and flung the door open. Clutching the music box, I threw myself out of the moving car. The hippies pounced on the car and pulled the guy out. I guess he thought they were going to beat him up, but hippies don't do that sort of thing. They believed in messing up minds instead of bodies. I felt sort of sorry for the guy because I knew he wasn't real bright, so I knew he was scared.

When I got home, a bit shaken once again, everybody was shooting up crystal methadrine. They got upset for a minute when I told them the rape story. Kirk asked me why I was the one to have all the fun. I told him I was the lucky one, but I didn't feel lucky. I felt slightly ajar.

They offered me some meth and we ushered in the dawn talking about aesthetics and Far Eastern spiritualism. We recorded the conversation— not realizing what seemed like earth-shattering insights on methedrine would sound foolishly cyclical the next day.

But it was already the next day . . . time for me to go back out on Haight Street and get lucky again.

DUTCH PROVOS

Teun Voeten

January 1990

IT'S NO SECRET THAT Holland has the most liberal drug laws in the world, especially when it comes to cannabis. What you may not realize, however, is that these laws were enacted thanks to the effort of the Dutch Provos. The Provos set the stage for the creation of the Merry Pranksters, Diggers, and Yippies. They were the first to combine non-violence and absurd humor to create social change. They created the first "Happenings" and "Be-Ins." They were also the first to actively campaign against marijuana prohibition. Even so, they remain relatively unknown outside of Holland. Now, for the first time, their true story is told.

It all started with the Nozems. Born out of the postwar economic boom, the Nozems were disaffected Dutch teens armed with consumer spending power. Part mods, part '50s juvenile delinquents, they spent most of their time cruising the streets on mopeds, bored stiff and not knowing what to do. Their favorite past-time? Raising trouble and provoking the police.

"Provo" was actually first coined by Dutch sociologist Buikhuizen in a condescending description of the Nozems. Roel Van Duyn, a philosophy student at the University of Amsterdam, was the first to recognize the Nozems' slumbering potential. "It is our task to turn their aggression into revolutionary consciousness," he wrote in 1965.

Inspired by anarchism, Dadaism, German philosopher (and counter-culture guru-to-be) Herbert Marcuse, and the Marquis de Sade, Van Duyn, a timid, introverted intellectual, soon became the major force behind *Provo* magazine. But while Van Duyn presided over the Provo's theoretical wing, another, more important, element was provided even earlier by its other co-founder, Robert Jasper Grootveld, a former window cleaner and the original clown prince of popular culture.

More interested in magic than Marx, Grootveld was an extroverted performance artist with a gift for theatrical gesture. During the early '60s, he attracted massive crowds in Amsterdam with exhibitionistic "Happenings." At the core of Grootveld's philosophy was the belief that the masses had been brainwashed into becoming a herd of addicted consumers, the "despicable plastic people." According to Grootveld, new rituals were needed to awaken these complacent consumers. While the writings of Van Duyn greatly appealed to the educated crowd, Grootveld found his followers among street punks.

The Provo phenomenon was an outgrowth of the alienation and absurdity of life in the early '60s. It was irresistibly attractive to Dutch youth and seemed like it would travel around the world. However, in only a few short years it disappeared, choked on its own successes.

"Every weekend in 1962, I paid a visit to a police officer named Houweling," explains Grootveld. "During these visits, I often dressed like an American Indian. We always had very friendly chats about marijuana. Houweling didn't know anything about it, so I could tell him anything I wanted."

Thus began the "Marihuettegame," a disinformation game played by Grootveld and his friends. The idea was to demonstrate the establishment's complete ignorance on the subject of cannabis. The players were supposed to have fun, fool the police and, of course, smoke pot. Other than that, there were no rules. Anything that looked remotely like pot was called "marihu": tea, hay, catfood, spices, and herbs included. Bonus points were collected when a smoker got busted for consuming a legal substance. The players often called the police on themselves. A raid by blue-uniformed nicotine addicts, looking for something that didn't exist, was considered the ultimate jackpot.

"One day a whole group of us went by bus to Belgium," says Grootveld. "Of course I had informed my friend Houweling that some elements might take some pot along. At the border, the cops and customs were waiting for us. Followed by the press, we were taken away for a thorough search. The poor cops . . . all they could find was dogfood and some legal herbs. 'Marijuana is dogfood,' joked the papers the next day. After that, the cops decided to refrain from hassling us in the future, afraid of more blunders."

The following year, Grootveld and artist Fred Wessels opened the "Afrikaanse Druk Stoor," where they sold both real and fake pot.

The marihuettegame became the model for future Provo tactics. Surprisingly, games proved to be an effective way of shattering the smug self-righteousness of the authorities. The police would usually overreact, making themselves seem ridiculous in the process. There was, however, a seriousness underlying the method. The ultimate aim was to change society for the better.

In the late '50s, Grootveld was already well-known as a kind of performance artist. His inspiration, he claimed, derived from a pilgrimage to Africa, where he'd purchased a mysterious medicine kit formerly owned by a shaman. Somehow, the kit helped Grootveld formulate a critique of Western society, which, he came to believe, was dominated by unhealthy addictions. A short hospital stay soon convinced Grootveld that the worst of these was cigarette smoking. "All those grown-up patients, begging and praying for a cigarette was a disgusting sight," he recalls. (Even after this realization, however, Grootveld remained a chain-smoker.)

Smoking, according to Grootveld, was an irrational cult, a pointless ritual forced upon society by the tobacco industry for the sole purpose of making profits. The bosses of the "Nico-Mafia" were the high priests of a "cigarette-cult"; advertisements and commercials were their totems. Ad agencies were powerful wizards, casting magic spells over a hypnotized public. At the bottom of the heap lay the addicted consumers, giving their lives through cancer to the great "NicoLord."

Grootveld began a one-man attack on the tobacco industry. First, he scrawled the word "cancer" in black tar over every cigarette billboard in town. For this, he was arrested and put in jail.

After his release, Grootveld began going into tobacco shops armed with a rag soaked in chloroform. "I spread that terrible hospital odor all around," he says. "I asked if I could make a call and spent hours on the phone, gasping, coughing and panting, talking about hospitals and cancer and scaring all the customers."

A rich, eccentric restaurant owner named Klaas Kroese decided to support Grootveld's anti-smoking crusade. He provided him with a studio, which Grootveld dubbed the "Anti-Smoking Temple." Declaring himself "The First Anti-Smoke Sorcerer," Grootveld started holding weekly black masses with guest performances by poet Johnny the Selfkicker, writer Simon Vinkenoog, and other local underground artists.

But Grootveld was soon disappointed by the small media coverage these performances received, blaming it all on the Nico-Mafia who controlled the press. He decided to do something really sensational. After a passionate speech and the singing of the "Ugge Ugge" song, the official anti-smoking jingle, Grootveld set the Anti-Smoking Temple on fire, in front of a bewildered group of bohemians, artists, and journalists. At first everyone thought it was a joke, but when Grootveld started spraying gasoline around the room, the audience fled to safety. Grootveld himself came perilously close to frying, saved only by the efforts of the police who came to rescue him. Although the crusade had only begun, the fire cost him the support of Kroese, his first patron.

In 1964, Grootveld moved his black masses, now known as "Happenings," to nearby Spui Square. At the center of the square was a small statue of a child, "Het Lievertje." By coincidence, the statue had been commissioned by a major tobacco firm. For Grootveld, this bit of evidence proved the insidious infiltration of the nico-dope syndicates. Every Saturday, at exactly midnight, Grootveld began appearing in the square, wearing a strange outfit and performing for a steadily growing crowd of Nozems, intellectuals, curious bypassers, and police.

Writer Harry Mulisch described it this way: "While their parents, sitting on their refrigerators and dishwashers, were watching with their left eye the TV, with their right eye the auto in front of the house, in one hand the kitchen mixer, in the other *De Telegraaf,* their kids went on Saturday night to the Spui Square . . . And when the clock struck twelve, the High Priest appeared, all dressed up, from some alley and started to walk Magic Circles around the nicotinistic demon, while his disciples cheered, applauded, and sang the Ugge Ugge song."

One night in May 1965, Van Duyn appeared at one of the Happenings and began distributing leaflets announcing the birth of the Provo movement. "Provo's choice is between desperate resistance or apathetic perishing," wrote Van Duyn. "Provo realizes eventually it will be the loser, but won't let that last chance slip away to annoy and provoke this society to its depths . . ."

Grootveld read the first Provo manifesto and decided to cooperate with the publishers. "When I read the word anarchism in that first pamphlet, I realized that this outdated, nineteenth-century ideology would become the hottest thing in the '60s," he recalls.

The leaflets were followed by more elaborate pamphlets announcing the creation of the White Plans. Constant Nieuwenhuis, another artist, was instrumental in shaping the White Philosophy, which considered work (especially mundane factory labor) obsolete. Provo's renunciation of work appealed to the Nozems—and marked an important ideological split with capitalism, communism, and socialism, all of which cherished work as a value in itself. Provo, however, sympathized more with Marx' anarchist son-in-law Paul Lafargue, author of "The Right to Laziness."

The most famous of all White Plans was the White Bike Plan, envisioned as the ultimate solution to the "traffic terrorism of a motorized minority." The brain-child of Industrial designer Luud Schimmelpenninck, the White Bike Plan proposed the banning of environmentally noxious cars from the inner city, to be replaced by bicycles. Of course, the bikes were to be provided free by the city. They would be painted white and permanently unlocked, to secure their public availability. Schimmelpenninck calculated that, even from a strictly economic point of view, the plan would provide great benefits to Amsterdam.

The Provos decided to put the plan into action by providing the first 50 bicycles. But the police immediately confiscated them, claiming they created an invitation to theft. Provo retaliated by stealing a few police bikes.

The White Victim Plan stated that anyone causing a fatal car accident should be forced to paint the outline of their victim's body on the pavement at the site of the accident. That way, no one could ignore the fatalities caused by automobiles.

Other White Plans included the White Chimney Plan (put a heavy tax on polluters and paint their chimneys white), the White Kids Plan (free daycare centers), the White Housing Plan (stop real estate speculation), and the White Wife Plan (free medical care for women).

Some White Plans were elaborate, others were just flashes of inspiration. "It seemed that proposing a White Plan was almost a necessary exam to becoming a Provo," says Grootveld. The most hilarious of all was the White Chicken Plan, proposed by a Provo subcommittee called Friends of the Police. After the police began responding to Provo demonstrations with increased violence, the Provos attempted to alter the image of the police, who were known as "blue chickens." The new white chickens would be disarmed, ride around on white bicycles, and distribute first aid, fried chicken, and free contraceptives.

The police failed to appreciate this proposal. At one demonstration they seized a dozen white chickens which had been brought along for symbolic effect.

Van Duyn's theories of modern life were quite similar to Grootveld's: labor and the ruling class had merged into one big, gray middle-class. This boring bourgeoisie was living in a catatonic state, its creativity burnt out by TV. "It is impossible to have the slightest confidence in that dependent, servile bunch of roaches and lice," concluded Van Duyn.

The only solution to this problem lay with the Nozems, artists, dropouts, streetkids, and beatniks, all of whom shared a non-involvement with capitalist society. It was Provo's task to awaken their latent instincts for subversion, to turn them on to anarchist action.

As later became clear, Provo didn't really enlighten the street crowd, although they did offer an opportunity to intellectuals and punks alike to express their feelings of frustration and rage.

Van Duyn's writings combined an equal mixture of pessimism and idealism. Too much a realist to expect total revolution, he tended to follow a more pragmatic and reformist strategy. Eventually he advocated participating in Amsterdam council elections. Other Provos denounced this as an outrageous betrayal of anarchist ideals.

One Provo leaflet hit the newsstands folded between the pages of *De Telegraaf*, Amsterdam's biggest newspaper. The perpetrator of this action, Olaf Stoop, was immediately fired from the airport newsstand where he worked. No big deal for a Provo. It was important to demonstrate a disdain for careerism in general.

When the next leaflet, Provokaatsie #3, was published it aroused indignation all over the Netherlands by alluding to the Nazi past of some members of the Royal House, a sacred institution in Dutch society. Provos threw the leaflet into the royal barge as it toured the canals of Amsterdam. Provokaatsie #3 was the first in a series of publications that were immediately confiscated by police. The official excuse was that Provo had used some illustrations without permission. A lawsuit followed and Van Duyn was held responsible. But instead of showing up in court, Van Duyn sent a note stating it was ". . . simply impossible to hold one single individual responsible. Provo is the product of an everchanging, anonymous gang of subversive elements. . . . Provo doesn't recognize copyright, as it is just another form of private property which is renounced by Provo. . . . We suspect that this is an indirect form of censorship while the State is too cowardly to sue us straight for *lese majeste* [an offense violating the dignity of the ruler]. . . . By the way, our hearts are filled with a general contempt for authorities and for anyone who submits himself to them . . . ."

In July 1965, the first issue of *Provo* magazine appeared. "It was very shocking to the establishment," recalls Grootveld. "They realized we were not mere dopey scum but were quite capable of some sort of organization."

The first issue contained out-of-date, nineteenth-century recipes for bombs, explosives, and booby-traps. Firecrackers included with the magazine provided an excuse for the police to confiscate the issue. Arrested on charges of inciting violence, editors Van Duyn, Stoop, Hans Metz and Jaap Berk were released a few days later.

Actually, Provo had an ambivalent attitude toward the police, viewing them as essential non-creative elements for a successful Happening. Grootveld called them "co-happeners." "Of course, it is obvious that the cops are our best pals," wrote Van Duyn. "The greater their number, the more rude and fascist their performance, the better for us. The police, just like we do, are provoking the masses. . . . They are causing resentment. We are trying to turn that resentment into revolt."

By July 1965, Provo had become the national media's top story, mostly due to overreaction by the city administration, who treated the movement as a serious crisis. Even though only a handful of Provos actually existed, due to Provo media manipulation it seemed as though thousands of them were roaming the streets. "We were like Atlas, carrying an image that was blown up to huge proportions," recalls Van Duyn.

At the early Spui Square Happenings, the police usually responded by arresting Grootveld, which was no big deal. Grootveld was considered a harmless eccentric and always treated with respect. Privately, he got along quite well with the police. "They gave me coffee and showed me pictures of their kids," he says. And Grootveld remained grateful to the police for rescuing him from his burning temple.

However, trouble started at the end of July. A few days before, the White Bike Plan had been announced to the press. The police were present, but hadn't interfered. At an anti-auto happening the next Saturday, however, the police showed up in great numbers. As soon as some skirmishing began, the police tried to break up the crowd.

The following week, after sensational press coverage, a huge crowd gathered at Spui Square. Again the police tried to disperse the crowd, but this time serious fighting broke out, resulting in seven arrests. The next day *De Telegraaf*'s headlines screamed, "The Provos are attacking!" Suddenly, the Provos were a national calamity.

In August 1965, some Provos met with the police to discuss the violent interventions in the Happenings. "Since Amsterdam is the Magic Center, it is of great cultural importance that the Happenings will not be disturbed!" declared the Provos in a letter to the commander of police. Unfortunately, the talks produced no results. "We stared at each other in disbelief like we were exotic animals," says Van Duyn.

The same night, the police surrounded the little statue in Spui Square, Rob Stolk recalls, "like it was made out of diamonds and Dr. No or James Bond wanted to steal it."

About two thousand spectators were present, all waiting for something to happen. At exactly twelve o'clock, not Grootveld, but two other Provos showed up. As they tried to lay flowers at the Het Lievertje statue, the crowd cheered. The police arrested them on the spot, after which a riot broke out. Thirteen were arrested, four of whom had nothing to do with Provo, but just happened to be hanging around the square. They all ended up serving between one and two months in jail. In September 1965, Provo focused their actions on another statue, the Van Heutz monument. Although Van Heutz is considered by most Dutch to be a great hero of their colonial past, Provo branded him an imperialistic scavenger and war criminal. The following month the first anti–Vietnam war rallies were organized by leftist students who were slowly joining Provo. "Our protests against the Vietnam war were from a humanistic point of view," recalls Stolk. "We criticized the cruel massacres, but didn't identify with the Vietcong like Jane Fonda. That's why later on we didn't wind up on aerobics videos."

Although the Happenings at the Spui Square were still going on, the Vietnam demonstrations became the big story of 1965. Hundreds were arrested every week. Meanwhile, the Provo virus was spreading throughout Holland. Every respectable provincial town boasted its local brand of Provos, all with their own magazines and statues around which Happenings were staged.

At the end of the year the administration changed tactics. Instead of violent police interventions, they tried to manage the Provos. Obsolete laws were uncovered and turned against Provo. But when a demonstration permit was refused on this basis, the Provos showed up with blank banners and handed out blank leaflets. They still got arrested. Provo Koosje Koster was arrested for handing out raisins at a Spui Happening. The official reason? Bringing the public order and safety into serious jeopardy.

Public opinion on the Provos began to get more polarized. Although many were in favor of even harsher measures against the rabble-rousers, a growing segment of the public sympathized with the Provos and began having serious doubts about police overreaction.

The monarchy became the ultimate establishment symbol for the Provos to attack. Royal ceremonies offered ample opportunities for satire. During "Princess Day," when an annual ceremonial speech was delivered by the queen, Provo made up a fake speech, in which Queen Juliana declared she'd become an anarchist and was negotiating a transition of power with Provo. Provo Hans Tuynman invited the Queen to hold an intimate conversation in front of the palace, where he and some other Provos had assembled some comfortable chairs. Although the Queen did not show, the police did, quickly breaking up the Happening.

The climax of this anti-royal activity came in March 1966, when Princess Beatrix married a German, Claus von Amsberg, a former member of Hitlerjugend, the Nazi youth organization. Coincidentally, Grootveld had been doing performances based on "the coming of Klaas," a mythical messiah. Sinterklaas, the Dutch version of Santa Claus, and Klaas Kroese, Grootveld's former sponsor, served as the inspirations for these performances, but by March, Provos identified the coming of Klaas with the arrival of von Amsberg.

"Grootveld objected to this corruption of his symbolic Klaas mythology," recalls Jef Lambrecht. "He wanted to keep Klaas pure and undefinable, but the link was soon established."

The Provos spent months preparing for the March wedding. A bank account was opened to collect donations for an anti-wedding present. The White Rumor Plan was put into action. Wild and ridiculous rumors were spread through Amsterdam. It became widely believed that the Provos were preparing to dump LSD in the city water supply, that they were building a giant paint-gun to attack the wedding procession, that they were collecting manure to spread along the parade route, and that the royal horses were going to be drugged. Although Provo was actually planning nothing more than a few smoke bombs, the police expected the worst acts of terrorism imaginable. Foreign magazines offered big money to Provos if they would disclose their secret plans before the wedding, plans that didn't exist.

A few days before the wedding, all the Provos mysteriously disappeared. They did this simply to avoid being arrested before the big day. Meanwhile, the authorities requested 25,000 troops to help guard the parade route.

On the day of the wedding, Amsterdam—the most anti-German and anti-monarchist city in the country—was not in the mood for grand festivities. Half the City Council snubbed the official wedding reception. A foreign journalist put it this way: "The absence of any decorated window, of any festive ornament, is just another expression of the indifference of the public."

Miraculously, by dressing up like respectable citizens, the Provos managed to sneak their smoke bombs past the police and army guards. "The night before, the cops made a terrible blooper by violently searching an innocent old man who was carrying a suspicious leather bag. So the fools gave orders not to search leather bags any more, fearing dirty Provo tricks!" says Appie Pruis, a photographer. The first bombs went off just behind the palace as the procession started. Although the bombs were not really dangerous (they were made from sugar and nitrate), they put out tremendous clouds of smoke, which were viewed on television worldwide. "It was a crazy accumulation of insane mistakes. Most of the police had been brought in from the countryside, and so were totally unable to identify the Provos." A violent police overreaction ensued, witnessed by foreign journalists, many of whom were clubbed and beaten in the confusion. The wedding turned into a public relations disaster. "Demonstrations of Provo are Amsterdam's bitter answer to monarchist folklorism," commented a Spanish newspaper.

The week after the wedding, a photo exhibition was held documenting the police violence. The guests at the exhibition were attacked by the police and severely beaten. Public indignation against the police reached new peaks. Many well-known writers and intellectuals began requesting an independent investigation of police behavior.

In June, after a man was killed in a labor dispute, it seemed as if a civil war was ready to erupt. According to *De Telegraaf,* the victim was killed not by the police, but by a co-worker, an outrageous lie. A furious crowd stormed the offices of the paper. For the first time, the proletariat and Provo were fighting on the same side.

By the middle of 1966, repression was out of control. Hundreds of people were arrested every week at Happenings and anti-Vietnam rallies. A ban on demonstrations caused them to grow even bigger. Hans Tuynman was turned into a martyr after being sentenced to three months in jail for murmuring the word "image" at a Happening. Yet around that time, a Dutch Nazi collaborator, a war criminal responsible for deporting Jews, had been released from prison and a student fraternity member received only a small fine for manslaughter.

Finally, in August 1966, a congressional committee was established to investigate the crisis. The committee's findings resulted in the Police Commissioner's firing. In May 1967, the mayor of Amsterdam, Van Hall, was "honorably" given the boot, after the committee condemned his policies. Strangely enough, Provo, which had demanded the mayor's resignation for over a year, liquidated within a week of his dismissal.

The reason for Provo's demise, which was totally unexpected by outsiders, was its increasing acceptance by moderate elements, and growing turmoil within its ranks. As soon as Provo began participating in the City Council elections, a transformation occurred. A Provo Politburo emerged, consisting of VIP Provos who began devoting most of themselves to political careers. Provos toured the country, giving lectures and interviews. When the VIP Provos were out of town attending a Provo congress, Stolk staged a fake palace coup by announcing that a new Revolutionary Terrorist Council had taken power. Van Duyn reacted furiously, not realizing it was a provocation against Provo itself. When the Van Heutz monument was damaged by bombs, Provo declared that "although they felt sympathy for the cause, they deeply deplored the use of violence." The division between the street Provos and the reformist VIPs began growing wider. Some Provos returned to their studies, others went hippie and withdrew from the movement.

Provo was a big hit as long as it was considered outside of society. But as soon as the establishment began embracing it, the end was near. Moderate liberals began publicly defending it and social scientists began studying the movement. The former Secretary of Transportation joined forces with Provo. "As a real supporter, he should have proposed a crackdown on Provo," Van Duyn said later.

Provo's proposal to establish a playground for children was now greeted by the City Council with great enthusiasm. The real sign of Provo's institutionalization, however, was the installation of a "speakers-corner" in the park.

Van Duyn encouraged this development, but Stolk saw it as a form of repressive tolerance—the Provos were now free, free to be ignored. "Understanding politicians, well-intentioned Provologists and pampering reverends, they were forming a counter-magic circle around us to take away our magic power," says Stolk. So Stolk and Grootveld decided to liquidate Provo. "The power and spirit had vanished," says Grootveld. "Provo had turned into a dogmatic crew. Provo had degenerated into a legal stamp of approval."

At the liquidation meeting, Stolk said: "Provo has to disappear because all the Great Men that made us big have gone," a reference to Provo's two arch-enemies, the mayor and commissioner of police.

Provo held one last stunt. A white rumor was spread that American universities wanted to buy the Provo archives, documents that actually didn't even exist. Amsterdam University, fearing that the sociological treasure might disappear overseas, quickly made an offer the Provos couldn't refuse.

HERBERT HUNCKE

An Interview

Steven Hager

September 1990

BACK IN THE 1950s, when Jack Kerouac, William Burroughs or Neal Cassady returned to New York City after a trip on the road, the first person they looked up was Herbert Huncke, a streetwise hustler who could usually be found hanging out in Times Square. Huncke served as mentor and guide to the Beat Generation and, according to Kerouac, even invented the term "beat." Last summer Paragon House published Huncke's autobiography, *Guilty of Everything,* an entertaining trip through the drug subculture, from Prohibition-era Chicago to New York in the '60s. Huncke recently came to the offices of *High Times* to discuss the book. Although addicted to hard drugs for much of his life, he was surprisingly chipper, witty, and entertaining.

High Times: When and where were you born?

Herbert Huncke: In Greenfield, Massachusetts, on January 9th, 1915. My father was from Chicago. He had a conservative German-Jewish background but I didn't find out he was Jewish until I was fifteen. He always denied it. My mother was of English and French descent and was from a fairly well-off family. Her father was a cattle baron.

High Times: You started running away at an early age.

Herbert Huncke: I started when I was twelve. I went off to see the world and got as far as Chicago.

High Times: When did you first smoke pot? Do you remember the first experience?

Herbert Huncke: No, I can't recall the first time. I do remember the feeling of hilarity I got from it. One image rather clear in my mind is the feeling that my face was frozen into a smile I couldn't break. You could buy six sticks for a quarter on West Madison Street in Chicago. And it was good pot. Mostly from Mexico. It was mostly Mexicans who dealt it. A Prince Albert can filled with pot sold for $1.50.

High Times: What was cannabis called back then?

Herbert Huncke: It was referred to as "tea." A joint was called a "stick." As in "I'll take a stick of tea."

High Times: When did you first find out about other drugs?

Herbert Huncke: I first read about opium when I read *The Little White Hag*. Don't ask me the author's name. It was an adventure story about opium dens and it was very lushly described. Smuggling on the high seas with Chinese pirates. Good escape reading.

High Times: How did you get involved with opiates?

Herbert Huncke: When I was fourteen I developed a friendship with a boy a year older than me and his sister. The three of us discovered a lot of things together. John Phillips was his name. Johnny died while making a delivery to a prostitute in a hotel. As he handed the delivery over, an agent stepped out. Johnny started to run. The agent shot and killed him.

High Times: What drugs had you tried at this point?

Herbert Huncke: At that point I'd tried cocaine a couple of times, but I didn't cotton to it. It was expensive and the sensation didn't last long.

Morphine, heroin. Those were the two main ones. I had tried some barbiturates. We were shooting right from the beginning.

High Times: How did you end up in New York?

Herbert Huncke: New York was always my dream. Every time I broke free, I'd head for New York.

High Times: The story goes you introduced William Burroughs to hard drugs.

Herbert Huncke: That's true. My friend Phil and I had just come back from a trip to sea with the merchant marine. This was 1945, or '46. Burroughs was introduced as a young man who'd taken care of Phil's apartment. He supposedly had a sawed-off shotgun and a gross or two of morphine syrettes for sale. Phil and I had been using syrettes on the ship. We'd gone to sea to kick a heroin habit and ended up getting addicted to morphine. Bill had one stipulation before he sold the syrettes. He wanted to find out what shooting morphine was like. So Phil and I obliged.

High Times: How was it Burroughs and you ended up going to Texas to grow pot?

Herbert Huncke: Well, we didn't go together. He went with Joan. This is a long story.

High Times: That's okay. I think our readers might be interested.

Herbert Huncke: Bill's family had decided after a couple of his escapades with the law that he should stay outside of New York. So he and Joan decided to go to Texas. Joan wanted to go to Mexico. She had always been interested in the Mayas. They got to looking around and decided to settle on a little piece of property outside of a town called New Waverly, about fifty miles from Houston. A beautiful place surrounded by bayous with raven-infested pine woods and cedar clusters, with a tiny weatherbeaten cabin on it. They sent for me, which was kind of interesting. I was on my way to Shanghai, but went to Texas instead.

High Times: How did you get the seeds?

Herbert Huncke: I scuffled around Houston and made contact with a shoeshine man. I built up a friendship with him. Got my shoes shined and rapped with him. I told him I wanted some reefer. Then I asked for seeds. He gave me a bag of seeds for $40.

High Times: Who tended the plants?

Herbert Huncke: We both did. Bill and I turned the soil over. I liked the digging part.

High Times: Did either of you have any experience growing?

Herbert Huncke: I can't speak for Bill. I didn't have much. I'd been around gardens as a child, but hadn't grown anything myself.

High Times: Did you know the difference between male and female plants?

Herbert Huncke: Later on. By the time the plants started to grow the information seeped in from somewhere. It was all guesswork. The plants grew to around five feet in three months and then we harvested. We cut them down close to the ground, turned them upside down and hung them in a shed.

High Times: Did you smoke any of it?

Herbert Huncke: Yes, of course. I always had a stick of it hanging out of my mouth. Bill was a latecomer to pot. He didn't care for it. Now I understand he likes it quite a bit. We put it in mason jars, stalks and all, before it was completely cured. Neal Cassady, myself, and Burroughs filled a jeep with calfskin bags stuffed with it. There was just enough room for us to squeeze into the jeep. We drove back to New York. We gave some away, downed a few jars ourselves.

High Times: I read somewhere that you sold the entire carload for fifty dollars to a bellhop in Times Square.

Herbert Huncke: Oh, please. That sounds like a Ginsberg statement.

High Times: Can you tell me some of the famous beat books you're in, and what the name of your character is in each book?

Herbert Huncke: I was Elmo Hassle in Kerouac's *On the Road*; Herman something in Burroughs' *Junky*; I don't remember what I was called in *Go* [by John Clellon Holmes]. There are more of them, but I can't remember if I'm even in Kerouac's first book *The Town and the City*.

High Times: Who is your favorite writer of the period?

Herbert Huncke: I have so many. Ed Dorn. His books have a certain warmth. Bill [Burroughs] has always fascinated. He's incredibly facile as a writer, well informed and a good sense of wit. Genet of course. Sartre. Colette. Paul Bowles, Malcolm Lowry.

High Times: Can you give me your impressions of a few people? How about Jack Kerouac?

Herbert Huncke: Enthusiastic, energetic. Had an intense desire to be creative, to express himself. He had many personal things that hung him up.

High Times: Were Cassady and Kerouac lovers?

Herbert Huncke: Not to my knowledge. I'd doubt it very much. I don't know why I'm so sure. But I just am. I think the extent of Kerouac's homosexual experiences would have been a fast blow job. Cassady made no bones about being bisexual. I think Cassady was basically heterosexual.

High Times: Allen Ginsberg.

Herbert Huncke: This is going to be a little tough. I respect Allen and admire his works. I don't always agree with his viewpoints. We disagree on almost everything. I always thought he was a bit deceptive in the way he presents himself. He can be evasive.

High Times: Neal Cassady.

Herbert Huncke: Just the opposite. He was like a big baby, bright-eyed and looking at the world with love and hope.

High Times: How do you feel about the current war on drugs?

Herbert Huncke: I think they should legalize drugs. That might be a huge answer to the problem. It's so riddled with politics, money, and corruption. I don't know how to talk about drugs anymore. Everything is based on falseness anyway. I don't like what's happening with drugs. I think Thailand must be ideal. Nice little hill villages with the poppies growing right outside. Easygoing lifestyle and close to nature.

High Times: What drugs do you still like?

Herbert Huncke: I smoke pot, drink alcohol—but not a lot. I don't particularly like methadone, but I have a lot of respect for it. It's kept me from suffering in a lot of cases. It's legal—that's the biggest advantage. I don't think it's done any real harm. My major objection is that it's synthetic. But it's the best thing they've got going now. I'm a heavy smoker of cigarettes. Drink coffee, tea. I guess I would like to be free to just smoke opium. But [*laughs*] other than that, I'll take anything I can get. I like hard drugs. I like cocaine, contrary to the way I started out. But I think it's probably one of the most destructive drugs in a funny way. No mercy shown there.

High Times: Did you ever consider yourself a beatnik?

Herbert Huncke: No. I didn't like the name. Or "beats."

High Times: But a lot of people consider you a prototype for the beatniks.

Herbert Huncke: I guess they do. In a way, I think it's more Ginsberg than me.

High Times: What do you think of the different generations that have come and gone in New York?

Herbert Huncke: All these generations passed by and they were all about the same to me. The first time I became conscious of something different was when the yuppies first emerged. [*Laughs.*] First time I heard the word "yuppie" I didn't want to tell the person I didn't know what it meant. I kept looking for the type. All of a sudden I became aware that I was surrounded by them in every direction. The other day I met three guys from Princeton. They dressed alike, looked alike, spoke alike. And in three hours they didn't say anything of substance. It's pretty scary to see a whole generation that's almost identical. But there's still a lot of individuality on the Lower East Side in New York.

I don't know much about today's younger generation. I used to pride myself on being in touch with the young crowd. But now they are talking a language that I don't savvy quite as thoroughly as I once did. We all know drugs are symptomatic of a badly adjusted society. We're going to have this problem as long as our society remains as it is. You cannot have money as the only factor in life and expect anything but shit as a result.

What kind of civilization are we heading toward, with thirteen-year-old drunkards? Today, liquor is the big problem. I don't see anything clearly, except that I believe somehow underneath it all there's something there that is good. I would like to see man find his niche in the scheme of things. Maybe he has found it—maybe this is the way it should be. Maybe all this confusion is necessary. Something good may come out of it, but I guess we won't know about it. Perhaps this will all explode and enrich some other planet somewhere else. I don't think anything is wasted, that much I do believe. But in the meantime, we try to get by the best way we can.

THE GREAT CANNABIS COLLECTION

Steven Hager with Carlo McCormick

January 1993

CANNABIS IS NOT EASY to collect. I've never been able to keep a sample for more than a few months. Shortly after coming to *High Times*, however, I began hearing stories about an awesome stash of the best buds from an entire decade. I didn't take these rumors seriously. Well, not until I received a strange visit from one of our regular contributors, Carlo McCormick.

"Do you remember how we started our search for the legendary LSD museum, that no one believed existed? I know you've heard the myth of 'The Great Cannabis Collection.' Well, I have reason to believe it *does* exist. All I need is the necessary travel and expense budget to find it."

"How much money would it take?" I wondered.

Unfortunately, Carlo never got the money. To his credit, however, he never gave up and exhaustively tracked down every possible lead. His obsession became something of a joke around the office. Few of us ever expected him to find his mythical collection.

Suddenly, around noon on a hot, humid, summer day, I received a mysterious phone call.

"Is this *High Times*?"

"Yes."

"This is 'The Collector.' I've been told Carlo McCormick is looking for me."

My first reaction was that Carlo, one of his friends, or someone in the office was playing a phone prank, but I decided to play along. The voice on the phone told me to have Carlo and a *High Times* photographer meet him on the corner of Fifth Avenue and 42nd Street at 9:00 P.M. that evening.

"Is it okay if I come too?" I asked.

"Yes," he said. "But don't bring anyone else."

Several hours later Carlo, Kent Sea, and myself were sitting blindfolded in the back of a van. The ride took about four hours. We were led into a house and taken downstairs into a basement. When the blindfolds came off, we were confronted by a tall, well-built man wearing a Ronald Reagan mask and a black Ninja outfit. Behind him was his collection.

"I don't want you to say anything about me," said The Collector while shaking our hands. "Just take whatever photos you like."

Carlo was already fingering a jar of puffy, purple, *sativa* buds. "Is it all right if we test a few samples?" he said staring at a label marked: *Hawaiian '83, Super Sweet, Deliciously Delirious.*

I picked up a nearby jar and handed it to Carlo. The label read: *Kauai, Sweet Sinse, A plus plus plus.*

"You're sure you don't want to try this instead?" I asked.

"We can try anything you like," said The Collector. "But you've got to leave before dawn. Most of these jars have never been opened. There's no mediocre pot here. Only the most significant buds from the last ten years."

For the next several hours, we watched Kent arrange his equipment and take photos while The Collector guided us through a remembrance of highs past.

"You could buy a Mercedes with just ten of these jars," I gasped.

"Please don't emphasize the money aspect," said The Collector. "I don't know why I did this. I think I wanted to have enough pot so I'd never have to buy any ever again . . . What three-hundred-eighty buds would you take to a desert island? Recently, however, I opened one of my favorites and was disappointed. I wanted to get some expert opinions on how well pot ages."

"It is moments like this when I profoundly realize why I work for *High Times*," said Carlo. "It's not just a job. It's an adventure."

NOTES FROM THE TASTE TEST

1. **Clone, 1985, New York Outdoor Grown.** The clone blows away everyone's theory of what can be done. Pure *indica*. Grey-green color. Hasn't kept well, probably due to bad seal. No pop when jar was opened.

2. **Balls, Sinse, Fall 1981.** Not much odor. Small jars in the early '80s. The Collector couldn't afford to keep large samples. Spongy little buds; hybrid. Too old and dry.

3. **Shasta Platinum, Fall 1981.** Very, very dry. Just a hint of perfume. Mount Shasta, CA (Northeast corner of CA). Not terrific. Has lost some punch.

4. **Hawaiian, April 1982.** Pure *sativa*. No stickiness. Spicy smell.

5. **Kingsbread, Colorado, December 1981.** Thick, tight pure *indica* bud with lots of red hairs. More powerful smell. Better seal with the top. (All before had aluminum top seal, the rest have wax seals that seem to work better.) Very sticky. Spicy. Grown outdoors by a "big, surly, dreadlock Vietnam Vet, a Rambo of the Rockies." High mountain pot.

6. **Hawaiian, 1983, Super Sweet, Deliciously Delirious.** Good seal-pop on opening. Pure *sativa* bud. A lot more expansion. Most popular joint so far. (Four hits each.) Long, stringy, *sativa* buds. The Collector says: "I like *indica* more. I get too tense on some *sativas*."

7. **Brainfuck, Humboldt, A++++++, December 1983.** Hybrid; lots of red hairs. Totally dry. Still good taste. "It's some kind of heroic effort to keep some integrity after all these years," says The Collector. "The body was dead, but the soul was still there."

8. **Kauai, Sinse, December 1982, Sweet A+++.** This came from a Hawaiian family. Not commercially available. Very large, loose buds. Hybrid. Good seal. Sweet taste. Very hash-like. Three hits around.

9. **1984 Santa Cruz Primo. A Standard.** Gone. "Must be the seal." Dead, dead, dead.

10. **Indica Humboldt, August 1986. A Nice Space.** No comments. (Pot overload kicking in?)

11. **Peruvian Seabird Guano, August 1984. Fertilized Humboldt Hybrid. "Very fucking nice."** Looks like Skunk #1. Smells like Skunk #1. Didn't lose a trick. "This is the best yet," says Steve. "I second that," says Carlo. The Collector doesn't know Skunk #1, but this is it!

12. **Rogue River, May 1989, A!** Good seal. Grown on the back side of Trinity Mountain. The growers got pushed up to get farther away from CAMP. Wet inside; not sticky; but moist and hard. "Still happening. I love it," says Carlo. "Great taste."

13. **East Coast Hybrid Sinsimella, October 1984, Very Strong Space.** Good seal.

14. **Oregon, June 1988, A! Top 5 of the year.** The Collector: "This is at the point that I think this is more ripe and better than when I put it in the jar. Better to roll—they get so nice— to give it a long cure . . . they come out so rich, a seven-year spliff." "This is the one that kicked my ass," says Steve. "In the eighties there were tons of great buds. It was amazing how it was flowing. Then, after 1986, 1987, something happened." "When did the stock market crash?"

15. **Spud Bud, Late Summer 1988.** Steve: "I recognize this strain. It was on the cover of the November 1986 issue with Chef Ra." Laced with trichomes. Beyond stoned. Tripping.

16. **Hash-Kabul-Gold Seal (no date).** Nice hash.

17. **"Cousin of Clone," November 1984, Upstate New York.** Very spaced, *indica* hybrid, "A."

The Collector checked his watch and stood up, indicating it was time to leave. Although we certainly didn't require the blindfolds, we put them on anyway, mostly to protect our delicate eyes from the piercing rays of the sun.

"That would never be done today," sighed Carlo. "It's like a sign from the '80s, the decade of excess."

"Yeah," I said. "Pot's just too valuable. Do you think the value of his collection has gone up or down?"

"I imagine that the decrease in potency, or worth of the pot has gone down relatively equal to the inflation in its market value," mused Carlo. "But this collection is worth more than just money, it's about having a vision, an obsession, a love that has no price tag."

The next day, sitting at my desk, I almost believed I'd dreamt the whole story up. Then Kent walked in with his photos.

"It's the greatest centerfold of all time!" announced our publisher John Holstrom. And so it is.

HIGH TIMES &
THE GRATEFUL DEAD

STEVE BLOOM

NOVEMBER 1995

The ultimate band for heads and the penultimate magazine for heads should have been a marriage made. Why couldn't they just get along?

THE FIRST ARTICLE *High Times* ever published about the Grateful Dead was a news story in our September 1977 issue which appeared on the "High Society" page and featured a smiling Jerry Garcia at the opening party for *The Grateful Dead Movie* with a joint in his hand. "Between autographs," the story stated, "he passed around joints to other members of his band, all of whom were in attendance except for bassist Phil Lesh."

Two months later, in the November issue we reviewed *Terrapin Station*. Critic Larry Blasins liked the album. "The Dead succeed here on a level of instrumental complexity and technical proficiency at which their *Blues for Allah* album merely hinted," he wrote. "The Dead are beginning to function as a cohesive entity, no longer just a crew to accompany Garcia on his cosmic journeys."

Garcia's then-wife Mountain Girl also received a rave, in the May '78 issue for her book about organic sinsemilla cultivation, *The Primo Plant*. "The author includes hip secret info on pot strains, composting, ground preparation, greenhouses, soil mixes, pruning and of course the erotic art of flowering, with all those sex pistils and steamy stamens," reviewer Bob Harris explained.

In our next issue however, the reviewers were not so favorable about Bob Weir's solo album, *Heaven Help the Fool*. "Doc Rock," a pseudonym for music culture editors Harry Wasserman and Charlie Frick, panned the album for sounding too much like Fleetwood Mac. "Weir has certainly lost the kaleidoscopic sound of unadulterated Dead," Doc Rock wrote, "but he does have every spiffy gimmick."

Eight months later, the February '79 issue featured a sidebar article about Augustus Owsley Stanley III, the legendary LSD chemist who fueled the Acid Tests and the Dead's early days. A photo-collage accompanying the story included head shots of Garcia, Mickey Hart, and Bill Kreutzman. The next issue noted the Dead's Egypt tour with a photo of Garcia on a camel on the "High Society" page. Asked if the band still represented the ideals of the '60s, Garcia said, "I think we are trying to uphold something else. Not so much idealism, more a delicate state of anarchy. Anarchy in the USA."

Though *High Times* had been publishing since 1974, no effort was made to feature the Grateful Dead in a big way during founder Tom Forçade's tenure, before he died in November 1978. Forçade was more fascinated with the punk-rock revolution of 1977 than nostalgic for rock's fading heroes. Frick, who now works at PowerPlay Music Video television as a producer journalist, recalls about Forçade: "Tom was not that interested in the Dead. It was not his driving thing. He was busy chasing the Sex Pistols. His thing was: 'Get the punks.' The Dead were not news. They weren't that popular at the time."

John Howell, *High Times* editor in chief from 1985 to 1987, who was responsible for the Grateful Dead special issue in February '87, adds about Tom: "He followed the counterculture energy wherever it went. If the Sex Pistols were creating the energy, then he went for them. In 1977, CBGB's (the New York rock club) was in full flower. That was the *thing* that was happening. Talking Heads, Blondie, and all that kind of stuff. That's what you find as music coverage in the magazine then. Of course, a lot of hippies were put off by punk, from the style to its aggressiveness. Tom was interested in energy. I'm sure if he were around in the mid-'80s and the Grateful Dead were back with the kind of energy they had then, he would have been right there."

After Forçade's death, Andy Kowl took over as publisher and editor of *High Times*. In 1981, he decided it was time to interview and photograph the Dead, and an overture was made to the band's then-publicist, Ren

Grevatt. Recalls John Swenson, music editor from '80 to '84: "Back in those days the band was under a lot of investigative pressure and heat, so they really were loath to be identified directly with any pro-drug organization, believe it or not. That's why they would not cooperate with any direct *High Times* interviews. They were offered the cover. Kowl wanted to do a big photo shoot. But Ren Grevatt was dead set, so to speak, against the band appearing in the pages of *High Times*."

Grevatt, who has long headed his own New York–based publicity agency, Ren Grevatt Associates, agrees with Swenson that the Dead "were the target of a lot of heat at that point. In fact there was a time when they didn't even dare go into Canada because they were targets to be just picked up. But it wasn't my own personal feeling pro or con *High Times* or smoking dope, it was the fact that I thought it was inadvisable for them to do that, and Richard Loren, who I believe was the manager at that point, probably agreed with me. I never had anything against you guys."

According to the band's former manager Rock Scully, Grevatt was "an awful square." Scully—who primarily worked as road manager until 1985, but also handled publicity duties for the Dead before Grevatt—says he "never had a problem with *High Times*. I never thought about it politically, like what it was going to do to us if we were in *High Times*. That's not the way I looked at things. You reviewed Mountain Girl's book. There were other things too. We were certainly very supportive of NORML. And we never stopped smoking pot."

High Times responded to Grevatt's turn-down with a sarcastic editorial in the Sept. '81 issue entitled, "An Open Letter to Jerry Garcia." This humorous but low-brow attempt to shame the Dead into cooperating with *High Times* was the beginning of a chill between the band and the magazine that would never thaw. It read:

Dear Jerry,

Why won't you talk to us? Mick Jagger talked to us, and so did Bob Marley and Norman Mailer. Even G. Gordon fuckin' *Liddy*, the guy who organized the DEA and came up with Operation Intercept— even our worst, most deadly enemies, have talked to us.

You talked to Tom Snyder. You did a *whole show* with Tom Snyder. Do you think that Tom Snyder ever waited outside the Fillmore Auditorium or Madison Square Garden with a head pumped full of acid singing 'Riding that train, high on cocaine . . .' over and over and over again? You bet your Stratocaster he didn't.

But forget that. Forget about the dozens of pathetic little messages we sent backstage to you. Forget about your buddy from the Pranksters days, Paul Krassner, who we sent to your house only to be told by a Chicano cleaning lady with a rag on her head that you'd moved. Forget about our publisher, Andy Kowl, who as a youth did severe and permanent damage to his larynx screaming "Dark Star" across the continental United States, and who now sits alone in his office holding his head in his hands, muttering, "Why, why, why?" Forget all that shit. And think about "Captain Tripps." Remember *him*? The old Jerry would have talked to *High Times*. Pigpen would have seen to that.

What's happened? Is it something we've said, or something you've smoked? What's wrong with us? Have not *High Times* readers feelings? If you prick us will we not bleed? Are we not fed by the same food and driven to boogie down by the same guitar licks as viewers of the *Tomorrow* show? Why have you hardened your heart against us? Jerry, we swear by the four remaining fingers of your right hand that we wish you no harm. All we want is for you to like us and give us an interview.

If you'd like to see an interview with Jerry Garcia in *High Times*, write him and tell him so. Send your letters to Why Jerry Why? Dept., c/o *High Times*, and we'll make sure he gets them. Don't delay. Jerry's future is in your hands.

Apparently the column and letter-campaign backfired. Dead coverage would not be found again in *High Times* until nearly four years later, and it wasn't good news. A story headlined "Vicestyles of the Rich and Famous" documented Garcia's recent bust for coke and heroin in Golden Gate Park. "It's no surprise to see a member of the Dead in trouble with the law over dope," associate publisher David Harrison wrote. "It was the nature of the drugs involved that made it so shocking." (It should be noted that Harrison himself subsequently got strung out on crack cocaine before committing suicide a few years later.)

In July 1986, Garcia succumbed to a near-fatal diabetic coma. Coincidentally, fictional columnist Ed Hassle wrote in the August issue: "Let's face it! There's only one psychedelic band in America—The Grateful Dead!! And until *High Times* gives them the special issue they deserve, my byline will not appear in these pages."

Readers echoed Hassle's battlecry. Pippy the Deadhead responded with a letter in the November issue: "I'm ashamed my favorite magazine doesn't spend more time covering the Dead—especially with Jerry recovering from a coma!"

So plans were drawn up to devote an issue to the Dead the following February. John Howell recalls: "Since I came to *High Times*, people had been saying, 'We should do a Grateful Dead issue.' The impression was *High Times* had already covered the band but when I researched it we hadn't done the Dead. So I decided we should do something. Right about that time Jerry had a problem—he was found unconscious in his car of a drug overdose. It was a big scare. The band clamped all publicity down and everybody was very uptight. When we called we were met with: 'No, we don't want any connections with *High Times*, it's a very sensitive moment for us.' I said, 'It's all over the media. We're the magazine that would treat it properly, less sensationalistically than most of the mass media.' But none of that meant anything to them. At that time, they were feeling really allergic to any associations that would amplify any aspect of his problems."

That didn't stop Howell. His search for a qualified writer who could provide an "insider's point of view" stopped at Hank Harrison, a former friend of the Dead family, particularly of Phil Lesh's, who had been excommunicated. Harrison, the author of two books about his experiences, *The Dead Book* and *The Dead,* had fallen out of favor in 1972 after a Marin County drug bust that involved both him and Lesh. "Phil blamed me for not taking the fall on that," he claims.

Harrison, who has not spoken to Lesh for years, felt the Dead's media paranoia stemmed not from the band itself but from the "damn entourage, which had so much power forming opinion inside the family at that time that anything I did, or anything anybody did, without their approval got bad-rapped. I was no longer an insider—I was an outsider. *High Times* was an outsider. *Relix* magazine was an outsider. Everybody who wasn't just kissing ass was an outsider. And I think there were some real mediocre people running the show. The Grateful Dead stopped being the Grateful Dead after Pigpen died."

Be all that as it may, Harrison got the assignment. "We ended up having Hank write the story—kind of by default," says Howell, who last year [1994] returned to *High Times* as editorial director after six years at *Elle*. "He had a little bit of an axe to grind, but not too much of one. He was trying to give some kind of semi-objective assessment of the history of this band—what are they now, where are they going? You know, journalism."

The article, "An Appreciation," did not serve to ameliorate problems between *High Times* and the Dead. But that, of course, was not the point. About Garcia, he wrote with a hint of satire: "Rumors of Jerry Garcia's death are greatly exaggerated. He does not have brain cancer. He is not a drooling idiot. He was sick and now he is better . . . All the band members agree that a little thing like athlete's foot or even the clap will not hold up a gig, but if Garcia actually ever died that would be a different thing."

The bottom lime for *High Times* was sales. "The issue sold like crazy. Howell says. "It was the best-selling issue I ever put together. We got a lot of attention. Other magazines just weren't covering them. The only coverage they had gotten in years was: *Jerry Garcia Found Unconscious in Car*. I felt our kind of coverage was actually an antidote to that.

"Unfortunately, I think they lumped us with all the other media, and then there were probably extra layers because we were in New York, they were in California, and we did have a context of discussing various sorts of drugs. It wasn't *High Times*, The Marijuana Magazine back then. There were discussions about cocaine, ecstasy, and other drugs that were in the environment. I'm sure the crowning blow was Jerry having an overdose with, apparently, coke and heroin at the time when we were asking them to cooperate on a story. It didn't help things, did it? There wasn't much way around it as far as I could tell."

Howell contends that bands with fanatical followings such as the Grateful Dead must be responsible to their audience. "Our readers wanted to make contact with them," he explains. "They were going to take things about the Dead in our magazine differently from what anybody else said. That's why it was a best-selling issue. Our readers were really thirsty for that kind of contact. As artists, I don't think they owe anything to anybody, but as part of their job of being entertainers they do owe something to their audience. My feeling was: 'I'm sorry, you're public people. That's part of your job.'"

Nearly two years later, *High Times* scored an interview with Jerry Garcia, albeit unofficially. Legs McNeil, a *High Times* contributor for more than a decade, had spoken to Garcia for *Spin,* but when the magazine rejected his submission he offered it to *High Times.* The "Jerry Speaks!" cover story in the February '89 was another big seller. The next issue featured an interview with Mickey Hart, again conducted by McNeil.

I began to work at *High Times* as news editor in 1989. It soon came to my attention that Deadheads were being assaulted at shows by out-of-control security guards. Two deaths occurred, and I covered both: "Death of a Deadhead" and "Second Deadhead Death Under Investigation". This spurred me to write the cover story, "Deadheads: Alive and Well," for the June issue based on interviews I conducted at the Landover, MD shows in March of that year. With these investigations, I had become the magazine's liaison to the greater Deadhead community.

For the August '90 issue, once again a freelance writer turned to us with an unauthorized Grateful Dead interview, this time with Bob Weir. Jesse Nash had interviewed Weir for New York's then trendy tabloid for the homeless, *Street News.* The enterprising writer, knowing the material was right for *High Times* and hoping to resell it, called editor in chief Steven Hager, who quickly signed a contract with Nash. Hager then contacted the Dead's publicist, Dennis McNally, and informed him of the plan to run the interview.

"He said we couldn't and if we did they would take action," Hager recalls. "He threatened a suit. Our lawyer said they couldn't stop us from running the interview. Dennis was pissed off because the interview was done for *Street News* and he didn't feel it belonged in *High Times.* If we had dumped the interview and made nice-nice there might have been a chance for a relationship, but I doubt it. They didn't want to associate with us. They didn't want to be in a drug magazine."

Hager has long been convinced that the Dead's unwillingness to allow coverage in these pages was due to Garcia's drug problems. "That's what kept us at an arm's length from the beginning." he says, "It was their dark secret. It's sad. They got all their juice from LSD, yet never lifted a finger for the legalization movement. The band had no platform on drugs. I've had mixed feelings about the band, the whole scene, everything. To me it was a religion without a message. Jerry is God? So then God's a junkie?"

High Times continued to cover the Dead, despite Hager's reservations. The December issue included a brief article by Garcia titled "On the Road with Neal Cassidy." The following May I reported on the trials and tribulations of attending the Dead's New Year's Eve show in Oakland without a ticket, and in June we excerpted the Mountain Girl interview from Sandy Troy's book, *One More Saturday Night*.

Garcia's fiftieth birthday was sufficient cause for an essay by this writer in the September '92 issue. "Does he know that hemp can save the world?" I asked. "Does he care?"

In October '94, we devoted our interview slot to John Perry Barlow, one of the band's lyricists (and the founder of the Electronic Frontier Foundation). Barlow visited *High Times* several times in 1992 and 1993. I told him about our problems with the Dead and in particular with McNally. After speaking to McNally, Barlow concluded that "you've both been assholes." He said he felt there wasn't much he could do to remedy the situation.

I interviewed Barlow during his first visit to *High Times*. Garcia wasn't well at the time, and the band had suspended touring for six months. We talked about Jerry and other issues pertaining to the Dead, but when it came time for the official interview, Barlow concentrated exclusively on his cyberspace pioneering. Arguing that Deadheads would want to know more, I fashioned a sidebar out of my interview and added it to the layout. Hugh Haggerty, production manager and author of the cyber interview, sent the sidebar to Barlow, who responded thusly by e-mail:

This would NOT have helped. It would have exacerbated the already dismal mess between *High Times* and the Dead. Indeed, it would have strained my relations with them. The fact that Bloom would have thought it appropriate to jam into my interview a sidebar is all you need to know about why such problems exist between these two organizations. I'm beginning to think that the main source of difficulty is Bloom's judgment and lack of sensitivity.

With that, I threw up my hands in amazement and disgust. Again, someone connected to the Grateful Dead was attempting to control coverage in *High Times*. So as not to piss off Barlow, we scrapped the sidebar. And with that I lost complete respect for the man who wrote the words, "I need a miracle every day." Apparently, he felt the same about me.

We at *High Times* are certainly not perfect. Some of us get stoned too often and think we can change the world with a phrase. We do feel high and mighty at times, since *High Times* stands for a cause no other publication dares to champion. That sets us alone, just like the Grateful Dead. But geography and culture clash and drugs of choice and good-old fashioned drug-induced paranoia should never have stood between us. Perhaps if *High Times* and the Grateful Dead had gotten together, the laws we all agree are abominable might have changed by now.

After Jerry Garcia's death on August 8, 1995, we rushed a cover story to press for our November issue. This was the end, as Jim Morrison sang, the end of the Dead's long, strange trip. That eulogy and this tribute are probably our final words and photos about the Grateful Dead. I sign off with sadness in my heart that we never resolved our problems with the Dead. But, Jerry, if you're up there checking this out, we never meant any harm. We just wanted to roll with you.

DEBBIE HARRY

An Interview

<small>VICTOR BOCKRIS</small>

<small>NOVEMBER 1996</small>

I MET DEBBIE HARRY in 1977, and experienced a good deal of her
success with Blondie firsthand through 1978–1982. During this time, we
wrote the text for *Making Tracks: The Rise of Blondie,* a book of photographs by Chris Stein, Debbie's live-in collaborator on Blondie. They wrote
the band's hits together. After Blondie's break-up in 1982 (under sad circumstances caused largely by a mysterious illness that struck Stein down),
I kept in touch with Debbie sporadically. I approached her to do the *High
Times* interview with some delight since she was just reaching a peak in
her solo career thanks to the movie *Heavy,* in which she starred opposite
Liv Tyler, and *Individually Twisted,* her record with the Jazz Passengers.
Harry has been touring with the Jazz Passengers and is finding a cool, new
groove to work in.

The interview was conducted at the apartment of photographer David
Croland, and in Harry's own Manhattan apartment. Some of the material,
particularly the sidebar conversation with Stein, was recorded but never
released during the time we were working on *Making Tracks.* The new
Debbie Harry is in fact no different from the old Debbie Harry inasmuch
as she is Debbie—the singer, songwriter, actress, and comedienne who will
continue to tie us up in individually twisted stitches throughout the '90s
and into the next century.

High Times: What is the most important thing that's happened to you in
the last year?

Debbie Harry: Just this past weekend I had to drive upstate to see my
Mom and Dad. I sort of had the same feeling I had at the beginning of

Blondie. Then, I had this really wonderful instinctive drive, this guiding momentum, this energy, and I just had to use it. I was so instinctive. Everything was just there, you know?

Then, for a long time I didn't want any kind of energy like that. But all of a sudden, driving upstate, I thought, Gee, I wonder if I could do that again? And I just had this little feeling in the pit of my stomach that went, Yeah, I could, and maybe I would want to. But who focuses all their drive on work at my age? I was thinking, I want to do that, then I was thinking I'm already doing it.

High Times: With the Jazz Passengers?

Debbie Harry: Yeah. This technical jazz singing with the Jazz Passengers is more emotional, more delicate. The voice is in a different position within the instrumentation. You have an obligation to be creative and responsive. You have to respond to every particular feeling, because being there in the moment is really important. It's not just this section four times, the next section two times, then the last section. The parts are woven together, and what somebody else plays and how you respond to that is more like acting.

High Times: Is the process of writing jazz songs very different from writing rock songs?

Debbie Harry: With the Jazz Passengers. I stepped into a situation that already existed, and then tried to add something of my own to it. That's different than what I did with Blondie. My Blondie stuff was more personal and direct.

High Times: How did you get involved with the Jazz Passengers?

Debbie Harry: [Producer] Hal Willner introduced me to them. Hal called me from London and said, Why don't you come and sing a track on this jazz album I'm doing? So he sent me the track and I thought, Oh, kinda weird, but it's pretty good. So I did it. And then from there I started working with them. I couldn't for the life of me have picked a better situation than the Jazz Passengers to experiment and to sing in a different way and perform in a different way and to know exactly what I wanted to do. It's very nice for me. It's like a great period of creative discovery.

High Times: Was *Heavy* a good role for you?

Debbie Harry: Getting a real acting part in *Heavy* was a revelation to me. Being other people is really the best thing for me. Being somebody else. I think the picture turned out well and I think the director, James Mangold, is a brilliant guy. Both of his parents were painters, and he's wonderful to work with. I was surprised when I saw the film. I had no idea what the pacing would be like. I was really moved.

High Times: Are you addicted to your work?

Debbie Harry: I guess I am, but I just think it's the best thing to be productive and to be creative. What else are you gonna do?

High Times: What is your daily life like these days? When you're living in New York and you're not touring, do you have any practical schedule?

Debbie Harry: Well, I swim every day. If I'm not working that night, performing or going to a club to see a band, I'll get up at about seven-thirty, eight o'clock. I take my dog for a walk and feed the cat. Then I get the newspaper and read it for an hour. I drink coffee and have a pastry. Then I just do phones or tour plans or clean up the apartment. Try to get jobs. Rearrange traffic. I'm trying to organize doing a book of my own again.

High Times: You want to do your autobiography?

Debbie Harry: Yeah, but I'd like to have more of a sex life before I write it. I mean, the book should be banned somewhere!

High Times: When did you break up with comic magician Penn Gillette?

Debbie Harry: A year ago. Basically, we were in a relationship where we planned to meet in airport lounges, which I thought was cool. But then we had trouble on the sex front because he's kind of big, and it was difficult to find a place to squeeze into, you know?

High Times: Have you been seeing anybody else?

Debbie Harry: No, not really. Dates here and there. Nothing much.

High Times: Are you working with Chris?

Debbie Harry: We haven't really done anything lately, but we did do some rock shows at SqueezeBox [at Don Hill's, the New York club] last year. And the last record we did, *Double Vision,* we worked on together. It's sort of an ongoing thing between the two of us, although we're not really super-active right now.

High Times: What do you remember about your teenage years?

Debbie Harry: At sixteen, I found out about pot, which was unbelievable because nobody did it. I lucked out. I had a girlfriend, Wendy, who was a year older than me and she had an older sister who was a real beatnik painter who lived in New York in a loft on Grand Street on the Lower East Side. She had traveled in Mexico and taken magic mushrooms and smoked pot.

High Times: What was it like when you first smoked grass?

Debbie Harry: I first smoked grass when I was eighteen. It was like an acid trip. I took about three hits off a joint and it lasted for hours and hours and it was great. My whole life just ran in front of me and I realized a lot of things in a flash. I could see a lot of things very clearly. It didn't answer everything, though. I still had some emotional problems and a lot of pain in my body.

High Times: Did you go out with a lot of different guys in high school?

Debbie Harry: When I was a freshman, my town had these stifled sexual appetites. It was really awful. No matter who you were, if you went out with a lot of guys you would get talked about and people would say you were a whore. It was this big paradox. So I ended up going out with one guy for a couple of months and then another guy for a couple of months. In my junior and senior years, I pretty much had one boyfriend.

High Times: Were you attracted to a particular type?

Debbie Harry: No. But I was really oversexed. Really charged, hot to trot. Later on, when I got my driver's license, I used to drive up to this sleazy town near Paterson [New Jersey] and would walk up and down this street there called Cunt Mile. I would get picked up and make out with different guys in back seats of cars to get my rocks off, because I was so horny and I couldn't make out with anybody in my town.

High Times: Did you always have this idea of going to New York and becoming a star?

Debbie Harry: There was quite a big jazz scene in 1965 on the Lower East Side when I moved there. I was into music more and more even though I was painting then. After taking my first acid trip, I started painting sound and decided I wanted to be in music. I hung out with bands and didn't paint anymore. But I had to learn how to feel good about myself, because I didn't like myself. To break up these patterns, I had to become what I wanted to be and who I wanted to be, and it took a long time. I felt that I was another person inside and that I wanted to come out, that I was in pain and always depressed and feeling terrible. Sometimes I was comfortable within my body. Sometimes I didn't like to feel at all. That's why taking drugs had a very strong attraction for me, because it made me bodiless, which is very nice.

High Times: When did you first get involved in the music scene?

Debbie Harry: In 1967. But I was so depressed and so upset, I knew that I would do it wrong and get so far in one direction that it would make people think of me in another way. This happens to many people, like Lou Reed. I knew I couldn't do it the way I wanted to, so at the end of the '60s I stopped doing music. I had come to a point that seemed like a tunnel. I was at the entrance, and I could either go down into the tunnel and continue or I could take this little winding road off to the side. So from '69 to 73, I took a sabbatical.

High Times: When you came back out in '73, what was the first thing you did?

Debbie Harry: That was the early glitter period when I used to hang around the [New York] Dolls. They were put down by the critics, but they were the pets of the New York scene. That period—T. Rex, Jonathan Richman, the Dolls—was when I jumped back in mentally. I had a little car and used to drive them around, but I was more on the fringes of everything. When I started performing with the Stilettoes in 1973, my intuition was no one was dancing to rock 'n' roll. And that was what the Stilettoes wanted to do—bring back rock dancing.

High Times: How did you learn to become a singer?

Debbie Harry: In the early '70s, when I was living with a guy who was a musician from when he was four years old, I used to practice all the time with earphones on. I was always going to rehearsals and watching people play, trying to learn about the structure of music. That was my musical training period, and it was really necessary. I knew I had to really learn how to sing more and I had to learn how to sing with all different attitudes. I could only sing in a very soft voice. I could never express a lot of emotion, otherwise I would start to cry, so I could only sing like a nice, sweet girl. I could never really let go, so I would practice shouting and singing as loud as possible whether it sounded good or not.

High Times: When you started Blondie, what was your motivation?

Debbie Harry: I wanted to be successful, but success was not my goal. That was not my obsession. My obsession was actually to just do it and everything else was secondary. I survived the hard times by not being obsessed. I was afraid of not being good enough musically. Blondie were never touted as being musical innovators, but we really had a terrific amount of feeling for the songs and the lyrics we did. They really meant something to us, and we did them with everything we could put into them. That's what made it happen with the audiences.

High Times: How do you reconcile carrying around the enormous shadow of the legend of Blondie?

Debbie Harry: That's funny, because to me it's grossly out of proportion. It's ridiculous and preposterous, yet it's totally accurate in relation to what is considered really vital and really valuable in the culture. But it just seems totally absurd to me that I should be considered anything other than another singer. The mythologizing of it is absurd. I was just being a driven, obsessed, star-crazed rock 'n' roller, and doing my best to be part of all that, and wanting to say a few things that were relevant at the time, and now it's gone way out of proportion.

The concept of the youth culture has an awfully powerful effect, which is incredibly fucking misleading. It's so boring, so incredibly ridiculous, but it controls many people's lives. They think they better get it done now because when they get to be forty-five they're not going to have anything.

High Times: Where do you see rock heading?

Debbie Harry: The only place left for rock to go is toward more girl stars. There's nothing left for men to do. There's bound to be more male stars, but they can't express anything new. What girls are saying is: "Don't treat me like that, treat me like this." Which Nancy Sinatra initially did with "These Boots Were Made for Walking"! That's the sort of predominant attitude. It's not the same as "Take another little piece of my heart now," or "Baby love, baby love"—all that kind of gush. It's giving girls a chance to develop, get to the stage where their style of living and thought is the same [as men's], not some clandestine activity.

The rules of the game nowadays are: If you can screw somebody and get away with not paying for something and make somebody else pay the price that's cool. It's a horrible, rotten status quo and it's not going to get any better by itself. That's the really bad thing about the downfall of religion. Religion said everybody must be good so that everything would stay in balance. I can look at it like a scientist, but still have respect for the powers that would be gods.

Maybe more ritual would install a sense of order and balance. If the proper ritual is followed it has some kind of electromagnetic implication that further on down the line more and more of your circuits will be completed so that you'll be able to do more of the things you want, and more of the things you want to happen will happen. This is what magic really is. You should always strive to summon up your own magic on a daily basis.

High Times: I'm confused by the '90s. Historically, the last five years of any decade are supposed to be a fantastic time. But nothing's happening!

Debbie Harry: There's so much information, Victor. People are too aware of history, too informed. There's going to be a new perception, a new idea of what people are. People will be a different thing. The human race will be a different thing. It will be much more sophisticated and aware of its animal motivation. It'll become more intellectual.

High Times: That's the greatest non sequitur I've heard in a long time: Aware of animal motivations so it will become more intellectual.

Debbie Harry: The human animal is motivated by food and sex, right? And now because we're so informed about political history—the nature of people going after money power and sex—everybody's exposed. There's no way you can actually do those things without a secretive, animal, clandestine thing. It's just a different kind of behavior. We're going to have to be very psychic and slinky.

'WILL YOU SHUT UP?!'
The following conversation between Debbie Harry, Chris Stein and Victor Bockris was recorded at Harry and Stein's penthouse apartment on West 58th Street in 1980, when Blondie was the No. 1 rock band in the world.

As Harry and Stein lay in bed, we discussed the text for *Making Tracks: The Rise of Blondie.*

Chris Stein *[to Debbie]*: At the beginning here you definitely should say I experimented with drugs. Everybody knows it. If you leave it out it's just a fucking whitewash. You say if you didn't try [drugs] you'd have ended up killing yourself, and yet there's nothing in the first page to suggest why you're miserable enough to want to kill yourself.

Debbie Harry: I was miserable. I just thought that's the way everybody was.

Chris Stein: If you don't say you took drugs and you were depressed and you couldn't sing and you couldn't talk . . . if you don't put the negative side in, it just comes off like a normal life.

Debbie Harry: It was normal. Why don't you put in the nitty-gritty about *your* life then, Chris?

Chris Stein *[switching the subject]*: This stuff on writing a popular song is a little cheerleady.

Debbie Harry: The method of writing a hit song is to fucking die and then come alive again. Just experience as much pain as possible, then you could write a hit song right. Get four Stella D'Oro breadsticks and a big jar of Vaseline and wait for the full moon in Cancer on a warm night and go down to the street and ram the breadsticks up your ass and then lie down in front of the taxicab so it runs over your stomach and makes the sticks into crumbs. Then belch, throw them all up, take the breadcrumbs, and cook them into a cookie and mail it to Ahmet Ertegun. After he eats the cookie, you bring in your tape. This is the magical formula. Or, get a big jar of peanut butter and plug it into the wall. Spread it all over your face while you're holding onto an electrical wire. Rent a twenty-dollar-per-month one-room apartment without a bathroom, lock yourself in with a year's supply of Dexedrine and just sit there and never sleep and just bang on the guitar. Then, at the end of the year, just take the last three minutes of the session and that'll do it. Guaranteed hit.

Chris Stein: When you started Blondie, did you think it was going to be a big, international sensation?

Debbie Harry: Not at first. Things were picking up gradually, but everything was so burned out at the time I never thought, Wow! A hundred people are coming to see me. I'm making it. At that time, who cared? New York wasn't a place for live entertainment, except in cabarets. At first, we played around sporadically. Our first drummer used to pass out from anxiety. At the most important moment when we really needed him to play he would pass out. He was always lying on the dressing room floor after drinking half a glass of champagne. That's when we played at Brandy's. The biggest song we did was "Lady Marmalade." One night, this girl Maud Frank the Third came in and invited us to play at her townhouse for a party for the Equestrian Club. This was more or less Blondie.

Chris Stein: They offered us two hundred dollars, so we jumped at it.

Debbie Harry: We got more than that!

Chris Stein: The thing was, we were only supposed to play three sets.

Debbie Harry: We got FUCKING FIVE HUNDRED DOLLARS upfront, then we said: For a thousand we'll play all night.

Chris Stein: You're out of your brain!

Debbie Harry: I am not out of my brain.

Chris Stein: Are you just making this up? *[To VB]* She doesn't have a real good head for details, believe me.

Victor Bockris: *[To DH]* You mean this is just a little fantasy in your mind?

Debbie Harry: We did it for more than two hundred dollars.

Chris Stein: We got two hundred dollars for fucking three sets is the way I remember it, and then they said, "Well, play one more time and we'll give you another hundred dollars." We came out with three hundred or three-fifty. I certainly don't remember getting a thousand dollars—for anything at that period!

Debbie Harry: Well, I guess you're right.

Victor Bockris: You only had a couple of songs. How could you play all night?

Debbie Harry: Victor, what are you talking about? You don't even know what our repertoire was. We did "Poor Fool." We did Tina Turner songs. We did "Narcissima" and . . .

Chris Stein: We didn't do any of those songs! We never did "Narcissima." C'mon, Debbie.

Debbie Harry: I'm beat now.

Chris Stein: So shut up! Why don't you watch TV? *[To VB]* The thing is, when we played at Brandy's we did cover material like "The Little Tootsie Roll Song" and "Honeybee."

Debbie Harry: The early disco stuff that came out in '73 and '74 more or less overlapped into Blondie. We just jammed out.

Victor Bockris: So you really were drawing an audience that early on?

Chris Stein: Around this time Patti Smith said to Debbie: I love you, come away with me. We'll live as lesbos. Let's stick our tongues down each others' throats. Shall we put that in?

Victor Bockris: *[To DH]* Why can't you just tell the story that Patti Smith came up to you and told you to get out of rock 'n' roll?

Debbie Harry: 'Cause it's tacky.

Chris Stein: Yeah, just leave it out.

Debbie Harry: Just say around this time people came up to me and told me to get out of rock 'n' roll. Patti wasn't the only one. I was pretty horrible. I deserved to be told to get out of rock 'n' roll. I was pathetic. Horrible and pathetic. I was very shy and stiff.

Victor Bockris: You weren't good enough for rock 'n' roll?

Chris Stein: No, that didn't have anything to do with it. Everybody knew she was too good-looking and she was a threat. Our bass player Fred's last show was Jungle Night when Debbie, Tish, and Snooky dressed up as jungle girls.

Debbie Harry: We all wore leather thongs. Fred quit that night.

Chris Stein: He didn't really quit.

Debbie Harry: He *quit*.

Chris Stein: He didn't.

Debbie Harry: He stopped playing, didn't he?

Chris Stein: Well, he ran off the stage.

Debbie Harry: For God's sake, when did he quit?

Chris Stein: He ran into the street in the middle of a song because the set was so horrible and disgusting.

Debbie Harry: It was always disgusting! To say we were a garage band was a compliment, because we were a gutter band. We were a sewer band. We were disgusting.

Chris Stein: But all this stuff about us being shattered and blown out wasn't any more than usual.

Debbie Harry: You know that's true, Chris! It's true! It was so, because all we did was lay in bed for a while.

Chris Stein: What are we doing now?

Debbie Harry: That's all *you* ever do!

Chris Stein: That's all *we* ever do.

Debbie Harry: Bullshit! It was a new thing to me then. I wasn't into it then. I had a day job.

Chris Stein: Shut up! *[To VB]* Just say that Fred quitting really ripped the bottom out from underneath us. Period.

Debbie Harry: It ripped the bottom out from underneath *me!*

Chris Stein: Will you shut up?

Debbie Harry: Because it meant the bass part went out.

Chris Stein: Stop it! There's not much tape left. *Please!* I don't want to do this if you're going to keep carrying on, Debbie!

Debbie Harry: *[In a very small voice]* Sorry.

Chris Stein: You gotta shut up and stop it! If you don't, I'll kick your fucking ass! Now shut up. Watch *Meteor* on TV. Look, look!

D. A. PENNEBAKER— LOOKING BACK

CARLO McCORMICK

JULY 2001

AT THE 2ND ANNUAL Stony Awards, *High Times* had the honor of presenting a Lifetime Achievement Award to one of America's greatest living documentary filmmakers, D. A. Pennebaker. Known best for *Don't Look Back*, his 1967 portrait of Bob Dylan; *Monterey Pop* in 1969; and *The War Room*, his Oscar-nominated portrait of the Clinton presidential campaign, in 1993, Pennebaker has also captured David Bowie, in *Ziggy Stardust and the Spiders from Mars*, and the raw experiments of the Plastic Ono Band in *John Lennon*. For five decades, he has defined our collective history with an honesty and immediacy that transcends time. Now seventy-one, Pennebaker lives in a Manhattan brownstorn with his wife and partner, Chris Hegedus.

High Times: Are you able to enjoy filming, or is it always about doing the job at hand?

D. A. Pennebaker: For us it's never a job. We're there because we have to be. We don't know where else to be. Our role was not to comment on what we saw, just to watch it.

High Times: You perfected that fly-on-the-wall perspective, but was it participatory as well?

D. A. Pennebaker: You participate in that you're hanging out with these people. It's a dialogue. In the second half of most of my films I go from the long photographic zoom lens, where you get people's faces recognizable up on stage, to a wide-angle lens. With the wide-angle, which is a fixed lens, you not only don't have to focus or do any of the other things a lens requires, you don't even have to look through it. You can pretty much hold the camera wherever you want, so you can face the people you're filming and become more of a participant in what's going down. It creates more of a sense of being in an inner circle, which is what you want—to be in a place where most people can't.

High Times: This kind of documentary intimacy that your generation created with the direct cinema, or cinema verite, is something you helped develop by coming up with a new camera technology that allowed filmmakers to go into situations that were previously inaccessible. Though unwieldy by today's standards, your camera was suddenly portable.

D. A. Pennebaker: We wanted something you could use to shoot in the desert or the Metropolitan Opera House. There was no such camera, so we invented one. It didn't exactly come about overnight, but by the time we got that camera to work it was very portable and quiet. I used that same camera to make *Don't Look Back* and *Monterey Pop*. You could still use it today.

High Times: Everyone now looks to verite as a style, the fluid mobility and rough, hand-held look. But I also think of it as a philosophy.

D. A. Pennebaker: The philosophy follows. You tend to justify what you do. We didn't set out to make shaky, bad-focus narrative films, though people still think we did. It wasn't anything we intended to do, it was all we could do. You couldn't carry tripods or lights around, you couldn't even take a person to do the lights. We developed everything down to a carryable state, which meant there were certain things you weren't going to do with a camera, and that determined our style. We never even remotely examined the aesthetics of how a picture should look.

High Times: As much as it was practical more than aesthetic, wasn't it also about going against Hollywood's fictional construct of reality?

D. A. Pennebaker: I've always hated that. When I see the lighting in most Hollywood movies, and the camera that never shakes, it's all so dead. I like to see some life behind the camera. For years I listened to my 78 records, and I never heard the surface noise. It's the same when it becomes the defects in our filmmaking. The shaking, the zooms you get when you have to focus, I don't notice them. All I see is that these films are alive in ways you can't help. Now they have shake-masters for tripods and you can reproduce a lot of these effects with video. People have accepted them, so you no longer have to fight for them. But in the beginning it was a struggle. People would say, "It makes my eyes hurt."

High Times: Your pioneering work has had considerable influence. I don't know how much you want to take credit or even responsibility for what has followed, but French New Wave cinema, the reality-based TV of *Cops* and *Survivor* and music videos all owe you a considerable debt. What do you think of these things?

D. A. Pennebaker: It's like MTV using the beginning of *Don't Look Back*. I don't feel that I totally own this anymore. You put something out, it's like a footpath. If enough people use it, it becomes public property. I don't take credit for it particularly, but I don't feel guilty about it. Occasionally you do something that becomes fixed. Why? I don't know. But everyone says that's the way it should be done, until somebody else comes along with a better way. I think what people saw in my earlier films was that finally it wasn't what the actors do in carrying out a writer or director's vision. They could see these people we've come to adore, in ways that don't require any of that theatrically, and make their own judgments about them.

It's as simple as this: In the '60s, every kid would buy certain records. To their parents, the record covers were just pictures. But for them it was a whole secret symbolic language that told them what kind of dope to smoke, where things were hidden, where to go and all kinds of things they naturally needed to know. Film is one more way you can convey secret information. *Don't Look Back* provided coded information for people who didn't want the other generation to know what they were really into. When the older generation looked at it, all they saw was out-of-focus, shaky pictures they weren't used to. But younger audiences dug it because this was not the old, it was something new. That it lasted this long is not just a test of the process, it's a test of Dylan.

High Times: Allen Ginsberg was in *Don't Look Back*, and Dylan certainly took a lot of his persona from Jack Kerouac. In terms of the evolving lineage of this coded language, what sort of influence did you take from Beat literature?

D. A. Pennebaker: Allen was a Kerouac kid. I knew Jack. In fact, for a long time Jack wanted me to make a film of *On the Road*. Of course, I had to say, "I don't know how to do that kind of movie. That's actors, and you don't want to do that with me."

High Times: You also did three films with Norman Mailer that make me think a bit of Beat films, like Robert Frank's *Pull My Daisy*.

D. A. Pennebaker: I knew Robert. It was different with Norman, because he saw that we had succeeded with *Monterey Pop*. He thought, if they can do it with their home movies, with my literary connections I can put something together using this inexpensive technique, put it in the theaters and make a lot of money. His lawyer was not so sure. In fact, by the third film he was forbidden to do it again. It was a funny problem for me, because I wanted Norman to direct, and I would shoot it for him. But he didn't know how to direct, and I didn't know how to tell him how to direct, because I didn't know how to direct either.

High Times: When it came to these private signifiers of '60s youth culture—the politics, music, drugs, lifestyle and philosophy—how did you try to relate all this in visual and narrative terms?

D. A. Pennebaker: *Don't Look Back* was an attempt to do that in the only way I knew how, by watching somebody who's inventing themselves as they go along. What you look to in artists, or anybody else you follow, is if they know something. And if we think they do, then we better figure out a way to find it out. It goes back to when the guy who threw the spear best was the one everyone else watched.

High Times: *Monterey Pop* certainly offered that opportunity.

D. A. Pennebaker: No one had ever made a film about a festival before. I knew that it would be difficult. We had some cameras that could shoot only ten minutes at a clip, and we weren't going to shoot 35-mm. So how were we going to do it? We also had to have some sort of recording set up. Luckily Brian [Wilson, of the Beach Boys] lent us his two Ampex 8-tracks. He had the first two 8-tracks in California, and if we hadn't gotten them, I'm not sure what we would have done. Things like this hadn't been solved yet, but I thought this is where we ought to be. So you work out a little construct that helps you make the film. In the case of *Monterey Pop*, I wanted it to be a momentary history of music and I knew I had to end up someplace that people had never seen before. That of course was Ravi Shankar. So Hendrix and all the rest had to build in that order. Generally in this type of film you have a narrator, but what was wonderful was I had the music, and that became my narration.

High Times: You left some bands out of the movie. How come?

D. A. Pennebaker: In the case of Moneterey we shot a lot of bands, like Electric Flag and Paul Butterfield Blues Band. Paul was a friend, and Electric Flag I had spent three days with in L.A. while they were rehearsing. Everyone thought then that they were going to be *the* big band of the whole thing. So Electric Flag, as well as Butterfield, were in an early version of the film, and it wasn't until it was almost released, when Truman Capote pointed it out to me that they didn't belong in there. Electric Flag was kind of now, but you couldn't do that and then go with a half-hour of raga music. And Paul's band was really good, but who needs that when you've got Otis Redding? I had to make choices that I never thought I'd have to make, but in the end the film kind of made itself. A lot of people got left out, but when we do the DVDs, we'll put them all on there after the film.

High Times: Having shot all these pop stars and even future presidents, what sort of boundaries between what's private and personal, versus public, have you had to be aware of?

D. A. Pennebaker: I don't know what those boundaries are. It probably depends on how you're brought up. I don't think porno films are necessarily evil, but I don't want to make them. Certain things are hard for me to embrace, and you have to be ready to embrace what you film. That has something to do with where you go and where you don't, but what really determines it is access.

High Times: So there isn't an unseen inventory of scandalous footage hidden somewhere here?

D. A. Pennebaker: Not at all.

High Times: How about all the footage of Bob Dylan and John Lennon?

D. A. Pennebaker: That was for the film Bob was making that never got finished but sort of came out as *Eat the Document*. And the reason it wasn't included in that was John was so nervous about Dylan, and Bob was really sick. I have no interest in filming people shooting up. The only things I have are these all-night music sessions with them where they clearly had some source of energy. And I was actually kind of in awe of it. I thought, "Jesus, this is what drugs can do? It's incredible, I'm all for it." But I knew that there was a heavy price to pay, and it never interested me to pay the price.

I never got into drugs. I knew they were around. I sometimes carried them for people. Every once in a while someone would pass me a joint and I'd puff on it to be social, but I didn't even smoke pot. From time to time I'd encounter drugs. Aldous Huxley tried to interest me in peyote. I tried mushrooms once and they made me really sleepy. I know that they laced my drink at [Timothy] Leary's wedding. At Monterey they slipped me Owsley's Purple Haze that Jimi was on—but it didn't affect me. I was always so involved in my own head, trying to figure what to do next for the film, the last thing in the world I wanted was to be removed from that.

High Times: Looking at your films from the '60s, I can't help but think it was a more innocent time. I don't know if it's my nostalgia, but people just seem not as self-conscious or aware of the camera.

D. A. Pennebaker: I wonder about that also, and I don't know if it's nostalgia. They certainly didn't know what our cameras looked like in general. There were television people going around sometimes with sort of similar cameras, with wires going into tape recorder, and they were really clumsy. But if anyone did notice us, they probably just associated it with TV.

High Times: Politics has also gone from an age of innocence to media savvy. You filmed the young Kennedy for *Primary* and *Crisis*. You caught the birth of the Clinton era with *The War Room*. And, it seems that Rip Torn playing a celebrity turned president in your Norman Mailer film, *Maidstone,* is in retrospect certainly very prescient of Ronald Reagan. How did you skip Nixon?

D. A. Pennebaker: I would have loved to make a movie with Nixon. I tried for years, but they thought I was out to trash him. I wanted to have Thanksgiving dinner with him. To think about all that he knew, it's incredible, and he'd sit at the table with all his relatives who never wanted to hear a word from him. Losers are interesting too.

High Times: Young people today inherit the '60s like this split-screen projection, Monterey Pop meets Altamont, the Mamas and the Papas next to Manson, the optimism and the disillusionment simultaneously. When did it all change for you?

D. A. Pennebaker: What guides me is the Byronic paradigm that the artist has to create his own paradigm in any way he can. That's what you do, and if somebody like a Manson comes along with a different paradigm that by contrast is dark and grisly, the only way you can deal with that is to bolster your own. I was approached to do the Altamont movie. I spent two weeks out there with Jagger and the Stones, and I walked on it.

High Times: You could feel the bad vibes already?

D. A. Pennebaker: Very bad. I didn't want to do anything with Mick, and I still don't. They asked me recently, but they just don't interest me. I'd rather hang out with someone like John Lennon, who was really nuts. In the end John was in such questionable shape I think somebody did him a favor by knocking him off. He was so crazy, he couldn't tell up from down, but you couldn't help love the guy.

High Times: Part of the Byronic paradigm some take too literally is the heroic romance of a tragic end. In your experiences with Janis Joplin and Hendrix, did you ever get a sense of this pathos?

D. A. Pennebaker: Not really. I knew Jimi here in New York, and he was very laid back, not at all the wild tempestuous rock star sort. Once when we were shooting down at the Generation Club and I couldn't get anyone to do the sound for me, Jimi ran the tape recorder. He was supposed to be up there on stage, but that was the kind of guy he was—not at all full of himself.

High Times: Speaking of death, your friend and Monterey organizer John Phillips recently passed away.

D. A. Pennebaker: I really loved John. He was a consummate songwriter with that wonderful sense that when it was there he knew it, and all he needed was to get his hands on the music. But at the same time he had that crazy Indian thing, that I'm going to beat myself to death and go over the cliff with it.

High Times: So many of the people you have worked with have become revered icons. When we look at your films what we see is Hendrix, Bowie, Lennon, Kennedy, Dylan. Do you wonder what it might be like if we could watch them now without all the fame, personality and history attached?

D.A. Pennebaker: I don't think you can strip them of what it is they're recognized for. You can't take Kennedy outside his surroundings any more than you can separate Hendrix from his performance. In the end, it is up to the people to make up their own mind. Working as an independent filmmaker, sometimes it's hard to get my films to an audience. But I know the audience is always out there, and I trust them. That's the only thing I trust.

WHAT'S SO FUNNY ABOUT RACE?

An Interview with Dave Chappelle

DAVID KATZ

MARCH/APRIL 2004

DAVE CHAPPELLE IS ONE achingly funny dude.

Just ask viewers who have tuned into *Chappelle's Show,* his Comedy Central hit, where they make the acquaintance of characters like Tyrone, "the goofiest crackhead in the town," who is lured to an intervention by the prospect of, what else, free crack. ("Is this the five o'clock free crack giveaway?" he pants breathlessly, as he barges through the door.) He's confronted by various former friends and victims, such as Rhonda, who "was very hurt that you carjacked me that time," and Ginny and Rob, the liberal white couple who took him in so he could study for his real estate license ("You sold our house and kept the money. Four hundred and fifty thousand dollars!"), and his supervisor at the post office, who had to let Tyrone go when he snorted up an anthrax letter meant for Senator Tom Daschle. The cunning but irredeemable addict ("You all act like crack is so bad!") fervently agrees to go into rehab, right after a visit to the men's room ("But first step is first; I need to go to the bathroom!"), where he escapes by flushing himself, feet first, down the toilet bowl.

Or meet Clayton Bigsby, a blind Ku Klux Klansman, author of *I Smell Nigger, Nigger Stain, Nigger Blood* and *Dump Truck;* a driving force behind the Southern re-emergent white supremacy movement, and the subject of a parody "Frontline" documentary, complete with the palpably anguished white narrator. There's only one minor problem: Clayton Bigsby is black, having been raised in an all-white orphanage for the blind, where, as the director states, "We figured we'd make it easy on Clayton by just telling him, and all the other blind kids, that he was white." So when he "smells nigger" at a truck stop where the only black person in sight is himself, you know something is definitely askew.

And please don't bother telling legally challenged R&B singer R. Kelly what a pisser Dave is, unless perhaps you want a punch in the mouth. The raunchy Romeo was accused of shooting homemade hidden camera video-tapes that show him having sex with a fourteen-year-old girl and then uri-nating on her face. He was mercilessly skewered by Chappelle in his now infamous faux R. Kelly music video, "Piss on You," in which Dave, as Kelly, sprays dancing homegirls with a garden hose from a yellow barrel labeled "Kelly's Urine" as he croons lines like, "Gonna pee on you. Drip. drip, drip," and "Your body, your body . . . is my Porta Potty," and "Only thing that make my life complete is when I turn your face into a toilet seat," all in Kelly's soulful falsetto style.

Also on the underage sex trip is a dead-on expose of the sexual molesta-tion of young Jedi Knights by their masters, complete with a press confer-ence from Skywalker Ranch featuring Yoda's denial, in perfect Yodaspeak: "No have sex with boys, Yoda did not. Tired Yoda is. Resign he will." How-ever, reporter Chuck Taylor (Chappelle, whitened-up in a blond wig) rolls a hidden camera videotape of Yoda and apprentice Qui-Gon Jinn quaffing coke and getting stupid. "Get down do you? Good blow this is! Horny it makes me," says Yoda, stuffing The Force up his itty-bitty nose.

A natural mimic whose droll stand-up delivery is blessed with pitch-perfect vernacular and precision timing, the thirty-one-year-old Chappelle's sidesplitting sketches also serve as caustic critiques of America's cultural and political contradictions, sparing neither racial nor sexual sensitivities. Not down with pallid, politically correct bullshit, Chappelle's audacious, ironic satire implodes stereotypes and unhinges the squeamish with its irreverent, obscenity-laced hip-hop argot and gross-out, no-holds-barred potty humor.

Laughs are job one to Chappelle, a comic wunderkind who began telling jokes on the street and later progressed to performing in local comedy clubs at the age of fourteen, chaperoned by his mother, a Unitarian minister who bet the dank, smoky, boozy, sexually charged atmosphere of a comedy dive was a better backdrop for her son than the crack-crazed, crime-driven, gun-crammed Washington, DC, streets of Ronald Reagan's 1980s "Morning In

America." Wanted for scene-stealing in films like *Robin Hood: Men In Tights* (1993) and *The Nutty Professor* (1996), in which he played opposite one of his personal idols, Eddie Murphy, Chappelle made the most of his roles. With comedy partner Neal Brennan, Chappelle co-wrote *Half Baked,* a 1998 homage to Cheech and Chong, in which Chappelle portrayed good natured, chronic-crazed janitor Thurgood Jenkins. The film is now considered an herbal classic, the DVD a must-own for college students matriculating in marijuana.

But it was his 2000 HBO comedy special, *Killin' Them Softly,* with its outrageous bit about a baby in diapers selling weed on a ghetto street corner, and a deconstruction of Sesame Street (that labeled The Count a pimp and deplored the hideous persecution of Oscar the Grouch by the other Muppets), that put Chappelle on the stand-up map. This led to appearances on *Def Comedy Jam,* and eventually his own show on Comedy Central, where laughs are real. "I show those sketches to a live audience," says Chappelle. "We don't use a laugh track. The laughs we get on TV are the real laughs from the audience."

Many of Chappelle's sketches are what-ifs: What if Wu Tang Clan ran a financial services company dispensing investment advice to white suburban families? ("Smith Barney is a bunch of bitches, old-time farts. Yo, you need to diversify your bonds. This ain't *Trading Places,* nigger, this is real fucking life.") Or this one: What if MTV's *The Real World* surrounded one clueless white guy with five "of the craziest black people we could find?" instead of the other way around? Hapless whitey Chad is introduced to his roommate: menacing, spliff-puffing, doo-ragged ex-con Tyree, who gives him a mean look and tells him: "Lookee here, *Chad,* for the entire period you in my room, I better not catch you standing up peeing. You sit down when you pee, you understand? That's right. Now get your fat ass out of here, white boy." Poor Chad.

And what if, as in an upcoming show, there was a blissful, wholesome, white Ozzie and Harriet–style 1950s American family who just happened to be named The Niggars? ("Hi, Niggars!" happily shouts Chappelle, the milkman, in an all-white uniform, a giant grin on his shiny black face, as he drops in on the family to make his delivery.)

Chappelle traces his comic lineage from Lenny Bruce through Richard Pryor and Eddie Murphy, with Bill Murray, Cheech and Chong, and old Bugs Bunny cartoons in the mix. Richard Pryor was an especially important influence. "I liked him when I was a kid, but I didn't understand the depth of what he was doing until I was an adult." Has comedy changed since Pryor, and even Murphy? "Crowds don't listen like that anymore. This is the MTV generation; they got a shorter attention span. I try to do it my way; I think I got a slower cadence, more deliberate than a lot of my contemporaries. They say you gotta train people to listen to you."

High Times sat down with Chappelle in New York City during the week the new season of his Comedy Central *Chappelle's Show* was being taped.

High Times: Let's begin with Tyrone the Crackhead, perhaps the Ultimate Crackhead. Did any black people give you shit, saying this was not the most complimentary picture of the black experience, even though it's funny as hell?

Dave Chappelle: Naw. As a matter of fact, I got a letter from a teacher who sent a letter that a student wrote about me, just saying how great that was and how it persuaded him to never do drugs, which made me laugh. But I said, That's kind of deep, you know?

Tyrone. Man, you know I grew up in DC in the eighties, man, during that crack epidemic; I seen this guy. I've never seen somebody desire something like they did crack in the eighties.

High Times: Like the itchy, impatient, cock-sucking Crack President in *Killin' Them Softly*?

Dave Chappelle: Yeah. Crack, man, it was so overwhelming, and it's tragic, and I guess those are the things that lend themselves to elements of comedy. Originally, Tyrone was a piece I did in my act. First sketch he did was the one where he went to the school and spoke to the kids during the Drug Awareness Week. And something like that actually happened to me when I was in school, during the Nancy Reagan years, and they sent this guy who was a recovering addict to talk to us about the ills of drugs, but the way he was saying this shit? Made drugs sound fun? Like I can't even describe. He's talking about doing acid, and him and his friends were laughing, and then he said "I talked to a guy for two hours and then I realized he wasn't there, like I'd hallucinated it." I guess that was meant to scare us, but all the guys were like, "Damn, look it, we gotta get some acid!"

High Times: Like Scared Straight. To some kids it made prison look bitchin'.

Dave Chappelle: Exactly. It backfired. And I mean, that's one of those things that stays with you, and Tyrone actually grew out of that.

High Times Did you have many eye-opening racial incidents when you were younger? Not something dire or drastic, but something like your "chicken" bit, where the white guy at the fast food place in Mississippi just assumes you want the chicken special?

Dave Chappelle: Oh yeah, I had a bunch of those. But I think overall, more than any one incident, was just what I saw around me. A lot of shit is unfair, man. Like I wasn't always a famous comedian. When you're nobody, and you look around at what the world is, and you're black, man, it just seems real daunting. Like how could I ever matter in a world like this? You know what I mean? Like, how many troops have died in Iraq as of today?

High Times: Almost five hundred, I think.

Dave Chappelle: Close to five hundred? When I was in high school in my freshman year, maybe over five hundred kids—*kids*—got murdered in the Washington, DC, area. They're all black! No national outcry, no nothing. This wasn't Baghdad; this was the nation's capital, man! I mean, there are so many inequities like that. You know crack wasn't a problem until suburban kids started smoking crack.

High Times: Do you have any political thoughts on crack?

Dave Chappelle: I know the conspiracy theory. You know, it wouldn't surprise me if it ever came out one day that crack was placed in the community like a scourge put on it. But even still, even if the powers-that-be did that,

I mean, even the country at large, it just seemed like they didn't care. It's just something that happens to "them." I can always see things big enough to not take that personal, which is why I think I can talk about it. I'm not gonna say I never take it personal, but for the most part I think I can see the bigger picture.

You know, I've hung out with people that I consider racist; I've smoked weed with racists of all different colors. I know it's not personal, I think it's just the broad strokes of the world. It's so ingrained in our culture; it's got such deep roots in American life. And the thing is that it's always kind of under-recognized; we don't like to deal with these things in our past. But if America was a dude, the best thing to do would be to confront your problems and admit that you have these problems, and then that's how you get past them.

High Times: Should America go into psychoanalysis?

Dave Chappelle: I say it's about time! If America was a single dude, he'd be overworked, he'd be a drug addict, he'd have a pussy problem, he wouldn't be able to keep his dick in his pants, he'd be burnt out, and he'd be about ready for a nervous breakdown. He'd be paranoid as shit. If America was a dude, that's pretty much what his character would be like.

High Times: The chronic. It figures in your work?

Dave Chappelle: Yeah. *Half Baked* and all that.

High Times: Did herb hit you hard when you first did it, as in the movie?

Dave Chappelle: When I first smoked weed I didn't like it so much. First time I smoked I was twelve. It didn't really do anything for me. You hear stories, "I was paranoid, I was this, I was that." Nothing. Then I smoked pot once in high school. I think the first decent experience I had with weed was when I was nineteen. I started smoking again, and that's when it was like, "Hey, this is not bad." By time that the chronic had come out, and

I loved it. *Half Baked,* man, I wrote that movie, my buddy and me did. I was livin' that lifestyle, I wasn't just *imitating* that lifestyle.

High Times: Did you have any qualms about making a drug movie?

Dave Chappelle: Oh, was I nervous about it? Not at all. Not at all. I didn't see anything wrong with smoking pot, you know. I mean, now I'm older, I can see where it can be less than beneficial. I still don't necessarily feel like it's *criminal.* Should Tommy Chong be in jail right now? Naw! I still can't believe it! I'm surprised you don't see more Free Chong shirts. You know, this is like crazy! Like I said, I can see where it's less than beneficial for the corporate schedule. But nine months in federal prison? *For selling bongs?*

High Times: If pot were legal, would that do good things for race relations?

Dave Chappelle: I think potentially it could. I mean, socially, when I think about the people I have smoked pot with, they are such an eclectic mix of people that I probably never would have spoken to a lot of them if it weren't for pot. Alcohol doesn't bring people together like that. You put these same people together, they're drinking alcohol, they end up fighting. So I mean, do I think it's the cure-all for America's problems? No. Do I think this shit is a good way to relax after a stressful day? Sure! In a live-and-let-live society I don't know if it should be considered criminal. It's not like people are breaking into cars to get pot money. If Tyrone smoked as much weed as he did crack, he'd fall asleep long before he committed a crime. *[Laughs]*

High Times: You do white people very well.

Dave Chappelle: Thank you.

High Times: There's Chip, your drunken white buddy, and Johnson the Cop. And Ralph Henderson, the Pop Copy training manager who's black but talks white. Where did you learn their odd inflections and bizarre pro-nunciations? Is it a matter of listening?

Dave Chappelle: I grew up in DC. In elementary school I lived in Silver Springs, Maryland, which is a pretty mixed area, black and white. Then in middle school, I lived in Ohio. Near Dayton. It's very white. And then in high school I was in DC; it was very black. But I guess I grew up in so many different places, and met so many different kinds of people, well, that white cadence was something I picked up.

And then I watched television a lot. I used to watch *Miami Vice,* and *Sanford and Son*—that was always a big one in the house, a lot of *Saturday Night Live, Arsenio Hall.* I used to watch an incredible amount of TV growing up, incredible; way more than is healthy. Bugs Bunny cartoons— I watched all of them, for hours. I like the older ones.

High Times: Dave, what have you got against the Ku Klux Klan? [*Laughs*]

Dave Chappelle: [*Laughs, Gives me funny look*] Damn!

High Times: Only kidding.

Dave Chappelle: Well, I guess they embody a particular brand of hatred that's very misguided, and the fact that they organize behind something like that is very unfortunate. But they're very intertwined in our history, after Reconstruction, and the Civil War, where these hate groups emerged. It's not that I have anything against them, as much as the ideology or the philosophy that makes people join an ill-informed, misguided philosophy.

High Times: That brings us to Clayton Bigsby. Were the people at Comedy Central squeamish about the nigger word being thrown around so much?

Dave Chappelle: Actually they were surprisingly receptive to it. Not gonna say they weren't nervous. I think the first fight about it was I wanted to put it on the first episode, and I think that's when they were like "Whoa!" That and the fact that they thought that the sketch was too long. They wanted me to cut certain parts of it out, which I absolutely didn't want to do.

High Times: Did you feel it was shocking when you did it?

Dave Chappelle: If I did it at a nightclub? It wouldn't be shocking at all. But somehow in the context of television, suddenly it takes on this whole 'nother, like, "This is crazy, this is shocking." I think if I polled my family of people that actually watched this show to see *me*, I don't think they're shocked. I think they laughed, they enjoyed it. But I don't think that I ever shock. It's hard to shock people nowadays.

High Times: How many of your characters are based on people, or things you've seen?

Dave Chappelle: Tyrone, I've seen. Bigsby was from a story my grandfather told me. My grandfather actually may be white, I don't know. He was born in a white hospital in 1911. He's at least half black.

High Times: His mother couldn't have been black, right?

Dave Chappelle: There's no way. There is no way a black woman under any circumstances could have a baby in a white hospital then. But he looks like a white dude, and he was blind from birth. But as far as he knows, you know, he grew up in DC. Black dude. As far as he's concerned, he's a black guy. And he was on the bus the day after Martin Luther King got shot, and all the brothers were like, "What you doing on the bus, you cracker, you honky?" And all this, and my grandfather was saying like, "What is a white person doing on the bus? Is he crazy?" He had no idea they were talking about *him*. So he told us that story, and I just did the inverse of that for Bigsby.

High Times: If white people didn't exist, would black people still be funny?

Dave Chappelle: *[Laughs]* That's hard! That's a big If! Wow, if white people didn't exist, that's a huge If! I can't imagine a world without white people! I'm gonna go out on a limb and say yes. Yes, 'cause I'm sure there were funny black dudes in Africa, before they met white people. They might not be as funny.

High Times: If white people didn't exist, would black comedians need to invent them?

Dave Chappelle: If white people didn't exist, who would we beat in the Olympics?

High Times: *[Laughs]* What do you make of the 'wigger' phenomena? Aka white niggers? As in the Bigsby sketch, when four white guys in knit caps and hoodies, blasting hip-hop in their convertible, pull up next to Clayton's pick-up truck, and he starts going berserk, and they high-five each other for being called nigger?

Dave Chappelle: Man, it's crazy! I like it, actually; all in all, I'd say I like it. The sad part about it is that they'll enjoy black culture as they grow up, but at a certain point, as soon as it's time to get a job or move on in their life, they'll throw this culture aside like they had never participated in it, and maybe even look down on it later in their life, and look down on the people who are in it. And that's unfortunate, but as a young person I gotta say I enjoy seeing black culture in the mainstream right now.

High Times: It's kind of a compliment.

Dave Chappelle: More than kind of. I think it's good for race relations that so many white kids' heroes are black dudes.

High Times: Did you ever think you'd see that?

Dave Chappelle: There are black people throughout popular culture who whites and blacks have been unanimous on. I mean guys like Eddie Murphy, whereas that could have been the kiss of death years ago if you're a black entertainer, because once that white audience embraces you, a black audience might lose respect for you.

High Times: And guys like Eddie Murphy didn't pander; they stayed black.

Dave Chappelle: Yeah. They stuck to their guns, man. A Richard Pryor, or any of these guys. So I think it's a beautiful thing, man. It brings a lot of people together. Like I said, I don't know how binding it is. After a certain point, they just might give up on us!

High Times: Just to go back to wiggers, do you think white people are ever qualified to use the word nigger?

Dave Chappelle: It's funny, I was having a conversation with Mos Def, who's a rapper, actor, comedian, and he said that it was an excluding word, originally. To call you a nigger is kind of like, "Get out of here; we don't want you." Now instead it's cool to be black, and we call it "Yo' one nigger;" and now it's still exclusive, but it's the other way, and we can say this, but you can't say that. And in a very personal situation, maybe I'll let it slide, but in general I don't want to hear white people say that. It's because, again, it could be a fad they're going through.

But in a way, I like the fact they're calling you that, and it's a positive connotation, because nigger is a word they use for black people that weren't down with their program of slavery. If a slave gave them a hard time they called him a "nigger." And that's the kind of slave you wanna be. You don't want to be the agreeable, smiling motherfucker; you want to be that disagreeable, ornery—if you would—get-out-of-my-sight mother-fucker. All these things are contextual, man. You can say most anything so long as you're not malicious about it. But you know, your intentions make or break everything, man.

High Times: Are there times you hear people say it, and you go "How's this guy saying it?"

Dave Chappelle: Yeah. If you have to ask, they probably didn't do it right. You know what I mean? You know, there are some people who can just get away with it. Lenny Bruce got away with it in the sixties. Pryor got away with it, I get away with it, you know, and it's just 'cause it's no malice, man.

High Times: What do you think of Lenny Bruce?

Dave Chappelle: Imagine, that was the first time anyone ever talked like that, in public, and as a comedian, up until that point. And Richard Pryor more so. I think that Richard completely stretched that out.

High Times: Cursing?

Dave Chappelle: Not just the cursing, but the shit they used to talk about! Lenny Bruce was talking about the Kennedy Assassination like it was funny, *after it happened!* Richard Pryor talks about the cops beating up Negroes, and "Can we break a nigger? It's in the rulebook: Oh, it says right here we can break a nigger." I mean, the substance of the shit they were saying, that's what I was impressed with. And not just that it was only daring; it was daring, but the shit was really funny, man, above anything—it was just funny.

High Times: Is that the most important thing? Beyond social implications?

Dave Chappelle: I mean look, whether you pull shit out of a box like Carrot Top, or juggle, or talk about politics, I still feel like the crowd just wants to be entertained. For instance, I'm doing a special in June. I'm not gonna go and deliberately write war jokes, unless there's something, an angle I see, like, *Oh, this is really funny. And it's a good point.* Like Piss on You? Hey, like, I almost didn't do it, just because I felt bad for R. Kelly. Yeah, like before we shot it. But after we recorded the song, I felt weird, like, man, I don't know if I should do this, I got all the guy's records, it's a terrible time in his life. Am I kicking a man when he's down? Was it wrong to kick a guy when he's down?

But when I thought about it, I literally was like, this shit is too funny, if I don't do it, I'll be mad at myself. 'Cause it's too funny. And the other thing was, I didn't think it was the worst. I figure, that's the least of his problems. It might actually help him to give people an opportunity just to laugh it off.

High Times: Get it into perspective.

Dave Chappelle: Yeah, exactly. You know, that's terrible, to pee on that damn girl.

High Times: Do you think this R. Kelly, Michael Jackson, Kobe Bryant shit, this media focus on "famous negroes gone wrong," is all distraction? Like, let's get some black guy fucked up so the public doesn't fixate on the fact that everything else is going to shit?

Dave Chappelle: That's funny, because the last time we heard from Michael Jackson in such a big media frenzy was right at the beginning of the invasion of Iraq. And right when it was happening, that's where that special came out with the boy that made the allegations. And I just remember thinking: "We're on the brink of a war, and Michael Jackson is the lead story on three networks?" Like he was on two networks at the same time, two of the big four. I think he's America's scapegoat, Michael Jackson. He's just somebody to hate when shit's going wrong.

High Times: What are some of the drawbacks of being famous?

Dave Chappelle: Obviously, less privacy. Scrutiny. Scrutiny is a form of oppression in a way, even if it's unintentional, because a scrutinized person will never act natural. If you know somebody's watching you eat, you're gonna start thinking, "How am I chewing my food?" Things that you normally just do and are natural about. So like, in my personal life, I used to be one of the funniest dudes you'd ever want to hang out with, but now I just save it for the stage 'cause it's safer. I feel too inhibited when I'm around strangers or something because I feel like, you know, you never know, one out of ten people are always out to get you. Two out of ten, five out of ten—as you go up the ranks it seems like there's more malicious people. You gotta be so cautious. That's no fun, man.

High Times: Is that a jealousy factor, you think?

Dave Chappelle: I think it's jealousy, I think it's desperation. Look, man, like I said, sometimes the idea of mattering in this society is daunting. When you meet a person who's famous, all kinds of different shit comes into people's minds. Take a totally nice, benign person who begins hanging 'round a famous person; you might see a dark side they never had. You see the best in people—sometimes they're very accommodating, maybe even too accommodating—and then you see the worst in people. Like maybe they figure, "If I can trip this guy I can get something." You know, it's par for the course, but it's a lot of scrutiny, and it forces you to be more self-aware. And I'm not interested in that. I like just living my life, spouting my opinion like I really mean it, and then changing my mind the next day. You know what I mean? [*Laughs*] I change my mind all the time. I believe what I believe, until I see a better way.

LOSING THE PLOT
Fear and Loathing in Baghdad

DAVID ENDERS

MAY/JUNE 2004

OCCUPIED BAGHDAD IS A lot like Detroit. You can replace "white flight" and "hollow urban core" with "We leveled heavy sanctions" and "We bombed the hell out of it," but the results are pretty much the same: lots of empty buildings, a police force you can't trust and lots of people who take the law into their own hands. Squatters live in the bombed-out and looted ministries and government buildings. They are forced to move occasionally so troops can clear out the unexploded bombs dropped last year that they've known about for months but are just getting around to dealing with.

Though the army has been here since April, the city is still in chaos. People drive on any side of the road they like, dodging the tank and Humvee patrols that run twenty-four hours a day. The official curfew has been lifted, but virtually everyone is off the streets by 11 P.M. CNN reporters are not allowed out after dark. Most people have not bothered to take down the brown packaging tape from their windows that they put up last March, before the bombing began. It's a little like Christmas lights that are left up all year. But the tape hasn't remained out of apathy—it's because the war isn't over. The tape will come down when the war is over.

The war won't be over for a long time. At the very least, it won't be over until foreign troops leave the country. (That said, please note any reference to "troops" in this article is a reference to U.S. troops, who are in charge of Baghdad and most of the rest of the country. I know that during his State of the Union address, George W. Bush read off that silly list of all the countries that have sent troops to Iraq, but what he didn't mention was that the troops from El Salvador were forced to ride into the country on a bus and wait inside a U.S. base for a month because they had no uniforms. It's a coalition like Simon and Garfunkel was a coalition. How many Art Garfunkel records do you own?)

So a sort of Robocop future has become Baghdad's present, as post-invasion confusion gives way to occupied hedonism. It's the kind of situation that lends itself to the bizarre, the banal, and situations so absurd that while there is no Godot in Baghdad, this is probably a pretty logical place to wait for him. (Or her.) Meanwhile, though, people have to find something to keep themselves occupied. On that note, my friend Rory has actually planned to kidnap a kid.

The translator is in on it. The driver is in on it. (In fact, I think he figures we're planning to ransom the kid or something. He fully approves.) I'm just along for ride. This is the turn the story I was working on about street kids has taken. It started innocently enough—in May, there were a lot of them out on the streets, panhandling money from foreign journalists. They would nick your satellite phone if you weren't paying attention, but they'd always give it back. They just wanted some attention. Some of them left the orphanages when they were looted after the invasion; some of them were just kids looking for a little bit of extra freedom. Most of them have gone home or found a place to stay now that it's gotten cold, but I'm working on a story about the real hard cases, the ones that slipped through the cracks.

Rory is a sixty-three-year-old ex-con with a slight history of addiction. He was a human shield during the war and helped bury the bodies of men from Lebanon, Egypt, and Syria who came to fight the American army in Baghdad. He has been fired on by American troops (of course, by now, we've all been fired on by American troops at some point) and is entirely unapologetic about his past.

"I was kind of like Robin Hood. I robbed the rich to pay my dealer," he says.

Rory did time in the States for a post office robbery (he dropped the gun) and time in the UK for possession. He says he's going to start a hash farm near Nasiriyah, and I think he may. He's already managed to make a documentary about the war and it's quite good, so he's working on another. If he finds a couple people he can trust, a hash farm should be no problem at all before the second doc is finished.

But for now, thoughts of hash farms and documentaries are far off. Rory is stoned—I mean focused.

Rory is planning to kidnap twelve-year-old Latifa (surname unknown) from the Al-Sadr House of Mercy, a home for street children. She is there against her will. The group is known to be fundamentalist, and hey—that's exactly the type of fight a sixty-three-year-old Scot should be picking with the local heavies. Rory has considered being armed for this event, but no one offered to lend him a gun. Better that way, I figured.

Rory met Latifa while he was working on his documentary. She was living on the street near the hotel he was staying in. Rory's got compassion for the down-and-out, so he started feeding the group of street kids Latifa ran with. He got to know them, know their addictions and looked out for them when they were in danger of taking a beating from the cops or from one of the taxi drivers who hung out by the hotel. Latifa has a family, and that is where Rory is planning to take her.

I play soccer with some of the kids from the home while Rory talks to the oldest boy. He's sixteen, but he's bigger than Rory. He says none of the home's supervisors are around and that Rory should come back on Saturday. Rory peers about for a glimpse of Latifa, but sees nothing and agrees to come back. He films the kids running back and forth on the dusty, makeshift field for a while and then we leave.

One more Iraqi remains unliberated. But don't worry, she'll escape from the home and find Rory when she needs money. He'll give it to her, buy her some new clothes and try and convince her to go with him to see her family. Then she'll disappear and we won't see her for a while. She sniffs a lot of glue and doesn't really want to go home. Rory is heartbroken.

On the bright side, at least Rory is back in Baghdad. He's happiest here. For some reason, there are a lot of people like that. Even I can't deny that it's good to be back, war or no. I've been here since May, then left for a month and a half in September—and when I got back, I knew things had changed. I bumped into Rory when I got to Amman, Jordan—and because Amman is the most boring city I've ever been to, I rode into Baghdad with him in the car he had already hired for that evening.

The moon hung low over the desert and there was a brief eclipse as we left Jordan. Jordan looks like Utah with mosques. It's almost as dry—and if you can manage to find a beer, it's not very good. Worse yet, I was there during Ramadan, everything closes from sunup to sundown, one of the local cable channels plays a different movie every night, so everyone stays home and watches it with their family. It was no small relief when we were out of Jordan, despite the sudden increase in probability we'd be shot before having a chance to figure out what's going on.

Rory, oblivious to the natural phenomena, handed me a spliff as soon as we crossed the border. It wasn't easy to get hash inside Iraq before the invasion—Rory even tried asking the secret police at one point and was informed that possession was punishable by death—so now it is to be savored. (Note to the War on Drugs cum War on Terror: An entire country has now been opened up to illicit consumerism—and guess who controls the supply? Brilliant job, guys.)

Most things hadn't changed in the month and a half I'd been gone, but a few things had. The economy picked up a little—there are now healthy black and consumer goods markets—and women feel safe enough to walk the streets now, some even wearing the same kinds of outfits you'd see on women in the U.S. or Europe rather than the traditional black, full-length abbiyas that cover everything but their face. That's a welcome change, but there are other things that I find less than encouraging.

The kids walking home from school stick out their hands as if to give me a high five and then pull back at the last minute, laughing. Gone are the people who will stop me on the street and shout "Amreekee good!" while giving a hearty thumbs-up.

The American army has arrested kids during class. Saddam would at least come knock on your door and would never, ever arrest a kid from school. No child left behind.

Every time I walk by a kilometers-long petrol queue, there are ugly, sidelong glances that didn't exist before. Ajnabi. Foreigner. This is your fault, however indirectly.

I had to do something. Things had become much worse. There was only one solution.

Mo was our first hash dealer. He was teaching English in Kuwait before the invasion when the *Los Angeles Times* asked him to be a translator. He was a tall guy with slicked hair, a pair of yellow-tinted glasses he almost never took off, and thick, tattooed biceps (a picture of an Egyptian courtesan on one arm) that he liked to flex. He brought the stuff in whenever he went back to Kuwait and sold it to journalists and NGO workers—basically, foreigners desperate to get high. Mo lasted a month or two.

"Have you talked to Mo lately?" another writer asked me when he noticed our stash was running out.

"He sent me an E-mail the other day."

"Where's he been?"

"He's in Kuwait. He got shot in the leg near Amara. Carjacking."

"Jesus. Is he okay?"

"Yeah. All he really said was that he shouldn't have taken that road."

After some nervous laughter, we found another hash dealer.

The hash trade in Iraq is mostly guys from other Arab countries bringing in the goods and selling to foreigners—NGO workers, journalists, contractors. I've been looking for the good Lebanese stuff, the kind Hezbollah grows in the Bekaa Valley, but that all gets exported to Europe. All I can find is the Afghan and Pakistani (still not bad) weed that comes through the gulf. The holy grail would be selling to soldiers, but it doesn't seem anyone's worked that one out yet. There are few laws in Iraq right now, so although drug possession was punishable by death before, you can now pass a spliff openly in front of the cops.

"This is the freedom," says my friend Hamid sarcastically. Hamid is a twenty-six-year-old translator/bodyguard/heavy-metal fan (yes, there are Iraqi metal bands) who lived for a couple years in the States when he was in his teens. He's a former member of the Fedayeen Saddam, the most loyal unit of the Iraqi army—"the suiciders" is how he translates the name. He's thrilled he can smoke hash now, but a bit dismayed he still can't elect his own leaders. "This is the freedom they promised us."

One of the favored words in Arabic for a spliff is saroukh. It means "missile." The first time we got Hamid stoned, the saroukh destroyed him. It was the day the army announced the capture of Saddam Hussein, and Hamid was shocked. He doesn't love Saddam per se, but he wasn't thrilled to see another Iraqi in US custody. He didn't like the idea of the president of his country being publicly humiliated on television.

"Would Iraqis be allowed to show American prisoners of war having their teeth examined on TV?" he asked. "How would you feel if that was George Bush instead of Saddam Hussein?"

While my friends were filming in his neighborhood, Hamid helped incite a demonstration in support of the deposed president that grew into a group of men, some firing Kalashnikovs and others carrying grenade launchers. Afterward, Hamid definitely needed something to calm him down.

He was still grappling with the feeling the next morning.

"Before I went to bed last night, I ate an entire box of cookies. I'm not sure why, but I just couldn't stop eating them," he said.

"That's called the munchies," I explained.

"The munchies? How do you spell that?" he asked, writing the new word in his notebook.

"Losing the plot" is what we say here when someone's gone nuts. It only applies to foreigners, because, in a sense, every Iraqi has lost it. Going crazy here isn't really going crazy, it's the logical reaction to having lived here for more than two decades under the leadership of a man whose primary objective was making war and having pictures of himself commissioned. As your prize for surviving all that, you get an occupying army staffed mostly by guys who never thought very highly of traveling abroad (and most of whom will never leave the States again, if they can help it). Iraqis can't really go crazy, because this place is already nuts.

Jim got arrested for tagging one of the blast barriers in front of the Baghdad Hotel (widely regarded by Iraqis as CIA headquarters) with graffiti. His mates spent three days looking for him, but since they didn't know his surname, it wasn't too productive—though how many Brits can there be in Baghdad with a shoulder-length ponytail and a penchant for urban art and expletives?

"I fookin' got arrested by the fookin' Americans. Quite fookin' boring, really," he says, when he turns up at the apartment after spending three days in a cage.

"Were you in a cell with other guys?"

"Yeah, at first. None of 'em fookin' spoke English, and I think at first all of the fookin' soldiers thought there was going to be fookin' trouble, because I was looking around and noticing that all the guys had what they were suspected of written on a little tag pinned to their chest. Theirs all said fookin' 'bomb making,' and mine fookin' said 'spray painting.' But after a little while we got on fookin' famously, so they fookin' moved me to me own fookin' cell."

Jim pauses and notes with dismay that in his absence, his roommates have finished his bottle of arak—a clear liquor, made locally from dates, that turns milky white when mixed with water. It's less than three dollars a bottle. Arak is very Hemingway. Think of the absinthe that gets considerable mention in *For Whom the Bell Tolls*.

"Fook. Guess I'll have to fookin' go get another fookin' bottle. That's your fookin' mates for ya, huh?"

Jim and Rory are quite sane—but there are a bunch of expats showing up these days who have totally lost the plot. I'm told the same thing happens in Palestine and Chiapas (where they call them "Zapatourists"): There are people who don't really have a clue about what to do with themselves but come out to "help." Some of them are adrenaline junkies, some of them are looking for self-aggrandizement, some of them have death wishes. They show up on the doorsteps of NGOs or just sort of hang about, complicating things far more than they need to be complicated. This place doesn't need any more lost people, and Iraqis don't need foreign advocates, they need a little bit of direct help. Just as there are Iraqi engineers perfectly capable of putting things back together so long as they have the funds, there are plenty of Iraqi activists and intellectuals who just need a little support and they can go ahead and take it from there. It needs to happen quickly. A lot of the Iraqis who can travel have begun to leave. Something needs to be done before all of them are gone.

The desire to leave is the only thing U.S. soldiers and Iraqis have in common. The troops intimate this in offhand conversations as they protect the perimeter of an area where a Humvee has been blown up or when you catch them standing guard at a checkpoint or a gas station, a job that brings mostly tedium.

"Look at all these ladies with their shoes," said a soldier from Ohio as he held back a group of Iraqi women in high heels waiting to return to their homes. The women were anxious to see their families, but they're probably lucky they weren't around when the explosion happened—a car bomb was set off as a U.S. patrol passed by. There was a Humvee lying upside-down, and another one had fully burned. Troops were searching every home in a two-block area and had already rounded up forty or so suspects for questioning and detainment.

I don't usually follow attacks, I don't like having to scrape assorted viscera off my shoes, and I don't like having to write stories that have leads like "One U.S. soldier and three Iraqis were killed as . . ." Why can't it just say four people were killed? Does it somehow make it more acceptable that one was a soldier? Are the three Iraqis less important? Yes, as far as politics in the States are concerned, they are; pressure is measured in soldiers, not civilians.

We didn't hear the bomb, we were driving by afterward when we saw the barriers the troops had set up. I get interested when I see them doing house searches. That's how I found myself talking to the soldier from Ohio, who was trying to hold back the ladies as politely as possible. Expletives were noticeably absent when he addressed them, and he commented on post-invasion Iraqi fashion from a standpoint that showed he had no knowledge of pre-invasion fashion.

"They've all gone out to buy fancy shoes now that they're allowed to show their ankles," he said.

"Actually, they were always allowed to show their ankles—Iraq's been a secular society for years. Now it's worse. In some places, people have been forcing women to cover up," I told him, trying at the same time to explain to the women that they were going to have to wait at least another half an hour. Soldiers in these situations often don't have translators. I don't speak much Arabic, but I know more than the soldiers.

Angry journalists standing with the women pointed to a man filming inside the cordon and asked the soldier why he wouldn't let them in. "That's probably one of our guys," the soldier said. "For future intel. There's nothing you could film here right now that you'd be allowed to show on TV anyway." The frustrated journalists decide to walk to the other side of the perimeter and see if the soldiers there will let them in. I decide to stick around and smoke cigarettes with the soldier from Ohio, who has decided he's going to sound off.

"Is CNN here yet?" the soldier asks. "Those guys are usually the first ones here. I've had it to here with journalists. I was at Red Cross after the explosion there." (The Red Cross headquarters in Baghdad was car-bombed in August). "That's the worst stuff I've seen out here. And there's that girl who works for Fox News—you know the one. She's filming on the roof of the building, and I had to go up and get her. 'Can't I just get a little bit more footage?' she says, and I tell her, 'You can stand fast if you want, bitch, but this thing's going to collapse. An I-beam just fell out. I'm getting out of here, even if you're not.'"

When the journalists have gone, the soldier from Ohio offers to escort me across the cordon. Bored soldiers sit around after finishing house searches. One of them yells at me: "Hey, man, you like to smoke pot? You look like you like to smoke pot." I don't think I look like a pothead. But apparently I do. There's no dress code in occupied Iraq, so I guess I've sort of let myself go—hair nearly to my shoulders, a rip in the knee of my jeans, unshaven, a wool sweater that's got a hole in the elbow and a cigarette burn or two and shoes that have been without laces for months. I certainly don't look like Special Forces.

"Yeah, that's the reason I didn't join up like you guys," I reply.

There are some days, though, when it feels a bit like I have joined up. It wasn't long after the military entered Baghdad that journalists began lining up to take orders. The press conferences are held at the convention center, a piece of modern architecture with sweeping curves and a nicely wrought garden on the south side of the Tigris that any American city would be proud of. Saddam was a megalomaniac, but he had good taste in con-structing public buildings.

The convention center is now home to the Coalition Provisional Authority, which is the political wing of the US military. Hezbollah has elected members in the Lebanese Parliament, the IRA has Sinn Fein—think of the CPA along the same lines.

After making it through the rows of barbed wire and the three body searches, men and women of rank, of the press or of varying degrees of usefulness to the

U.S.-led administration are allowed to pass through the sometimes-working automatic doors into the convention center's main hall, which is lovingly decorated with a banner sent by fourth graders from some school in Kansas. The American kids professed their support for Iraqi children in red, white, and blue marker. No Iraqi child will see this banner.

The convention center is where the press conferences are held, where the dictums of the occupying authority are delivered. US generals cite made-up statistics and simply refuse to answer questions if they're too complicated or put the generals in a position where they can't answer truthfully without making the army or the CPA look bad.

A journalist sitting next to me at a press conference declares he's "inspired" and decides to pop a Valium. The press conferences are kind of like having your intelligence insulted and your shins kicked at the same time. The CPA is not a legitimate governing body, but it acts as one and uses the military to enforce its rules. Should I report what they say and support their feigned legitimacy? Or is it better to tell the truth, since they'll find out what the CPA said while staring down the barrel of a gun. I want the Iraqis to overrun the convention center, to accept that this is just a subtler form of the fascism that they've been dealing with for the last twenty-five years, and to resist. But they will not overrun this place. The army has won. Challenging authority is dangerous, the military has made it clear that it will shoot first and ask questions later. They took a good look at how the last guy controlled the population and decided it made sense. "People in this country have a great fear of the state," says Womidh Nidhal, who has taught political science at Baghdad University for twenty-eight years.

My Iraqi friend Hamid walks into my hotel room singing his rendition of a Pink Floyd song:

"We don't need no occupation. We don't need no CPA. Saddam Hussein will return to Baghdad. Hey! Soldier! Leave those kids alone!"

Hamid hates what is happening to his country. He hates the occupation, hates the humiliation. He knows he's lucky to have a job because he speaks English, but wakes up and thinks about leaving every day. He knows the war is far from over.

Hamid shot himself in the leg a few days before the American army entered Baghdad. "I was waiting for the Americans to enter. The last night I went out to stand guard like I did every night," he says in American-accented English, tears coming to his eyes. "The night was the darkest night I had ever seen. All my friends had already escaped. My mom was standing in the door and she was saying that if I went out, I was going to die, and she was crying.

"What's the point of fighting and dying? My people are tired. I am fighting. I'm fighting to get medicine for my mom." Hamid's mother has multiple sclerosis. "I'm working to get money for my family.

"I lost a lot of innocent people in this war. A lot of people died and what did it change? Nothing."

WHY DO THEY CALL IT DOPE?

LUC SANTE

NOVEMBER/DECEMBER 2004

YOU HAVE TO KEEP your eye on the past. Not only is it not dead yet, but it can sometimes jump up and bite you on the ankle. Not long ago, while reading the 1921 memoirs of James L. Ford, a New York theater critic and man-about-town, I ran across the following:

> Many years ago, when prairie schooners were the means of transit across the continent, there hung from the axle-tree a bucket of black wagon grease containing what was called a daub stick with which the lubricant was applied. The earliest American frequenters of the Chinese joints in San Francisco were men who had crossed from the east in these prairie schooners and as the word 'daub' had become corrupted into 'dope'[,] the opium paste which looked exactly like the axle-grease acquired its name by a quite natural process.

I promptly looked up dope in an etymological dictionary, which told me that the word derives from the Dutch doop, meaning "sauce" (Ford was wrong about daub).

Instantly I saw before me a panorama, like a post-office mural painted by the WPA: Dutch burghers in New Amsterdam, wearing high-crowned hats and knee breeches, spooning gravy over the Sunday roast, merged into pioneers, in homespun and gingham, on a dusty track in an endless field of waving rye, swabbing the wheel assembly of a Conestoga wagon with some kind of black gunk. These blended into a shadowy crowd, some wearing queues and skullcaps, others in derbies or picture hats, bent over long bamboo pipes of burbling yen pock from which plumes of smoke curled up into a cloud that, as it drifted through time, collected spiraling fumes from the reefers of Harlem rent-party revelers, the joints of Human Be-In votaries, and the blunts of an assortment of O.G.'s on a stoop. There was your cavalcade of American history, all bound together by one simple monosyllabic word!

The word may have gone out of business in Dutch (doop now means, of all things, "christening"), but in America its career has been even more dizzyingly various than my tableau would suggest. Not so long ago, it referred to molasses, to ice-cream toppings, to soda pop—was it the gooey syrup or the onetime cocaine content that caused Coca-Cola to be called "dope" in the South for most of the twentieth century? It has meant any kind of lubricant, glue, poison, insecticide, incinerant, medicine, liquor, coffee, or unidentified gumbo. It has signified information, news, esoteric lore—even spread out amorphously to take in just about any sort of thing, stuff or business. As a verb, meanwhile, it could mean "to poison," "to lubricate," "to medicate," "to adulterate," "to predict," "to figure out" or "to dawdle." At least for the first half of the twentieth century, it was the all-purpose tool, the Swiss Army knife of the American language, and no substitute—not even shit—has been able to cover all of its many functions. Yes, the word also means "idiot," but that sense is from the British Isles and has a completely different etymology, either from dupe or from daup, an English dialect word meaning "carrion crow."

But all of those other denotations and connotations derive from the transsubstantiation of axle grease into opium. The meanings related to cognition, for example—"data," "inside knowledge," "to suss out," "to prognosticate"—ultimately descend from the unfortunate practice of hopping up racehorses, information pertaining to which could make anyone a mahatma at the track. Every other application of the word refers to substances—dark, viscous, sticky and of complex, multifaceted, uncertain, dubious, speculative, or hazardous composition or employment. You could say that dope, a purely and utterly American word, stands for the familiar unknown. It is the stuff in the cabinet, under the stairs, out in the tool shed, in an unlabeled jar, pooled at the bottom of an old tin can; stuff you use without really knowing much about it, stuff that works but that you don't care to inquire too deeply about. This describes an enormous category in American life.

In our society, a great deal of business is concealed under ten-dollar words, trademarks, cop talk, and quasi-scientific jargon that to the lay ear simply registers as "dope." The ingredients list on a box of cookies might as well read, approximately: flour, butter, sugar, dope. Much breathless packaging says, in effect, "Now With Added Dope!" Spokespersons for energy companies, being lobbed softballs by congressional subcomitees on C-SPAN, reply with verbiage that can nearly always be translated as: "We plan to invest in more dope." If pharmaceutical advertising were stripped of its misleading charts and perspiration-free images, the industry would be stuck with saying pretty much the same thing in every instance: "Our dope is really great!" Of course it's nice that we can establish the presence of, for example, potassium sorbate, D&C Red No. 40, chlorinated isocyanurate, and dextromethorphan hydrobromide, and have the ability to look them up and maybe figure out what they might do to us, but unless you're a chemist or a consumer advocate, how often have you bothered? It's all dope.

Think again of that miracle, when axle grease was transformed into opium. The throng in attendance included people who had abandoned everything they had known growing up in order to make a better life for themselves, had hocked most of their assets to pay for the journey, had crossed the plains, the high desert and the Sierra Nevada in rattling wagons subject to the elements—or had crossed the Pacific in the sweltering, overcrowded holds of sailing ships with few rations and zero comforts. Now, at the end of the journey, having ascertained that El Dorado was nowhere in sight, they decided they might as well go kick the gong around. The Chinese, who supplied the stuff, had had it foisted upon them long before by the British East India Company, but the Americans would probably only know of it as a tincture, dissolved in alcohol, available at drugstores. Now they took a look at the black gunk and it reminded them of the substance that greased their wheels. After a few puffs, they decided that the similarity extended to function: This shit would grease their wheels as well, in a different sort of way. And so it has. Dope—meaning everything from nicotine to serotonin-reuptake inhibitors and from silicone implants to petroleum additives—has been doing the job for well over a century. You just can't call it dope anymore. You wouldn't want people to think it had anything to do with pleasure.

NORMAN MAILER ON POT

RICHARD STRATTON

NOVEMBER/DECEMBER 20004

THIRTY YEARS AGO, WHEN *High Times* was in its infancy, I did a long interview with Norman Mailer that was published in two parts in *Rolling Stone* magazine. Mailer and I first met in Provincetown, MA, in the winter of 1970 and have been close friends ever since. At one time we owned property together in Maine, which was put up as collateral for bail when I got busted for smuggling marijuana in the early '80s. The Feds were all over the connection between Mailer and me; he testified for the defense at the trial of my partner in Toronto, Rosie Rowbotham, who ended up doing over twenty years for importing hashish. Mailer later testified at my trials in Maine and New York. The government became convinced that he was some sort of hippie godfather to the sprawling marijuana-trafficking organization Rowbotham and I ran, along the lines of Timothy Leary's figurehead status with the Brotherhood of Eternal Love conspiracy out of Laguna Beach, CA.

But Mailer was more a friend of the cause than a co-conspirator. He certainly had what to an assistant United States attorney might qualify as "guilty knowledge." He knew what I was up to. I remember standing with him on the balcony of his Brooklyn Heights apartment one night, looking out at the glittering behemoths of the Lower Manhattan financial district, then down at the containers stacked on the Brooklyn docks below like mini-skyscrapers and telling him, "Right down there, Norman, in those containers, there's seven million dollars' worth of Lebanese hash. All I have to do is get it out of there without getting busted." The novelist in him was intrigued, but the criminal in him would always remain subservient to the artist. The government put tremendous pressure on me to give them

Mailer, as though he were some trophy I could trade for my own culpability. They were star-fucking: John DeLorean had been busted in a set-up coke case; Mailer's head would have looked good mounted on some government prosecutor's wall.

When I went to prison in 1982, Mailer became—after my mother—my most loyal visitor and correspondent. And when I was released in 1990, I stayed in his Brooklyn Heights apartment while the Mailer family summered in Provincetown. I've known Mailer's youngest son, John Buffalo, since he was born and turned to him when I needed someone to act in my stead here at the magazine while I finished work on the TV show I produced for Showtime. But, as with my criminal enterprise, Mailer has no financial stake in the outcome of the *High Times* mini-media-conglomerate conspiracy. He's an interested observer and adviser.

All this by way of saying there's real history here, so much so that there was never any pretense at making this a typical interview; it's more like a master speaking to an apprentice about what he has learned. I'd read Mailer extensively before I met him. His writing, in essays such as "The White Negro" and "General Marijuana," his nonfiction *The Armies of the Night* and *The Executioner's Song,* and the novels *The Naked and the Dead, An American Dream, Why Are We in Vietnam?* and *Ancient Evenings,* to mention just a few Mailer works, have reshaped post–World War II American literature. Mailer's whole notion of the existential hipster living in the crucible of his orgasm probably contributed as much to my fascination with the outlaw life as the cannabis plant itself.

I've smoked pot with Mailer on a number of occasions and have always been impressed with where it took him: to the outermost reaches of the universe and back to the murky depths of the human psyche. But I had never really sat with him and got his thoughts on pot until we met, almost thirty years to the day of that first interview, and I asked him to expound on his views of the plant that became the inspiration for this magazine.

Norman Mailer: Looking back on pot—is it thirty years since I smoked?—by the '70s I began to feel it was costing me too much. We'll get to what I got out of it and what I didn't get out of it—but by the '80s, I just smoked occasionally. And I don't think I've had a toke—and this is neither to brag nor apologize—in ten years. But I look back on it as one of the profoundest parts of my life. It did me a lot of good and a lot of harm.

What I'd like to do today is talk about these dimensions of pot. People who smoke marijuana all the time are, as far as I'm concerned, fundamentalists. Their one belief is that pot is good, pot takes care of everything—it's their gospel. I think they're about as limited—if you want to get brutal about it—as fundamentalists. Fundamentalists can't think; they can only refer to the Gospels. Pot people can't recognize that something as good as that might have something very bad connected to it—which is not to do with the law, but what it does to you. That's what I'd like to talk about. The plus and minus.

The other thing I'd like to talk about is the cultural phenomenon of pot. That is rarely gone into. Instead, people are always taking sides—pot's good, pot's bad; pot should be outlawed, pot should be decriminalized—there's always this legalistic approach. But I think marijuana had a profound cultural effect upon America, and I wouldn't mind seeing this magazine exploring all that pot did to the American mentality—good and bad.

Richard Stratton: Marijuana is already a huge cultural phenomenon. In the thirty years *High Times* has been around, pot has gone from a marginal anomaly in our society to something that's almost mainstream.

Mailer: Yeah, only not mainstream yet. Too many attitudes have settled in on pot, and there's too much dead-ass in the thinking of pot smokers now. Some thirth years ago when it was all new, we really felt we were adventurers—let's say forty years ago—we really felt we were on the edge of startling and incredible revelations. You'd have perceptions that I still use to this day—that's part of the good. When I first began smoking, I was a typical liberal, a radical rationalist. I never believed in a Higher Power. I still dislike those two words—Higher Power. I didn't believe that God was there. I couldn't explain anything, because when you're an atheist, you're living without a boat on an island in the Pacific that's surrounded by water: There's nowhere to go.

It's hard enough to believe in God, but to assume there is no God, no prime force—how can you begin to explain anything that way?

I was a socialist, more radical than most liberals, but I was altogether a rationalist. I was also at the point of getting into one or another kind of terminal disease, because my life was wrong. My liver was lousy and I wasn't even drinking a lot. My personal life was not happy and I was congested, constricted. I couldn't have been tighter. Then pot hit.

In the beginning, I remember that pot used to irritate the hell out of me, because nothing would happen when I smoked. I've noticed that intellectuals with highly developed minds usually have trouble turning on. The mental structure is so developed, so ratiocinative. So many minefields have been built up to protect the intellect from pot, which is seen as the disrupter, the enemy. The first few times I smoked, I just got tired, dull and irritated. I was angry that nothing had happened. It went on like that for perhaps a year. Three, four, five times I smoked, and each occasion was a blank.

Then one night in Mexico I got into a crazy sexual scene with two women. We were smoking an awful lot of pot. Then one of the women went home and the other went to sleep and I felt ill and got up and vomited. I'd never vomited like that in my life. It was exactly as if I was having an orgasm of convulsive vomiting. Spasmodically, I was throwing off a ton of anxiety. I've never had anything like that since and I wouldn't want to. Not again. Pretty powerful convulsive experience.

Afterward, I rinsed my mouth out, went downstairs to where my then wife was sleeping on one couch, and I lay down on the other and stayed there. Then it hit—how that pot hit! I don't know if it ever hit any harder. It was incredible: I was able to change the face of my wife into anyone I wanted. It went on before my eyes. I could play all sorts of games in my mind. Whole scenarios. It went on for hours. When it was over, I knew that I was going to try this again.

A couple of days later, I was out in the car listening to the radio. Some jazz came on. I'd been listening to jazz for years, but it had never meant all that much to me. Now, with the powers pot offered, simple things became complex; complex things clarified themselves. These musicians were offering the inner content of their experience to me. Later, when I wrote about it, I would say that jazz is the music of orgasm. Because that was what it seemed to me. These very talented, charged-up players full of their joys and twists and kinks—God, they had as many as I did—were looking for the musical equivalent of an orgasm. They would take a song, play the melody, then go into variations on it, until they got themselves into a tighter and tighter situation with the take-off on the melody. I can't speak musically, but I can tell what was going on in that odyssey. They were saying: This is very, very hard to get out, it's full of knots—but I'm going to do it. And they'd climb a tower of music looking to reach the gates at the top and break through. It wasn't automatic; very often they failed. They'd go on and on, try more variations, then more. But often they couldn't solve the problem they'd set themselves musically, whatever that problem was. And sometimes, occasionally, they would break through. Then it was incredible, for they would emerge with you into a happy land just listening to music. Other times they'd stop with a little flair, a sign-off, as if to say: That's it, I give up. All that was what I heard while high, and I loved it. I became a jazz buff.

Over the next couple of years, I went often to the Five Spot, the Village Vanguard, the Jazz Gallery. I'd hear the greats: Thelonious Monk, Sonny Rollins, Coltrane, Miles Davis. Those were incredibly heady years, listening to those guys for hours on pot, or without it, because once pot had broken into my metallic mental structure, it had cracked the vise, you might say, that closed me off from music. I had become such a lover of pot that I broke up with a few friends who wouldn't smoke it. At the end of a long road—ten years down that road—I committed a felony while on pot. That didn't stop me, but I did smoke a little less as the years went on.

I'm a writer: The most important single element in my life, other than my family, has been my writing. So as a writer, I always had to ask: Is this good for my writing? And I began to look at pot through that lens. It wasn't all bad for editing—it was crazy. I'd have three or four bad ideas and one good one, but at the same time I was learning a lot about the sounds of language. Before, I'd been someone who wrote for the sense of what I was saying, and now I began to write for the sound of what I was writing.

Stratton: Like a jazz musician.

Mailer: Well, I wouldn't go that far, but to a degree, yes. I'd look for the rhythm of the long sentence rather than the intellectual impact, which often proved to be more powerful when it came out of the rhythm. So occasionally the editing was excellent. But it was impossible to write new stuff on pot. The experience was too intense. On pot, I would have the illusion that you need say no more than "I love you" and all of love would be there. Obviously, that was not enough.

Stratton: Let's talk about the detrimental aspects of pot, how you feel it worked against you.

Mailer: Well, the main thing was that I was mortgaging time, mortgaging my future. Because I'd have brilliant insights while on pot but could hardly remember any of them later. My handwriting would even break down. Then three-quarters of the insights were lost to scribbles. Whenever I had a tremendous take on pot, I was good for very little over the next 48 hours.

But if you're a novelist, you have to work every day. There are no easy stretches. You do the work. Marijuana was terrible for that. So I had longer and longer periods where I wouldn't go near pot—it would get me too far off my novelistic tracks. When it hit, three or four chapters of my next book would come into my head at once. That would often be a disaster. The happiest moment you can have when writing is when a sense of the truth comes in at the point of your pen. It just feels true. As you are writing! Such a moment is most certainly one of the reasons you write. But if I received similar truths via pot, I was no longer stretching my mind by my work as a novelist.

In fact, with the noticeable exception of Hunter Thompson, who has broken—bless him—has broken every fucking rule there is for ingesting alien substances . . . indeed, there's nobody remotely equal to Hunter—I don't know how he does it. I have great admiration for his constitution and the fact that he can be such a good writer with all the crap he takes into himself. Unbelievable, unbelievable—but no other writer I know can do it.

Stratton: So you believe that, if you were to smoke some good pot right now, you'd let your mind go—and you might see the rest of the book in your head, but you might not have the impetus to sit down and write it?

Mailer: That's right. One mustn't talk about one's book. For instance, I'm doing one now where I haven't even told my wife what it's about. She's guessed—she's a very smart lady, so she's guessed—but the thing is, I know that to talk about this book would be so much more stimulating and easy and agreeable than to write it that I'd end up talking to people about what a marvelous book I could have done. I believe pot does that in a far grander way—it's the difference between watching a movie on a dinky little TV set and going to a state-of-the-art cinema.

Stratton: Most the writing I'm doing these days is screenwriting. And because of the nature of the material I'm working on, I usually have a detailed outline. I know where I'm going, I've already seen the movie in my head. So when I write, after having smoked some pot, I find that what it does for me is I can just sit back and watch the scene play out in my mind. And I don't have to worry about getting lost, because I've got the structure of the screenplay holding me in check.

Mailer: I can see that would work for screenplays, but in a novel you've got to do it all.

Stratton: What about sex on pot?

Mailer: Sex on pot was fabulous. That was the big element. I realized I hadn't known anything about sex until I was able to enjoy it on pot. Then again, after a few years, I began to see some of the negative aspects. Once, speaking at Rice High School—I had a friend, a priest named Pete Jacobs, who'd invited me to speak there; it's a Catholic high school run by the Christian Brothers in Manhattan, and it's a school well respected by a lot of Irish working class all around New York, Staten Island, Queens, because they give you a very good, tough education there. The Christian Brothers are tough. But Pete told me, "Say what you want to say. These kids will be right on top of it." They were. They weren't passive students at all. One of them asked me, "How do you feel about marijuana and sex?" And I gave him this answer: You can be out with a girl, have sex with her for the first time on pot and it might be fabulous—you and the girl go very far out. Then two days later you hear that the girl was killed in an automobile accident and you say, "Too bad. Such a sweet little chick." You hardly feel more than that. The action had exhausted your emotions. On pot, you can have a romance that normally would take three to six months to develop being telescoped into one big fuck. But over one night, there's no loyalty or allegiance to it because you haven't paid the price. About that time, I realized that fucking on pot was crazy because you'd feel things you never felt before, but on the other hand, you really didn't attach that much loyalty to the woman. Your feelings of love were not for the woman, but for the idea of love. It was insufficiently connected to the real woman.

It bounced off her reality rather than drawing you toward it. Other times, you could indeed get into the reality of the woman and even see something hard and cold and cruel in her depths, or something so beautiful you didn't want to go too near it because you knew you were a lousy son of a bitch and you'd ruin it.

One way or another, I found that pot intensified my attitudes toward love, but it also left me detached. It was a peculiar business. So there came a point where I began to think: Who gave us pot? Was it God or the devil? Because by now, I was my own species of a religious man. I believed in an existential God who was doing the best that He or She could do.

God was out there as the Creator, but God was not all powerful or all wise. God was an artistic general, if you will—a very creative and wonderful general—better than any general who ever lived. By far. But even so, generals finally can't take care of all their troops. And the notion of people praying all the time—begging for God to watch over them, take care of them—so conflicted with what I felt. I felt that God cannot be all good and all powerful. Not both. Because if He's all good, He is certainly not all powerful. There's no way to explain the horrors of history, including the mid-century horrors of the last century, if He is all good. Whereas if God is a great creator—not necessarily the lord of all the universe, but let's say the lord of our part of the universe, our Creator—then God, on a grander scale, bears the same relationship to us that a parent does to a child. No parent is all wise, all powerful, and all good. The parent is doing the best that he or she can do. And very often it doesn't turn out well. That made sense to me. I could see our relation to God: God needs us as much as we need God. And to me, that was exciting, because now it wasn't a slavish relationship anymore. It made sense.

Stratton: You feel marijuana helped you discover this existential God?

Mailer: No question. That was part of the great trip. But I began to brood on a line that I'd written long before I'd smoked marijuana, a line from *The Deer Park*. The director who was my main character was having all sorts of insights and revelations while dead drunk, but then said to himself, "Why is my mind so alive when I'm too drunk to do anything about it?" That came back to haunt me. Because I thought: Pot is giving me so much, but I'm not doing my work. I don't get near enough to the visions and insights I'm having on pot. So is it a gift of God—pot? Or does it come from the devil? Is this the nearest the devil comes to being godlike? It seemed there were three possibilities there: One could well be that marijuana was a gift of God and, if so, must not be abused. Or was it an instrument of the devil? Or were God and the devil both present when we smoked? Maybe God needed us to become more illumined? After all, one of my favorite notions is that organized religion could well be one of the great creations of the devil. How better to drive people away from God than to give them a notion of the Almighty that doesn't fit the facts? So, I do come back to this notion that maybe God and the devil are obliged willy-nilly to collaborate here. Each thinks that they can benefit from pot: God can give you the insights and the devil will reap the exhaustions and the debilities. Because I think pot debilitates people. I've noticed over and over that people who smoke pot all the time generally do very little with their lives. I've always liked booze because I felt: It's a vice, but I know exactly what I'm paying for. You hurt your head in the beginning and your knees in the end, when you get arthritis. But at least you know how you're paying for the fun. Pot's spookier. Pot gives so much more than booze on the one hand—but on the other, never quite presents the bill.

Stratton: I'm not sure that's true of everyone who smokes pot.

Mailer: I'm sure it's not.

Stratton: A lot of people are motivated by pot. I am, for one.

Mailer: What do you mean, "motivated"?

Stratton: I mean that it doesn't debilitate me. I don't want to sit around and do nothing when I'm high. I get inspired, energized. I don't subscribe to the theory of the anti-motivational syndrome. If anything, when I'm straight, I'm often too hyper and too left-brain-oriented. I go off on tangents and I don't stop to look around and try to find a deeper meaning in what I'm doing. Marijuana will slow me down and allow me to connect with the mood of what's going on around me. And that, in turn, inspires me to go further into what I'm trying to do.

Mailer: I ended a few romances over the years because when I got on pot I couldn't stop talking. And finally I remember one girl who said, "Did you come to fuck or to knit?"

[Laughter]

Stratton: That's one of the interesting things about marijuana—how it affects everyone differently. It seems to enhance and intensify whatever's going on in the person at any given moment. Let's say that we were going to do some stretching right now and we did it straight. We'd be like, "Oh, man, this hurts. This is an ordeal." Now if we smoke a little pot and then stretch, it would feel good and put us more in touch with our bodies and the deeper sensations of the activity.

Mailer: I learned more about my body and reflex and grace, even, such as I have—whatever limited physical grace I have, I got it through pot showing me where my body, or how my body, was feeling at any given moment. Here, I can agree with you. Dancing—I could always dance on pot. Not much of a dancer otherwise, but on pot, I could dance. There's no question it liberated me. All of these good things were there. All the same, when it comes to the legalization of pot, I get dubious. Pot would be taken over by media culture. It would be classified and categorized. It would lose that wonderful little funky edge that once it had—that sensation of being on the edge of the criminal. All the same, the corporate bastards who run most of America will not legalize it in a hurry. Pot is still a great danger to them. Because what they fear is that too many people would no longer give a damn about the corporation—they'd have their minds on other things than working for the Big Empty. To the suits, that makes pot a deadly drug. The corporation has a bad enough conscience buried deep inside to fear, despite their strength, every type of psychic alteration that they haven't developed themselves.

1974   COLLECTOR'S **30**ᵗʰ**ANNIVERSARY** EDITION   2004   no. **347**

CELEBRATING FREEDOM
NOVEMBER / DECEMBER 2004

HighTimes

IGGY POP
NORMAN MAILER
HUNTER S. THOMPSON
JIM JARMUSCH
LUC SANTE
TOM FORÇADE

WWW.HIGHTIMES.COM
US $4.99 | FOR $5.99 | CAN $6.99

0 735878

1 2>

ABOUT THE CONTRIBUTORS

As the man who introduced Allen Ginsberg to Bob Dylan, Dylan to the Beatles, and the Beatles to marijuana, **Al Aronowitz** likes to boast: "the sixties wouldn't have been the same without me." He also claims to be the invisible link between the Beats and the Beatles.

Ruth Baldwin is the associate editor of Nation Books.

Ann Louise Bardach is the author of *Cuba Confidential: Love and Vengeance in Miami and Havana*, and currently covers politics for *SLATE*. Previously, she was a contributing editor to *Vanity Fair* for ten years and wrote for the *New York Times*.

Chip Berlet is a former Washington editor from *High Times* and board member of the Underground Press Syndicate. He continues to write about right-wing social and political movements.

George Barkin edited *High Times* in 1984. He went on to edit *National Lampoon* magazine and currently writes and produces films.

Steve Bloom has been with *High Times* since 1988, and is currently coeditor. Bloom is the author of *Watch Out for the Little Guys*, a portrait of basketball's shortest players.

Michael Bloomfield (1943–1981) was an influential, Chicago-born blues player and was considered by many to be the first premiere rock/blues guitarist in America. He played with Bob Dylan and others, and was a member of the Paul Butterfield Blues Band. His albums include *Super Sessions* with Al Cooper.

Victor Bockris has spent over thirty years writing about the cultural heroes of the twentieth century. He is the author or coauthor of biographies of Andy Warhol, Lou Reed, John Cale, Patti Smith, Muhammad Ali, Keith Richards, the Velvet Underground, William S. Burroughs, and more.

William S. Burroughs (1914-1997) was the author of numerous books, including *Naked Lunch, Nova Express, The Ticket that Exploded, The Soft Machine*, and *The Wild Boys*. He was a member of the American Academy of Arts and Letters and a *Commandeur de l'Ordre des Arts et des Lettres of France*.

Mark Christensen is the author of several books including the novels *Aloha* and *Mortal Belladaywic*, and the nonfiction *Super Car*.

Editor of *High Times* for its first two years, **Ed Dwyer** then served as special projects editor until the death of magazine founder Tom Forçade in 1978. He has since held senior-level editorial positions at many magazines, and has been published in *Penthouse, Playboy, Men's Health, Variety*, and other publications. He is currently a features editor at *AARP the Magazine* in Washington, D.C.

Bruce Eisner has been a journalist covering psychedelics, consciousness, and the alternative culture since 1971. From 1977–1978, he was a contributing editor for *High Times*. Eisner published his book, *Ecstasy: The MDMA Story*, in 1989. He currently lives in Las Vegas, Nevada, where he is completing his dissertation for a Ph.D. in psychology. His blogs can be found on Bruce Eisner's Vision Thing at www.bruceeisner.com.

David Enders is a freelance journalist from Grand Rapids, Michigan. Between April and September 2003, he was the editor of the *Baghdad Bulletin*, Iraq's first post-invasion English-language publication.

Bruce Jay Friedman is a novelist, playwright, screenwriter, and journalist. His last publication was the novel *Violencia*. He is the author of many other novels, including *The Lonely Guy's Book of Life* and *The Current Climate*, short story collections, and screenplays including *Stir Crazy* and *Splash*. A collection of his nonfiction was published in 2000.

Josh Alan Friedman is the author of *When Sex Was Dirty*, and the subject of *Blacks 'N' Jews*, a new feature documentary based upon his 1997 blues album of the same name.

Kinky Friedman is the next governor of the great state of Texas.

Steven Hager has a Masters in journalism from the University of Illinois and was editor of *High Times* for over fifteen years. His most recent book is *Adventures in the Counterculture: From Hip Hop to* High Times.

Debbie Harry was the lead singer and co-creator (with Chris Stein) of the iconic band Blondie, founded in 1974. Their most recent album is *The Curse of Blondie*. She is also a writer and an actress.

J. Hoberman is senior film critic for the *Village Voice*; his books include *The Dream Life: Movies, Media, and the Myth of the '60s*.

Mark Jacobson is the author of *12,000 Miles in the Nick of Time*, and the coeditor of *The KGB Bar Nonfiction Reader* and *American Monsters*. He is a contributing editor to *New York* magazine.

David Katz has written for a variety of publications, including *High Times*, the *Village Voice*, the *Lower East Side Review*, *Rap Express*, *Circus*, and *Girls Over 40*. He lives in Manhattan.

Paul Krassner is the author of *Murder at the Conspiracy Convention and Other American Absurdities*. His new collection is *Magic Mushrooms and Other Highs: From Toad Slime to Ecstasy*. His latest comedy album is *The Zen Bastard Rides Again*.

Dean Latimer wrote stories for *High Times* from 1975 until 2002. He was also *High Times'* sordid affairs editor.

Carlo McCormick is a senior editor of *Paper* magazine.

Barry Miles was the cofounder, in 1966, of Indica Books and Gallery, where John Lennon first met Yoko Ono, and was cofounder of *International Times* (IT), the first European underground newspaper, where he interviewed Paul McCartney, George Harrison, Mick Jagger, among others. In 1968 Paul McCartney appointed him head of Zapple, the Beatles' spoken word label. He specializes in writing about the Beat Generation and is the author of biographies on Ginsberg, Burroughs, Kerouac, among others. His best-selling *Paul McCartney: Many Years from Now* was written in close collaboration with McCartney. His latest books are *Hippie* and *Zappa*.

Cookie Mueller (1949–1989) was best known for her work in the films of director John Waters, including *Pink Flamingos* (1974). Mueller performed both on and off-Broadway, was an art critic, and advice columnist. Her books include *Fan Mail, Frank Letters*, and *Crank Calls* and *Garden of Ashes* (Hanuman).

Annie Nocenti was the editor of *High Times* (2003–2004), the editor of *Scenario* magazine, and editor at large at *Prison Life*.

Glenn O'Brien is a regular columnist for *GQ, Paper* magazine and *Vanity Fair Italia*. He is editor and publisher of *Bald Ego*, a literary magazine, the author of a book of essays, *Soapbox*, and a book of poems, *Human Nature*.

Joey Ramone (1951–2001) was a founding member and lead singer of the seminal and influential 1970s punk rock band, the Ramones.

Ron Rosenbaum is a columnist for the *New York Observer* and the author of many books including *Those Who Forget the Past* and *Explaining Hitler*.

Jerry Rubin (1938–1994), one of the founders of the Yippies, was an antiwar activist, Chicago 7 defendant, and entrepreneur.

Luc Sante's books include *Low Life, Evidence* and *The Factory of Facts*. He lives in Ulster County, New York.

Larry "Ratso" Sloman edited *High Times* from 1979–1984, before he left to edit *National Lampoon*. He's the author of the award-winning *On the Road with Bob Dylan, Reefer Madness,* and *Steal This Dream,* an oral biography of Abbie Hoffman. Sloman is best known for his collaborations with Howard Stern on *Private Parts* and *Miss America*. His latest book, with Anthony Kiedis, is *Scar Tissue*.

Terry Southern (1924–1995) was the coauthor of the films *Dr. Strangelove* and *Easy Rider*. His novels are in print through Grove/Atlantic. His novel *Candy* is the subject of a new book, *The Candy Men: The Rollicking Life and Times of the Notorious Novel* Candy by Nile Southern.

Peter Stafford, who fancies himself a "P.I." (psychedelics investigator, chronicler and storyteller), is the coauthor, with Bonnie Golightly, of *LSD—The Problem-Solving Psychedelic,* and author of *Psychedelic Baby Reaches Puberty, Psychedelics Encyclopedia,* and *Psychedelics and Magic Mushrooms*. He is currently completing an update of his former writings about DMT, Ayahuasca, Ibogaine, and other entheogens, called "Heavenly Highs."

Richard Stratton was one of original contributors to *High Times* in 1974, and returned as publisher and editor in chief in 2003–2004. Stratton was an international pot smuggler who served eight years in federal prison, where he wrote the cult novel *Smack Goddess*. He was the publisher/editor of *Prison Life* magazine, the creator and writer of the Showtime series *Street Time,* and the producer and cowriter of the Cannes and Sundance film festival winner *Slam*. His journalism has appeared in *Rolling Stone, Penthouse, Spin, Details, Esquire,* and *GQ*.

Teun Voeten is a writer, photographer, and anthropologist who covers armed conflicts worldwide. He is the author of *How de Body? One Man's Terrifying Journey Through an African War.*

Andy Warhol, a painter and graphic artist, also produced a significant body of film work, including his famous *Chelsea Girls.* Equally well known in the late 1960s and early 1970s as resident host at his studio, the Factory, Warhol died in New York in 1987.

Andrew Weil is a pioneer in the field of Integrative Medicine. Dr. Weil is also a best-selling author and editorial director of www.DrWeil.com, the leading online resource for Integrative Medicine.

Robert Anton Wilson is author of thirty-five books and founder of the Guns and Dope Party [www.gunsanddope.com]

An innovative iconoclast, **Frank Zappa** (1940–1993) founded the classic 1960s rock band Mothers of Invention, whose albums include *Hot Rats, Waka/Jawaka,* and *The Grand Wazoo.*

ACKNOWLEDGMENTS

We would like to thank Victor Navasky, Carl Bromley, John Buffalo Mailer, Richard Stratton, and Michael Kennedy for making this book happen. A great appreciation goes to Ed Dwyer, Larry "Ratso" Sloman, A. Craig Copetas, Carlo McCormick, Paul Krassner, Mike Wilmington, and Michael Simmons for their invaluable help in leading us to important articles and help in tracking down authors. And a big thank you to Justin Taylor and Michelle Zaretsky for all their editorial and production help.

A note on the editorial selection process:

With thirty years of *High Times* archives to choose from, this anthology could have filled many volumes. *High Times'* stellar drug news coverage and groundbreaking cultivation articles alone could fill their own volumes. Instead, this collection goes back to the magazine's roots, and is guided by Tom Forçade's ideal for *High Times*—that it represent a "new consciousness," and be "far more than a 'dope' magazine." This anthology's selections were all written originally for *High Times*, (reprints and advance book chapters were excluded). Stories were chosen for their excellence, or to illuminate the profound effect that drugs have had on journalism, politics, literature, music, history, the law, comedy, sex, activism, and more. A few stories chosen simply to show how dope journalists have more fun.

—The editors

PERMISSIONS